Pro PerformancePoint Server 2007

Building Business Intelligence Solutions

Philo Janus

Apress®

Pro PerformancePoint Server 2007: Building Business Intelligence Solutions

Copyright © 2008 by Philo Janus

ISBN-13 (pbk): 978-1-59059-961-7

ISBN-10 (pbk): 1-59059-961-6

ISBN-13 (electronic): 978-1-4302-0588-3

Lead Editor: Jeffrey Pepper
Technical Reviewers: Dana Hoffman, Phillip Taylor
Editorial Board: Clay Andres, Steve Anglin, Ewan Buckingham, Tony Campbell, Gary Cornell, Jonathan Gennick, Matthew Moodie, Joseph Ottinger, Jeffrey Pepper, Frank Pohlmann, Ben Renow-Clarke, Dominic Shakeshaft, Matt Wade, Tom Welsh
Project Manager: Richard Dal Porto
Copy Editors: Damon Larson, Heather Lang
Associate Production Director: Kari Brooks-Copony
Production Editor: Katie Stence
Compositor and Artist: Van Winkle Design Group
Proofreader: April Eddy
Indexer: Broccoli Information Management
Cover Designer: Kurt Krames
Manufacturing Director: Tom Debolski

Distributed to the book trade worldwide by Springer-Verlag New York, Inc., 233 Spring Street, 6th Floor, New York, NY 10013. Phone 1-800-SPRINGER, fax 201-348-4505, e-mail orders-ny@springer-sbm.com, or visit http://www.springeronline.com.

For information on translations, please contact Apress directly at 2855 Telegraph Avenue, Suite 600, Berkeley, CA 94705. Phone 510-549-5930, fax 510-549-5939, e-mail info@apress.com, or visit http://www.apress.com.

Apress and friends of ED books may be purchased in bulk for academic, corporate, or promotional use. eBook versions and licenses are also available for most titles. For more information, reference our Special Bulk Sales—eBook Licensing web page at http://www.apress.com/info/bulksales.

The source code for this book is available to readers at http://www.apress.com. You may need to answer questions pertaining to this book in order to successfully download the code.

For Pamela Janus, my mother, who sparked my love of logic, mathematics, and reading.

Contents at a Glance

Foreword xv

About the Author xvii

About the Technical Reviewers xix

Acknowledgments xxi

Introduction xxiii

CHAPTER 1   Business Intelligence 1

CHAPTER 2   Overview of Microsoft's Business Intelligence Platform 17

CHAPTER 3   SQL Server 33

CHAPTER 4   SQL Server Integration Services 53

CHAPTER 5   SQL Server Analysis Services 83

CHAPTER 6   SQL Server Reporting Services 125

CHAPTER 7   Data Mining 165

CHAPTER 8   Business Intelligence in Excel and SharePoint 189

CHAPTER 9   ProClarity Analytics Server 211

CHAPTER 10   PerformancePoint Monitoring 255

CHAPTER 11   Advanced Scorecarding 303

CHAPTER 12   Dashboards and Reports 333

CHAPTER 13   Planning 367

CHAPTER 14   Management Reporter 421

INDEX 435

Contents

Foreword xv

About the Author xvii

About the Technical Reviewers xix

Acknowledgments xxi

Introduction xxiii

■CHAPTER 1   **Business Intelligence** 1

What Is Business Intelligence? 1
Scorecards vs. Dashboards 2
Key Performance Indicators 5
    KPIs and Business Process 6
    The Law of Unintended Consequences 7
Strategy Maps 8
Data Silos 10
Data Marts 11
Why Do I Care? 13
The Microsoft Business Intelligence Stack 13
    SQL Server 2005 14
    Microsoft Office 2007 14
    Microsoft Business Intelligence 15
A Successful Business Intelligence Engagement 15
Conclusion 16

■CHAPTER 2   **Overview of Microsoft's**
Business Intelligence Platform 17

SQL Server 17
    SQL Server Integration Services 18
    SQL Server Analysis Services 18
    SQL Server Reporting Services 21
SharePoint Integration 22
Excel Services 24
SharePoint KPI Lists 25

ProClarity 6.3 26
PerformancePoint Server 2007 28
    Monitoring and Analytics 29
    Modeling and Planning 31
Conclusion 32

■CHAPTER 3   **SQL Server**................................... 33

Overview 33
SQL Server Editions 33
    Compact Edition 35
    Express Edition 35
    Workgroup Edition 36
    Standard Edition 36
    Enterprise Edition 37
    Developer Edition 38
Tools 38
    Management Studio 38
    Business Intelligence Development Studio 40
    Profiler 42
Programmability 43
    Stored Procedures 44
    Service Broker 44
    Web Services 45
    Query Notifications 45
    Database Mail 45
Security 45
XML 46
    XML Datatype 46
    Schemas 46
    XQuery and Data Manipulation Language 46
    XML Best Practices 47
High Availability 47
    Mirroring 47
    Failover Clustering 47
    Online Index Operations 47
    Database Snapshots 47

Service Pack 2 48
    Reports 48
    Best Practices Analyzer 49
    Data Mining Improvements 49
SQL Server 2008 51
    Data Platform 51
Conclusion 52

CHAPTER 4   **SQL Server Integration Services** 53

Overview 53
    Why Integration Services? 53
    Editions 59
    Data Sources 59
About Data Transformation Services 60
Architecture 62
Getting Integration Services 63
Business Intelligence Development Studio 64
Flows 67
Program Flow Components 70
    Containers 70
    Tasks 71
    Executing Other Code 71
    Transferring Things 72
    Maintenance 72
Data Flow Components 72
    Data Flow Sources 72
    Data Flow Transformations 73
    Data Flow Destinations 74
Scripting Tasks 74
Custom Tasks 77
Error Reporting 78
Scalability 79
Deploying and Executing Integration Services Packages 80
Conclusion 82

CHAPTER 5   SQL Server Analysis Services 83

What Is a Cube? 84
Facts and Dimensions 89
Star Schema or Snowflake Schema? 90
BIDS and Analysis Services 91
Building a Cube 91
    Creating the Project 94
    Creating a Data Source 96
    Creating a Data Source View 99
    Dimensions 104
    Creating the Cube 114
Calculated Measures 122
Multidimensional Expressions 122
Key Performance Indicators 122
Perspectives 123
Conclusion 123

CHAPTER 6   SQL Server Reporting Services 125

Architecture 128
    Report Server 128
    Report Manager 129
    Report Designer 130
    Report Builder 131
    Reporting Services Configuration Manager 132
    Extensibility 134
    Summary 136
Creating Reports 136
    Table and Matrix Reports 137
    Reporting Services 2008: Tablix 138
    Multidimensional Reports 147
    Charts and Graphs 160
SharePoint Integration 163
Conclusion 164

CHAPTER 7   **Data Mining** 165

SQL Server Implementation 166
Data Mining Algorithms 168
    Decision Trees 168
    Association Rules 172
    Naive Bayes 172
    Clustering 175
    Sequence Clustering 175
    Time Series 176
    Neural Networks 176
Choosing an Algorithm 177
Mining Accuracy 178
Mining Model Prediction 178
Data Mining in Integration Services 178
SQL Server 2005 SP2 Excel Add-Ins 180
    Table Analysis 181
    Data Preparation (Data Mining Tab) 183
    Data Mining Tools 185
Publishing to Reporting Services 186
Conclusion 187

CHAPTER 8   **Business Intelligence in Excel and SharePoint** 189

Business Intelligence in Office 190
Excel 2007 191
    Data Connections 192
Excel Services 197
    Why Excel Services? 197
    Configuring Excel Services 200
    Publishing to Excel Services 203
MOSS Business Intelligence 206
    KPI Lists 206
    Dashboards 207
Conclusion 210

■CHAPTER 9   **ProClarity Analytics Server** 211

ProClarity Analytics Server Overview 211
    ProClarity Charts 214
    Web Standard 222
    Web Professional 224
    Architecture 225
    Using ProClarity Web Professional 228
    Publishing and Briefing Books 234
Advanced Visualizations 236
ProClarity and SharePoint 244
Installing ProClarity Analytics Server 246
Conclusion 254

■CHAPTER 10   **PerformancePoint Monitoring** 255

Scorecards 255
Strategy Maps 259
Installing PerformancePoint 262
    Prerequisites 262
    Installation 262
Running Dashboard Designer 269
Tour of Dashboard Designer 271
    Server vs. Workspace 272
    The Fluent User Interface 272
    Connecting to a Monitoring Server 274
    The Workspace Browser 275
    Editor and Properties 276
    The Details Pane 278
Creating a Scorecard 278
    Indicators 278
    KPIs 281
    Scorecards 294
Conclusion 302

CHAPTER 11   Advanced Scorecarding 303

Hooking KPIs to Data 303
    ODBC (Access Database File) 303
    Excel 2007 Spreadsheets 307
    Excel 2007 Scorecards 315
Analysis Services 321
    Creating an OLAP Scorecard 327
Reporting Services 332
Conclusion 332

CHAPTER 12   Dashboards and Reports 333

Overview of the Dashboard Editor 333
Reports 336
    Analytic Grids 338
    Analytic Charts 345
    Excel Services 348
    PivotChart, PivotTable, and Spreadsheet Reports 349
    ProClarity Analytics 350
    SQL Server Reports 352
Creating Dashboards 356
    Filters 358
    Linking Dashboard Items 362
Publishing Dashboards 363
Summary 366

CHAPTER 13   Planning 367

    Why Plan? 368
    PerformancePoint Planning Server Scenarios 369
    PerformancePoint Planning Server Architecture 371
Installation 371
    PerformancePoint, Windows 2008, and 64 Bits 372
Working with Planning 375
    Creating a Model 381
    Importing Data 396
    Designing Forms 399
    Workflow 408
    Entering Data 412
Business Rules 417
Conclusion 419

■CHAPTER 14 **Management Reporter** 421

Creating Management Reports 421
Connecting to PerformancePoint Server 431
Exporting to Reporting Services 434
Conclusion 434

■INDEX 435

Foreword

One element of Bruce Springsteen's showmanship involves the soliloquies he recites before introducing the members of his band. In one of these, he recounts being a young man standing before a dark grove of trees. He tells about being afraid to pass through the trees. As he tries to get his courage up, a gypsy appears before him and asks him for his story. As she realizes he is afraid to pass through the trees, she tells him, "You need a man. You need someone who can help you." And then Bruce goes on to introduce the members of the band. If you are contemplating your first business intelligence or performance management project, or maybe your largest or most complicated project to date, Philo Janus is "your man." He's here to help you pass through the figurative dark grove of trees. He is a solution specialist at Microsoft, focusing on business intelligence. More than that, Philo is a trusted confidant of the BI product development teams at Microsoft. He is able to provide guidance to our teams based on his years of field experience and his ability to synthesize input from diverse customers into patterns and trends that help us build better products. We always appreciate his insights; I believe you will come to as well as you read this book and work through the examples.

This book is based on Philo's experience with the entire Microsoft business intelligence offering and his work with many Microsoft customers. He starts with the foundation of Microsoft BI, SQL Server (including its major BI components), Integration Services, Analysis Services, and Reporting Services. In doing so, Philo helps you build a robust base for your own projects. He also covers data mining, an increasingly used feature of BI applications. From there, Philo works "up the stack," bringing in elements of Microsoft Office and Performance-Point Server 2007, Microsoft's entry into the performance management market. He includes coverage of Management Reporter, the very newest component of the offering as of this writing. We built the Microsoft BI offering to provide every aspect of a complete BI solution, from acquiring and managing data, to adding value through analytics, to presenting results to end users and business people in ways that both guide and inspire action and results. Only a book (and a guide like Philo) that covers the whole spectrum of Microsoft BI can help you provide a complete solution for your company and end users.

Philo tells it like it is. With the product team, he is plainspoken about where and how we can do better for our customers. Alas, software is an imperfect art and we are always improving. In this book, Philo guides you through the few tricky spots in the technology with practical steps you can use to make progress in your projects. He also imparts wisdom he's gained both from experience and from just being smart. For example, in Chapter 1, he explains the Law of Unintended Consequences as it applies to BI projects. Put quickly, what you measure becomes important to a lot of people in your organization. They will change their behavior as performance management takes hold in the team or company. As an implementer, you need to anticipate these changes and ensure that they are meaningful and actually lead to better performance—not shallow and easily "gamed." Philo provides examples and practical advice on how to do this.

In addition to imparting wisdom and big-picture guidance, your author supplies the practices, tips, and how-tos you need to make progress with your own projects. Philo gives you insight into the structuring and layering of the elements you will use to build your application. Building the application objects in the right order will save you time and reduce your testing efforts. In the per-component chapters, you'll find advice on which components to use for each job and which to not use at all. Philo will help you future-proof your application so it grows gracefully as the Microsoft product offering continues to evolve.

While much of this book necessarily addresses the foundations of any BI application, ETL, OLAP, reporting, and so on, it has a particular focus on performance management. As the worldwide economy goes through the various stresses of rapidly rising energy prices, recession, competition for resources, and turmoil in the financial markets, companies need agility, accountability, and alignment to maximize their use of limited resources and compete most effectively *and* efficiently. PerformancePoint Server 2007 is Microsoft's platform for performance management. If you are charged with bringing performance management into your corporation, PerformancePoint is for you. Philo is an excellent guide to performance management and PerformancePoint. You are in excellent hands.

Bill Baker
Distinguished Engineer, Microsoft

About the Author

PHILO JANUS is a senior solution specialist with Microsoft. Over the last five years, he has had various roles including evangelist for Office as a developer platform, teacher of SharePoint development, technology specialist for the Business Intelligence product group, and finally application and platform solution specialist.

Philo graduated from the US Naval Academy with a BSEE in 1989 to face a challenging career in the US Navy. His first assignment was on the USS Midway (CV 41), where he had 52 direct reports, four chief petty officers, and several million dollars of equipment to keep track of. All the maintenance was tracked on note cards and grease pencil whiteboards. This heritage may be where Philo's interest in automated monitoring was born.

Philo's software development career started with building a training and budgeting application in Access 2.0 in 1995. Since then, he's worked with Oracle, Visual Basic, SQL Server, and .NET building applications for federal agencies, commercial firms, and conglomerates. In 2003, he joined Microsoft as an Office developer evangelist. When Business Scorecard Manager was released, he quickly found happiness talking to enterprise customers about managing their metrics with this new software. Microsoft quickly grew its business intelligence practice, and Philo has been happier than ever as more capabilities get added to the newly christened PerformancePoint suite.

About the Technical Reviewers

Born in Brooklyn, New York, **DANA L. HOFFMAN** often jokes that her name should have been "Data." She has always had a sharp eye for detail and an avid desire to create systems that are not just workable but intuitive and easy to use. She always tries to see things from the user's point of view, and sees technical reviewing as an excellent opportunity to put her nitpicking skills to good use. With a background in programming and database development, Dana currently works as a data analyst. She lives in Connecticut and is nearly finished raising two sons.

PHILLIP TAYLOR is an independent IT consultant providing database systems development services to several large government agencies. Specializing in data warehouse and business intelligence, he has spent the last ten years building solutions using Microsoft SQL Server.

Acknowledgments

This is often the hardest part of writing a book. You live in fear of who you're going to forget. Last time I forgot my mom, so I think I've pretty much set the upper limit on embarrassing omissions.

First and foremost, I could not have done this without the support of my family. My kids endured another year of "Daddy is working on his book." Hopefully it was a little easier this time having the last book on hand as a concrete reminder that it's actually possible. Antoinette and Samantha, thank you so much for understanding.

What my wife has put up with is nothing short of amazing. Suffice to say that Chapter 9 was written in the Bahamas and Chapter 13 was written in a hotel room in London. She's been a real trooper in putting up with my absences, even on vacation. Christine, I love you, babe.

Big thanks to my project manager, Richard Dal Porto, for dealing with my incredibly erratic writing schedule.

And anyone who buys this book owes my technical reviewer, Dana Hoffman, a bouquet of flowers. Dana was relentless in letting me know when text didn't make sense, when I was using jargon I hadn't defined, and when exercises didn't work. If you find the exercises and walkthroughs in this book valuable, and get through them having learned something, it's thanks to Dana's work.

Finally, another shout-out to my cheerleaders at the Design of Software: Rui Pacheco, John Haren, Aaron F. Stanton, PhD, Ricardo Antunes da Costa, Colm O'Connor, Mark Theodore Anthony Wieczorek, Peter Lorenzen, Andrei Tuch, Tim Becker, Geert-Jan Thomas, Tapiwa Sibanda, Christopher Boyle, Luis Zaldivar, and David J Donahue.

Introduction

"**B**usiness intelligence" is a nebulous, scary term that is often brandished as something that you need an MBA and 20 years of experience in the field to implement. As I've dug my way around the field in the three short years since Business Scorecard Manager was released, what I've found is that the *technology* does not have to be that hard. I'm not saying it's always easy, but it's definitely approachable and accessible to the average developer or DBA.

The issue with business intelligence is that the *business problem* is hard. There are issues of metrics, what to measure, how to measure it, where to get the data, how to get the data securely, how to apply the data, how to analyze the data, how to get value out of the analysis, and so on. The important things—and I try to reiterate these throughout the book—are focusing our attention on the business problems and trying to make the technology as unobtrusive as possible.

That is what Microsoft is doing with PerformancePoint. By commoditizing what was previously a premium software field, they are trying to make business intelligence available to the masses, so we can think in terms of "How do I measure performance" instead of "How can I afford business intelligence software and consultants?"

Who This Book Is For

My target for this book is really the jack-of-all-trades developer or DBA: developers who set up their own servers and databases, and DBAs who write code, reports, and so on. There are parts that will appeal to more structured team types, but other parts that won't. But if you're a "I want to solve this problem and learn what's necessary to do it" type, then I hope I've hit your sweet spot.

Although fairly technical in a lot of areas, this book may also serve folks who want to understand business intelligence and the interface between business intelligence and technology.

I appreciate any feedback from readers on how you found the book—what worked and what didn't. You can get in touch with me at philo89@msn.com.

How This Book Is Structured

My main goal with this book was that readers be able to actually read it from front to back. I try to tell a story, building from some business intelligence basics, to how the Microsoft platform works, and finally to how PerformancePoint delivers the best solution overall. While I think individual chapters stand on their own, it really works best as a whole work.

The book breaks down as follows:

- Chapters 1 and 2 introduce you to business intelligence and the Microsoft solution.

- Chapters 3 through 7 cover SQL Server and the services that make it a business intelligence platform.

- Chapter 8 is a quick overview of the business intelligence capabilities in SharePoint, especially Excel Services.

- Chapters 9 through 14 cover PerformancePoint.

Prerequisites

To work with the exercises in this book, you'll need the following:

- SharePoint version 3; either Microsoft Office SharePoint Server (MOSS) 2007 or Windows SharePoint Services (WSS) version 3 will suffice, except in Chapter 8, which requires MOSS

- SQL Server; either 2005 or 2008 will do

- PerformancePoint Server 2007, including ProClarity 6.3

Of course, you'll need Windows Server, either 2003 or 2008. If you haven't delved into virtualization yet, I highly recommend investigating Windows Server 2008 and its Hyper-V technology.

Downloading the Code

The downloads for this book are available from the Source Code/Download page of the Apress web site, at www.apress.com. The most notable of these are the Texas Healthcare data set for Chapter 5; the scorecards and dashboards developed in Chapters 10, 11, and 12; and the planning solution created in Chapter 13.

Contacting the Author

Philo is always available via philo89@msn.com. Feedback and questions are welcome.

■■■

CHAPTER 1

Business Intelligence

Before we can talk about implementing business intelligence solutions, it's important to have an understanding from the business perspective on what our users are trying to accomplish. A repeating theme throughout this book will be that business intelligence is about solving business problems. So it's important that the business intelligence architect, DBA, developer, and so on be in tune with the problems involved on the business side as much as the technical side.

What Is Business Intelligence?

The IT industry has spent the last two decades getting data off of desktops and out of filing cabinets, and into relational databases. We've been very successful, and most business processes today are run from electronic data stores.

Unfortunately, as data has been moved by various initiatives and different groups into products by various vendors and integrators, we've ended up with huge collections of transactional silos. The data serves those who use the system—the warehouse can generate pick lists with bin numbers from orders, the financial group can generate invoices and checks, HR can manage employee records, and so on. But what about managers and executives who need an "all-up" perspective on their organization? They need to see current staffing levels and how they may compare to shipping times, order error rates, and stock levels, and how those numbers relate to truck loading rates and fuel usage. They will ask questions about how numbers interrelate, and will also want to perform analysis on relationships among data that may not be intuitive or obvious (data mining).

The problem domain can be summed up very simply: "I have several piles of data, and I want to get some value out of them."

BUSINESS INTELLIGENCE VS. PERFORMANCE MANAGEMENT

A lot of words have been written about the difference between business intelligence (BI) and performance management (PM), regarding where and how they overlap. One general theory is that BI is about delivering information while PM is about acting on that information.

My personal take on this: who cares? I feel that it's an esoteric exercise that doesn't really deliver any value to the people who need to run their companies. Whether you call a dashboard BI, BPM, or a dashboard, the important point is that it delivers the information necessary for people to monitor their business and make decisions on how to run it.

As I said, this is just my opinion.

Scorecards vs. Dashboards

The root of a BI solution (and often the impetus for a BI initiative) is the scorecard. There is often some confusion about when to use a scorecard and when to use a dashboard. Again, a lot of opinions exist about which is which, so let me share mine.

© Scott Adams, Inc./Dist. by UFS, Inc.

A *scorecard* (Figure 1-1) is a small, direct application that tracks a collection of *key performance indicators* (KPIs), and shows current actual values and target values, and a score for the KPI. KPIs may then be aggregated into *objectives* and/or *perspectives* with scores rolled up in either an average, a weighted average, or a bubble-up exception (showing the worst child score for a parent). Scorecards are strategic—they show long-term values, goals, and trends. Data in a scorecard should not be the type of data you would want to see in real time, but rather data that you monitor on a weekly or even monthly basis.

	Q1-06 Actual	Q1-06 Target	Q2-06 Actual	Q2-06 Target	Q3-06 Actual	Q3-06 Target	Q4-06 Actual	Q4-06 Target
⊟ **Financial Objectives**		●		●		△		●
⊟ **Revenue**		△		△		△		△
Sales Amt	$25,663,364	△	$34,366,793	△	$48,122,573	△	$72,000,830	△
Units	14,005	△	18,752	△	24,057	△	37,164	△
⊟ **Margins**		●		●		△		●
Gross Margin %	19.89%	●	19.84%	●	16.52%	△	17.37%	△
Gross Profit %	24.83%	●	24.76%	●	19.78%	△	21.02%	●
⊟ **Costs**		●		●		●		●
Cost	$20,558,319	●	$27,546,799	●	$40,174,195	●	$59,493,287	●

Figure 1-1. *A scorecard*

A *dashboard* (Figure 1-2), on the other hand, is more tactical. This is where you'll see your near-real-time data. You'll want charts and graphs that show data changing over hours, and how the data interrelates. A scorecard may be part of a larger dashboard as a means of giving an overarching perspective to the more tactical data displayed in the dashboard.

A good analogy is that a dashboard in a car shows real-time data: oil pressure, speed, RPMs, and so on; while a GPS display and maintenance record are similar to a scorecard—showing where you've been and the long-term trends of your performance.

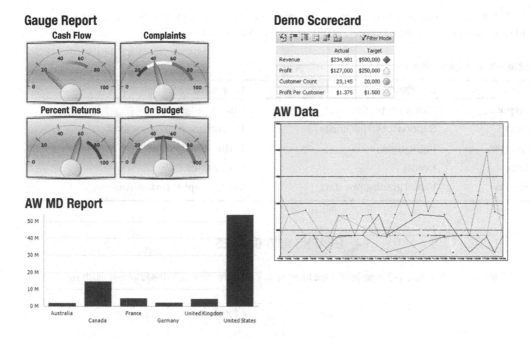

Figure 1-2. *A dashboard*

THE BALANCED SCORECARD

You will also hear about a special case of scorecard called a *balanced scorecard*. The balanced scorecard was created by Robert Kaplan and David Norton in 1992. Their goal was to pull the focus of management off the balance sheet (profit/loss) and pay attention to those factors outside finance that are indicative of the health of the company. To do this, they created what they called *perspectives* to aggregate KPIs and/or *objectives* (collections of KPIs).

Following are the four perspectives in a balanced scorecard:

Financial: Standard profit-and-loss type data

Customer: Measures indicative of customer satisfaction

Internal business processes: The health of the company's processes

Learning and growth: Primarily focused on employee quality and satisfaction

The goal of a balanced scorecard is to identify factors that are critical to the success of a business (and that will affect profit and loss down the line) *before* they become critical problems. For example, excessive employee attrition and turnover will eventually show up in decreased customer satisfaction, increased loss rates, and ultimately lower profits. Instead of waiting for it to become such a problem that it shows up on the balance sheet, by measuring attrition directly, management will get an advanced "heads up" when it becomes a problem.

Note that from a technical point of view, a balanced scorecard doesn't have any special requirements—it is simply a special case of scorecard. PerformancePoint Server allows you to build balanced or "unbalanced" scorecards.

For more information about balanced scorecards, check out the Balanced Scorecard Institute at www.balancedscorecard.org/.

Wayne Eckerson presents a straightforward chart comparing scorecards and dashboards in *Performance Dashboards* (Wiley, 2005) (shown in Table 1-1).

Table 1-1. *Comparing a Dashboard to a Scorecard*

	Dashboard	Scorecard
Purpose	Measures performance	Charts progress
Users	Supervisors, specialists	Executives, managers, staff
Updates	Right-time feeds	Periodic snapshots
Data	Events	Summaries
Display	Visual graphs, raw data	Visual graphs, text comments

GRAPHS AND GAUGES

Note the gauges in Figure 1-2. How helpful are they? Now look at the gauges in the following illustration:

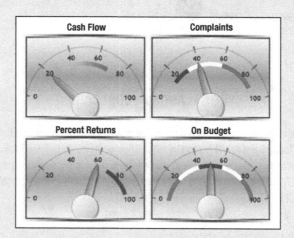

Note the labels—they may work well as reminders, but they are not very descriptive as to what the gauge is measuring, or how. If the gauges were self-describing (as we usually like graphical indicators to be), the labels would be incidental to what the gauges meant. Cash Flow is 20 and out of the red, but what does that mean? And what is the trend of the value? Is the Percent Returns gauge moving into the green or out of it?

If you'd like to really dig into maximizing the value from visual representations of data, I recommend *Information Dashboard Design*, by Stephen Few (O'Reilly, 2006), which walks through a number of dashboard designs by various vendors (sadly published before PerformancePoint was available), and discusses pros and cons of each design.

Once you have dashboard design down, dig into your indicators and charts with *Show Me the Numbers*, by Stephen Few (Analytics, 2004), which picks apart the various ways of representing data (including our favorite—the gauge).

Key Performance Indicators

We mentioned KPIs before, but what are they?

A KPI is where the business meets the data (see Figure 1-3). While a scorecard can have perspectives and objectives as business drivers, the actual metrics—the KPIs—are going to be data driven. The underlying principle originating here is, "You cannot manage what you cannot measure." So, while we may want happy customers and content employees and satisfied shareholders, those subjective concepts won't help us run our business.

| Units Sold | 16,878 | ○ | ↗ |

Figure 1-3. *The center of a scorecard—the KPI*

So we must identify the data-driven "things" that will help us guide our business decisions. A standard mnemonic that is used to evaluate KPIs is *SMART*. Spelled out, indicators must be

- Specific

- Measurable

- Achievable

- Realistic

- Timely

Some examples of good KPIs include customer attrition, cost of acquiring a customer, employee retention, percent of late deliveries, average wait times, and revenue growth. These may seem intuitive, but you should recognize the various pitfalls associated with each.

"Customer attrition" seems like a great metric; however, if you are a retail store, how do you define a lost customer? Just because a customer hasn't visited the store in a month doesn't necessarily mean they've decided to never visit again. (If you're a tire store, you may only see customers once a year.) In addition, if you're a brick-and-mortar store, how do you even track customers (this explains affinity cards, doesn't it?)?

"Employee retention," by comparison, is pretty straightforward—you want to just look at employee turnover. However, the danger here is assuming one metric can serve the whole company. You have to be cautious to set baselines—it may turn out that while turnover in accounting is very low, the shipping dock is always churning employees. Before you try to hold the shipping dock to the standards set by the accounting department, do some research—it may turn out that shipping departments always have high turnover rates; it's the nature of the work. In that case, you can work on getting turnover *lower*, but you don't want to set the accounting department's numbers as a goal if it's unrealistic.

"Percent of late deliveries" is pretty much a line drive down the middle. All you have to be sure of is that you have the data to measure what a late delivery is.

In addition, since we're discussing wiring scorecards to data, keep in mind that a KPI must have the data to drive it. (You could factor this under "measurable" and "achievable.") An interesting aspect of this approach is how it can help keep KPIs honest—when an indicator is suggested, identify where the data is going to come from. If that data doesn't currently exist, you have to ask a series of questions:

- Why isn't the data currently being captured?

- Should it be captured?

- If not—if this data isn't worth building a business system for—should we be driving our business from it?

In other words, the need to have the data acts as something of a sanity check on the KPI itself.

As you start to look at KPIs, you may be quickly overwhelmed, especially if the organization does not currently have a scorecard or has never evaluated performance metrics.

KPIs and Business Process

David Parmenter, in his book *Key Performance Indicators: Developing, Implementing, and Using Winning KPIs* (Wiley, 2007), recommends a 12-step process that covers major success factors, such as stakeholder buy-in, organic growth, and iteration instead of "get it right the first time." His 12 steps for identifying and implementing KPIs are as follows:

1. Senior management team commitment

2. Establishing a "winning KPI" project team

3. Establishing a "just do it" culture and process

4. Setting up a holistic KPI development strategy

5. Marketing a KPI system to all employees

6. Identifying organization-wide critical success factors

7. Recording performance measures in a database

8. Selecting team-level performance measures

9. Selecting organizational winning KPIs

10. Developing the reporting frameworks at all levels

11. Facilitating the use of winning KPIs

12. Refining KPIs to maintain their relevance

The reason I list these is to drive home the point that KPIs, objectives, scorecards, and dashboards constitute a *business problem*. They will require significant effort by business stakeholders to get right, and they will require maintenance in the long term to continually reevaluate the indicators and ensure they are guiding the business appropriately. I highly recommend Parmenter's book as a good foundation of how to build a solid collection of KPIs.

The Law of Unintended Consequences

One final warning regarding KPIs is to be wary of creating unexpected behaviors. Since you can't always anticipate how people will react to metrics, this again points toward the issue that you cannot create KPIs and walk away—reevaluation of the intent and effects of KPIs must be part of the scorecard business process.

Here are a couple examples of unintended consequences:

A company has a metric of "number of cases held over 20 days." The net result of this metric is that when your case is 18 days old, you'll see a flurry of activity, but when you hit the 3-week mark, it will suddenly go dead. Why? Because there is no metric to differentiate between a case that's 21 days old and one that's 90 days old. Once you're past the magic 20-day mark, there is no incentive to work on your case.

One computer manufacturer implemented a metric on its support line counting "number of calls lasting more than 10 minutes." Their cost of support skyrocketed. When they dug into the background, they found that their support technicians would work hard to help customers for 9 minutes. As the clock entered that ninth minute, they would simply offer to ship the customer a new system to get them off the phone.

A classic example of unintended consequences is counting lines of code. Many development managers come to the conclusion that a good metric for developers is counting the lines of code they write every week. In the initial part of a development project, this may even render what appears to be good performance data.

However, there are a number of factors to consider that pretty much invalidate the use of "lines of code" as a metric:

- A lot of development is about solving a problem, so a developer may go a whole day and write four lines of code, but those four lines may be a very tight loop that fixes a performance bug.

- Other optimizations may involve deleting large chunks of code and replacing them with a few lines, for a net negative.

- A lot of development now is template-based—if a developer spends a day just setting up form templates where a tool generates 5,000 lines of code, does that count?

- While I would be loathe to suggest that developers often game the system, there are a lot of ways to write code such that what should be one line of code comes out as ten. Is that a desired outcome?

So, the unintended consequence of measuring "lines of code" as a developer metric is that you're rewarding developers that just stamp out template code or find ways to game the system, while you're penalizing the superstars who have a negative metric.

Another example of a unintended code-related consequence is in counting bugs. If "bugs reported" is used as a metric, with lower numbers being better, what you end up with are fights between the developers and testers over every bug reported as to whether it's really a bug. Developers should not have a vested interest in hiding bugs.

A better metric might be "function points delivered" or accuracy of project estimates (too many days over *or* under yielding a bad metric). There are a number of essays and commentaries about using metrics on software development projects. Here are some examples:

- "In pursuit of code quality: Monitoring cyclomatic complexity," by Andrew Glover (`www.ibm.com/developerworks/java/library/j-cq03316/index.html`)

- "Lines of code," from the c2 wiki (`http://c2.com/cgi/wiki?LinesOfCode`)

- "Hitting the high notes," by Joel Spolsky (`www.joelonsoftware.com/articles/HighNotes.html`)

To sum up, determining the KPIs for your organization is a nontrivial problem. If there are no KPIs currently, then there's a lot of work to be done on the business level. Even if your organization already has a scorecard and KPIs, but it's driven manually, you will find that many things will have to shift as you try to move the scorecard to a data-driven environment (e.g., the first time a reported green KPI goes red when the real data is hooked up).

Do *not* quote the implementation time or development time as a timeframe for scorecard implementation. Be sure that the proper business process analysis and implementation is being considered or else you'll be a software project manager being held up by a business process you have no control over.

Strategy Maps

Strategy maps were created by Robert Kaplan and David Norton (yes, the balanced scorecard guys). Kaplan and Norton, while working on balanced scorecard implementations, noticed that successful business implementations were the result of *focus* and *alignment*.

We're all familiar with the concept of a mission statement—most businesses have some form of mission or vision. They are traditionally the butt of many jokes, as they are often perceived as fluffy or obvious. What is often missing is the linkage between a company's mission statement and what the company actually does. It's easy to have a mission statement of "Provide valuable services to our customers," but this begs the question of how?

Strategy maps are designed to link a company's high-level goals (*perspectives*, in balanced scorecard parlance) to the KPIs that measure how the company is performing on the measures that drive the business. A strategy map shows how KPIs relate to objectives and then to perspectives (Figure 1-4).

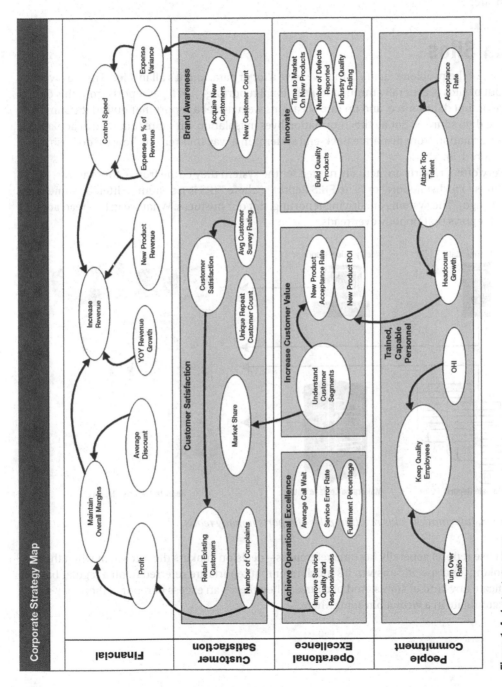

Figure 1-4. *A strategy map*

Very often, a company will build a strategy map before attempting a scorecard, as a way to formalize the company's strategy and how these factors interrelate. Strategy maps are generally drawn in a simple drawing package (like Microsoft Visio), but are increasingly included in a scorecard implementation to actually show the relationships between KPIs and the corporate strategy.

Data Silos

The root of the problem, again, is that we have a lot of data, and it's all in silos. The way we get data out of silos is generally through transactional reporting—we'll get reports from this data source or that data source, and on rare occasions we may get a report that pulls data from two or more data sources. But all the information lives in isolation—it's rare that we can actually view information from disparate back-end systems in a way that reflects how we do business (see Figure 1-5).

Very often, reports are actually named for the system they come from—for example, "The Warehouse Picklist Report" or "The FIPS Report" (where FIPS is a system written by some guy 10 years ago). The systems are driving reporting, not our business. What we get instead are piles of reports that nobody ever reads.

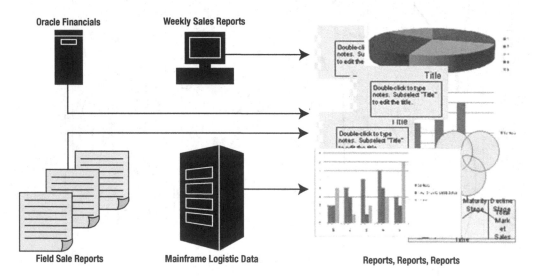

Figure 1-5. *Information silos result in piles of reports nobody reads.*

These reports generally become references—decision-makers dig into them when they are looking for a specific answer. It's much rarer that reports are referred to on a regular basis to indicate any kind of status. And of course, when there's an excess of reports, then they simply accumulate in a virtual bin somewhere.

Data Marts

What we want is a way to pull this stuff into one place, in a way that makes sense. The industry solution to this problem is the *data mart*. You may also hear references to OLAP (online analytical processing, as coined by E.F. Codd & Associates in 1994) or dimensional data storage. The fundamental idea is that we are starting to break down the system barrier and look at our information in ways that make sense to our business.

Tip I prefer to use the term *data mart* or *cube*. I've found that if you try to talk about a "data warehouse" anywhere near an executive or a consultant, they will immediately launch a 3-year project to build the "Corporate Data Warehouse," and you're stuck at square one. The other possible sticking point if you use the "DW" phrase is that your initiative will be shut down with the statement "We already have a data warehouse project in progress." Data warehouses have their place, but there is no reason an agile data mart project cannot happen in tandem.

Instead of getting reports named after the system that produced them, we want information structured similarly to the way we do business. We want to be able to break down warehouse delivery by customer type, order volume by warehouse location (or vice versa), and processing backlog by customer order amount. Where the data comes from or how it's stored in each system isn't a concern for a business user; all they want to do is use the data in the ways they run their business.

OLAP cubes seem complicated, but once you understand the basics, they are pretty straightforward. The fundamental concept is similar to pivot tables—we want to aggregate relational data by the dimensions we are interested in. For example, we may have a list of purchases made in a store. While that list of purchases is good for stock checking or auditing, simply having a list of 1,000 (or more) individual purchases doesn't tell us a lot—what did people buy a lot of? Is there a time of day that's busiest? Are people buying a lot of goods at once or are most purchases in the express lane (12 items or less)?

Using a pivot table in Excel, we can group purchases by item or by checkout aisle. But grouping by time is problematic—every purchase timestamp is to the second, so unless two people are buying at the exact same instant, the rollup will simply be the same list again. We could create a calculated column to pull out the hour of purchase and aggregate by that, but doing that every day would be painful, and it quickly bogs down if we start to talk about multiple stores and hundreds of thousands of purchases.

So the idea is to get away from the reams of relational records (as shown in Figure 1-6) and give our users the ability to work with data in a format that makes sense to them (as shown in the cube browser in Figure 1-7).

ProductKey	OrderDateKey	DueDateKey	ShipDateKey	ResellerKey	CustomerKey	EmployeeKey	PromotionKey	CurrencyKey	SalesTerritory	SalesC
372	762	774	769	97	(null)	282	1	100	4	SO517
287	762	774	769	97	(null)	282	1	100	4	SO517
380	762	774	769	97	(null)	282	1	100	4	SO517
390	762	774	769	97	(null)	282	1	100	4	SO517
525	762	774	769	99	(null)	285	1	100	5	SO517
599	762	774	769	99	(null)	285	1	100	5	SO517
549	762	774	769	99	(null)	285	1	100	5	SO517
361	762	774	769	100	(null)	291	1	19	6	SO518
598	762	774	769	100	(null)	291	1	19	6	SO518
516	762	774	769	100	(null)	291	1	19	6	SO518
513	762	774	769	100	(null)	291	1	19	6	SO518
359	762	774	769	100	(null)	291	1	19	6	SO518
551	762	774	769	100	(null)	291	1	19	6	SO518
353	762	774	769	100	(null)	291	1	19	6	SO518
596	762	774	769	100	(null)	291	1	19	6	SO518
363	762	774	769	100	(null)	291	1	19	6	SO518
402	762	774	769	100	(null)	291	1	19	6	SO518
290	762	774	769	100	(null)	291	1	19	6	SO518
511	762	774	769	100	(null)	291	1	19	6	SO518
592	762	774	769	100	(null)	291	1	19	6	SO518
591	762	774	769	100	(null)	291	1	19	6	SO518
517	762	774	769	100	(null)	291	1	19	6	SO518
532	762	774	769	100	(null)	291	1	19	6	SO518

Figure 1-6. *Rows and rows and rows of relational records*

	Calendar Year ▼				
	⊞ CY 2001	⊞ CY 2002	⊞ CY 2003	⊞ CY 2004	Grand Total
Group ▼	Internet Sales Amount	Internet Sales Amount	Internet Sales Amount	Internet Sales Amount	Internet Sales Amount
⊞ Europe	$709,947.20	$1,627,759.71	$3,382,979.27	$3,209,356.08	$8,930,042.26
⊞ North America	$1,247,379.26	$2,748,298.93	$3,374,296.82	$3,997,659.37	$11,367,634.37
⊞ Pacific	$1,309,047.20	$2,154,284.88	$3,033,784.21	$2,563,884.29	$9,061,000.58
Grand Total	$3,266,373.66	$6,530,343.53	$9,791,060.30	$9,770,899.74	$29,358,677.22

Figure 1-7. *Browsing a cube in Analysis Services*

Note how the table in Figure 1-7 uses terms that a business user would be comfortable with. While the table in Figure 1-6 has ProductKey and SalesTerritory by number (meaning that we have to find the tables they map to), the table in Analysis Services has sales territory groups, fiscal years, and Internet Sales Amount columns (properly formatted). Later, we'll see that once a cube is built, creating information like this is incredibly easy.

■**Note** We have discussed the problems with time fields in Excel, and yet Analysis Services has rolled our records by time up to the fiscal year. We can drill down by quarter, month, day, and so on. Analysis Services understands time implicitly, but this can be tricky to accomplish properly. We'll cover time dimensions in Chapter 5.

Why Do I Care?

So far, we've talked about managing business through metrics, how to best determine those metrics, how to aggregate metrics and align KPIs to corporate strategy, and the problems with trying to connect business drivers to the data we want to drive those indicators with. Just as a strategy map aligns KPIs and their data to business strategy, we need to align the products we're going to discuss with a BI solution.

This next section will give you some guidance before we start to dive into the really techie stuff behind the scenes.

The Microsoft Business Intelligence Stack

The BI solution from Microsoft is as shown in Figure 1-8.

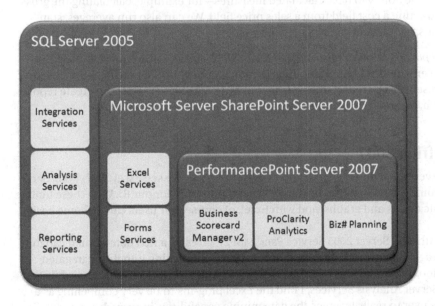

Figure 1-8. *The products in a Microsoft BI solution*

My goal is to cover these products and give some baseline understanding of how they fit into a BI solution. The most compelling part of Microsoft's BI platform is SQL Server and the capabilities that it gives you in a SQL Server license.

SQL Server 2005

The foundation of our solution is SQL Server 2005. In addition to the relational database capabilities we're all familiar with, SQL Server offers powerful BI services included in the licensing for a server. While not installed by default, it is very straightforward to install and configure these additional services.

SQL Server Integration Services (also referred to as SSIS): This is an enterprise-class ETL (extract, transform, load) tool that enables you to extract data from one location, process it, and push it to another location. While neither endpoint is required to be SQL Server (e.g., you could use Integration Services to move data from Excel spreadsheets to Oracle), in this book we'll be using Integration Services to pull data from data sources and load it into a staging database in SQL Server. Integration Services is the first step in getting our data out of the silos we have and together in some form of homogenous data store.

SQL Server Analysis Services (also referred to as SSAS): This is where we build our data marts. Analysis Services allows us to map various data sources together for use as the facts and dimensions in our cubes. In addition to building and managing OLAP cubes, Analysis Services offers the ability to have calculated measures—for example, calculating the gross profit by subtracting a cost field from a sales price field. We can also run averages, standard deviations, averages of child values, and so on.

SQL Server Reporting Services (also referred to as SSRS): This is a powerful web-based reporting server. The most important thing to understand about Reporting Services is that the data represented in a report does *not* have to be in SQL Server—you can create reports on Sybase data, for example, and simply use SQL Server as a report server.

Microsoft Office 2007

On top of SQL Server (most notably on top of Analysis Services), we see Excel 2007, Excel Services, and SharePoint. These make up the basic presentation layer for our BI. With these tools, we can create basic charts and graphs, and with Excel, of course, our users can do some basic analysis.

Excel 2007, with SQL Server 2005 Service Pack 2 (SP2), gives us a rich data mining capability. Once we have aggregated our data into a cube, we can start digging into the aggregated information and looking for various patterns. This is referred to as *data mining*, and while the engine is in SQL Server Analysis Services, I find the Excel plug-ins to be very compelling as a way for a business user to really leverage the data mining capabilities in a much easier-to-use fashion.

The next layer, however, is where we really want to focus our attention for display and visualization.

Microsoft Business Intelligence

This is where Microsoft's BI capabilities really show their mettle:

Business Scorecard Manager (BSM) 2005: This grew out of a solution accelerator designed to show off Analysis Services. It became so popular that Microsoft made it into a supported product. BSM's main purpose is to display standard red-yellow-green scorecards. The solution accelerator only displayed data from Analysis Services, and BSM works best on Analysis Services, but it is capable of using any ODBC data source for both actual values and targets.

ProClarity Analytics Server 6.3: This was acquired by Microsoft in June 2006. The ProClarity corporation carried a suite of products including a dashboard server, desktop analytics, and other servers. However, the primary product Microsoft has concentrated on, and is moving forward with, is Analytics Server. ProClarity Analytics Server provides rich, powerful visualizations on Analysis Services data. It also empowers end users to build their own analytic charts and dig into the dimensional data, and publish those charts and graphs for others to view.

Capabilities from both BSM and ProClarity Analytics Server are being rolled into PerformancePoint Server 2007. In addition to monitoring (scorecards) and analytics (detailed charts and graphs), PerformancePoint adds a robust planning and modeling system to enable end users to build dimensional models on their own, publish those models, make assignments, collect input, and roll data together. It's a powerful tool for "what-if" and forecasting scenarios. Code-named Biz# (pronounced *biz sharp*) in development, this will round out the capabilities of PerformancePoint.

By combining all the capabilities of SQL Server, SharePoint, and PerformancePoint, we can build a truly robust BI system—aggregating data, storing it, creating a strong analytical data mart based on the data gathered, and presenting that data in a myriad of ways through reporting or embedded in SharePoint sites where users can create their own dashboards (see Figure 1-8, shown previously).

A Successful Business Intelligence Engagement

Incidentally, one very powerful aspect of Microsoft's BI solution is that it's "a la carte"—you can implement it piecemeal and build up to a fully automated BI solution. Many products (and many consulting engagements) take an all-or-nothing approach—they need to gather all the requirements, define all the objectives and KPIs, identify all the data sources, and design all the dashboards, and then they will go to work on the whole thing for a number of months before finally delivering a "completed" product. Of course, unveiling a "completed" product for the first time will indicate just how incomplete it is from the customer's perspective.

PerformancePoint scorecarding gives you the capability to build a scorecard manually—so you can work with the customer to define a rough outline of their scorecard in a way that brings it to life. Once the scorecard is built and published on a web site (even if only with hand-coded numbers), then stakeholders can see the scorecard and understand it as presented, encouraging feedback and review of the metrics and objectives.

At the same time, the IT department can identify the business systems that will provide the data for the scorecard. As the scorecard survives its initial review, IT can start evaluating the actual sources of the data and identify "quick wins" for pulling data into data marts to serve the scorecard. What we want to do is build foundations in technology, knowledge, and process that we can build our BI solutions on in an iterative way.

Once we've identified business data we want to put in a cube, we can build some Integration Services ETL packages to pull the data from its source location, scrub it, and load it into a staging database. We can then build a data mart using the data from the staging database—build some cubes and perhaps some KPIs inside Analysis Services.

Finally, we wire the scorecard KPIs we've addressed to the cube, as well as provide additional analytic reports and drill-down capabilities.

This is step one. From here it's a degree of "lather, rinse, repeat," except that we want each iteration to be a growth activity—identify what worked and what didn't work so that the next round of implementation goes more smoothly. In the meantime, we can expect our business stakeholders to be evaluating the KPIs we've wired up and giving us feedback on how they need to be adjusted.

The overriding goal here is to make a slow, gradual transition from existing processes (often a pile of spreadsheets and a scorecard in PowerPoint) to a formal, fully automated BI process that simply renders scorecards and dashboards with near-real-time data. We want to do this in a measured way such that we minimize work that's going to be thrown away, and we also want to build the processes necessary to *maintain* the products that are built.

Conclusion

From here, we'll be focusing much more on technology (a sigh of relief from the geeks in the house). We'll dive into the various platforms and products I've discussed, and I'll give you a functional overview of how they work, how to get started with them, and how to best take advantage of them from a BI point of view.

These chapters are only meant to be introductory chapters—helping you to understand the capabilities and give you a running start. There is a wealth of information available to dig deeper on each technology, both online and in book stores.

With that, let's take a look at the technologies involved.

CHAPTER 2

■ ■ ■

Overview of Microsoft's Business Intelligence Platform

In 2005, Microsoft formally entered the business intelligence (BI) world with Business Score-card Manager (BSM), an outgrowth of the former Business Scorecard Accelerator. While SQL Server Analysis Services was a formidable BI engine, it was BSM that put a face on this power-ful back end.

Soon afterward, while developing a business process management (BPM) planning engine (code-named Biz#), Microsoft acquired ProClarity, a company that had made its name offering a rich analytics suite for Analysis Services cubes. While Microsoft continued to offer the ProClarity products as a stand-alone offering, the interesting stuff was going on behind the scenes—folding ProClarity and the next edition of BSM into Biz#. The suite was officially branded PerformancePoint, with the first release, PerformancePoint Server 2007, launching in late 2007.

This product places Microsoft firmly among the industry BI powerhouses, and it is only enhanced by the SQL Server stack underneath it, and SharePoint as a collaborative framework hosting it.

In this book, I'm going to walk you through an entire BI solution, including pulling data together, building it into a data mart for analysis, creating reports, building a scorecard and dashboard, and even developing a model for performing forecasting and what-if analysis.

Let's take a quick look at the products that comprise Microsoft's BI suite, as described in Chapter 1, which we're going to explore further in the coming chapters.

SQL Server

All the services that we will cover are part of the SQL Server licensing—there are no additional costs to leverage these capabilities. (A proper implementation will require additional servers for proper scalability, but you get the idea.) As I like to say, "If you're running SQL Server now, you can start working with these technologies this afternoon!"

By itself, SQL Server offers the ability to aggregate and clean data, build analytical data marts or cubes, and create reports on either transactional or dimensional data. These abilities are embodied in SQL Server Integration Services, SQL Server Analysis Services, and SQL Server Reporting Services. Let's take a little closer look at each of these.

SQL Server Integration Services

Integration Services offers a robust enterprise capability to move, translate, and clean data from a number of sources (most notably ODBC sources and flat files). The standard term for this capability is *extract, transform, and load*, or ETL. You can build data flows using Business Intelligence Development Studio (BIDS), which is a modified version of Visual Studio 2008 that is installed with the client tools.

Using a flowchart metaphor, you can perform any number of tasks in sequence or parallel with the data—manipulating and cleaning it as necessary. We will also cover the ability to use data mining tasks to clean data in accordance with existing data. Figure 2-1 shows an Integration Services project in BIDS.

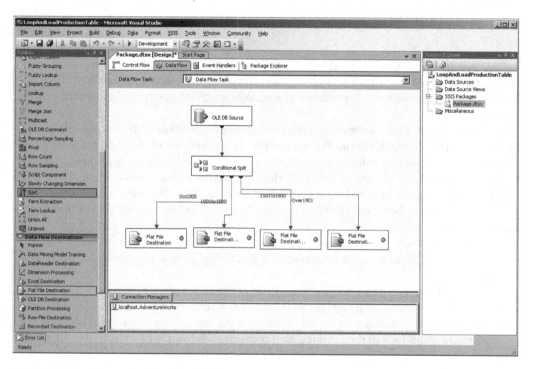

Figure 2-1. *The Integration Services designer*

SQL Server Analysis Services

Analysis Services is the jewel of our BI adventure. Often referred to as "pivot tables on steroids," Analysis Services enables the building of dimensional data stores, frequently referred to as cubes or data marts. You may also hear the term OLAP (online analytical processing) used to describe this method of aggregating data.

SQL Server Analysis Services provides a server-based method of crunching large amounts of data to get past the record-based focus of the existing data and provide aggregated views of the information necessary to truly understand how the data relates to the business. Figure 2-2 shows a browser view of OLAP data in Analysis Services.

Once a dimensional model is designed in Analysis Services, it becomes extremely straightforward for users to consume that data through reports, scorecards, dashboards, analytics, and even Excel 2007, as shown in Figure 2-3.

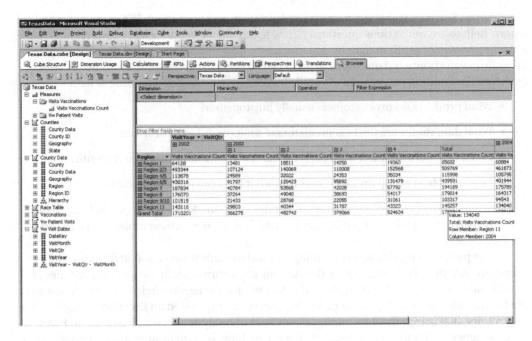

Figure 2-2. *Browsing a cube in BIDS*

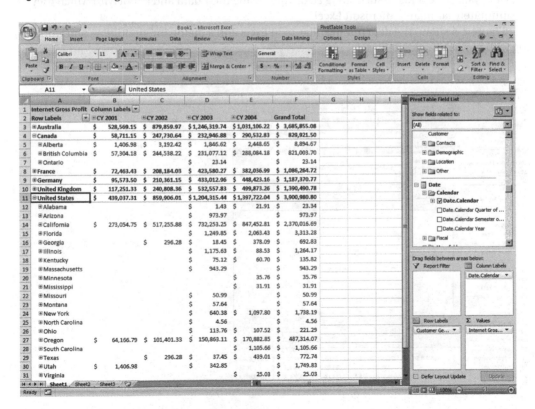

Figure 2-3. *An Analysis Services cube in Excel 2007*

Analysis Services also offers a very powerful data mining capability. While analytics and reports help to answer various questions ("How much did we produce last quarter?" or "What is the breakdown of profit margin by department?"), data mining will guide the user when they don't even know what questions to ask. The following list gives some examples of questions that data mining can generate to guide investigation and understanding of data:

- What products do my customers usually buy together?

- What data values are the best predictors of a successful assembly line?

- Given past performance, what performance can I expect for the next 3 months?

- How can I best group my customers into what their buying habits will be?

The data mining algorithms in Analysis Services help to identify patterns and trends in data, and can identify whether these types of questions are even answerable, as well as showing the answers.

In the past, data mining was something you had to really understand before you could even start working with it—designing data mining algorithms meant answering a number of esoteric questions and fully building out the data mining dimension before you could see any use from it. Starting with SQL Server 2005, SQL Server incorporated an Excel 2007 plug in for data mining that brings the data mining capabilities of Analysis Services forward into Excel. My experience is that this really broadens the accessibility of data mining fundamentals—now data analysts can explore data mining algorithms using their data and a tool with which they are intimately familiar—Microsoft Excel.

Figure 2-4 shows the data mining plug-in in Excel and a dialog for identifying and working with outliers in data tables.

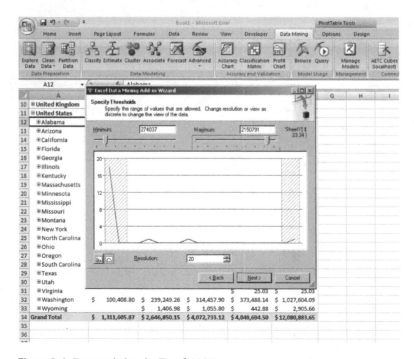

Figure 2-4. *Data mining in Excel 2007*

SQL Server Reporting Services

Reporting Services is a web-based enterprise reporting engine. After designing reports in BIDS (Figure 2-5), you can publish them to the reporting server, where they are available to users with appropriate security restrictions. Users can also subscribe to reports on a recurring basis or a data-driven basis (e.g., "When purchases exceed $1 million, e-mail me this report.").

■**Note** SQL Server 2008 includes improvements to the charting control, as well as map control and gauge controls acquired from Dundas for richer reporting, and new capabilities for authoring and delivery of reports in Word or Excel.

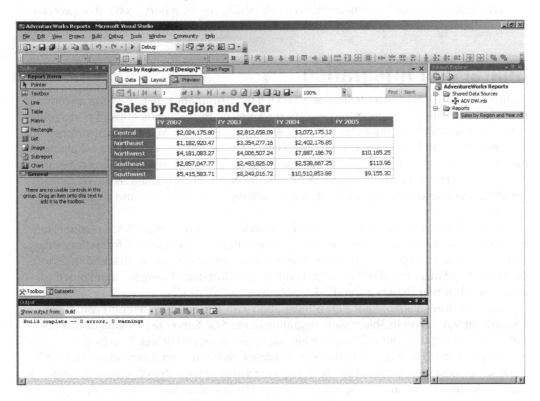

Figure 2-5. *The Reporting Services designer*

While most users will probably view SQL Server reports in the browser, they may want to export the report data in order to work with it in other ways. Out of the box, SQL Server Reporting Services 2005 supports export to the following:

- HTML

- MHT (Microsoft single-file web export)

- PDF

- XLS (Excel workbook)

- CSV

- XML

With SQL Server 2008, end users also have the ability to edit reports in Word or Excel and generate them dynamically.

SharePoint Integration

"Scorecards do not exist in a vacuum" is what I tell my customers. When you have a scorecard or a dashboard, the stakeholders responsible for acting on the KPI s and objectives are going to have to collaborate on their plan of action. A compelling part of Microsoft's BI strategy utilizes SharePoint as the centerpiece. Microsoft Office SharePoint Server 2007 is a collaborative framework—it offers web-based sites that end users can personalize with various types of information—task lists, contacts, calendar items, document libraries, and so on. Of course, with SQL Server and PerformancePoint you can add reports, scorecards, and dashboards to the list.

By hosting the corporate scorecard in a collaborative portal, it enables stakeholders to comment on performance, discuss and assign action items, track related information, show contextual charts and graphs, and so on. SharePoint is also so easy to use that end users will be able to build their own dashboards by combining all this data. Example SharePoint dashboards are shown in Figures 2-6 and 2-7.

A new feature in SharePoint 2007 is integration with SQL Server as a report center. By configuring SQL Server in SharePoint integration mode, SQL Server uses SharePoint as the publishing and hosting point for reports instead of the report server web interface.

In turn, SharePoint's Report Center site template provides a central location for hosting reports. Previously, reports may have been scattered across various shared folders, business systems, web sites, and so on. Finding a particular report was problematic and strongly dependent on bookmarks. With Report Center, all reports can be published to the same location and found in the same place. You may still link to reports from other locations and embed reports in other dashboards, but if you're looking to browse existing reports or trying to find a specific report, you only have one place to look. Figure 2-8 shows a SharePoint Report Center site.

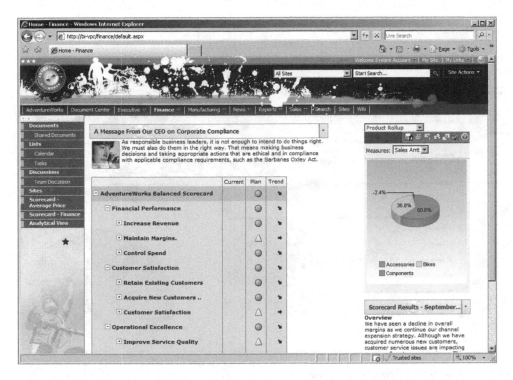

Figure 2-6. *Using SharePoint as a BI platform*

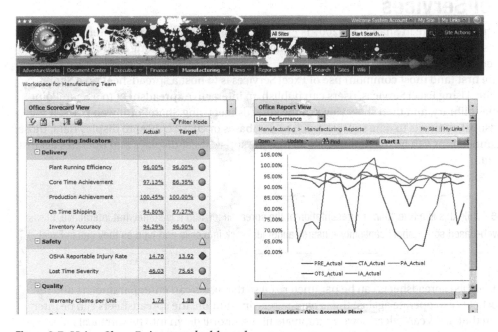

Figure 2-7. *Using SharePoint as a dashboard*

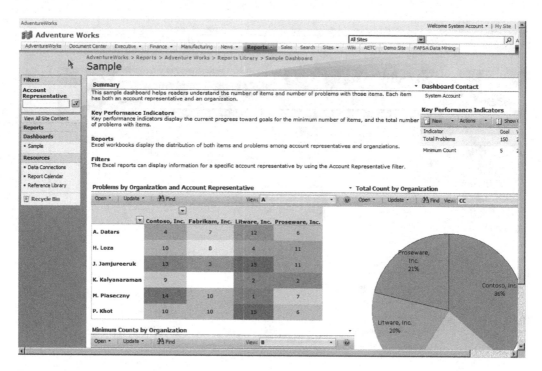

Figure 2-8. *A SharePoint Report Center site*

Excel Services

Another new feature in SharePoint 2007 is Excel Services. As part of the new enterprise-level features in SharePoint, Excel Services creates new capabilities for working with spreadsheets at the enterprise level.

The first (and most common) use of Excel Services is to host a spreadsheet on a Share-Point site. Using Excel Services, users can publish an interactive spreadsheet to a SharePoint document library, and then show views of the spreadsheet using SharePoint web parts. If the spreadsheet connects to data sources (such as databases or OLAP cubes) to display data, those data connections can be maintained live so that the spreadsheet displays and operates against live data.

■**Note** While this is a true "thin" representation of the spreadsheet, and it is somewhat interactive, this is not a web-based spreadsheet capability—users cannot just click into cells and type as they can in Excel.

Published spreadsheets can be parameterized so that users can enter parameters and the spreadsheets can operate against those parameters. In addition, the spreadsheets can be interactive in that users can select views, manipulate filters, or drill down into hierarchical data.

Figure 2-9 shows an Excel workbook published to a SharePoint site using Excel Services.

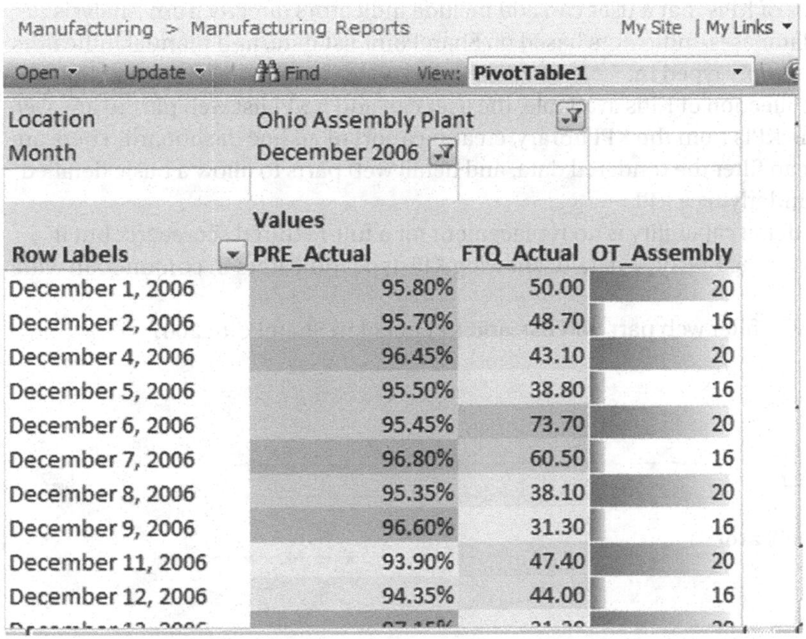

	Values		
Row Labels	PRE_Actual	FTQ_Actual	OT_Assembly
December 1, 2006	95.80%	50.00	20
December 2, 2006	95.70%	48.70	16
December 4, 2006	96.45%	43.10	20
December 5, 2006	95.50%	38.80	16
December 6, 2006	95.45%	73.70	20
December 7, 2006	96.80%	60.50	16
December 8, 2006	95.35%	38.10	20
December 9, 2006	96.60%	31.30	16
December 11, 2006	93.90%	47.40	20
December 12, 2006	94.35%	44.00	16

Figure 2-9. *Excel Services displaying a spreadsheet in SharePoint*

A final use case for Excel Services is the ability to publish a *snapshot view* of a spreadsheet. This allows users (perhaps external users, or internal users who should not have access to proprietary business logic) to view a spreadsheet and even download a copy of it. However, when they download the spreadsheet, they are only getting a snapshot—the contents of the cells, but none of the formulas or back-end calculation logic that renders the values. Thus, they have access to the numbers for their own use, but the proprietary business logic is scrubbed before the data is shared.

Another use for Excel Services (which we won't be covering in this book) is publishing a complex spreadsheet to a server to be calculated. Power analysts often have immense, complicated spreadsheets with cross-references, deep calculations, statistical analysis, and so on. Traditionally, they would calculate these spreadsheets on their desktop machines overnight with a sign on the monitor that reads "Do not turn off." Now, Excel Services enables them to publish these complex documents to a server where they can be run on true server-class hardware as services.

SharePoint KPI Lists

Another feature of the Enterprise SharePoint licensing is the ability to build simple, ad hoc dashboards.

SharePoint has a new library type called a KPI list. This is oriented toward KPI-type representations of data. A KPI list contains individual items (KPIs) that have an actual value, a target value, and a status indicator. Depending on the type of KPI added, a user may have the ability to design one or more of these values (e.g., SharePoint can read native KPIs from SQL Server Analysis Services, but those KPIs cannot be edited in SharePoint).

The various types of KPIs that a user can add include indicators directly from Analysis Services, relational databases, indicators based on SharePoint list data, and manual indicators where the values are simply typed in.

Once there is a collection of KPIs available, the user can add a KPI list web part to any web part page and pull the KPIs from the KPI library, creating a sort of ad hoc dashboard. There are filter web parts that can filter the rendered data, and detail web parts to allow a basic detailed analysis of the data underlying a KPI.

The KPI list and detail capability is no replacement for a full-featured scorecard, but it makes a nice way of pulling KPI-type data or showing KPI-type indicators in conjunction with other content.

Figure 2-10 shows a filter web part, KPI list, and KPI detail in SharePoint 2007.

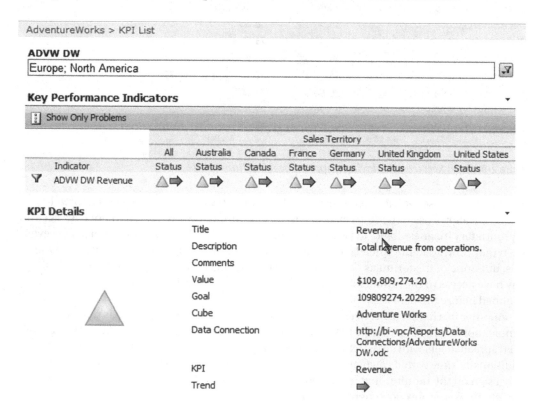

Figure 2-10. *KPI list web parts in SharePoint*

ProClarity 6.3

In 2006, Microsoft acquired the ProClarity corporation. ProClarity made its name by providing advanced visualizations, and charting, graphing, reporting, and dashboarding tools based on SQL Server Analysis Services cubes. In SQL Server 2000, Analysis Services was very powerful. Unfortunately, there was no capability out of the box to even view the results of a cube once it was processed (there was a free Visual Basic project that you could download and build to browse the cube, but still).

Leaping into that gap, ProClarity produced a product that had two primary sales points:

- It was incredibly flexible and displayed intuitive visualizations for Analysis Services data.

- It was incredibly easy to use.

In effect, they put a face on the powerful cubes that could be rendered with Analysis Services.

In addition to traditional types of graphs and charts (Figure 2-11), ProClarity had advanced visualizations that gave users powerful new ways to view and gain value from their data.

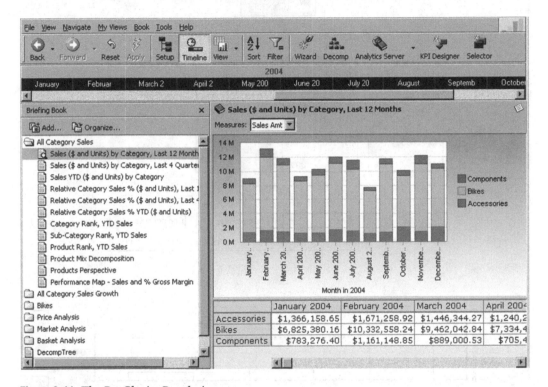

Figure 2-11. *The ProClarity Pro designer*

The decomposition tree (Figure 2-12) offered a completely intuitive way to drill into data. More than just walking down a predefined hierarchy, the decomposition tree allowed a less technical user to point and click and drill across dimensions, viewing how the components that make up their business contributed to the numbers they were seeing.

Other visualizations provided by ProClarity include a performance map, which displays a heat map–style display based on underlying dimensions in the cube, and a perspective view, which plots data in a scatter chart manner to identify clusters of values, outlying data points, and other relationships.

While some of ProClarity's capabilities are being rolled into PerformancePoint, and the long-term goal is for PerformancePoint Server to take over all of ProClarity's functionality, the limited implementation in version 1 of PerformancePoint makes ProClarity Analytics Server a continuing necessity in a BI implementation. As a result, we'll cover ProClarity Analytics Server and how it can be integrated with a PerformancePoint dashboard.

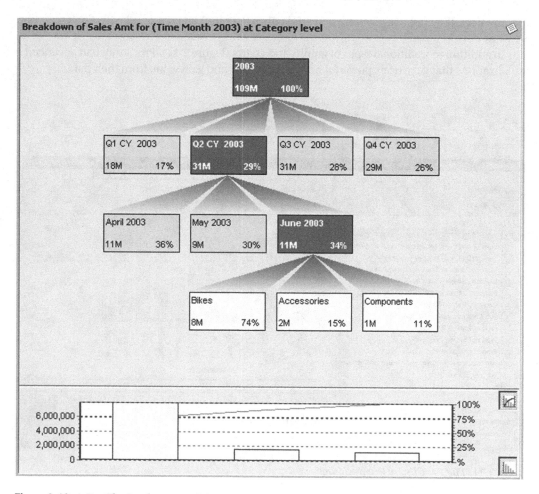

Figure 2-12. *A ProClarity decomposition tree*

PerformancePoint Server 2007

PerformancePoint Server is Microsoft's first full-blooded entry into the BI arena. Building upon the foundation of SQL Server and Analytics Services, it blends the scorecarding capabilities of BSM 2005 and ProClarity Analysis Server.

Often, a BI implementation (or more likely a simple scorecard implementation) is designed to be wholly reactive—a KPI turns yellow, everyone rushes around to figure out why, the cause is identified, and the status goes back to normal—watching the scorecard.

Microsoft's goal with PerformancePoint Server 2007 is to bring more process to a BI solution—instead of a loop consisting of "watch scorecard" and "react," the planners behind PerformancePoint Server wanted a product that encouraged more process—the ability to monitor one's business, analyze why certain results were the way they were, and plan a course of action that was organized, data driven, and repeatable. This cycle has been distilled down to *monitor, analyze, plan*, or MAP (see Figure 2-13).

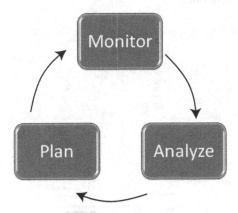

Figure 2-13. *The Microsoft BI cycle*

This cycle roughly maps as shown in Table 2-1.

Table 2-1. *Mapping Microsoft BI Products*

Step	Previous Version	PerformancePoint Term
Monitor	BSM 2005	Monitoring (scorecard)
Analyze	ProClarity 6.3	Monitoring (analytics)
Plan	Biz#	Planning

PerformancePoint really has two segments: *monitoring and analytics* (sometimes referred to as M&A) and *planning* (or P).

Monitoring and Analytics

The monitoring and analytics module of PerformancePoint will feel somewhat familiar to anyone who's used BSM—it derives from the same designer. However, it has been thoroughly overhauled, and has evolved from a simple scorecard designer to a full-featured dashboard builder.

The designer (Figure 2-14) is a Windows client application that is delivered via "click once" install from the monitoring server web site. The dashboards, scorecards, and analytic charts you design are then published back to the analytics server for consumption via Share-Point, SQL Server Reporting Services, or a simple ASPX web page.

Scorecards can aggregate data from any number of back-end data sources, including Excel spreadsheets, SharePoint lists, ODBC data sources, and of course SQL Server Analysis Services. The scorecards can be designed in a drag-and-drop fashion, and the builder offers a live preview.

Associated with scorecards (and what makes them dashboards) is contextual amplifying information such as reports, charts, and other content. You can associate this content with a scorecard using the builder and publish the whole thing at once.

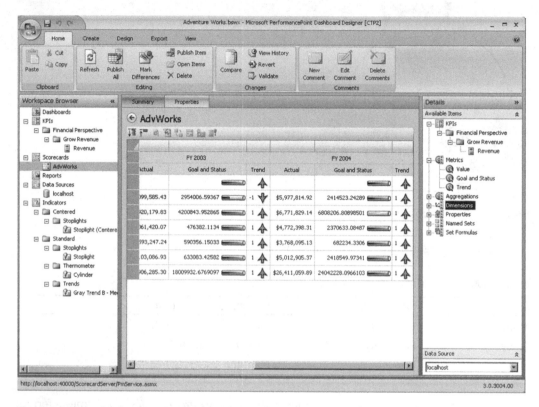

Figure 2-14. *The PerformancePoint Dashboard designer*

PerformancePoint dashboards can be exported by the user into Excel or PowerPoint.

Once a scorecard indicates a problem, we want to be able to drill into the underlying data to identify a root cause. PerformancePoint provides some capability for analytic charts (and even predictive charts using data mining techniques), but the real power is associating ProClarity charts and visualizations with a scorecard, empowering an end user to really dig into the underlying data in an intuitive way.

Once a business user has identified a root cause, they will probably want to do some forecasting or what-if analysis to identify potential solutions to the problem and the effects they would have on other areas of the business. That's where the modeling/planning part of PerformancePoint Server comes into play.

Modeling and Planning

The modeling and planning module of PerformancePoint Server is a powerful new paradigm to leverage SQL Server Analysis Services. The idea here is to allow a business user to design and deploy an OLAP cube. While this was previously only the province of DBAs and data architects, Microsoft's goal here is to commoditize OLAP technology and make it accessible to the masses.

A business user can design a "model" for a business process, consisting of dimensions, measures, and scenarios. Once they have designed the model (which is really an OLAP cube under the covers—shhh!), they can deploy it to a server and build data entry forms to leverage the cube technologies.

Here are two examples of problems that a modern CFO may face:

You are the CFO for a large organization. When preparing the budget, you would like to get inputs from each of the 20-something regions that make up the company. However, in practice this quickly becomes untenable—getting 20 spreadsheets with cross-linked formulas from each region and rolling them all together is just too hard. So instead you simply guesstimate budget numbers based on last year's expenditures and hope for the best.

Now you're the CFO of a government agency. With a presidential election coming up, it's anyone's guess which way the agency's budget will go next fiscal year. The director of the agency asks you to prepare three annual budgets—one assuming a 5 percent cut, one assuming the same budget as this year, and one assuming a 2 percent increase. You now have to create and manage three separate budgets, how they'll break out to your regions, and so on.

Traditionally, these problems have been very hard (in general, so difficult that they're simply not solved). PerformancePoint planning is designed to enable exactly these scenarios:

PerformancePoint has the capability of splitting out and delegating assignments from the model. So, you (the corporate CFO) can assign a request for budget inputs to each region. The CFOs for each region can then have a form built in Excel that they use to prepare their budget submissions (see Figure 2-15). After they submit their budgets, you can review each submission (via the server; no e-mailing documents around) and roll them together automatically using Analysis Services technology to produce your own budget.

PerformancePoint has a scenario-based capability that enables you (the government CFO) to create a baseline budget, and then simply select different scenarios to adjust the numbers as you see fit. You can also delegate scenarios to subordinates or federate the budget among regions just as in the corporate CFO scenario.

The idea is to take what has traditionally been a spreadsheet and e-mail performance and bring it into the 21st century by using a client-server process with workflow, business rules, and data mining to truly empower business users and planners to make data-driven decisions and poll their subordinates for input, without having to cut and paste from a pile of spreadsheets.

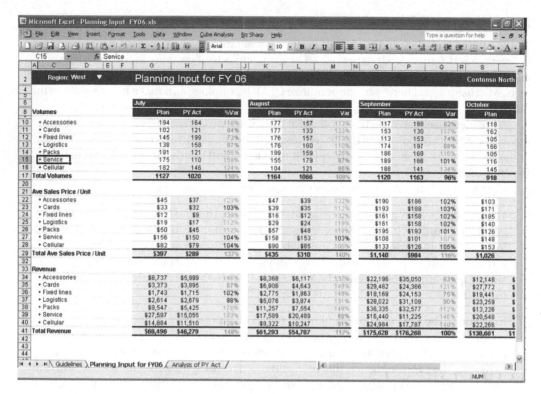

Figure 2-15. *An Excel input form for PerformancePoint planning*

Conclusion

In the chapters that follow, I will do an overview of SQL Server. We'll focus on SQL Server 2005 for this book, but I will point out differences that arise in SQL Server 2008 when appropriate.

■Note The SQL Server overview will be fairly brief—a high-speed fly-by, if you will. The SQL Server relational engine is immensely powerful and a great friend to have for staging, reporting, and so on. If you'd like to dig deep into the capabilities of the SQL Server relational engine, I recommend *Pro SQL Server 2005*, by Thomas Rizzo (Apress, 2005).

The chapters following the overview of the SQL Server relational engine will delve into Integration Services, Analysis Services, and Reporting Services, covering the concepts you need to know for a BI implementation.

After the SQL Server grand tour, we'll do a light overview of SharePoint as it pertains to BI—exploring web part pages, Report Center sites, KPI lists, and filters.

Then we'll dig into the meat of the book: ProClarity Analytics Server (including installation and configuration) and PerformancePoint Server (monitoring, analytics, and planning). We'll also cover integration and how these pieces work together.

CHAPTER 3

■■■

SQL Server

Overview

Microsoft SQL Server originated with a partnership with Sybase, writing SQL Server for OS/2. Later, Microsoft and Sybase parted ways, and Microsoft focused on SQL Server for the Windows platform. The most well-known versions started with SQL Server 6.5 in 1996, followed by 7.0 in 1999. In 2000, Microsoft released SQL Server 2000, another evolutionary step in moving SQL Server into the enterprise RDBMS arena.

SQL Server 2005 was launched late in 2005, and was a revolutionary step forward for SQL Server, and placed the platform solidly in the enterprise relational database market, while also broadening the appeal with versions addressing each level of platform (mobile, embedded, workgroup, and so on).

The most recent edition of SQL Server is SQL Server 2008, released in mid-2008. SQL Server 2008 is more evolutionary than revolutionary, with a focus on compatibility and ease of migration from SQL Server 2005. However, there are still significant investments in the data platform and pages of new features covering everything from developers to maintainability and high availability.

■**Note** I won't be doing a deep dive into SQL Server, such as installing it, writing T-SQL, or other aspects of the transactional database. My only goal with this chapter is to give a broad overview of the platform our BI will build on. For more information, I recommend browsing www.microsoft.com/sql or digging into any of Apress's many SQL Server titles.

Let's start our tour by taking a look at the various SQL Server editions.

SQL Server Editions

There are a number of editions for SQL Server 2005, and when first contemplating the choices, they may seem a bit confusing. We're going to review each of the editions—for a quick comparison, see Table 3-1.

When choosing an edition, you'll need to keep a number of factors in mind, including the following:

- Hardware allocation

- Standards requirements

- Type of application (departmental, enterprise, mission critical)

- Estimated data size and growth

- Type of programming (queries, stored procedures, embedded CLR)

- Maintenance requirements

- Features

- Price

The range of possibilities for various projects is why Microsoft offers the various editions of the database engine. You can start with Express or Developer Edition to learn your way around, build and test some proofs of concept, and even deploy small-scale applications. From there, as requirements demand, your group can grow to Workgroup Edition, and on to the Standard. For those applications that are mission critical or have large-scale requirements, Enterprise Edition is a real workhorse.

Table 3-1. *Comparing SQL Server Editions*

Version	Cost	Max Database Size	Max CPUs	Max RAM	64-Bit	Notes
Compact	Free	4 GB	1	N/A	N/A	Small footprint
Express	Free	1 GB	1	1 GB	No	Full T-SQL
Workgroup	$4,000/CPU	Unlimited	2	3 GB	No	Simple applications
Standard	$6,000/CPU	Unlimited	4	OS max	Yes	Integration Services, Analysis Services, Reporting Services
Enterprise	$25,000/CPU	Unlimited	OS max	OS max	Yes	
Developer	$50/machine	Unlimited	OS max	OS max	Yes	Same as EE, limited by licensing

■**Note** Prices are, of course, as of the date of publication, and always subject to change.

Compact Edition

SQL Server Compact Edition is designed for use on compact devices (smartphones and Pocket PCs). The runtime is under 1 MB in size, and the engine runs in-process on the compact device. The benefit is that compact application developers can work with an engine they understand and are familiar with.

Of course, given the target platform, the engine is limited to a single user and a 4 GB maximum database size. In addition, there are no advanced features (such as stored procedures or triggers). Pricing is easy enough—SQL Server Compact Edition is free for development and deployment.

For more information about SQL Server Compact Edition, see www.microsoft.com/sql/editions/compact/default.mspx.

Express Edition

SQL Server Express Edition was created to offer low-end entry into developing on and working with SQL Server. This is the newest incarnation of Microsoft Data Engine (MSDE), and has been reengineered to, again, align more closely with how SQL Server operates, to maintain a uniform interface from compact through entry level and up to enterprise.

Note MSDE will not be supported on Microsoft Vista.

Express Edition also includes a lightweight version of SQL Server Management Studio to act as an interface to the databases you create. There is no limit to the number of users or connections to the engine, but as scalability is limited, don't expect to run the next Amazon.com on it. This edition does include advanced database capabilities such as stored procedures, views, triggers, cursors, active directory support, and so on. Express Edition also supports SQL Server's 2005 XML capabilities and CLR stored procedures.

Express Edition is limited to a single CPU and a maximum database size of 4 GB. It will also only take advantage of 1 GB of installed memory, and is not available for 64-bit machines. This edition can be used, embedded, and deployed for no charge (redistribution requires registration for redistribution rights at www.microsoft.com/sql/editions/express/redistregister.mspx).

There is a rich site detailing SQL Server Express Edition, as well as tutorials and in-depth technical articles to learn SQL Server, at www.microsoft.com/sql/editions/express/default.mspx.

Express Edition with Advanced Services

SQL Server Express Edition with Advanced Services adds Management Studio Express to the client components available for Express Edition. In addition, it enables full text search and reporting services. This is a separate download to enable developers to leverage a lightweight data engine if they choose (Express Edition), or add text search and reporting if their requirements demand it (Advanced Services).

Other than the additional services, all the other fundamentals are the same as Express Edition, and Express Edition with Advanced Services is still free to use and distribute (with registration).

Workgroup Edition

SQL Server Workgroup Edition is the first licensed version we've covered that you have to pay for.

■**Note** SQL Server is licensed in two ways: per CPU, with unlimited connections, or per server, which requires a client access license (CAL) for each user or device that authenticates against the server. Microsoft only requires licensing physical CPUs, regardless of the number of cores, so a quad-core single CPU box will cost the same as a single-core single CPU box. A "server" license licenses the entire server machine, regardless of the number of processors or cores, and is significantly cheaper than even a single CPU license, but you do have to license every user who accesses the server, so it's a trade-off that you have to evaluate. For more information, including how to buy and from where, please see www.microsoft.com/sql/howtobuy/default.mspx.

Workgroup Edition is targeted toward, as named, workgroup applications—simpler applications that only need a relational database and perhaps basic reporting. It raises the limit on CPUs to two, and can use up to 3 GB of installed RAM. It only supports 64-bit in emulation mode—Windows on Windows (WOW)—and has no limit on the size of the database. For failover or high availability, Workgroup Edition offers log shipping, which provides some standby capability, but not mirroring or failover clustering like Standard or Enterprise Editions.

Workgroup Edition includes the full client components install, including SQL Server Management Studio and Business Intelligence Development Studio (BIDS). However, this edition does not include Analysis Services, Integration Services, or data mining capabilities.

Standard Edition

SQL Server Standard Edition and Enterprise Edition are the top end of the scale—they both have the full complement of services, but differ in the factors that govern truly enterprise databases and requirements for high uptimes.

■**Note** For a complete comparison of SQL Server editions, see www.microsoft.com/sql/prodinfo/features/compare-features.mspx.

Standard Edition includes Integration Services, Analysis Services, and Reporting Services. While it is limited to four CPUs, there is no limit on the size of the database or RAM that the server can access. This edition offers mirroring, but only a single redo thread. It also offers clustering, but only two nodes. Other availability features such as online indexing, restore, and fast recovery are only available in Enterprise Edition.

■**Note** Standard and Enterprise Editions add SQL Server Notification Services. However, as Notification Services are being removed in SQL Server 2008, I advise against investing too heavily in them.

SQL Server Standard Edition also adds Integration Services (albeit with a limited set of transforms) and Analysis Services. With SQL Server Analysis Services comes a very powerful set of data mining capabilities. Standard Edition also adds the capability for SQL Server to run native web services from the engine—it's possible to set up web services using HTTP endpoints and use T-SQL to process the response from a web service request.

Enterprise Edition

For truly business-critical applications, where emergency failover and uptime are of the utmost importance, SQL Server Enterprise Edition builds on Standard Edition, adding data partitioning to provide for very large databases. Fast recovery means that the database engine is engineered to allow the user to access the database during the undo or rollback phase of database recovery.

Enterprise Edition also adds advanced transforms to Integration Services, data-driven subscriptions to Reporting Services, writeback capabilities to Analysis Services cubes, and advanced data mining methods. It also allows integration of data mining capabilities into Integration Services transforms, which allows data cleaning based on existing data in the database instead of fixed business rules.

For example, imagine importing sales data from various stores around the United States. Looking at a long list of items and quantities, can you pick out the errors and define business rules? Probably not. However, you could set up a data mining query to test items and quantities against all the previous orders in the database—this would flag unusual sales as possible errors (e.g., a large number of surfboards sold in Montana, rock climbing gear sold in Florida, or sunscreen sold in Cape Cod in December). Note that these are *possible* sales, but should be flagged for manual review.

The high availability features in Enterprise Edition are the most compelling reasons for this edition, providing an effective always-on database server capability. This edition offers full failover clustering capability, up to nine nodes. Database mirroring is available in all modes. In addition, we have database snapshots, online index operations, parallel index operations, and table and index partitioning. We'll dig a bit into what these mean later.

An interesting "feature" of Enterprise Edition is unlimited virtualization. Normally, every server installed must be licensed, whether real or virtual. For example, if I have a server with 8 processors and I'm running 32 legacy virtual guest machines with SQL Server installed on each, I must license 32 instances of SQL Server. However, I could license the host server with Enterprise Edition (eight CPUs), and then I could install unlimited instances of SQL Server in the guest virtual machines. For heavy virtualization scenarios, this is definitely a compelling option.

The data warehousing/analysis services improvements with Enterprise Edition are so significant that I'll cover those in Chapter 5.

Developer Edition

SQL Server Developer Edition is effectively Enterprise Edition, with the exception that the engine and services are only licensed for a single user. This enables developers to work with SQL Server and learn and develop against all its capabilities for a very low price ($50 per user).

Tools

Now that you're familiar with the different editions of SQL Server, let's take a look at the tools you'll be using to interact with a database engine. You'll spend most of your time in SQL Server Management Studio for administering databases, and in the Visual Studio–based BIDS for development of Integration Services processes, Analysis Services cubes, and Reporting Services models and reports.

Management Studio

If you're familiar with SQL Server 2000, Enterprise Manager and Query Analyzer have been replaced with SQL Server Management Studio (Figure 3-1).

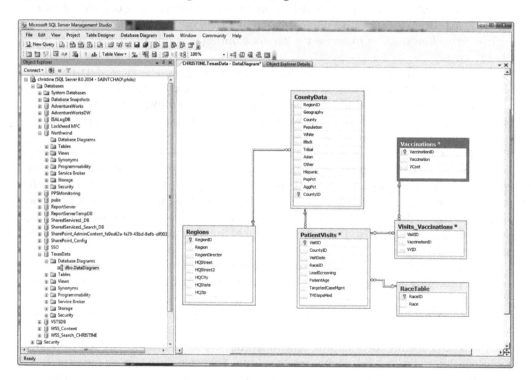

Figure 3-1. *SQL Server Management Studio*

Management Studio has a huge number of improvements over the SQL Server 2000 tools. Apart from uniting management and query editing into a single platform, there are improvements in diagramming (printing database diagrams is now native—no more screen captures!). You can also use Management Studio to manage the administrative aspects of Integration Services, Analysis Services, and Reporting Services, simply by using the Connect to Server dialog, as shown in Figure 3-2.

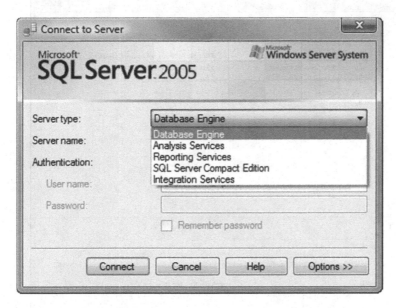

Figure 3-2. *Selecting services from the Connect to Server dialog*

■**Tip** Management Studio can take a little longer to connect to Reporting Services than the other services—it uses the web services, which need to compile the first time you access them. So be patient.

This enables Management Studio to give you a full bird's-eye view of your servers, as well as a quick-and-easy way to see what's going on across your enterprise.

The query editor is available through Management Studio as well, with an added bonus—if you're using Analysis Services, SQL Server Management Studio allows writing and running MDX (Multidimensional Expressions), DMX (Data Mining Extensions), and XML/A (XML for Analysis) queries.

Of course, there's far more to SQL Server Management Studio than I've covered here—again, my only goal is to give an overview.

Business Intelligence Development Studio

For a large portion of this book, we'll be spending our time in BIDS. BIDS is installed with the client tools of SQL Server, and is a specialized instance of Visual Studio 2005 with templates for the SQL Server services installed (Figure 3-3).

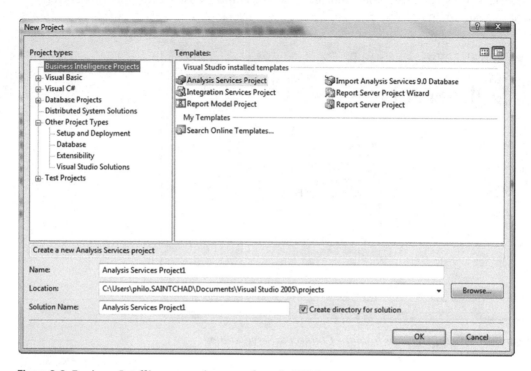

Figure 3-3. *Business Intelligence project templates in BIDS*

■**Note** If you already have Visual Studio installed, BIDS will merge the BI projects with the projects in your Visual Studio installation. From that point, opening Visual Studio and opening BIDS from the SQL Server Start menu will have the same effect. You will use Visual Studio 2005 for SQL Server 2005, Visual Studio 2008 for SQL Server 2008.

BIDS is a no-cost install as part of the SQL Server package, but without Visual Studio it can only be used to create projects in the Business Intelligence list (shown previously in Figure 3-3). This tool is exceptionally powerful, and a great aid for visual design of Integration Services flows (Figure 3-4), Analysis Services cubes (Figure 3-5), and Reporting Services reports (Figure 3-6).

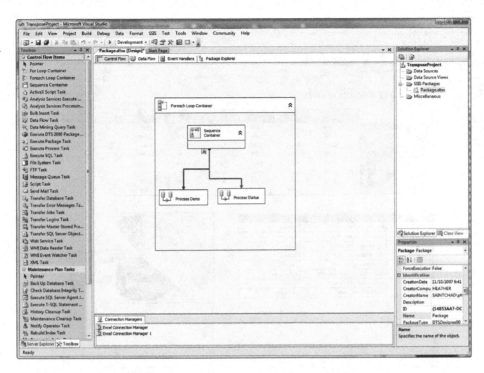

Figure 3-4. *SQL Server Integration Services control flow in BIDS*

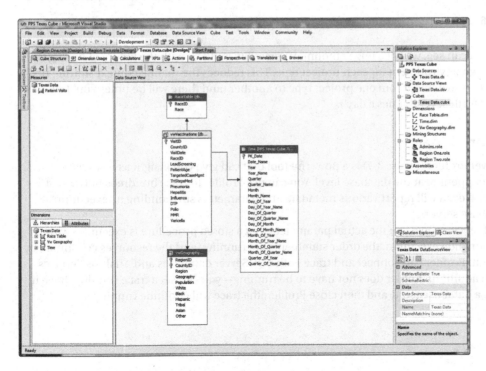

Figure 3-5. *SQL Server Analysis Services cube design in BIDS*

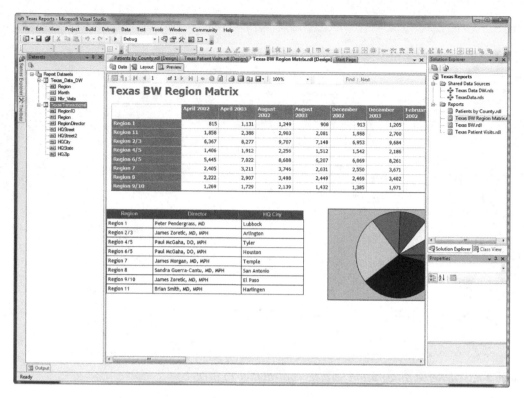

Figure 3-6. *SQL Server Reporting Services report in BIDS*

As you can see, we get a huge amount of versatility in BIDS, with the luxury of having the same design environment for each project type. This reduces the mental context shifting necessary when switching from one project type to another (and there will be times you'll switch back and forth several times a day!).

Profiler

SQL Server Profiler (Figure 3-7) is a powerful tool that can give you insight as to what is really happening at the database level. You can use Profiler to trace hundreds of types of events, and each will report various metadata and parameters surrounding its execution at the database server.

Profiler can show you the actual parameters that a stored procedure is executing with, timings for code execution, the order statements are running, and the resources consumed by each event. Profiler can connect and trace both SQL Server databases and Analysis Services cubes. In addition, Profiler does not have to be running—you can set a trace running, have it dump to a database table, and then close Profiler; the trace will continue running.

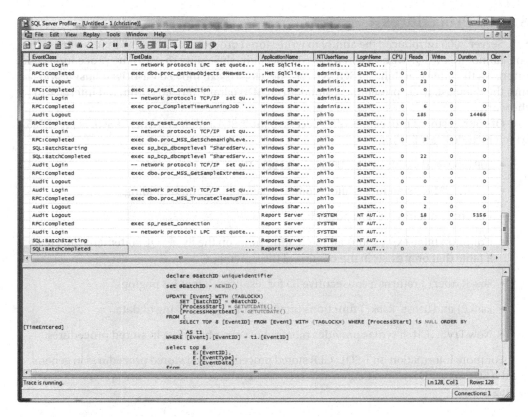

Figure 3-7. *SQL Server Profiler*

■Tip One of the greatest uses for Profiler is troubleshooting database connections. If an application can't connect to a database or cube, run a trace on the object watching for login failures—the event will show which account is failing connection, which will give you a good hint as to what's going on.

Programmability

Of course, RDBMSs aren't just about data storage anymore—they are as much application servers as data repositories. SQL Server 2005 offers a robust capability for automating processes, including significant improvements from SQL Server 2000. Again, I'll give a whirlwind tour just to acquaint you with the breadth of SQL Server's features.

■Note For those of you who are fans of the Northwind or Pubs sample databases, note that Microsoft is moving toward AdventureWorks as a standard sample database, and it is not installed by default! To install it, you must do a custom install—one of the options under the database engine is to install the sample databases. You can still download the Northwind and Pubs databases from Microsoft as well.

Stored Procedures

SQL Server 2005 introduced the ability to write stored procedures using .NET languages. While you cannot mix T-SQL with CLR in a stored procedure, the ability to use more procedural code improves the interoperability of SQL Server—developers can move data-driven business logic into the database while presenting a standard OLEDB parameterized command interface to the world.

Of course, stored procedures offer access to the T-SQL enhancements in SQL Server 2005, which include the following:

- `TOP` now works with `INSERT`, `UPDATE`, and `DELETE`.

- `PIVOT/UNPIVOT` statements allow complex data folding and unfolding.

- Recursive queries are now possible.

- Common table expressions allow creating views on the fly; a SQL statement can create a table that only exists in the context of the statement.

- `Row_Number()` returns a consecutive ID for resultsets (great for paging).

- `Rank()` and `Dense_Rank()` functions provide score-type ranking of data.

- New `Try...Catch` syntax provides more robust error handling in stored procedures.

For more information on T-SQL, CLR stored procedures, and stored procedures in general, see the SQL Server Developer Center, at `http://msdn2.microsoft.com/en-us/sqlserver/aa336270`.

Service Broker

SQL Server Service Broker was introduced with SQL Server 2005. Service Broker is a programmable application host that runs inside the database engine. This provides a platform for developers to locate tasks, actions, or processes that are asynchronous to database processing, but smaller scale, so a full-blown Windows Service would be overkill.

Some examples of uses for Service Broker include the following:

Data collection among disparate systems: For example, a centralized warehousing system that needs to poll various smaller stovepipe systems to update stock levels could initiate Service Broker queries to communicate with each subsystem, collect its information, and update the main stock level store.

Batch query processing: This allows a stored procedure or other process that depends on a query being processed to continue on and commit without waiting on the query.

Loosely coupled or occasionally connected systems: Service Broker queries can be initiated and wait on an intermittent connection without holding up other business logic.

For an in-depth understanding of SQL Server Service Broker, I recommend *Pro SQL Server 2005 Service Broker*, by Klaus Aschenbrenner (Apress, 2007).

Web Services

An awesome new capability in SQL Server 2005 is the ability to create HTTP endpoints and attach them to stored procedures. The net result is that you can access SQL Server and execute a stored procedure from any platform that can communicate with SOAP-compliant web services. You do not need IIS running to enable this capability, either—SQL Server creates and manages the endpoint completely.

Query Notifications

Query notifications build on the Service Broker architecture and allow developers to create notification events to applications when data has changed. A client can create a notification and then terminate—the query notification will survive the connection being closed. The application can then poll a Service Broker queue for available notifications.

Note A query notification terminates once its criteria have been met. To receive another notification when the data changes again, the notification must be set again by the calling application.

Database Mail

Database Mail (often called "SQL Mail") replaces the e-mail capability in SQL Server 2000, which required installing Microsoft Outlook on the server to enable the MAPI interfaces. Database Mail is an integrated part of SQL Server, and uses SMTP directly to send e-mail as required. However, Database Mail runs in its own process, so sending e-mail does not impinge on the RDBMS processes.

Database Mail works in the background and is asynchronous. You can specify failover servers in case a mail server is not available, and Database Mail is cluster-aware, enhancing its scalability.

Security

"Secure by design, by default, in deployment" is the catchphrase for Microsoft's Trustworthy Computing initiative, and this is absolutely true in SQL Server 2005. In fact, SQL Server 2005 SP2 has been certified against the EAL4+ of the Common Criteria Certification, and is FIPS 140-2 compliant.

New and enhanced security features in SQL Server 2005 include, but are by no means limited to, the following:

Granular permission control: Enhanced permissions make it easier to minimize the permissions that a DBA grants to users or processes to accomplish what they need to do.

Enforced password policy: By enforcing AD-type password policies on user accounts, 12345-type security risks have been removed.

DDL triggers: These allow for broader use of triggers for auditing.

Off by default: The services and features installed with SQL Server by default are limited subset of its full capabilities. As I mentioned previously, not even demo databases are installed by default.

Least privilege support: SQL Server Profiler no longer requires administrator rights to run.

For more information about SQL Server security, please see www.microsoft.com/sql/ technologies/security/default.mspx.

XML

XML is definitely a first-class citizen in SQL Server 2005. SQL Server understands XML natively, which gives database developers a huge boost in capabilities, especially when dealing with document-centric or XML-centric applications.

XML Datatype

First of all, SQL Server 2005 now has an XML datatype. This can be used to store entire XML documents or just fragments. XML datatypes can be associated with schemas and validated against them. XML datatypes can be used in table columns, variables, and parameters.

■**Note** A stored XML datatype cannot exceed 2 GB per instance.

XML datatypes can have default values and constraints, can be used in views (including query by XQuery) and computed columns (again, leveraging XQuery to modify the XML), and so on. Obviously, another great use for the XML datatype is in conjunction with SQL Server web services, mentioned previously.

Schemas

Schemas can be stored in SQL Server in Schema collections. These collections can be used to type XML data stored in database tables, variables, or parameters. Note that these are collections—you can have multiple schemas in a collection, and an XML instance associated with the collection need only validate against one schema.

XQuery and Data Manipulation Language

The best part about having XML in the database is the ability to use XQuery to query the XML instances.

Consider an example in which you accept purchase orders from a vendor that are submitted in XML. Normally, you might parse the XML upon receipt and just store the data you need in the database, or you might keep the XML documents in a file system for archiving.

With the XML datatype, you can store the originally submitted XML in the database in a typed field. This becomes very powerful when you realize there's a field in the XML documents that you are actually interested in and you want to run a query against them. Instead of batch processing thousands or tens of thousands of text files, you can simply run an XQuery query against the column to extract the data and do with it as you need.

XML Best Practices

The SQL Server Developer Center at MSDN has a number of best practices for using XML in SQL Server, including when to use XML vs. parsing the document and storing it as relational data, choice of XML technology, data modeling, granularity of the XML data stored in an XML column, and so on. The Developer Center is at `http://msdn2.microsoft.com/en-us/sqlserver/aa336270`.

High Availability

Once more, I'll give a very quick overview into a very serious topic. My only goal here is to acquaint you with the terms to enable more research. I will also recommend *Pro SQL Server 2005 High Availability*, by Allan Hirt (Apress, 2007).

Mirroring

Database mirroring was first made available in SQL Server 2005 SP1. The general concept is that transaction logs are transferred directly from one server to another, providing a hot backup should the primary database server fail. The two servers are called the *principal* and the *mirror*. An optional third server may be set up, referred to as the *witness*, which governs failover should the principal server fail.

More about mirroring is available at `www.microsoft.com/technet/prodtechnol/sql/2005/dbmirror.mspx`.

Failover Clustering

Failover clustering maintains uptime by having a number of servers, or nodes, that share storage (necessarily a high-availability storage solution). A failover cluster looks like a single server logically; should a single machine fail, the cluster will continue operation without a blip, operating from the common data storage.

A detailed whitepaper on failover clustering is available at `www.microsoft.com/downloads/details.aspx?familyid=818234dc-a17b-4f09-b282-c6830fead499&displaylang=en`.

Online Index Operations

Very simply—in the past, tables had to be taken offline while index operations were performed. In SQL Server 2005 (Enterprise Edition), users can still access table data and use other indexes while an index is being created, changed, dropped, or rebuilt.

Database Snapshots

Database snapshots allow a DBA to capture a full database at a point where the DBA can be confident about the state of the database—a current state of the data if all processing transactions were rolled back instantaneously. This provides a checkpoint to where the database can be rolled back if necessary. This is a great tool for implementing changes—take a snapshot before rolling out modifications to a production database.

Service Pack 2

SQL Server 2005 SP2 rolled out a surprising number of improvements and changes for the database and associated services. For a full review of what's new in SP2, see http://msdn2. microsoft.com/en-us/library/bb283536.aspx.

Reports

SQL Server Management Studio has had server reports for a while, but SP2 made them easier to find, as shown in Figure 3-8.

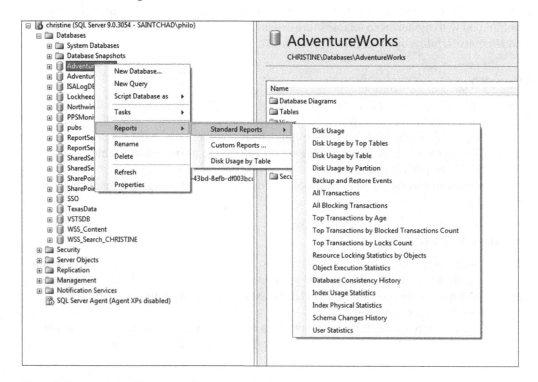

Figure 3-8. *Reports in SQL Server Management Studio*

SP2 also added custom reports, the ability to open multiple reports at the same time, and scalability improvements.

Best Practices Analyzer

The Best Practices Analyzer was much improved post-SP2. The Best Practices Analyzer (Figure 3-9) will review a SQL Server installation against Microsoft recommendations and produce a list of recommendations and issues to help groom your database servers.

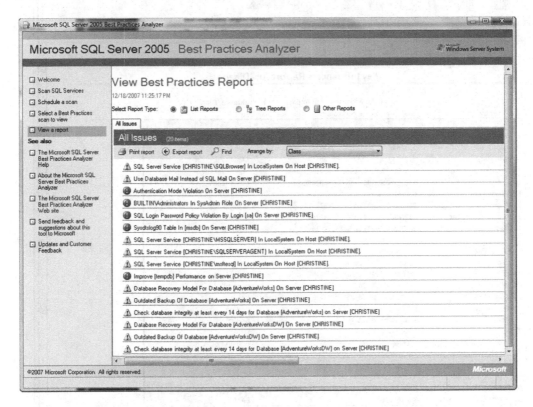

Figure 3-9. *The SQL Server Best Practices Analyzer*

Download the Best Practice Analyzer here: `www.microsoft.com/downloads/details.aspx?FamilyId=DA0531E4-E94C-4991-82FA-F0E3FBD05E63&displaylang=en`.

Data Mining Improvements

The data mining plug-ins for Excel 2007 and Visio 2007 introduce a huge improvement in SQL Server SP2.

Data mining is similar to Analysis Services in that it's simply not sexy or compelling without a "face." While the technology is very powerful, until there is some kind of visualization to really communicate what's going on behind the scenes, it's just another server.

The Excel 2007 data mining plug-ins give SQL Server data mining that face (see Figure 3-10).

Figure 3-10. *Data mining in Excel 2007*

Bringing data mining into Excel makes it accessible, and enables power users—and other users who may be capable of deriving value from data mining, but who don't know how to answer the first question in the data mining wizard ("What model do you want to use?")—to dig into SQL Server Analysis Services data mining and derive value from their data.

We'll cover data mining more in Chapter 7.

SQL Server 2008

With the release of SQL Server 2008, Microsoft has continued to mold SQL Server as a true enterprise data platform. There are refinements throughout, and a number of additions.

■**Note** An exhaustive list of the additions and improvements in SQL Server 2008 is available online at `http://msdn2.microsoft.com/en-us/library/bb500435(SQL.100).aspx`.

Data Platform

There are a surprising number of improvements in the data engine itself, serving both administrators and developers. Some of the highlights are discussed in the following subsections.

Spatial Datatype

SQL Server 2008 will offer new datatypes to support geospatial data. The two new datatypes are geography and geometry. This will enable T-SQL statements to deal with intersecting geographies, polygons, pathing, and so on.

MERGE Statement

The new MERGE statement will perform an INSERT, UPDATE, or DELETE as necessary based on the results of joining two tables. The WHEN MATCHED and WHEN NOT MATCHED phrases provide the tools to articulate how to merge the two tables.

Filestream Storage

Filestream storage completely blurs the answer to the question, "Should I store BLOBs in the database or the file system?" With filestream storage, you can do both (and reap the benefits of both). Filestream storage stores the BLOBs in the file system, where they are accessible outside the database server, but at the same time they are visible and maintainable from within the server.

Encryption

Transparent database encryption (TDE) encrypts the actual database and log files. The SQL Server engine provides on-the-fly encryption and decryption for applications and services, but if the physical media storing the database files were stolen, the database files would be encrypted and unusable.

Auditing

SQL Server has a vastly improved change data capture system that tracks inserts on, updates, and deletes records in SQL Server tables, making auditing data manipulation very straightforward.

Conclusion

By no means was my intent here to provide a full introduction to SQL Server 2005. This was simply an opportunity to cover areas of the platform that you may not be familiar with, and to pique your interest to follow up and do additional research. I hope the high-speed overview has been helpful in your discovery of some formerly unknown nooks and crannies of SQL Server. In the next chapter, we're going to look at SQL Server Integration Services, an extract-transform-load (ETL) service that is part of SQL Server, which we'll use to move data from our individual systems into a normalized model that we can use for BI analysis and reporting.

CHAPTER 4

■■■

SQL Server Integration Services

SQL Server Integration Services was introduced with SQL Server 2005 to replace Data Transformation Services (DTS) in SQL Server 2000. An extract, transform, load (ETL) tool, Integration Services is designed to enable moving, manipulating, and cleaning data before loading into a transactional database, staging database, or other repository.

Overview

SQL Server Integration Services runs as a service concurrent with SQL Server to provide a standardized way of loading batches of data from one data repository to another. While Integration Services is generally used to load data into SQL Server, it can also be used to dump data for consumption by other services, to move data into other systems, or even to move data from one system to another, acting solely as a stand-alone ETL tool.

A developer will build Integration Services packages in BIDS, and then load them to an Integration Services server. Jobs can be executed manually or on a schedule by the SQL Server Agent. Integration Services also provides a flexible connection architecture so that you can move integration packages from development to test and into production without having to rewrite connection strings every time. I'm going to cover some basic Integration Services concepts and introduce you to the tool you'll use to load data into the scorecard.

Why Integration Services?

As we look at various BI solutions, many times we are faced with the reality that the data we want to report on is not in the right place, not in the right format, or not "clean" enough for our needs. As a result, we need a process to move, transform, and scrub the data to get it into the shape we need for our reporting requirements.

Consider the order records in Table 4-1.

Table 4-1. *Sample Order Records*

Order ID	Customer ID	Product Name	Qty	Unit Cost	Ext Cost	Ship Weight
1	CFE	Mugs	25	$9.95	$248.75	2lbs
2	CFE	Mug Holders	25	$1.00	$25	24ozs
3	XYZ Corp	Muggs	12	$9.95	119.4	1.5kg
4	Naprixy	Mugs	15	995	14925	75

As you can see, there are various issues with the records:

- Record 1 has a shipping weight in pounds, while record 2 is in ounces, and record 3 is in kilograms. Record 4 doesn't have units at all.

- The extended cost in record 2 has no decimal places. While this is semantically accurate, it may cause problems with some systems.

- Compare the product names in record 1 and record 3. While it's possible the company has two products, "Mugs" and "Muggs," it's more likely one is a typo.

- The extended cost in record 3 has no dollar sign. Again, pure inference indicates the data itself is correct, but it's an inconsistency.

- Record 4 has no decimal points. Some business systems actually don't use decimal points, instead relying on a defined number of decimal places assigned by field. In this case, it looks like the Unit Cost, Ext Cost, and Ship Weight fields have some number of implied decimal places.

These records would take manipulation before they could be loaded into any business system. Now imagine documents with hundreds of these that have to be loaded weekly or even daily. The trick to identifying when to use Integration Services is when you can identify large numbers of repetitive actions to "clean" data. In the case of the preceding records, you can set up tasks to parse the shipping weight. A flowchart might look like Figure 4-1.

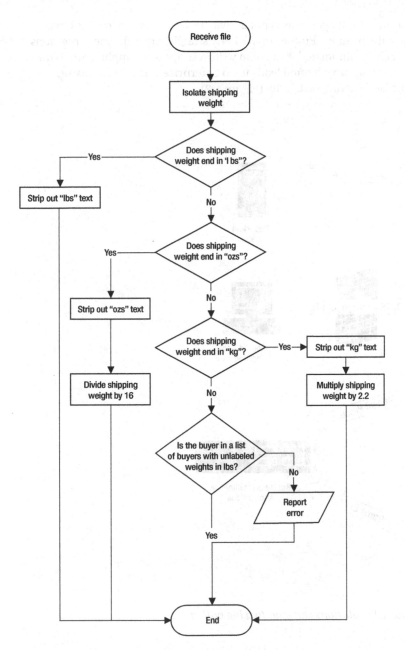

Figure 4-1. *Flowchart showing processing shipping weights*

Once the flow is identified (mind you, this is not a trivial task—see the following sidebar, "Technology Doesn't Solve the Business Problem"), it's fairly straightforward—the same steps over and over. This can easily be automated. You could write a script or an application to do it, but experience shows that this approach often leads to an enterprise strewn with custom code, individual solutions, and varying scalability (Figure 4-2).

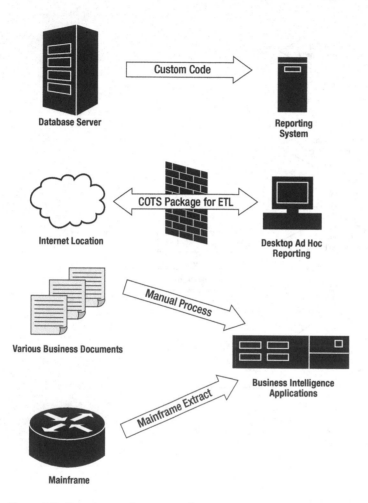

Figure 4-2. *Creating various ETL solutions can lead to a big ball of mud.*

As you can imagine (or perhaps have experienced), this ends up with code, connection strings, and implementations all over the enterprise. The goal of Integration Services (indeed, any enterprise ETL tool) is to centralize and normalize all this transfer and translation logic into a single location, as represented in Figure 4-3.

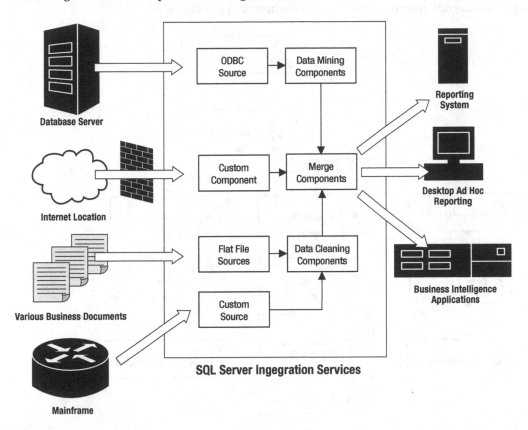

Figure 4-3. *Using SQL Server Integration Services to manage ETL tasks across the enterprise*

If a single architecture is used, then the system administrator has a one-stop shop for all ETL tasks.

In addition, SQL Server Integration Services uses a GUI to design ETL flows, making it much easier to move from a flowchart approach for data transformation and to logically lay out complex data migration and cleaning tasks. Integration Services jobs are called *packages* and are designed in BIDS, a SQL Server–specific implementation of Visual Studio. You can see what an Integration Services data flow job might look like in Figure 4-4.

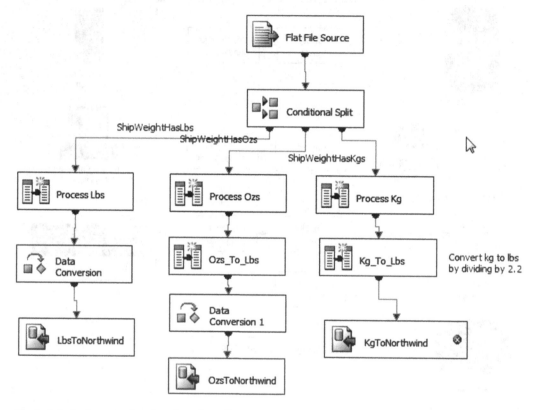

Figure 4-4. *An Integration Services data flow task*

In this chapter, you're going to look at Integration Services and learn how to build a basic transformation package. This is meant as a familiarization overview, not a deep dive—enough so that you'll understand the technology and can make an informed decision as to where it may fit into your BI solution (you'll hear that a lot in this book). For more information about Integration Services, I recommend *Pro SQL Server 2005 Integration Services*, by Jim Wightman (Apress, 2007).

■**Note** Integration Services needs an instance of SQL Server to operate (store package metadata, drive the engine, etc.). However, the data it is moving does not need to be coming from or loaded into SQL Server— you can use Integration Services solely as a data migration tool to, say, extract data from a collection of Access databases and dump CSV files in the input folder of a mainframe application.

TECHNOLOGY DOESN'T SOLVE THE BUSINESS PROBLEM

I'll repeat this comment several times throughout this book—these technologies do not solve every problem; they are just tools. I often tell folks that traditionally a BI solution is 90 percent business analysis, and the technical implementation takes the other 90 percent of the time (an astute reader may notice that needing 180 percent of the allocated time may cause scheduling problems . . .). A sad result is that so much time is often spent on technical implementation that business analysis is seen as a painful, disposable luxury.

The idea behind these tools is to shrink the required implementation time so that you have the time to do the business analysis. As the simple example at the beginning of this chapter shows, just one field in a single data feed needs analysis, research, and effort to positively nail down how the data should be processed. For data manipulation, you're going to have to find data sources, figure out how to get access to them securely, pick the data apart, design the required transformations and manipulations, set up error reporting, and so on.

So remember, the business analysis is a very hard problem—do not dismiss it.

Editions

SQL Server Integration Services editions follow the editions of SQL Server that they are installed with. Basic import/export functionality is available with SQL Server Workgroup Edition, but "real" Integration Services is only part of Standard and Enterprise Editions. Standard Edition includes the Integration Services engine and basic transforms, while Enterprise Edition adds, in addition to the scalability and fault tolerance features, advanced transforms in Integration Services (data mining, text mining, and data cleansing).

Tip For more information about SQL Server editions, see Chapter 3, or visit www.microsoft.com/sql/prodinfo/features/compare-features.mspx.

Data Sources

SQL Server Integration Services has a number of data sources and destinations out of the box—these are the interfaces you will use to build your data transformations. The data source components out of the box include sources for Excel spreadsheets, flat files, OLEDB databases, and XML. In addition, control tasks can pull data from other sources by extracting the data and dropping a formatted file to be parsed by a flat file data source. Some examples of these tasks include FTP and Web Service tasks.

Finally, as I'll note a few times, if none of the standard tasks will accomplish the data movement you are trying to build, you always have the option to write code, either in a one-off script task or by building your own custom task in .NET.

INTEGRATION SERVICES OR BIZTALK?

The #1 question I get asked during Integration Services presentations is, "When do we use Integration Services instead of BizTalk?" The answer, as always, is, "It depends."

The best way to decide is to look at the mainstream use cases. Integration Services is designed for bulk loading of data—when you get a flat file dropped into a shared folder, pick it up and parse it into a business system. You may have to translate parts of the file, clean some of the data, and report on out-of-band values, but for the most part, you are picking up a dump truck full of information and offloading it somewhere else.

BizTalk is designed for transactional work—processing invoices and purchase orders, tracking RFID tags, and running other automated document processing. Consider placing an order at your favorite online bookstore—the system has to check your credit card to see if it's valid and you have the credit available. It also has to check stock and location, and if an item is out of stock, check back order status and provisionally place the back order—all on an order-by-order basis.

So, at the center of the circles, Integration Services is used for large dumps of data; BizTalk is transaction by transaction. Obviously, there's overlap in the middle, but that should help you with a starting point.

About Data Transformation Services

SQL Server 2000 used DTS for ETL. However, DTS suffered from some issues resolved with Integration Services (most notably extensibility and manageability). If you're moving from SQL Server 2000 to 2008, and you have a number of DTS jobs to work with, the first and most important thing to realize is that Integration Services is *not* DTS 2.0—it is a ground-up rewrite of the ETL platform.

Some improvements that you'll find in Integration Services if you're used to DTS include the following:

Improved debugging: In DTS, you could really only examine what was going on by adding ActiveX scripts and creating traceability somehow (pop-up dialogs, writing to a log file, etc.). In Integration Services, you have those abilities, as well as breakpoints in script code, data flow visualizers, error messages, error outputs on tasks, and so on.

Looping: In DTS, you could only loop with a script. In Integration Services, there are first-class looping and foreach containers (Figure 4-5), with provisions for changing values inside the loop.

Extensibility: In DTS, you could write custom tasks and transforms, but it was nontrivial. In Integration Services, custom tasks and transforms are simply a matter of implementing the Integration Services task interface. In addition, you can create source adapters, destination adapters, loop enumerators, and log providers.

Deployment: Migrating DTS packages from development to test to production was basically the province of a few tricky how-to articles on the Web. Integration Services packages are designed to handle migration from development to test to production with support for variables, varying connection strings, and so on.

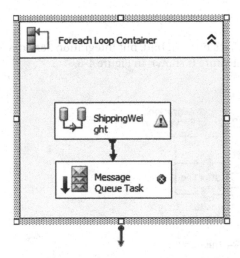

Figure 4-5. *A foreach loop container control flow task*

With that in mind, you have a few options for dealing with a collection of DTS jobs:

- Run DTS alongside your SQL Server installation. You can either install both DTS and Integration Services and use the DTS engine to run your DTS jobs, or use the Execute DTS 2000 package task in Integration Services to execute DTS jobs from Integration Services. For more information, see "Considerations for Upgrading Data Transformation Services," available on MSDN at http://msdn2.microsoft.com/en-us/library/ms143706.aspx.

- Migrate your DTS packages to Integration Services using the DTS Package Migration wizard. Note that the wizard will most likely not provide a full-fidelity migration—it's intended to be a "best effort" migration. For more information on this, see "Migrating Data Transformation Services Packages," available on SQL Server Books Online at http://msdn.microsoft.com/en-us/library/ms143501(SQL.100).aspx.

- Rewrite the package for Integration Services. This is really the best option, due to the architectural and design improvements in Integration Services over DTS. Especially with respect to logging and parallelism, it's really worth reviewing and rewriting your DTS packages to take advantage of the improvements in Integration Services. Of course, by running Integration Services side by side with DTS, you can keep the old packages running while you migrate them.

So, if we're going to invest in Integration Services, let's take a look at the architecture of what we're getting into.

Architecture

With great power, comes great complexity . . . Well, it's not that bad, but Integration Services is a more complex server application. A rough architecture is shown in Figure 4-6.

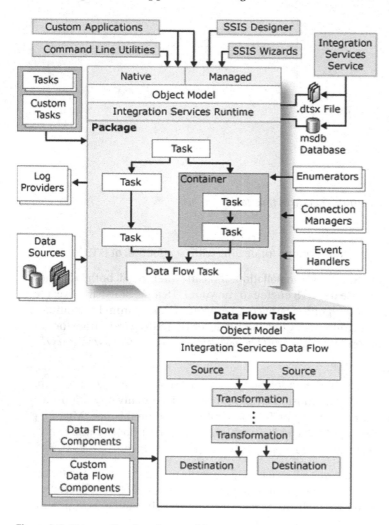

Figure 4-6. *Integration Services architecture*

Again, I won't dig too deeply into the architecture of Integration Services, but this should help guide you into understanding the workings and nomenclature of the services. It's also a good thumbnail to identify extensibility points and options while you're building packages.

Getting Integration Services

"OK," you say, "I want to use Integration Services and all its ETL goodness. Where do I get it?"

SQL Server Integration Services is a component of SQL Server, but it is not installed by default. If you try to run the SQL Server installer when SQL Server is already installed, you'll get a warning that SQL Server is already installed. The trick is to go through Add or Remove Programs (Figure 4-7).

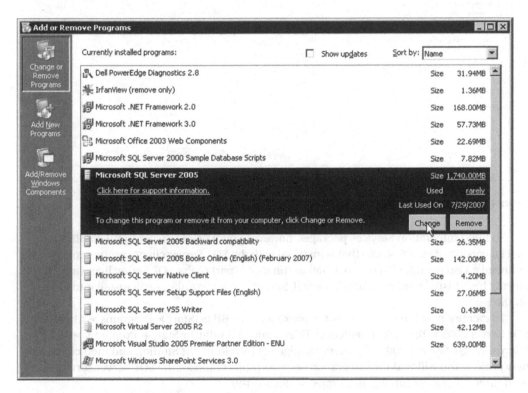

Figure 4-7. *SQL Server in Add or Remove Programs*

This will launch the SQL Server configuration wizard so you can choose additional services to install and configure. SQL Server Integration Services is very straightforward to install—pretty much a Next/Next/Next/Finish installation.

Business Intelligence Development Studio

Once you have Integration Services installed, there are two main interfaces for working with the service. The first is via SQL Server Management Studio (Figure 4-8), where you can review installed and running Integration Services packages.

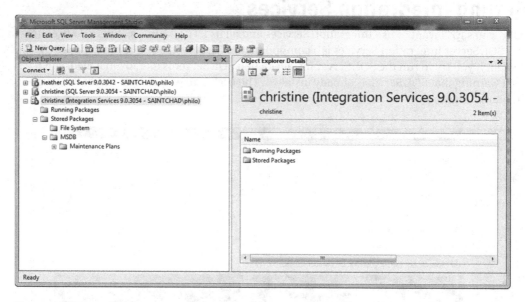

Figure 4-8. *SQL Server Management Studio*

To build Integration Services packages, however, you'll need to work in BIDS. BIDS is a special version of Visual Studio that is installed with the SQL Server client components. You do not need a Visual Studio license to install or run it—it's part of the SQL Server licensing. (If you already have Visual Studio installed, the SQL Server project templates will install into Visual Studio.)

To create a new Integration Services package, open BIDS (Start ➤ Programs ➤ Microsoft SQL Server 2005 ➤ Business Intelligence Development Studio, or Start ➤ Programs ➤ Microsoft SQL Server 2008 ➤ Business Intelligence Development Studio), and then create a new project. You will find the Integration Services project (and all the SQL Server services projects) under "Business Intelligence Projects" (Figure 4-9).

Select Integration Services Project, give the project a suitable name, and then click the OK button. You'll then have the Integration Services package designer open to a blank control flow (see Figure 4-10).

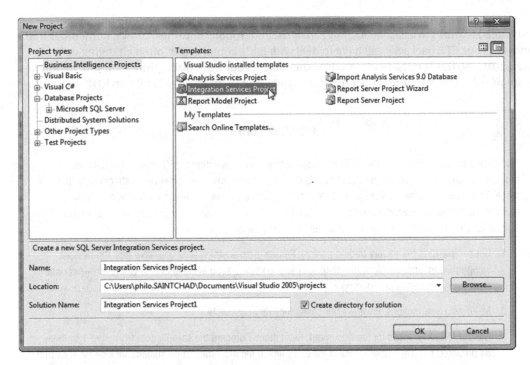

Figure 4-9. *The Business Intelligence projects in BIDS*

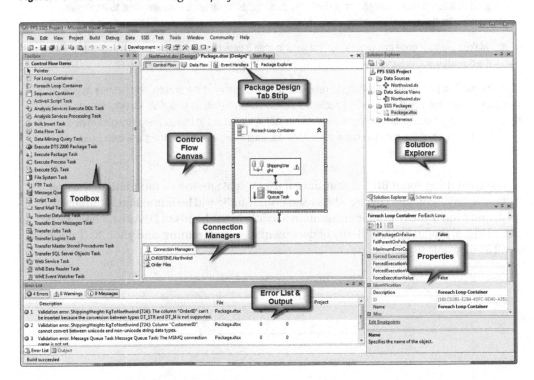

Figure 4-10. *The Integration Services package designer in BIDS*

BIDS allows you to design and debug Integration Services packages, and has a lot of advanced features to assist debugging, analysis, and troubleshooting of flows. Remember that most of your ETL packages will have to deal with fairly complex and often changing data structures, so this is not a place to skimp on making your work bulletproof—be sure to anticipate possibilities, variations, user mix-ups, typos, and so on (see the "Philo on EDI" sidebar).

PHILO ON EDI

I wrote this on a message board in 2004 in response to a newbie question on EDI (electronic data interchange—a structured messaging system dating back decades). I have pointed several other people to it since. This is really the best guide I've seen to setting up ground rules for building any kind of document translation. (I've also reposted this on my blog at `http://blogs.msdn.com/philoj/archive/2007/09/24/philo-on-edi.aspx` in case you need to refer your manager to it.)

1. Get sample data from every trading partner. Refuse to do anything until you have this. Claim work stoppage, announce loudly at meetings that you're stalled, send e-mails to VPs, whatever—*get data from every partner before starting*.

2. Make zero assumptions. Provide error cases for every possibility.

3. Get the ANSI X12 specs for the document. Read them. Compare the sample data from step 1 to them. Be prepared to create program flows for every line in the implementation guides, *but* look for lines that aren't used by your partners. Any line you can't find being used, document it. Once you have a full list, send that list to your manager for "I don't see these fields being used—do we need to implement them?" Get the answer in writing.

4. Make sure your code can provide for the lines in step 3 when some partner starts using one of them the day after you deploy.

The hardest part about EDI is that the rules are observed mainly in the breach, and nobody makes partners follow the rules. I built my 810/850 parser as a class hierarchy, which ended up serving me *very* well—it was very modular, and changes like those in step 4 turned out to be relatively straightforward.

As a final note, make sure you know what ANSI document versions the partners are using, too.

The great thing about BIDS is that since it uses Visual Studio as a foundation, the user interface is very familiar—anyone who's used Visual Studio will be immediately familiar with it, and even if you're putting Integration Services in the hands of DBAs who have never touched Visual Studio, there is plenty of documentation and training, and your .NET developers will also be able to help out.

Flows

The toughest thing to get used to with Integration Services is the way that flows work. When you first open an Integration Services package project, you'll want to start dragging data sources and destinations to the canvas to hook them together. This will quickly become frustrating as you look for data sources in the toolbox. Go ahead, look. I'll wait.

Hopefully you didn't find any. That's because when you create a new Integration Services package project, you are looking at the Control Flow tab—this is where you pin together the large-grained tasks you see in the toolbox (loop containers, Data Flow tasks, Message Queue tasks, etc.). Pulling, massaging, cleaning, and pushing data are a subset that is all contained inside a Data Flow task.

Take a Data Flow task from the toolbox and place it on the Control Flow canvas (Figure 4-11).

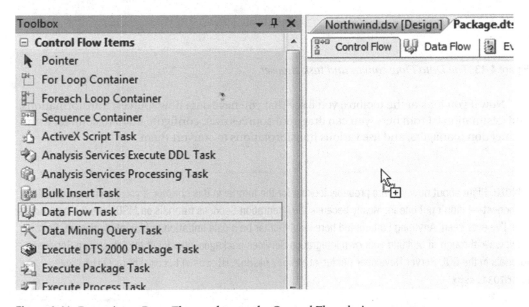

Figure 4-11. *Dropping a Data Flow task onto the Control Flow design canvas*

You will see the Data Flow Task icon with a connector arrow pointing out of the bottom (Figure 4-12). You can use the connector arrow to connect the flow of the Data Flow task to other control flow items (e.g., to trigger an e-mail upon completion, or perhaps to trigger another Data Flow task).

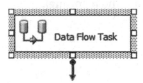

Figure 4-12. *The Data Flow task*

"I get it," you say, "but where do I connect my Excel spreadsheets to my databases?" Fair question. To open the Data Flow task, you can double-click it; right-click it and select Edit from the context menu; or simply select the Data Flow tab from the Package Design tab strip, and then select your Data Flow task from the drop-down box (Figure 4-13).

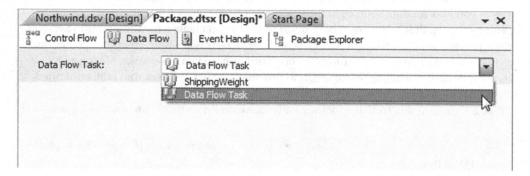

Figure 4-13. *The Data Flow canvas and task chooser*

Now if you look at the toolbox, you'll see that you have data flow sources, transformations, and destinations. From here, you can drag your sources over, configure them to connect with connection managers, and use various transformations to convert them.

Note Right about now you are probably looking for the tutorial in this chapter, if you haven't already. I'll be honest—I didn't put one in. Mostly because the Integration Services tutorials on MSDN are the best tutorials I've ever seen. Anything I attempted here would either be a pale imitation or blatant plagiarism. So for a good walk-through of building your own Integration Services packages, check out the Integration Services tutorials in the SQL Server Developer Center, at http://msdn2.microsoft.com/en-us/library/ms167031.aspx.

The few hints I do want to give about using BIDS for Integration Services packages require a bit of a walk-through.

Drag any data flow source to the canvas, and then any transformation (I used the Excel source and the Lookup transformation). Note that the Excel source has a green arrow and a red arrow at the bottom—the green arrow is the task output, and the red arrow is error output (you can configure a task to route records that fail to the error output for logging and reporting).

Drag the green arrow to your transformation. It should look like Figure 4-14. Now for a bit of magic: right-click the line connecting the two tasks, and then click Data Viewers. The Data Flow Path Editor will open, with Data Viewers selected in the left-hand pane. Click the Add button at the bottom. This will open the Configure Data Viewer dialog (Figure 4-15).

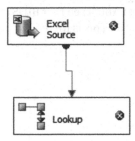

Figure 4-14. *Data source and data transformation tasks connected on the Data Flow canvas*

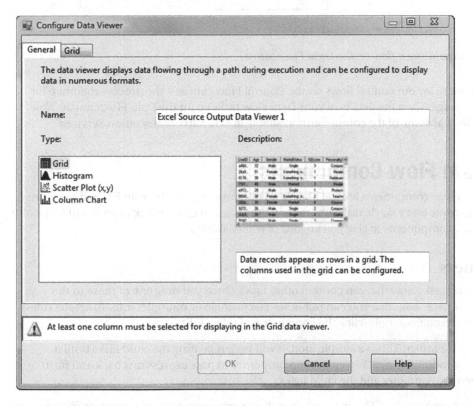

Figure 4-15. *The Configure Data Viewer dialog*

Data viewers give you insight into what's really going on between tasks—what the data looks like—while you are executing the task. It's a quick and easy debugger. (You can also use visualizations if you have large amounts of data—a histogram or scatter plot may tell you more than a simple grid view if you're testing 100,000 rows of data.)

The other tip is really simple and really easy to miss—click an empty space on the canvas (near one of the task boxes) and type a note (use Ctrl+Enter to wrap lines). You'll see that BIDS lets you add free-text notes anywhere you need to on a canvas (Figure 4-16). This is incredibly valuable for commenting more complex flows.

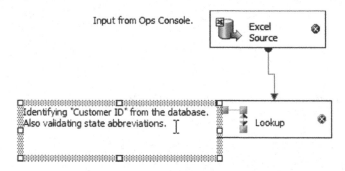

Figure 4-16. *Annotating a flow on the Data Flow canvas*

So to review, lay out control flows on the Control Flow canvas—the process roadmap for your ETL package. Then the details of your Data Flow tasks go on the Data Flow canvas. Now let's take a look at some of the components available in SQL Server Integration Services.

Program Flow Components

The program flow components are the high-level tasks available to drive an ETL package. I'm not going to cover every single task component, but I want to give a quick overview of some of the main task components to give you an idea of what's available.

Containers

Containers are task items that can contain other tasks. Once you drag one of these to the canvas, you have a "box" that you can put other tasks (single or multiple) into. To set the rules governing the container, right-click the container and select Edit.

For loop container: This is a simple loop. It will keep repeating the child tasks until a specific condition is met. You can set up properties to pass expressions back and forth between the container and the child tasks.

Foreach loop container: This is a container that loops over a collection, such as files in a folder. Again, you can set the properties, and then select expressions to pass the values of the current loop (e.g., the current file name) into the child tasks.

Sequence container: Use this container to group together a set of controls on the canvas. It doesn't loop, but it allows you to enable or disable a group of control tasks, set a transaction on a group of tasks, or create a set of common variables that all the tasks inside the sequence can read and/or alter.

Tasks

I've grouped these together here as simply "tasks to do things."

Data Flow task: To some degree, this is the reason you're reading this chapter. The Data Flow task is where you actually manage moving data around.

Data Mining Query task (Enterprise Edition only): This task allows you to run some predictive analysis based on mining models built in Analysis Services. The main idea here is to clean data based on data already in the database.

File System task: This allows you to interact with the file system—move files around and copy them; create, copy, and delete directories; and so on. One main use here would be to archive flat files after they have been bulk-loaded by a Data Flow task.

Send Mail task: This task is pretty straightforward—it allows you to send e-mail from within a package. It's useful for alerting in case of failure, posting success notes, and so on.

Web Service task: Use the Web Service task to fetch a value from a web service (which you can write to a variable), or to pull a dataset of records (which you have to write to the file system before you can use them in another task). Also note that the Web Services Description Language (WSDL) file for the web service must be available locally to configure a Web Service task.

XML task: This is a task for interacting with an XML document, including applying transforms or running an XQuery against the data. XML documents can also be data sources—you can use the XML data source in a data flow.

Executing Other Code

While Integration Services offers a number of structured tasks as the building blocks for your transformations, sometimes you need to do something that doesn't quite fit with any of the given components. As a result, there are a number of methods for embedding custom code into a package, as listed following:

ActiveX Script task: Note that this task is being deprecated. This task is for implementation of ActiveX scripts that you may have written in DTS. I would recommend strongly against using this task for new packages.

Execute Package task: This task selects another Integration Services package to run.

Execute Process task: This task is used to run an application. Obviously, since the application will be running on a server in the context of Integration Services, use judgment as to what applications you choose to run.

Execute SQL task: This task is used to run T-SQL on SQL Server. The SQL statement can be entered directly into the component, read from a file connection, or passed by variable.

Script task: This is one of your major extensibility points. If you can't do it anywhere else, you can do it in a Script task, which simply gives you free-form access to flows and data via VBScript.

Transferring Things

The Transfer Database, Transfer Error Messages, Transfer Jobs, and Transfer SQL Server Objects tasks all provide methods of moving objects from one instance of SQL Server to another.

Maintenance

The Maintenance Plan tasks are grouped into their own section in the toolbox—they are various tasks oriented toward maintaining databases. This allows you to build database maintenance jobs into Integration Services, making it more centralized and increasing the reusability of the jobs.

Data Flow Components

Once again, when you place a Data Flow component on the canvas, you will be able to configure the data flow within the task. This consists generally of sources, transformations, and destinations, and the tasks within the data flow are organized similarly.

■**Tip** SQL Server Integration Services is definitely one of those development environments where your life will be much easier if you understand "the way of Integration Services." The way to think of data flows is as collections of columns of data—that's how Integration Services looks at data. So long as you think in terms of columns, it's pretty straightforward. If you try to think of data flows as matrices, and look for ways to manipulate the data accordingly (most notably trying to transpose rows and columns), you'll end up very unhappy.

Data Flow Sources

Data Flow sources are the "from where" for your integration package. These provide a standardized format for accessing data that your data flows will use to process.

DataReader source: This consumes data from a .NET provider and makes it available to the flow.

Excel source: This opens an Excel spreadsheet and reads the data from it. Note that it can be tricky to get the *right* data out of Excel—it may be easier to just get a CSV file if you can arrange it (CSV files are much less prone to ambiguity).

Flat file source: This is what you'll use to read the CSV file mentioned previously.

OLEDB source: This is the default task for reading "other" databases. You can specify a particular table or view, or enter SQL directly.

Raw file source: Raw files are native to Integration Services—you can use raw file destinations and sources to move data between Integration Services packages or even between servers. They can be written and read much faster than any other file type, but they are not portable outside Integration Services.

XML file source: This is used to read XML files.

Data Flow Transformations

Out of the box, there are 28 data flow transformations. Again, I won't cover them all in detail (see SQL Server Books Online for full details on every task), but I'll try to give you an idea of what is possible.

Aggregate: This applies an aggregate function (such as SUM or AVERAGE) to a column and adds the value to the output (as a new column).

Conditional Split: This separates the data in the flow based on some criteria. One example might be that all records where the destination is overseas go through a separate pipe that deals with customs and foreign addresses.

Data Conversion: This makes an explicit cast to a column in your data (such as converting a value that comes in as a string to a decimal or date). It's also necessary for dealing with Unicode errors.

Lookup: The number one use of this is to replace explicit values with foreign keys.

Fuzzy Lookup: Similar to the Lookup transform, this one uses fuzzy matching to provide close matches from the lookup table. One example would be the problem we had with the dataset at the beginning of this chapter—matching "Muggs" to "Mugs" in our product catalog. Fuzzy Lookup transformations return similarity and confidence values you can work with. In addition, since fuzzy matching can get very expensive in terms of memory, you can set a limit on how much memory will be available for running the match.

Merge: This brings two sorted datasets together, inserting each record so that the output is still sorted on the same column.

Multicast: This is similar to the conditional split, except that this transform directs a copy of every row to each of multiple outputs.

Percentage Sampling: This takes a random sampling of the input rows (so, instead of loading 1 million rows into a database, you might only load a random selection of 20,000 rows).

Pivot: Just like a pivot table, this denormalizes data to provide pivoted output. (You might do this to dump a summary table into e-mail or Excel.)

Script: Similar to the Script task in the control toolbox, this gives you access to the dataset in the flow (record by record, cell by cell) so that you can write any code necessary.

Union All: Similar to the Merge transformation, this provides an unsorted blending of output records—for example, after you split input records and process them. You might also union a number of flat file or database inputs before processing.

Data Flow Destinations

Most of the destinations are similar to the data flow sources, but there are a few additional destinations worth noting:

Data Mining Model Training destination: This routes data through data mining model algorithms to help train them. More on this in Chapter 7.

Partition Processing destination: This loads and processes a SQL Server Analysis Services partition (to process the data you've just loaded into a staging or an underlying relational database).

SQL Server destination: There is an OLEDB destination that's database agnostic, but the SQL Server destination takes advantage of a fast-load data access mode, and has a number of additional options that affect how the data is bulk-loaded into SQL Server.

Scripting Tasks

I want to amplify a little more about the Script component in the Data Flow toolbox. If you drag a Script component to the canvas, the first thing you will see is a dialog for selecting the component type (see Figure 4-17).

■**Note** A Source component has no inputs and supports multiple outputs. A Destination component has a single input. A Transformation component has one input and supports multiple outputs. The Script component does not have error outputs.

After you select a component type, the component will drop to the canvas. You can open the component configuration by double-clicking it, or right-clicking and selecting Edit. The Script Transformation Editor has four panes: Input Columns, Inputs and Outputs, Script, and Connection Managers.

On the Input Columns pane (Figure 4-18), you can select which columns will be available to scripts. Note that the list of input columns won't be available until you connect a flow to the component, at which time it will list the columns in the flow for you to select from. Each column can be marked ReadOnly or ReadWrite.

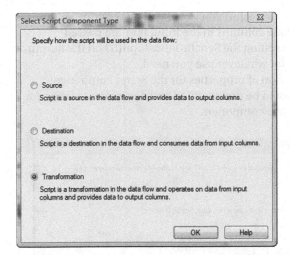

Figure 4-17. *Selecting the type of Script component to add to the Data Flow canvas*

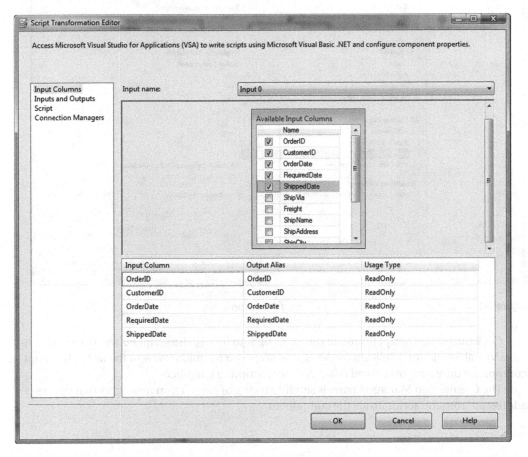

Figure 4-18. *Selecting columns in the Script Transformation Editor*

The next pane, Inputs and Outputs, shows the input you've created by selecting columns, and a default output. Note that by default, all the columns in the input flow are passed through to the output; you can change this by setting the SynchronousInputID on the output to None. You can also add additional outputs for whatever use you need.

The Script pane initially opens to a collection of properties for the Script component (Figure 4-19). You can indicate if the script should be precompiled and designate variables for the script to use that will be available outside the component.

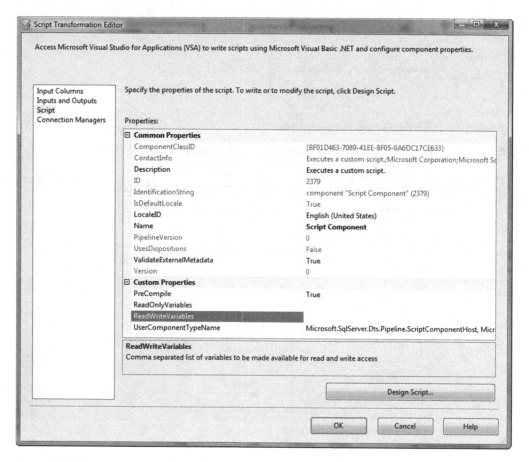

Figure 4-19. *The Script pane of the Script Transformation Editor*

Click the Design Script button in the lower right to invoke the script editor. The script editor is Visual Studio for Applications (VSA), and gives you a familiar view of the task. The Script component only supports Visual Basic .NET as a scripting language.

The Connection Managers pane is simply a listing of connection managers that can be addressed from the script inside the component.

Custom Tasks

Script tasks and components are good for solving one-off problems, quick fixes, or proofs of concept. However, if you are addressing something that is going to be a problem over and over (e.g., extracting business-specific data in a particular format from a flat file data dump), then it's best to invest the time and energy into writing a custom component.

Integration Services supports a number of custom components:

Custom Tasks: This is for use in the control flow.

Custom Connection Managers: This is for access to various types of back-end systems.

Custom Log Providers: This can be used, for example, if you have a specific log format in a specific database that you always want packages to write to.

Custom ForEach Enumerators: This can be used, for example, if you're working with SharePoint data, and you want to iterate over a number of SharePoint sites for some ETL work.

Custom Data Flow : This can be a data source, transform, or data destination.

SCRIPT COMPONENTS VS. CUSTOM COMPONENTS

A fairly standard refrain in development is, "When do I invest the time in doing this properly?" As I mentioned, Script components are great for one-off tasks. Something like, "I just need to grab a single value from somewhere," or "This particular task needs to report an audit of how many people named Smith ordered some particular brand of ham."

Generally, my advice is that the second time you find yourself writing the same code, you need to put serious thought into moving it into a custom component. In most cases, you can probably analyze ahead and determine if you're going to need to do the same thing over and over. In case you can't, use a Script component and be alert for the first time you want to open it up and copy the script to use somewhere else—move the code into a custom component.

By writing a custom component, you provide a standardized method for ETL developers to implement the business logic you direct. By writing a custom log provider, you provide the fields you want mapped and how the connection should be made. By writing a custom data flow transformation, you can provide additional functionality without reinventing the wheel over and over. For example, if you have a large number of Excel spreadsheets that are set up with records as columns instead of rows, you need to transpose the data. Writing a custom component to do so enables all your developers to reuse the same logic in an intuitive way.

A custom component will be available in the toolbox and provide a standard interface that your developers are comfortable with. They can drag it to the canvas, connect it to other components, and have a user interface to edit whatever properties are necessary.

To develop a custom component, you just need to create a standard .NET DLL in Visual Studio—there's no SDK or project template. Then you need to inherit the appropriate base class for the component you want to build (e.g., a Data Flow component inherits from the `PipelineComponent` base class). Then implement the necessary methods, create a user interface if necessary, build, and deploy.

■**Note** These directions are similar to directions on how to play the flute—blow in one end and move your fingers along the holes. For in-depth information on implementing your own custom components, see the article "Developing Custom Objects for Integration Services" on the SQL Server TechCenter at `http://technet.microsoft.com/en-us/library/ms403361.aspx`, as well as Jim Wightman's *Pro SQL Server 2005 Integration Services* (Apress, 2007).

Error Reporting

When you were dragging components to the Data Flow canvas, you probably noticed those little red arrows next to the green arrow connectors (Figure 4-20). Those are error outputs—you can leverage them to dump records that fail whatever transform you were attempting.

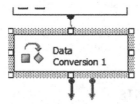

Figure 4-20. *Data Conversion task showing an error output*

In the properties editor of any given transformation task, there's a button in the lower left labeled Configure Error Output. Clicking this button opens the Configure Error Output dialog (shown in Figure 4-21). This is important to know about, because by default every failure results in the entire component failing—you can run a million rows through a component analyzing/transforming a dozen columns, and if one field fails, the whole process errors out and stops.

Using this dialog, you can change the way errors are handled. You have the option on each column to set whether a failure in that column will fail the whole process, whether the transform should ignore failures, or whether failed rows should be redirected to the error output (red arrow). This last option creates a recordset on the error output, which you can handle just like any other data flow (write it to a database, drop it to a flat file, send it in an e-mail, etc.). When you consider the ease and flexibility of handling errors, this is (in my opinion) part of what makes Integration Services so compelling.

■**Caution** Be careful with "Ignore failure"—the row will still go to the output of the transform. Since your transform logic was skipped, you now have a somewhat unpredictable chain of events. You might be tempted to use "Ignore failure" to deal with anticipated error conditions (e.g., a null value in a numeric field), but errors are agnostic. For example, when someone sends a date value in that numeric field, you'll get the same error, and now you'll have a date in your pipeline that's probably going to try to load that value into a numeric field in a database.

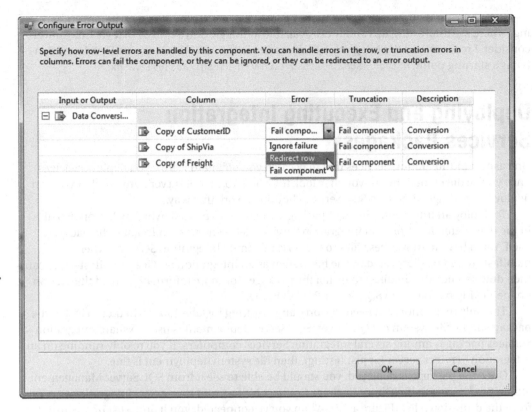

Figure 4-21. *The Configure Error Output dialog*

Scalability

Tip Early optimization is wasted effort.

I'd like to give a few thoughts about scaling Integration Services packages. As the tip says, the first note is not to worry about optimization too early in the development process. You may spend a week trying to get a loop from 5 seconds to 2 when your data read process takes 10 minutes under load. It's better to build the transformation package, evaluate execution time, and then optimize where the time is being consumed.

You *can*, however, optimize for parallelization early. Integration Services understands parallel processing and will take advantage of it where possible. Knowing this, you can do things like split incoming records (using a conditional split task) and run separate processing pipelines, which may be parallelized.

Once you have your package developed, you can start optimizing if necessary. Another reason to wait until the package is completed is that you may find more problems from interaction, race conditions, record locking, and so forth, than any single component gives you.

Scalability and optimization are areas that are well worth reading up on before embarking—there are interesting tips and tricks available in Integration Services that you may never consider. I recommend the Integration Services site in the MSDN SQL Server Developer Center as a starting point: http://msdn2.microsoft.com/en-us/sql/aa336312.aspx.

Deploying and Executing Integration Services Packages

One aspect of Integration Services that may catch you off guard is how you deploy packages once you've developed them—you may look for where to set the server name so that you can deploy the package directly to SQL Server. They don't work that way.

To deploy an Integration Services package, you need to build it, which will drop two files in the designated location—an Integration Services deployment manifest and the package itself. You'll have to move these files to the server running Integration Services, where the manifest should be discovered by the file system as an Integration Services manifest—you can then double-click the manifest to install the package. For more information, read the section on "deploying packages" in SQL Server Books Online.

The only real option you need to worry about during installation is whether to install the package in the file system or SQL Server. SQL Server deployment is used to share Integration Services packages among several Integration Services computers. If you're only running on an Integration Services server (or just testing), then file system deployment is fine.

Once the package is deployed, you should be able to see it from SQL Server Management Studio. Connect with the Object Explorer Connect button, and then select Integration Services from the drop-down list (Figure 4-22). When you've connected, you'll find a list of the installed Integration Services packages under Stored Packages.

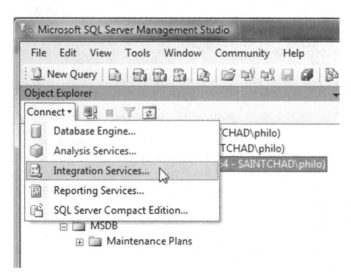

Figure 4-22. *Connecting to Integration Services in SQL Server Management Studio*

You can execute a package from Management Studio by right-clicking the package and selecting Run Package. This will give you a dialog with a number of options for executing the package (Figure 4-23).

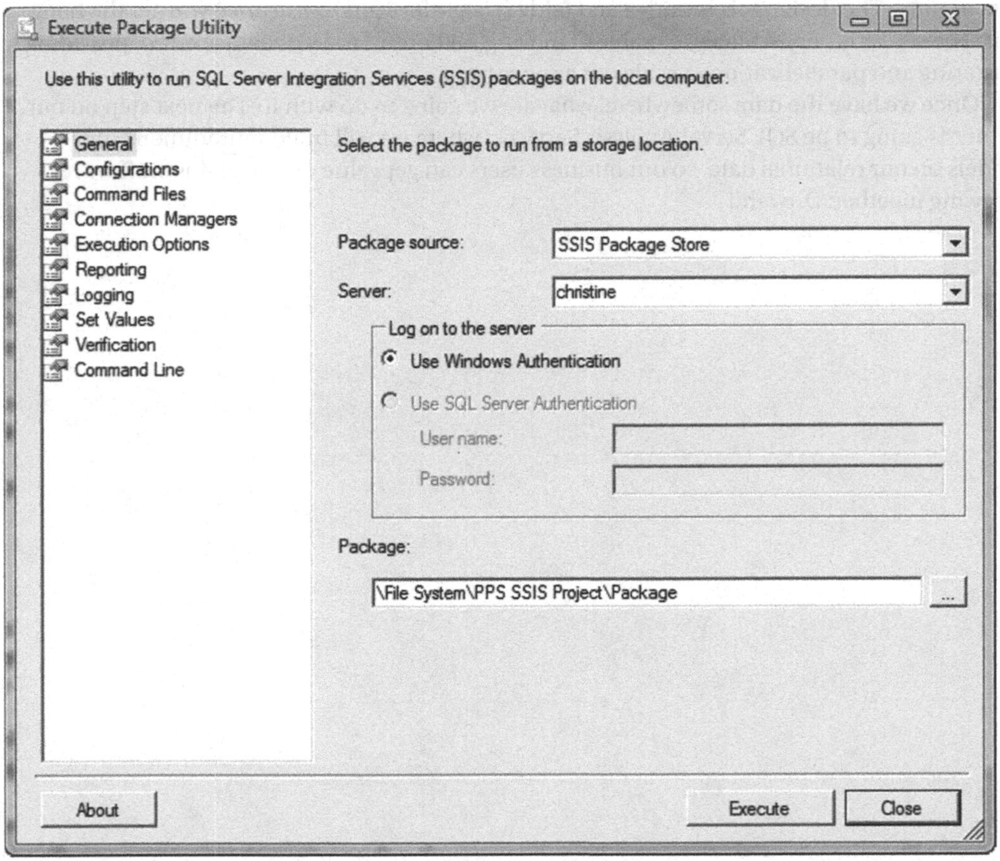

Figure 4-23. *Properties for executing an Integration Services package from Management Studio*

Something that's really powerful is the ability to change the connection strings of the embedded connection managers—set paths, server names, usernames, and passwords if necessary. You can also set warning levels, logging providers, values for variables, and even what versions of a package are allowed to run (if, for example, you have a configuration process that has validated version 2.0 of a package, you can lock out versions beyond 2.0).

You can schedule packages to run on a regular basis using the SQL Agent—this is very similar to how the Agent worked in SQL Server 2000. Be aware that you will need to have the appropriate roles and permissions in place to execute packages using the SQL Agent.

Conclusion

There you have it—a high-speed overview of the ETL package you may have available right now and not even know it. Integration Services is incredibly powerful and a great way to move data around. The designer is intuitive and fairly straightforward to use once you get the hang of it. The server is very scalable, capable of moving millions of rows of data around, providing clustering and parallelization to scale out as necessary.

Once we have the data somewhere, what are we going to do with it? The next step on our BI tour is going to be SQL Server Analysis Services, where we will build multidimensional models on our relational data, so our business users can get value out of all this stuff we're throwing together. Onward!

CHAPTER 5

■■■

SQL Server Analysis Services

Now that we have data aggregated into a convenient location (thanks to Integration Services), we want to do something with it. We can report on it—create plain old transactional reports and charts—but that sort of defeats the purpose of pulling all this stuff together in the first place.

Once we've aggregated our data, we want some way to maximize the utility of it. We want the following:

- To easily aggregate information in multiple ways that reflect the business

- To enable business users to perform analysis on the data

- To achieve different ways of visualizing data to gain insight

That's the idea behind OLAP technologies—aggregating data in a way that enables a business user to analyze and gain insight into the business processes underlying the data.

■Note Once again, this chapter is not meant to be a deep dive into OLAP and Analysis Services. Rather, my intent is to demystify Analysis Services and provide a stepping-off point for you to continue learning. OLAP is a deep, rich field with lots of nooks and crannies. You could spend months just trying to figure out where to start. This chapter will walk you through building a cube with just enough information to make you dangerous. Once you've done that, then you can start filling out your knowledge. For this, I recommend *Delivering Business Intelligence with Microsoft SQL Server 2005*, by Brian Larson (McGraw-Hill Osborne, 2006).

What Is a Cube?

Most IT users and developers are familiar with pivot tables—using Excel or other reporting solutions to show rolled-up data. For example, consider a listing of patient visits similar to Table 5-1, which shows rows and rows of patient visits—not a lot of use for analysis purposes (considering that there may be thousands or millions of records!).

Table 5-1. *A Listing of Patient Visits with Some Background Information*

Visit ID	Visit Date	Lead Screening	Patient Age	Targeted Case Management	County
14378	1/1/2002	TRUE	47	TRUE	Angelina County
14509	1/1/2002	TRUE	31	FALSE	Atascosa County
14745	1/1/2002	FALSE	33	TRUE	Atascosa County
14771	1/1/2002	FALSE	70	FALSE	Angelina County
14779	1/1/2002	FALSE	61	TRUE	Angelina County
14912	1/1/2002	TRUE	75	FALSE	Angelina County
14946	1/1/2002	TRUE	14	FALSE	Angelina County
15043	1/1/2002	FALSE	55	FALSE	Anderson County
15045	1/1/2002	FALSE	82	FALSE	Angelina County
15155	1/2/2002	TRUE	70	FALSE	Austin County
15168	1/2/2002	TRUE	28	FALSE	Anderson County
15263	1/2/2002	TRUE	81	FALSE	Anderson County

ABOUT THE DATASET

In this chapter, I'm working with a dataset that I generated to reflect patient visits and vaccinations in Texas. I used Texas healthcare regions and Texas counties, and then took the population distribution in each county by race and used that as a guideline to generate histogram-similar data. I've found it's a pretty good dataset for building cubes and reports. Most importantly, it's relatively straightforward, making the walk-through for building it easy to follow. After this chapter, I'll revert to using the AdventureWorks demo OLAP database.

I generated the data before Visual Studio Team System DB Pro (which can generate test data) shipped—that's why I wrote code to do so. If I were to do it again today, I'd use the extensibility of DB Pro to do it.

There are approximately 750,000 patient visits and 3.5 million vaccination records in the database; you can download it with the code for this book (from the Source Code/Download page on the Apress web site, at www.apress.com).

The first trick we learn is to use the pivot table. Let's say we want a breakdown of patients by county, by date seen. We can "pivot" the table so that the counties are down the side, while the dates are across the top, as shown in Table 5-2. (I used Excel 2007 to generate the pivot table—more about Excel 2007 in Chapter 7.)

Table 5-2. *A Pivot Table Showing Visits by Date*

Row Labels	1/1/2002	1/2/2002	1/3/2002	1/4/2002	1/5/2002
Anderson County	1	4	5	1	1
Andrews County				1	1
Angelina County	6	4	5	5	3
Aransas County					1
Archer County					
Armstrong County					
Atascosa County	2	1	1	2	4
Austin County		1	1	5	
Bailey County					2

Of course, one problem immediately shows up—if we have two years of patient data, that's over 700 columns of data, and not really something that's easy to scan or gain insight from. We can adjust the data to roll up monthly—add a calculated column in the table to show month and year, and then pivot on that field (Table 5-3).

Table 5-3. *Pivoting from a Calculated Date Field*

Row Labels	1/2002	1/2003	10/2002	10/2003	11/2002	11/2003	12/2002	12/2003	2/2002
Anderson County	67	63	125	111	80	85	71	101	66
Andrews County	17	22	23	21	24	15	16	24	20
Angelina County	134	82	187	143	107	143	100	122	90
Aransas County	29	25	40	33	38	34	27	51	31
Archer County	4	10	19	17	11	22	13	14	14
Armstrong County	1	3	1	3	2	2	1	4	4
Atascosa County	58	46	70	82	49	77	49	73	41
Austin County	43	26	47	49	38	47	41	46	30
Bailey County	10	5	15	14	9	13	6	16	13

Uh-oh. Now we have a different problem. The numbers are rolling up the way we want, but look at the sort order: 1/2002, 1/2003, 10/2002, 10/2003, . . . That's no good. To fix this, we can change the calculated column to add a leading zero, and we can change the column to be year/month so it sorts by year first.

Let me also point out that there are 254 counties in Texas, so the report will be 254 rows long, or at least four pages. A pivot chart might help, but then we lose the time dimension—the two axes in the chart will be county and number of visits (Figure 5-1).

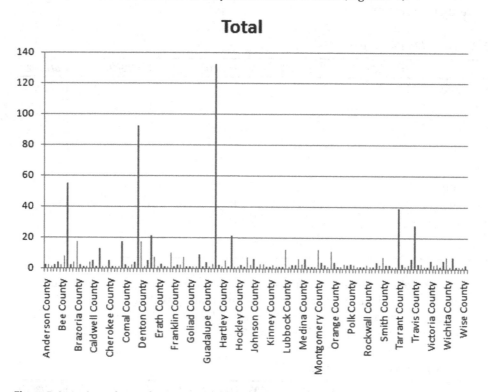

Figure 5-1. *A pivot chart of patient visits by county*

You'll note this may not be the most informative chart you've ever seen. To improve it, you could aggregate the chart into healthcare regions, since there are only eight. But then it's likely that someone doing analysis would want to "drill into" the counties underneath the regions. In addition, the time is broken down by month—what if we want to see the data by quarter or year? If we are looking at something that is driven by budgets, we may want to see the data by fiscal year, which means creating and calculating another column.

Perhaps we want to see the data broken out by race—we can add another column, or perhaps add a filter. What about looking at something like a comparison of vaccinations given vs. targeted case management scenarios? That would probably take a lot of trial and error to even get the data to lay out the way we want. Each time we want to see our data just a little differently, we have to add columns to the table, reconfigure the data, and redraw tables or charts—this is not a process conducive to analysis!

Then let's add into consideration that there are over 3 million rows in this dataset—Excel 2007 can only handle 1 million rows of data, and any kind of complex pivot on that much data is going to take significant time to run.

The solution is to move all of this work to a server. SQL Server Analysis Services (like any OLAP engine) is designed to allow you to build out the types of aggregations you will be interested in, and then process the underlying data to fill the aggregations. So, for example, if you will want to see data broken down by time (year, quarter, month, etc.) and county, then you can design "dimensions" to reflect those breakdowns. You can also create hierarchies, such as the Texas healthcare regions, which are aggregations of counties, or the time dimension (years have quarters, quarters have months, etc.). This enables us to present data similar to that shown in Figure 5-2.

Year ▼ Quarter		Calendar 2002	Calendar 2003		
			Quarter 1, 2003	Quarter 2, 2003	Quarter 3, 2(
Region ▼	Vw Geography	Vw Vaccinations Count	Vw Vaccinations Count	Vw Vaccinations Count	Vw Vaccinations
Region 1	Armstrong County	30	7	11	7
	Bailey County	101	23	22	28
	Briscoe County	30	4	4	5
	Carson County	110	30	25	21
	Castro County	131	31	40	27
	Childress County	113	20	28	23
	Cochran County	52	9	23	12
	Collingsworth County	52	7	12	14
	Crosby County	114	21	34	20
	Dallam County	87	20	18	20
	Deaf Smith County	303	66	97	72
	Dickens County	38	12	11	2
	Donley County	55	6	14	12
	Floyd County	132	31	31	23
	Garza County	72	12	13	12
	Gray County	382	98	106	86
	Hale County	632	126	196	130
	Hall County	59	9	18	15
	Hansford County	81	15	27	25
	Hartley County	83	19	26	23
	Hemphill County	51	10	14	14
	Hockley County	346	81	97	59

Figure 5-2. *Breaking down data by region, county, and time*

SQL Server Analysis Services is designed to be a "single version of the truth"—one place to aggregate business information in specific ways. In addition to simply rolling information together, you can design calculated measures to calculate averages, maximum values, standard deviations, and even advanced financial values.

The way to picture working with cubes is simply to picture a cube (Figure 5-3). In this drawing, we see something similar to our Texas data cube—the dimensions along the edges are for four calendar quarters, three regions, and three vaccinations. We can now select parts of the cube by designating what dimensions we're using. The darker area shows the results of asking for pneumonia vaccinations in region 4/5 in Q1.

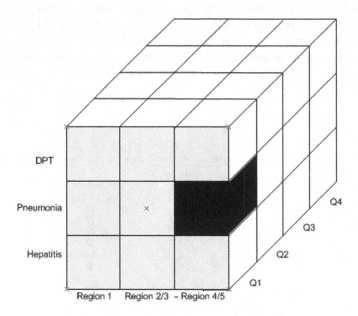

Figure 5-3. *A notional representation of an OLAP cube*

Note that we can slice the values ("facts" or measures) any way we like. For example, we may want a count of all the DPT vaccinations given in all the regions in Q1—that selection is shown in Figure 5-4.

This will return an array of values representing aggregations of the underlying values (e.g., we have not shown our Patient Race dimension, so those values are aggregated together).

Note Our relational records exist all the way down to where a single member of every dimension is specified. (Date, Region, County, Vaccination, and Race). The number at the finest granularity of a cube is called the *leaf-level member*.

The OLAP specification has a query language for selecting various combinations of measures based on the dimensions involved, called *Multidimensional Expressions*. We'll cover Multidimensional Expressions a little more later on.

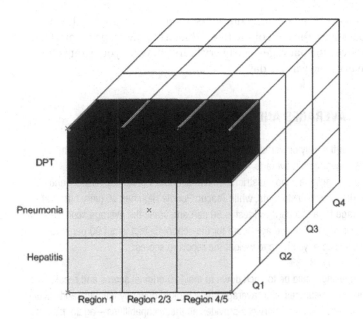

Figure 5-4. *Selecting measures using only two dimensions*

Facts and Dimensions

The two key parts of a cube are facts and dimensions. In the diagrams shown earlier, *dimensions* are the sides of the cube—the way you want to break down the data. They may be, for example, sales regions, states, dates, or personnel codes. *Facts*, on the other hand, are the contents of the cube—the numbers you are aggregating and reporting on. They could be, for example, sales amounts, number of people treated in a hospital, or number of cars on a stretch of highway.

Tip An easy rule of thumb regarding facts vs. dimensions is that facts are numbers and dimensions are strings.

In Analysis Services, you will define fact tables as the tables containing what you want to measure. They may have monetary amounts, quantities, or other measurements. One tricky aspect of working with fact tables is that you'll often want to count records. For example, if you are measuring the number of patients who visit a clinic, your fact table may be the table of patient records. However, there are no numbers in a patient record that you want to add together—you just want to count patients. The trick here is to add a column whose value is 1. Then, to count patients, you add the values in that column—if there are ten patient records, the sum of that column will be 10.

Analysis Services has other ways of aggregating numbers, including averaging. If you're measuring delivery times for packages, the sum of the times doesn't really help you out (e.g., "It took a total of 110 days to deliver 100 packages" isn't very helpful). What you want is the average—that the average delivery time was 1.1 days.

AVERAGES AND ANALYSIS

Once you start talking averages, one of the truly powerful benefits of Analysis Services shines through: aggregation. In other words, you can't average an average.

Let's consider scores in schools. Imagine a school district with two schools: Bruins High School and Teacup Poodle High School. Bruins High has 100 students, while Teacup Poodle High has 10 (very bitter) students. Bruins High reports their average for a standardized test is 80 percent, while the average score at Teacup Poodle High is 100 percent. Obviously, the average score for the school district is not 90 percent.

To calculate the district's average score, you have to weight the reported scores:

$((100\% \times 10) + (80\% \times 100)) / 110 = 81.8\%$

What would be even more compelling would be to back down to the 110 original scores and recalculate the total average. Then we could also get measures, like "average score broken down by teacher" and "average score broken down by classroom size." Analysis Services provides all these capabilities—again, it's not just returning the specific reports that business users ask for; it's enabling them to drill into the data and view it in unanticipated ways while following a line of research or inquiry.

Star Schema or Snowflake Schema?

When you actually build a cube, there are two types of schemas or layouts for the tables involved—the star schema and the snowflake. Basically, the star schema is a single fact table with dimension tables linked directly to it (see Figure 5-5). A snowflake schema, on the other hand, will have dimension tables linked to other dimension tables, generally to create a hierarchy (such as the CountyData and Regions tables in Figure 5-6). There is a lot of debate as to which is better. My advice is to stick with star schemas—functionally there's not much difference between the two, and you will find far more support in documentation and tutorials (and front ends) for star schemas.

■**Tip** Honestly, star and snowflake schemas have subtle trade-offs in the design and execution of the cube. Don't worry too much about it while you're learning—just take the design as it comes. As you gain experience, you'll be in a better position to understand the pros and cons of each schema style.

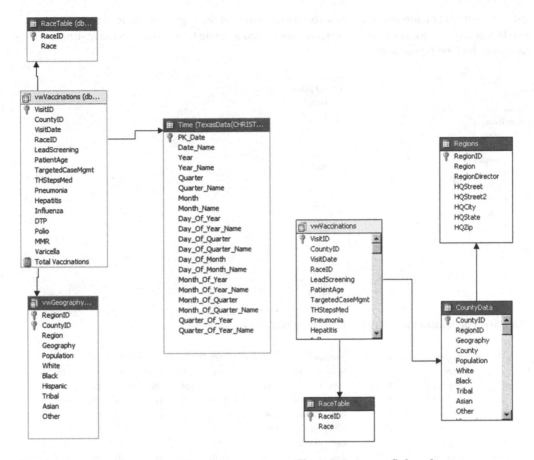

Figure 5-5. *A star schema*   **Figure 5-6.** *A snowflake schema*

BIDS and Analysis Services

Again, the main location for working with Analysis Services cubes is Business Intelligence
Design Studio (BIDS). You can install BIDS by running the SQL Server client installation,
which will fully provision BIDS if you don't have Visual Studio installed, or will add the BI
project types to Visual Studio if you already have it installed.

Building a Cube

So let's walk through building a cube from our Texas vaccination data. However, before we
start, we have a bit of work to do in the database itself. Our transactional database is normalized, which is not the optimal way to work with a cube data source, especially if we want a star

schema. Our first challenge is that our county records and our region records are in two tables (see Figure 5-7), so we want to denormalize them into a single table. This is a fairly simple view to write (see Figure 5-8).

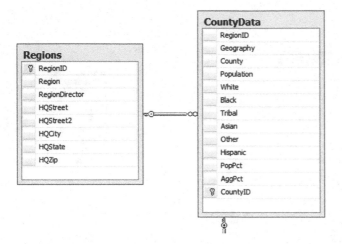

Figure 5-7. *The relational tables for Texas counties and regions*

RegionID	Region	CountyID	Geography	Population	White	Black	Hispanic	Tribal	Asian	Other
8	Region 4/5	1	Anderson County	55109	36617	12941	6705	350	246	4410
7	Region 9/10	2	Andrews County	13004	10024	214	5202	115	92	2183
3	Region 4/5	3	Angelina County	80130	60174	11792	11496	240	538	6230
8	Region 11	4	Aransas County	22497	19672	322	4571	131	623	1200
2	Region 2/3	5	Archer County	8854	8459	7	431	55	11	202
1	Region 1	6	Armstrong County	2148	2050	6	116	14	0	60
6	Region 8	7	Atascosa County	38628	28286	230	22620	310	121	8315
4	Region 6/5	8	Austin County	23590	18924	2509	3805	66	69	1649
1	Region 1	9	Bailey County	6594	4397	84	3119	43	9	1886
6	Region 8	10	Bandera County	17645	16590	58	2384	159	49	450
5	Region 7	11	Bastrop County	57733	46327	5072	13845	404	268	4385
2	Region 2/3	12	Baylor County	4093	3723	137	382	24	21	136

Figure 5-8. *Denormalized geographic data*

The next problem we have is that patient visits and vaccinations are normalized with a many-to-many relationship (Figure 5-9). If we try to bring this into Analysis Services as is, we're going to have problems aggregating our records, and we're going to have multiple fact tables (one for vaccinations and one for patient visits).

What we'd like to have is a table that aggregates all this information together, as in Table 5-4. Now we have each record as a patient visit, and each record showing a tally of the vaccinations given that we can total.

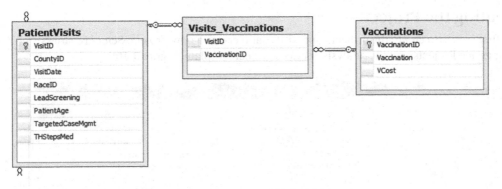

Figure 5-9. *The many-to-many visit/vaccination relationship*

Table 5-4. *Denormalized Vaccination Data*

VisitID	CountyID	VisitDate	Pneumonia	Hepatitis	Influenza	DPT
44075	105	1/31/2002 12:00:00 AM	0	1	1	0
44079	15	1/31/2002 12:00:00 AM	1	0	1	1
44093	61	1/31/2002 12:00:00 AM	1	0	1	0
44111	178	1/31/2002 12:00:00 AM	1	1	1	1
44126	101	1/31/2002 12:00:00 AM	0	1	1	0
44129	140	1/31/2002 12:00:00 AM	1	0	1	1

This could be a pretty tricky view to set up, but luckily SQL Server 2005 has the PIVOT function available, so we can define the view as follows:

```
SELECT VisitID, CountyID, VisitDate, RaceID,
LeadScreening, PatientAge, TargetedCaseMgmt, THStepsMed,
[1] AS Pneumonia, [2] AS Hepatitis, [3] AS Influenza,
[4] AS DPT, [5] AS Polio, [6] AS MMR, [7] AS Varicella
FROM
(SELECT     PatientVisits.VisitID, CountyID, VisitDate,
RaceID, LeadScreening, PatientAge,
TargetedCaseMgmt, THStepsMed, VaccinationID
FROM patientvisits INNER JOIN Visits_Vaccinations
ON PatientVisits.VisitID = Visits_Vaccinations.VisitID) v
PIVOT (COUNT(VaccinationID) FOR VaccinationID
IN ([1], [2], [3], [4], [5], [6], [7])) AS pvt
```

This aggregates our vaccinations into one place and pivots them to align them into the columns for each vaccination.

Now that we have our tables prepared, let's create a cube.

Creating the Project

The first step is to create the project. Open BIDS and create a new project. Select Business Intelligence Projects and the Analysis Services Project template (Figure 5-10).

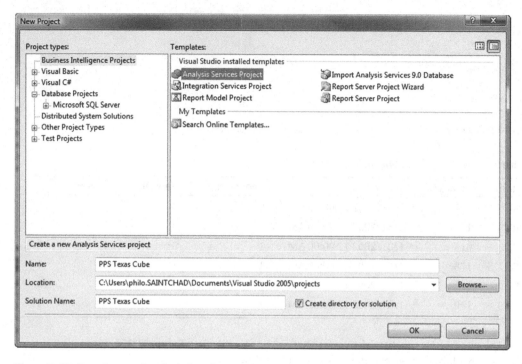

Figure 5-10. *Creating an Analysis Services project*

This creates a solution with folders for the various Analysis Services items, as shown in Figure 5-11. (If you don't see the Solution Explorer window on the right, open it by selecting the View menu, and then the Solution Explorer.) We'll walk through creating the necessary components in this chapter.

The folders in the project are as follows:

Data Sources: This is where you will create the various data connections necessary for your cube. Analysis Services can connect to any OLEDB data source directly.

Data Source Views: Once you have designated data sources and their connection details, you use the data source view to map out how Analysis Services will use the data. This allows you to leverage data from different data sources. You can even connect SQL Server data to Oracle data.

Cubes: This is the heart of why we're here. This folder will hold the cubes you create.

Dimensions: In SQL Server Analysis Services, you create discrete dimensions. You can either create them manually or have the Cube wizard create them for you.

Mining Structures: This folder holds data mining structures for performing advanced analysis on cube data. We'll cover more of this in Chapter 7.

Roles: This folder holds security roles for accessing the cubes.

Assemblies: This folder holds any .NET assemblies associated with the cube (for calculated measures, actions, or other functions associated with the cubes).

Miscellaneous: Just as it sounds, this folder is a catchall for other files in your cube structure.

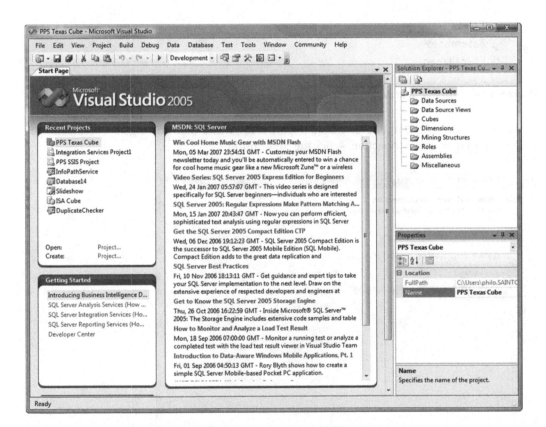

Figure 5-11. *The solution created*

Creating a Data Source

So let's create a data source. In the Solution Explorer, right-click the Data Sources folder and select New Data Source (Figure 5-12).

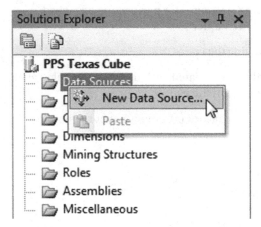

Figure 5-12. *Creating a new data source*

This will open the Data Source wizard (Figure 5-13), which lists existing data connections. We'll create a new data connection—click the New button.

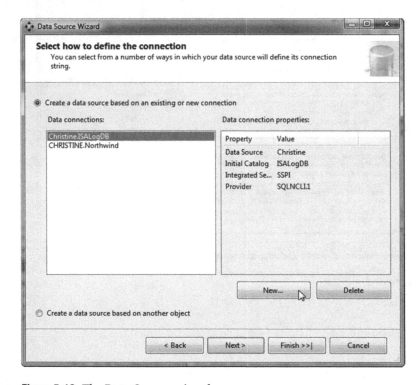

Figure 5-13. *The Data Source wizard*

The Connection Manager will open, as shown in Figure 5-14. If you click the Provider drop-down list, you will see the available data connection providers—by default, you'll see a number of Microsoft providers, and you will also see any other providers that you have installed, or that have been installed by other software packages.

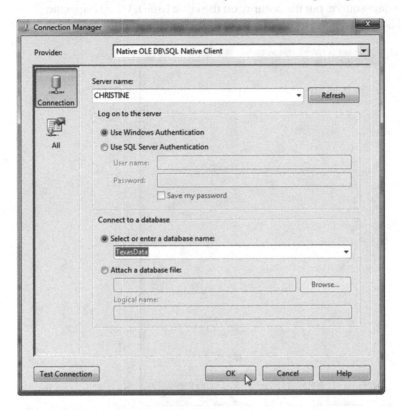

Figure 5-14. *The Connection Manager*

The connection options you're offered after selecting the provider will, of course, depend on the provider selected. The view in Figure 5-14 shows the options for the SQL Native Client. Select or type the server name. Check the Use Windows Authentication check box, and then select the database name (TexasData if you're using the Texas dataset). Click the OK button. This will return you to the data connections page of the wizard—make sure your new connection is selected, and then click the Next button.

■**Caution** You may be tempted to use localhost for the server name when you are working on a single server. While this makes the cube portable so long as the data source is on the same server as the cube, it can hide the fact that you need to change the connection information when moving cube solutions. If both your development and test environments are single-server, but your production environment uses multiple servers, then a localhost connection will pass tests fine, but fail in production. Using the server name will raise the issue sooner.

Figure 5-15 shows the Impersonation Information page of the Data Source wizard. This is the information Analysis Services will use to connect to the data source. The service account will work well provided you can give permission for the Analysis Services service account on the data source (remember, this is the information that Analysis Services uses to pull the underlying data from the data source, not the security on the cube itself). Using a specific username and password is risky when you consider password-changing requirements.

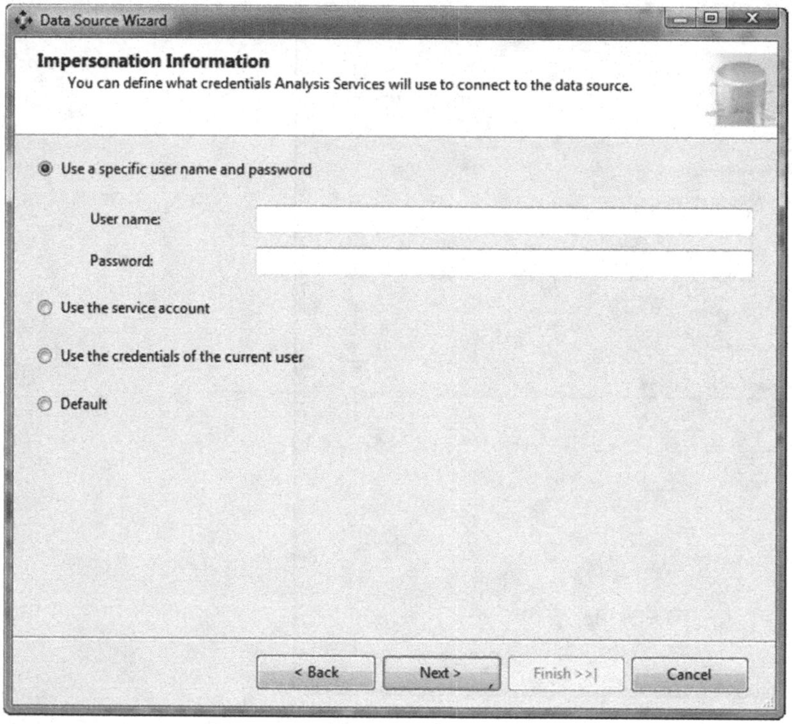

Figure 5-15. *The Impersonation Information page of the Data Source wizard*

The big consideration with the "Use the credentials of the current user" option raises the double-hop problem. If you will be connecting to Analysis Services across a machine boundary, and Analysis Services has to cross another machine boundary to connect to the data source, the connection will fail if you don't have Kerberos enabled.

Click the Finish button. Of course, if you need to, you can add additional data connections as necessary. Once you have one or more data sources, you'll need to map how Analysis Services will access the data you want in your cube—you need to create a data source view.

Creating a Data Source View

The data source view is where we indicate what tables and views we want our cube to use, and how they will map together. The data source view is the schema of the underlying data framework our cube will represent.

Many OLAP technologies require that the data they are aggregating be pulled from their data sources and loaded into a staging database. The staging database will have data structures to support an OLAP view, as opposed to the transactional view that supports the source database. This requires setting up an ETL process to load data from the transactional database to the staging database. The cube then uses that staging database as its data source.

SQL Server Analysis Services does not require that data be loaded into a staging database. Using a concept called the *Universal Data Model* (UDM), Analysis Services can map its cubes directly to the underlying data.

Nevertheless, you may want to create a staging database for some transactional data. Note that we did set up views to properly represent the transactional data for the cube—when the cube is processed, it will read those views to build the aggregations. This may create a greater load on the transactional database than you care to have. Alternatively, perhaps you don't have access to the database to create the views necessary. In this case, you may want to set up an intermediate database and an ETL job (using SQL Server Integration Services) to load the database. You have the option to work either way—do what works best for your situation.

Finally, if you are going to pull data from certain sources, such as Excel spreadsheets, web services, or data that is only accessible through transactional APIs, then you will have to load that data into a staging database—Analysis Services will not read that data directly through a data source view.

So, let's create a data source view—right-click the Data Source Views folder in the Solution Explorer, and then click New Data Source View (Figure 5-16).

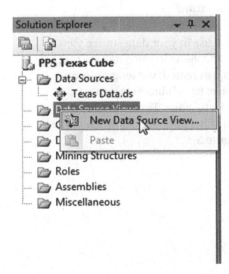

Figure 5-16. *Creating a data source view*

After the Welcome to the Data Source View Wizard page, you will see the Select a Data Source page (Figure 5-17). Select the data source created in the previous section, and then click the Next button.

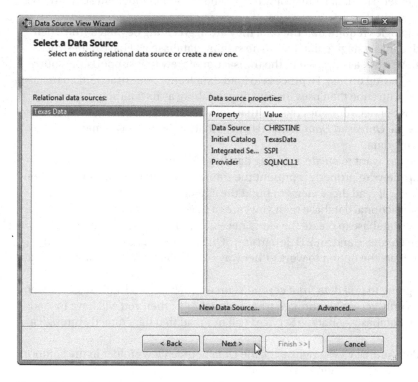

Figure 5-17. *Selecting a data source in the Data Source View wizard*

The next step is to select the tables and views you will use in your data source view (Figure 5-18). You'll be presented with a list of the tables and views in the database that the data source connects to. We're going to use the views we created: vwGeography and vwVaccinations, as well as the lookup table for patient race: RaceTable. Select these and click the > button to move them to the "Included objects" pane. Then click Next.

That's all you need to do here. Finish the wizard—the final pane will show the tables and views that will be added to the data source view (Figure 5-19).

Figure 5-18. *Selecting the tables and views we'll use in our data source view*

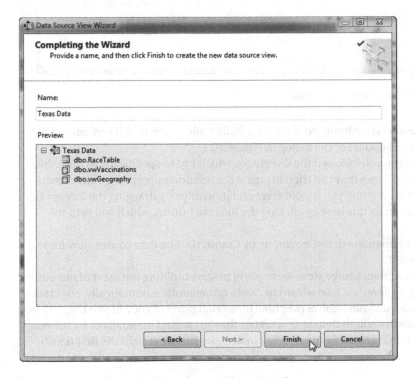

Figure 5-19. *Finishing the Data Source View wizard*

Once the wizard closes, you'll be shown the data source view on the design surface (Figure 5-20), with the views and table that you selected in the wizard. What you need to do now is create the relationships between them.

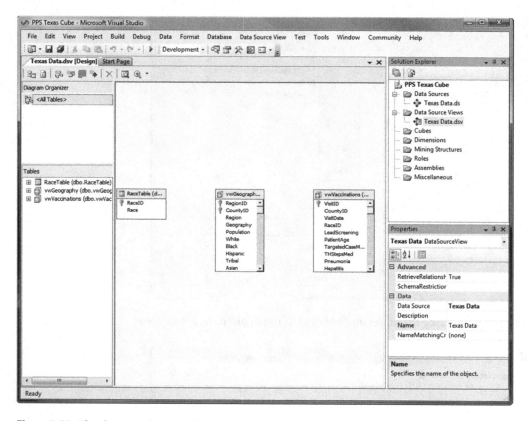

Figure 5-20. *The data source view design surface*

Click and drag the RaceID column from the RaceTable table to the RaceID column in the vwVaccinations view. You should see the dialog in Figure 5-21.

If you see the warning, you followed the directions, which I gave specifically to raise this warning. The warning indicates that you tried to create the relationship in the wrong direction. In the data source view pane, you should create relationships by dragging the foreign key to the primary key. You can fix this here by clicking the Reverse button, which will turn the relationship around.

Now connect vwVaccinations to vwGeography by CountyID. The data source view pane should look like Figure 5-22.

Now that we have our data source view, we're going to start building the meat of our cube: the dimensions. You can allow the Cube wizard to create dimensions automatically, but creating them manually gives you finer control over how these vital parts of your BI solution will be built. (While you can always edit dimensions, whether they're created manually or by the wizard, it's often easier to rebuild them from scratch—so why not just do it right the first time?)

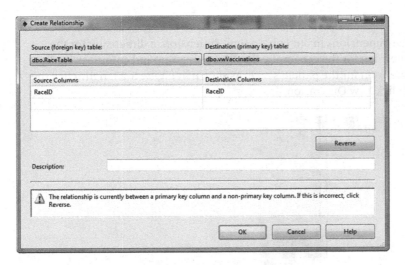

Figure 5-21. *The Create Relationship dialog*

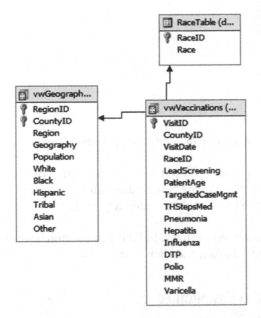

Figure 5-22. *The data source view with the tables and views connected*

Dimensions

We're going to have three dimensions in our cube: a time dimension, a dimension for the patient's race, and a dimension for the geography (healthcare regions and counties). We'll start by creating the dimension for the patient's race. As shown in Figure 5-23, right-click the Dimensions folder and click New Dimension.

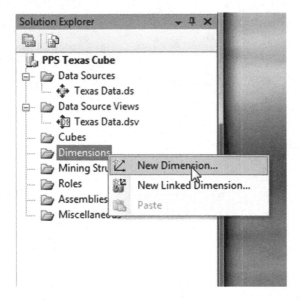

Figure 5-23. *Creating a new dimension*

This will open the Dimension wizard. Click past the welcome page to open the Select Build Method page of the wizard (Figure 5-24).

Select "Build the dimension using a data source," since you will base this dimension on the RaceTable table. Ensure that "Auto build" is checked. For the "Create attributes and hierarchies" drop-down selector, either choice is fine since there won't be a hierarchy in this dimension. Click Next.

The next page allows you to select the data source view you will build the dimension from (Figure 5-25). Select the data source view you created earlier, and click Next.

ABOUT ATTRIBUTES AND HIERARCHIES

Attributes are one of the core concepts of SQL Server Analysis Services, and attribute relationships (including hierarchies) are the primary tools in proper design and scalability of your cube solution.

You use attributes to define relationships between members (such as Year-Quarter-Month or Region-County). Attributes help the OLAP engine determine where to calculate aggregations, speeding response time for the end user.

For more information, read "Dimensions (Analysis Services)" on Microsoft TechNet, at `http://technet.microsoft.com/en-us/library/ms174527.aspx`.

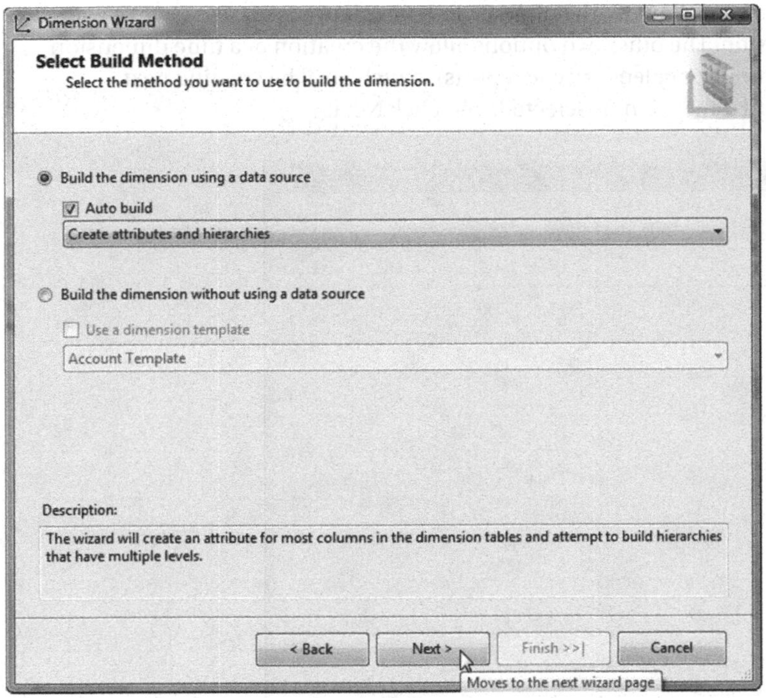

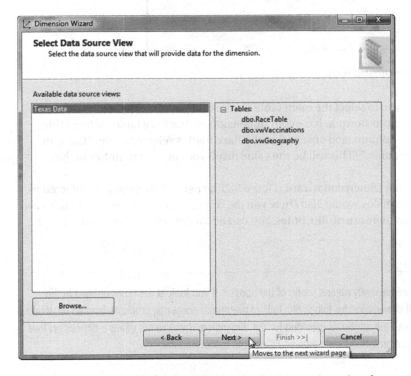

Figure 5-24. *The Select Build Method page of the Dimension wizard*

Figure 5-25. *Selecting the data source view in the Dimension wizard*

The next page allows you to choose the dimension type (Figure 5-26). First, we're going to create a standard dimension. The other two options allow the creation of a time dimension (which we'll need for getting our calendar-type reports), which we'll be creating next.

Ensure that "Standard dimension" is selected, and click Next.

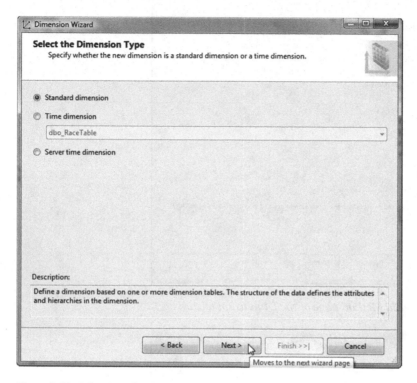

Figure 5-26. *Selecting the dimension type*

The next page asks you to select the main table for the dimension (Figure 5-27). Choose dbo.RaceTable from the drop-down to base your dimension on the RaceTable lookup table. Check RaceID as the key column, and ensure that the Race field is selected under "Column containing the member name." (This will be the value displayed for each member of the dimension.) Click Next.

In the next page of the Dimension wizard (Figure 5-28), ensure that Regular is selected as the dimension type. This dialog would also show you the dimension attributes, but in this case the table is very basic, so there are no attributes. You can add a description if you choose (or add it later). Click Next.

■**Note** "Regular" in this sense really means "none of the above." If you look at the other options in the selector, you'll see prebuilt dimensions for things like bills of materials, accounts, products, and so on. If you select one of these, you'll see the attributes provided for the dimension. If you're not using a dimension that conforms to one of these preformatted types, then you'll want to select Regular.

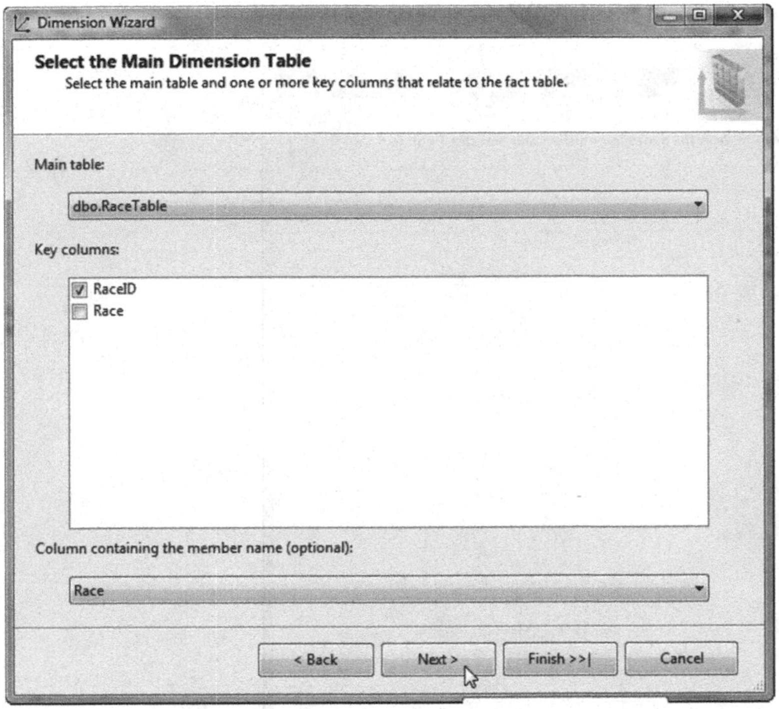

Figure 5-27. *Selecting the main table in the Dimension wizard*

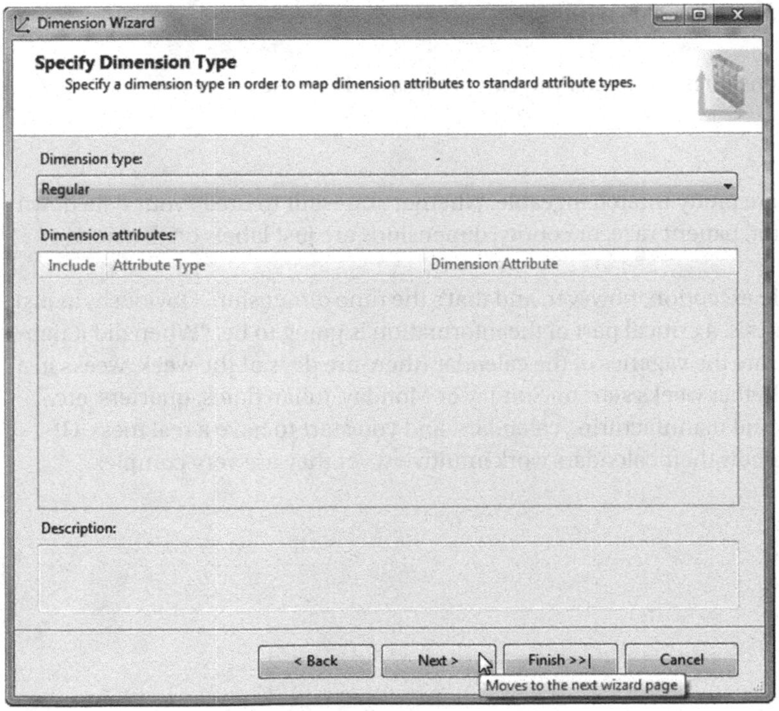

Figure 5-28. *Selecting the dimension type*

The final page (Figure 5-29) summarizes the dimension. Click Finish.

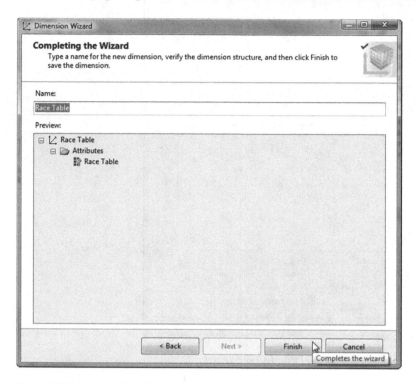

Figure 5-29. *Completing the Dimension wizard*

Now that your dimension is complete, you can process and browse it.

The Time Dimension

Dimensions in general are pretty interchangeable. Whether you want to break your data down by account, product color, patient race, or county, dimensions are just labels on divisions of data.

There is one notable exception, however, and that's the time dimension. Obviously, in just about any business analysis, a critical part of the information is going to be, "When did it happen?" In addition, there are the vagaries of the calendar (there are days of the week, weeks in a month, questions on whether weeks start on Sunday or Monday, Julian dates, quarters, etc.). Add on fiscal calendars and manufacturing calendars, and you start to have a real mess. Of course, everyone knows how their calendars work intuitively, yet they are very complex.

Given all that, it seems silly to have to reinvent the calendar wheel every time you create a cube, doesn't it? Of course it does. Luckily, Analysis Services has a method for creating a calendar, or time dimension, for you. Let's walk through it.

First, right-click the Dimensions folder, select New Dimension, and then click the Next button on the welcome screen of the wizard (if you haven't turned it off already). The Select Build Method page of the Dimension wizard will appear (Figure 5-30).

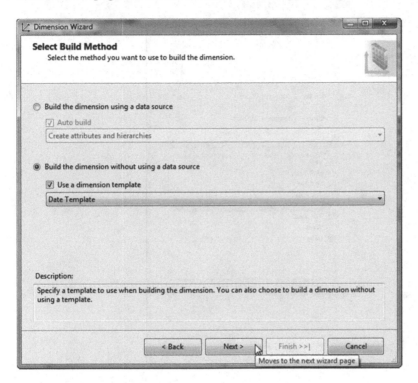

Figure 5-30. *Creating a time dimension*

Select "Build the dimension without using a data source." This taps into the predeveloped templates packaged in Analysis Services—the date template will create a table prepopulated with dates for a range you specify, as well as create attributes for the dates. Check the "Use a dimension template" check box and select Date Template from the drop-down list. Click the Next button.

The next page of the wizard allows you to select the time period you want the date table generated for (Figure 5-31). Set the first calendar day to January 01, 2001, and the last calendar day to December 31, 2005. This covers the data in the Texas dataset.

Leave the first day of the week as Sunday.

Under "Time periods," check the boxes for Year, Quarter, Month, and Date. This indicates which attributes to generate and populate. Click the Next button.

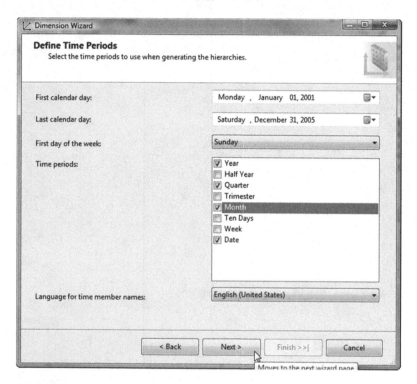

Figure 5-31. *Selecting the date range and time periods to generate the dimension for*

The next page allows you to add additional calendars (such as fiscal or manufacturing calendars). Analysis Services allows you to build reports using various calendars, so that you can look for patterns with respect to not just seasonality, but based on budget constraints or other calendars. Leave these unchecked and click the Next button.

The final page will review what the wizard will create (Figure 5-32). Note that in addition to the attributes for the dates, the wizard is also going to create a hierarchy for the time periods specified in the wizard. Check the "Generate schema now" check box at the bottom of the page—this will create the table and add it to your data source view (Figure 5-33).

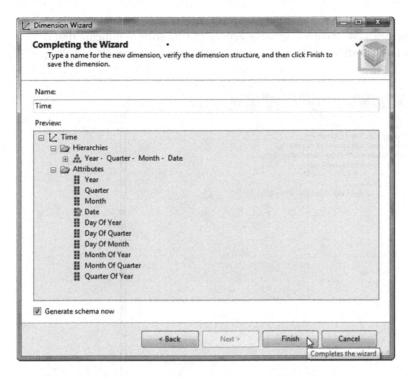

Figure 5-32. *Finishing the Dimension wizard for the time dimension*

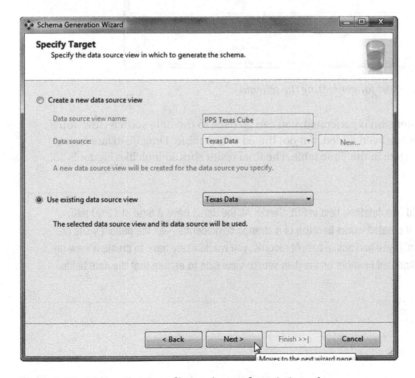

Figure 5-33. *Adding the time dimension to the existing schema*

When you generate the schema, you may get a warning on the RaceTable table—that's fine, it's expected (see Figure 5-34). Analysis Services generates this error to indicate that the dimension will be populated from the table, and so does not need to be generated by the OLAP engine.

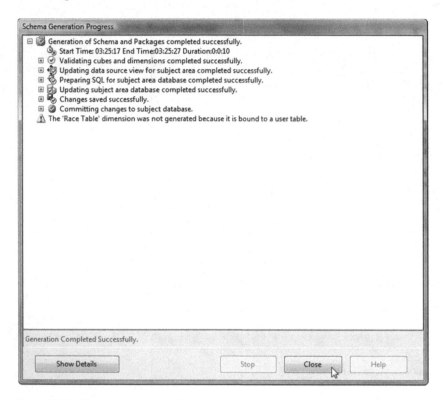

Figure 5-34. *The output report for generating the schema*

Once the time dimension is generated, you can go back to the data source view. You'll see that the Time table has been added, but not linked to any table. Drag VisitDate from vwVaccinations to PK_Date in the Time table. The final result should look like Figure 5-35.

■**Note** The PK_Date field is a datetime field in SQL Server. All the dates have a time of 12:00 a.m. (midnight). The join we just created works because of a strange coincidence—all the patient visits are timestamped at 12:00 a.m. If you had actual patient records, you would likely have to create a view on the database side or a calculated member on the data source view side to ensure that the date fields would map.

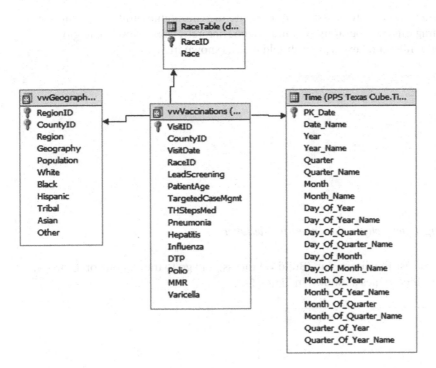

Figure 5-35. *The data source view with the Time table*

Dimension Hierarchies

Outside of the time dimension, you will want other hierarchies in your dimensions:

- Shipping containers have palettes; palettes have crates.

- Regions have states; states have counties.

- Companies have departments; departments have workgroups.

- Product lines have product types; product types have products.

Let's take our Texas healthcare geography, for example—we have regions and counties. Surely, the directors of various healthcare regions will want to be able to view their own region and drill down to the county level. So how do we create this type of hierarchy? It's actually pretty straightforward.

Create a new dimension based on the vwGeography table, just like you did for the RaceTable table. Once the dimension is created, go into the dimension designer. Drag the Region attribute from the attributes list on the left to the Hierarchies and Levels pane in the center. Then drag the vwGeography attribute to the Hierarchy box, below the Region attribute. The Hierarchies and Levels pane should look as shown in Figure 5-36.

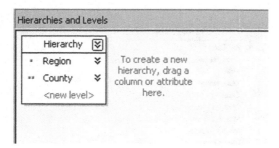

Figure 5-36. *Creating a hierarchy in the dimension designer*

Now if you reprocess the dimension (Build ➤ Process) and go to the dimension browser, you should see your hierarchies as shown in Figure 5-37.

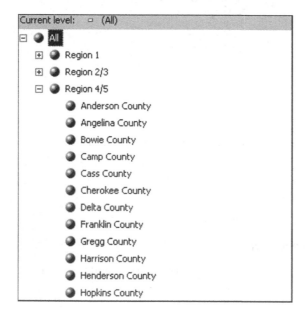

Figure 5-37. *Geographic hierarchy in the Texas dataset*

Creating the Cube

So now the part we've all been waiting for: creating our cube. Having laid the groundwork, creating the cube from our data source view and existing dimensions becomes very straightforward. Again, start by right-clicking the Cubes folder in the Solution Explorer and selecting New Cube (Figure 5-38).

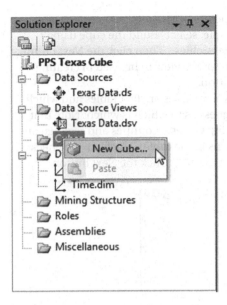

Figure 5-38. *Creating a new cube*

You will be greeted with the introductory page of the Cube wizard. Click the Next button to open the Select Build Method page of the wizard (Figure 5-39).

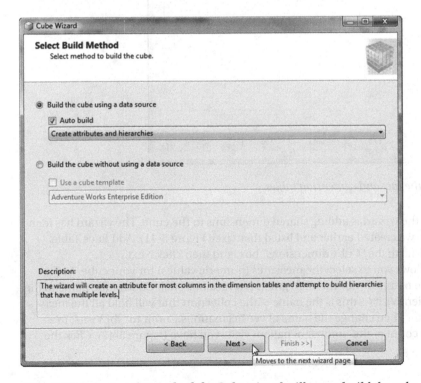

Figure 5-39. *Selecting the method the Cube wizard will use to build the cube*

Similar to the Dimension wizard, this wizard can operate from a data source view or generate a cube with no data source available. For this example, select "Build the cube using a data source," "Auto build," and "Create attributes and hierarchies." Then click the Next button. The next page of the wizard allows you to select the data source view to be used in creating the cube. Select your data source view and click the Next button.

The next page of the wizard is where you indicate which tables are fact tables and which are dimensions (Figure 5-40). The wizard makes a best guess as to which is which. Note that the Geography view is selected as both a dimension (string values—counties and regions) and a fact table (numbers—the county population breakdowns in the table). Uncheck the check box under Fact for vwGeography (we'll keep this straightforward). Click the Next button.

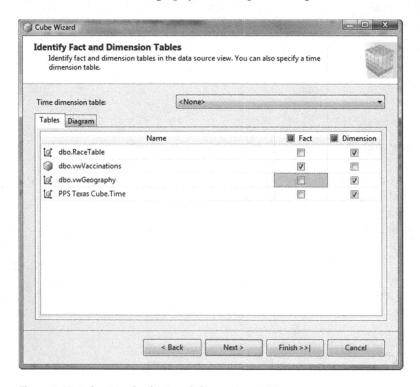

Figure 5-40. *Selecting the fact and dimension tables*

The next step in the wizard is adding shared dimensions to the cube. The wizard has identified the dimensions we created earlier and listed them (see Figure 5-41). Add Race Table, vwGeography, and Time to the "Cube dimensions" box, and then click Next.

The next page allows you to select the measures (numeric values) for your cube. At the top, in brackets, is the name of your measure group (vwVaccinations). Change the name to the more descriptive Patient Visits—this is the name of the collection that will hold all the measures listed underneath. Then change the name of vwVaccinations.Count to Nbr Visits, to indicate that this is a count of the number of patient visits you have (Figure 5-42). Click the Next button.

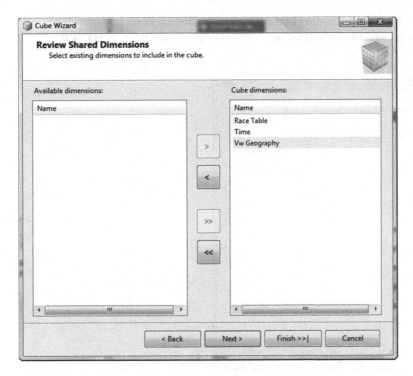

Figure 5-41. *Selecting dimensions to add to the cube*

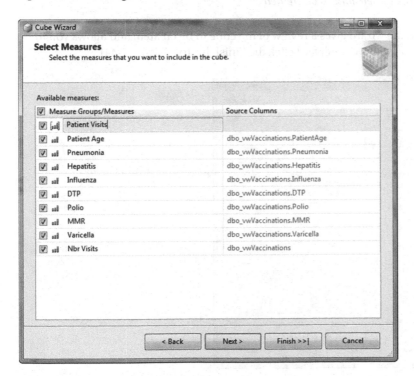

Figure 5-42. *Selecting measures for the cube*

We're almost done. Next, the wizard will ask you to review the dimensions that will be created and/or associated with the cube (Figure 5-43). Leave all the defaults and click the Next button.

Figure 5-43. *Reviewing the dimensions to be created*

The final screen in the wizard gives a review of the cube to be created, and allows you to give the cube a name. Leave the default and click the Finish button (Figure 5-44).

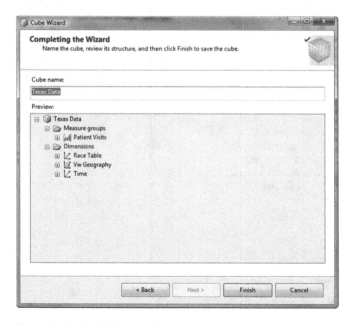

Figure 5-44. *Finishing the Cube wizard*

Once the wizard is finished, you're left in the cube design palette, which shows you the fact tables and dimensions created and associated by the wizard (Figure 5-45). Note the simple star shape (one central fact table with a group of dimension tables arrayed around it).

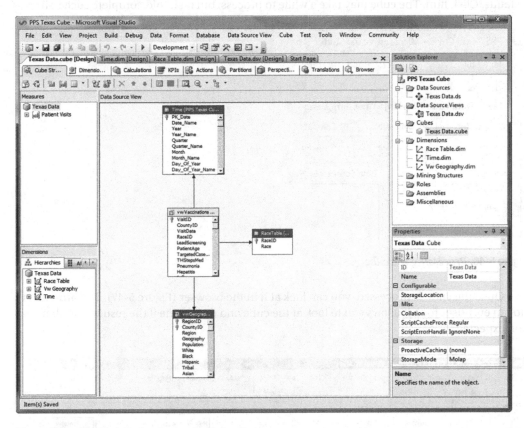

Figure 5-45. *The finished cube in the cube designer*

To see the results of your cube, you first need to process it. You can do this either from the Build menu, or by clicking the Process button (Figure 5-46). This will open the Process Cube dialog. There are a number of options here for processing cubes, but you can accept the defaults. Click Run. The cube may take a while to process, but it should complete successfully.

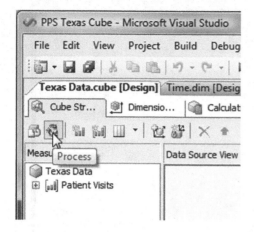

Figure 5-46. *Processing the cube*

Once the cube is processed, you can look at it in the browser (Figure 5-47). The browser is not an end-user tool; it allows you to look at the cube and determine if the results are what you expected.

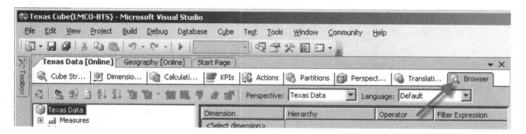

Figure 5-47. *Opening the cube browser*

■Tip If you are using the 2005 version of BIDS, and getting unusual results from the browser (errors or a blank page), then make sure you have applied Service Pack 2 to the client tools installation (I often patch the server but forget to patch the client machine).

The browser is pretty self-explanatory (Figure 5-48). If you're familiar with building pivot tables in Excel, this is very similar—open the Measures group and select a measure to drag to the area labeled Drop Totals or Detail Fields Here.

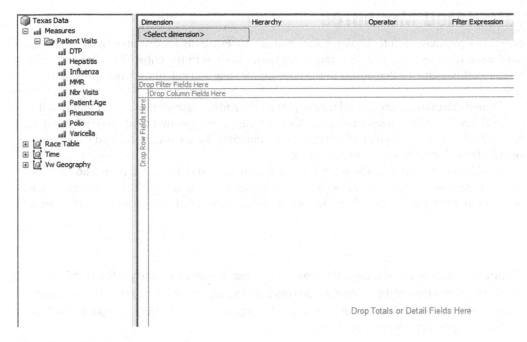

Figure 5-48. *The SQL Server Analysis Services browser*

Then you can either open up dimensions and drag attributes over, or simply drag the whole dimension over. For example, dragging Geography to the vertical area labeled Drop Row Fields Here, and Time to the area labeled Drop Column Fields Here, gives you a result similar to Figure 5-49.

Drop Filter Fields Here

Region ▼	Year ▼		
	⊞ Calendar 2002	⊞ Calendar 2003	Grand Total
	Nbr Patient Visits	Nbr Patient Visits	Nbr Patient Visits
⊞ Region 1	12146	12417	24563
⊞ Region 2/3	93416	96453	189869
⊞ Region 4/5	21556	21927	43483
⊞ Region 6/5	81433	83102	164535
⊞ Region 7	35571	36714	72285
⊞ Region 8	33352	33893	67245
⊞ Region 9/10	19216	19492	38708
⊞ Region 11	27068	27456	54524
Grand Total	323758	331454	655212

Figure 5-49. *The browser showing our cube*

Note that your regions have expansion (+) symbols. If you open them, you will see their subordinate counties in the hierarchy you created. In addition, each of the calendar year members can be opened to show quarters, and then months.

That's it! You've built a cube! Now for a quick review of some other aspects of cubes that are worth knowing.

Calculated Measures

Sometimes you may want to display values that are not expressly represented by the transactional data. You may want to derive additional values to show in the cube. There are two ways to achieve this: named calculations in the data source view and calculated measures in the cube.

Named calculations are a good way to provide an additional column of data that is still transactional in nature—a sales tax value, for example, or an extended total. In our Texas data, we could add a named calculation to total the vaccinations for each visit. Named calculations are calculated during processing of the cube.

Calculated measures, on the other hand, are more related to the cube/dimensional structure—for example, average values (which vary depending on the query). You define calculated measures on the Calculations tab of the cube designer. Calculated measures are calculated at query time.

Caution If you're playing with calculated measures, get lost, and decide to simply delete all the code, you'll find your cube stops updating when you process it. That's because there is a CALCULATE command in the code metadata that launches the cube processing. If you go into the code window and press Ctrl+A, and then Delete, you'll delete this command as well.

Multidimensional Expressions

Beyond the fun you can have with the browser, there is a rich query language behind the cube that allows a lot of magic. For example, you could return all pneumonia vaccination counts from counties where the Hispanic population is greater than the Native American population. If you had current data, you could define that query for "the past three months with rolling averages."

The language of querying cubes is called Multidimensional Expressions (MDX). It is a set-based query language that gives you great power and flexibility when dealing with cubes. The best book for learning MDX is *Fast Track to MDX*, by Mark Whitehorn (Springer, 2004).

Key Performance Indicators

A great new capability in SQL Server Analysis Services 2005 that we will exploit later is being able to define KPIs within the cube itself. This gives us "one version of the truth." For example, if we wanted to define a KPI dealing with workdays, do weekends count? How about holidays? Personal vacation days? Company training days? Rest assured that given five different departments, we will get five different answers. This is problematic for defining KPIs, since it makes it difficult to compare across the organization.

By defining the KPI in an Analysis Services cube, everyone leverages the same definition (for better or worse). KPIs in Analysis Services allow you to define targets, values, trends, and indicators. The KPIs can be surfaced in PerformancePoint Server, Excel, SharePoint, and other applications.

Perspectives

Just a quick note about perspectives—perspectives are not intended as a security feature. They are a way to group functionality to suit different users. For example, when considering a personnel cube, HR may have a hundred dimensions they use, contracting may have a few dozen, management may want a few dozen others, and so on. With all of those dimensions intermingled, it quickly gets frustrating for users to work with the cube on a regular basis.

Instead, Analysis Services provides a capability to create "virtual cubes," or perspectives, on a given cube. You can create additional perspectives of the cube, and select which measure groups, measures, dimensions, and members to include in the perspective. To the end user, the perspective will appear just like another cube available, except that it will have a sharply targeted set of features to better enable users to do their analyses. (And if they need features from the main cube, they can always open it as well.)

Conclusion

All of that, and we've only scratched the surface of SQL Server Analysis Services. It's almost criminal how much I've had to leave out. However, my main goal was to demystify OLAP and cubes—to give you the running start you need to understand the importance and power of Analysis Services, as well as its place in a BI initiative.

In addition, the planning components of PerformancePoint are Analysis Services cube–based, so a basic knowledge of Analysis Services is essential to tackling that part of PerformancePoint.

We have one more technology in the SQL Server package to cover before we move on to the good stuff. We've aggregated data and built it into a model we can use for reporting and analysis—now how do we use these cubes to provide value to our end users?

That's where SQL Server Reporting Services comes in.

CHAPTER 6

■■■

SQL Server Reporting Services

Once you've aggregated business data into one or more cubes, you'll still want a way to publish and share data from the cube (as well as a means of standard reporting against a relational source). The next step in our tour of SQL Server services is SQL Server Reporting Services—a web-based report engine built into SQL Server. In this chapter we're going to look at using Reporting Services, building reports, and using the report model to enable users to create ad hoc reports.

SQL Server Reporting Services presents users with a web-based administration interface (Figure 6-1) where they can run reports, subscribe to reports, and configure reports if they have the administrative rights. This is also where users can launch Report Builder if report models have been deployed.

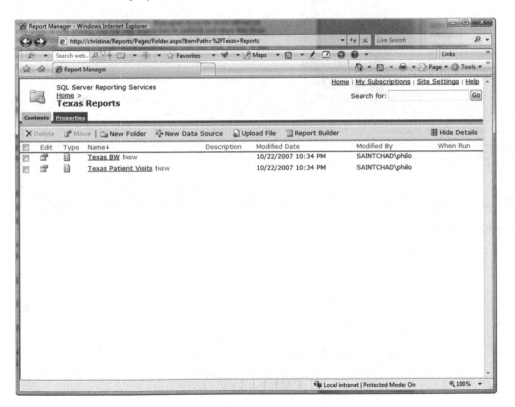

Figure 6-1. *Reporting Services Report Manager interface*

■Note This chapter is going to focus on Reporting Services 2005, but I will take time to point out significant differences in Reporting Services 2008.

Figure 6-2 shows our friend Business Intelligence Development Studio (BIDS)—this time with a Reporting Services project open. Getting basic reports out of Reporting Services is very straightforward, and the platform is very extensible to provide powerful reporting capabilities. Out of the box, Reporting Services includes basic design features like grids and charts; there are also third-party add-ins for advanced charting, maps, controls, and so on.

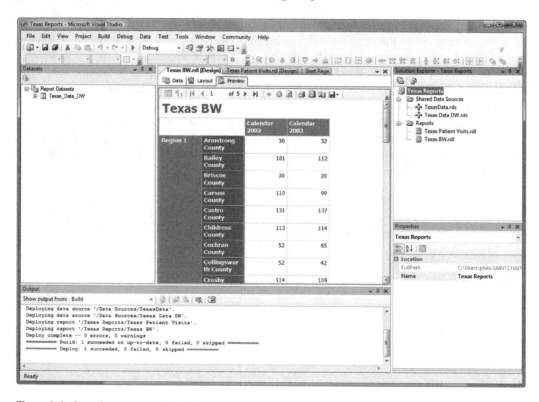

Figure 6-2. *Creating reports in BIDS*

Finally, Figure 6-3 shows Reporting Services Report Designer. You can also build a report model in Reporting Services, which end users can then use in Report Builder to design and publish their own reports. This is similar to the concept in Analysis Services where the heavy lifting is done in building the cube on the back end, enabling average users to perform ad hoc analysis on the front end.

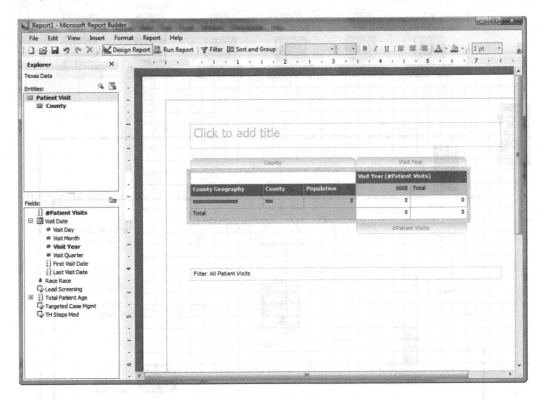

Figure 6-3. *SQL Server 2005 Report Builder*

Report Builder is a rich client application that is delivered with "click-once" deployment technology—when a user clicks on the Report Builder link in the Report Manager browser interface, the Report Builder application is downloaded and launched without even a Next ➤ Next ➤ Finish. From there, the user can select a model, build a report, and save it back to the report server for others to consume.

OK, let's take a look at how Reporting Services works.

Architecture

The conceptual architecture for Reporting Services is shown in Figure 6-4. I like this diagram because it clearly lays out the moving parts as well as the extensibility points.

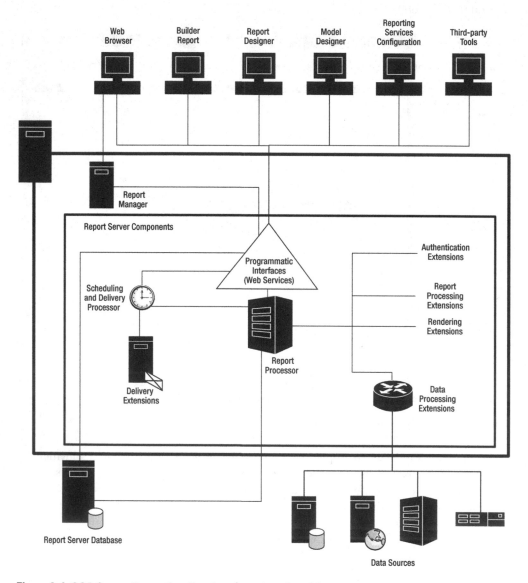

Figure 6-4. *SQL Server Reporting Services functional architecture*

Report Server

Report Server is obviously the main component of Reporting Services. It consists of a Windows service and a Web service that process report requests, compile the reports, and deliver them, either as scheduled or on demand. Report Server also allows you to build extensions for rendering, processing, delivery, and so on.

The Windows service has two components that do the actual ongoing work of Reporting Services: the Report Processor and the Scheduling and Delivery Processor. The Report Processor manages reports and requests. When a user (or process) requests a report, the Report Processor pulls the report definition from the database, uses the data connections to retrieve the data necessary, merges the data with the layout from the definition, renders the report, and delivers it to the output or Scheduling and Delivery Processor.

The Scheduling and Delivery Processor handles report subscriptions. It monitors events, data-driven notifications, and subscription timing. If a report is being requested directly by a user, the Scheduling and Delivery Processor isn't involved. Scheduled events are handled by being maintained in a queue; the Scheduling and Delivery Processor polls the queue at 10-second intervals (this is configurable).

While Report Server runs things behind the scenes, Report Manager is the user interface and truly the "face" of Reporting Services.

Report Manager

Report Manager is the web-based interface for Reporting Services (Figure 6-5). When you configure Reporting Services, Report Manager is installed by default at `http://server/Reports`, where you can see it as a virtual directory.

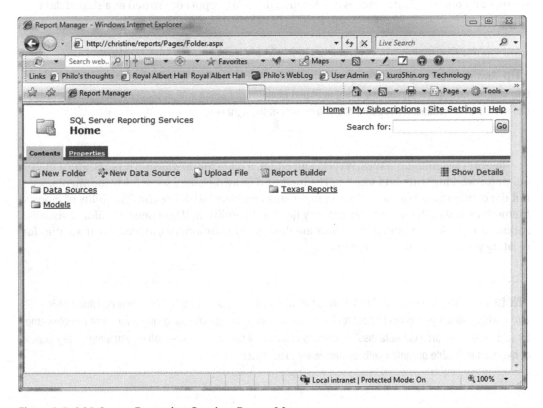

Figure 6-5. *SQL Server Reporting Services Report Manager*

■**Tip** A number of folks have issues with "losing" Report Manager when they install SharePoint. This is because SharePoint (WSS or MOSS) installs to the default IP and port, just as Reporting Services does. When it does this, it deactivates the web application where Report Manager was installed. A quick fix is to go to IIS Manager, change the port of the default web site to a different port (favored alternates are 81, 8080, and 8100), and then start the web site (right-click Default Web Site, and then click Start). For more information about working with the Report Manager virtual directories, see http://msdn2.microsoft.com/en-us/library/ms159261.aspx.

Through Report Manager, your users can access everything they need from the user aspect of Reporting Services—viewing reports, managing organization of reports (creating folders, moving reports among folders, etc.), role-based security, schedules and subscriptions, and so on. This is also the main interface for launching Report Builder.

Report Designer

BIDS is also where you can create reports. A report project can contain multiple shared data sources and reports. (Data sources can be embedded in a report or created as a shared data source.)

■**Tip** Always create your data sources as shared data sources. Besides allowing them to be reused, this also enables editing the connection string in Report Manager (for users with appropriate permissions), which can save a lot of headache regarding pointing reports at the right server.

Report Designer has a WYSIWYG layout editor, a pane for previewing reports, and a query editor for working with data sources. The toolbox (Figure 6-6) may seem fairly rudimentary, but the configuration of the toolbox components combined with the configurability of reports themselves makes Reporting Services very flexible. In addition, if you need additional visualization capabilities in your reports, there are third-party components, as well as capabilities for creating your own toolbox components.

■**Note** Reporting Services 2008 has more powerful charts, a gauge control, and a new construct called *tablix*, which allows you to nest tables and matrices in various combinations, giving a far more flexible setup for tabular and hierarchical data display. There isn't a control called "Tablix"—rather, you simply drag tables or matrices into table or matrix cells as necessary to nest them.

Once you've designed your report, it's a very straightforward exercise to configure your report project for deployment to your Reporting Services server.

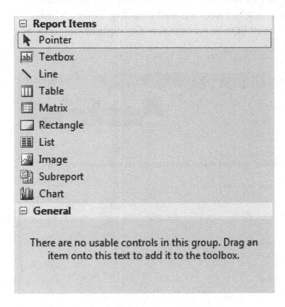

Figure 6-6. *The Report Designer toolbox*

Report Builder

If you create a *report model* (a dimensional construct similar to an Analysis Services cube), then your users will be able to use Report Builder to create their own ad hoc reports within the constraints of the model. A report model is a metadata description of a data source and its relationships—think of it as the schema for a data source (which can comprise data from multiple data sources) with annotations and user-friendly labels.

Report models are created using BIDS and the Report Model Project template. Once you've built a report model and published it to Reporting Services, your users will be able to launch Report Builder from Report Manager, select a model and report style, and build their own reports.

Reporting Services Configuration Manager

When you install Reporting Services on a server, you will have to run the Reporting Services Configuration Manager (Figure 6-7) to get Reporting Services up and running. You can find the Configuration Manager under Start ➤ Microsoft SQL Server 2005 ➤ Configuration Tools ➤ Reporting Services Configuration.

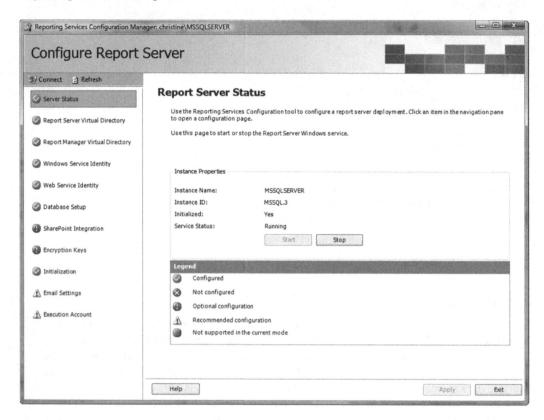

Figure 6-7. *Reporting Services Configuration Manager*

Once you're in the Configuration Manager, it's fairly straightforward to walk down the checklist in the left-hand panel. To get Reporting Services into a usable state, you need to at least complete the steps for the following:

Server Status: Simply ensure that you're connected to the right server and that it's running.

Report Server Virtual Directory: Connect to an IIS server and configure the virtual directory to be used for Report Server (the default is ReportServer).

Report Manager Virtual Directory: Do the same for Report Manager as you did with Report Server (the default is Reports).

Windows Service Identity: Configure the account used by the Reporting Services Windows service. Clicking the Help button here will open a great article discussing the issues around each type of account.

Web Service Identity: This pane will display the account that the web service will run under. You can set this by setting the application pool for the virtual directory where the web service is located.

Database Setup: This pane is where you set up the database that Reporting Services will use for its reports repository. You'll trip over an interesting situation here: if you are running the Configuration Manager on a remote machine from Report Server, or if you installed the client tools later (e.g., to set up Reporting Services), then there is a good chance that the client tools are not patched to the same version as the server, and your database setup will fail. Make sure that your client tools are patched to the same service pack as your server.

Initialization: Check the status of the server and configure a scale-out deployment.

SharePoint integration is only enabled if you change the server to SharePoint mode (see the "SharePoint Integration" section later in this chapter). Encryption keys are recommended to secure the reports in the server, the e-mail settings allow the reporting server to e-mail reports, and the Execution account is a low-privileged account that Reporting Services can leverage to run other processes.

Reporting Services 2008 has a significantly different Configuration Manager (Figure 6-8). If you're familiar with the settings in the 2005 Configuration Manager, then these will seem very similar, with one big gotcha, as shown in the figure. Reporting Services 2008 runs its own web services; it's not dependent on IIS. As a result, configuration of the web interface is done directly in the Configuration Manager, not in IIS Manager.

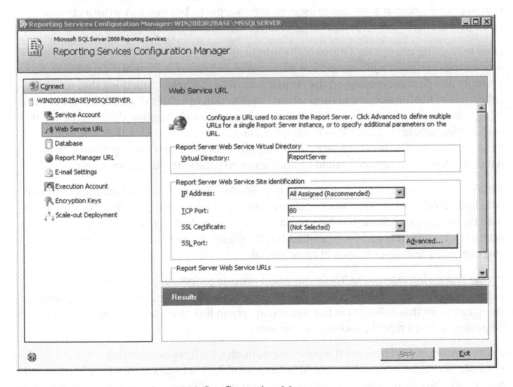

Figure 6-8. *Reporting Services 2008 Configuration Manager*

Once you've stepped through the Configuration Manager, Reporting Services should be up and running and ready to go.

Extensibility

Reporting Services has a great extensibility story. You can pretty much modify any aspect of the engine you need to. In addition to modules, you can write .NET assemblies to extend the fundamental capabilities. There are also APIs in the form of the .NET object model, URL-based commands, and web services.

Note In-depth extensibility is beyond the scope of this book; this is just meant to be an overview of the potential of Reporting Services. To dig deeper into customizing and programming SQL Server Reporting Services, start with the SQL Server Programming Reference, available online at `http://msdn2.microsoft.com/en-us/library/ms166342.aspx`.

Extensions

Each of the extensions is written as a .NET assembly that provides custom functionality to Reporting Services. You can write custom extensions for each of the following functions:

Authentication extensions: By default, Reporting Services uses IIS integrated authentication to authenticate and authorize users to access reports, but you can write a custom authentication provider if you need some other method of accessing reports.

Data processing extensions: These are the interfaces between a report and its data. A data processing extension will connect to a data source and return a flattened dataset. An example of a data processing extension you may want might be something that reads a collection of flat file documents and returns a collection of values (if you don't want to use Integration Services to load the data into a staging database). Another data source worth considering would be XML files—if you have a large collection of XML files, you could write a data processing extension to report on those files without loading them into a database. XML Web Services would be another good candidate for an extension.

Rendering extensions: Reporting Services uses rendering extensions to take the combined data and layout information and translate it into a format for the user. Reporting Services uses rendering extensions to deliver the standard reports. You may want to write a custom extension to write a report in a specified HTML format to a web server, for example; or you may want to deliver reports in Word format.

Report processing extensions: These extension provide processing for toolbox items. For example, suppose that you enable a user to embed a MapPoint map in Reporting Services, but want this delivered in the report with a map link to an online map. This would be performed in a report processing extension.

Delivery extensions: These are the pipelines through which reports are delivered. An example of a delivery extension would be an assembly that hooks an API for a high-speed printer and has reports printed and collated automatically.

That's the "heavy lifting" approach to customizing Reporting Services—it requires more code and testing, but a properly implemented extension will be as solid as Reporting Services itself. There are easier ways to manipulate Reporting Services, however, as you'll see in the following sections.

Web Services

The best way to interface with Reporting Services, outside of writing actual extensions, is via the embedded web service. The ReportService web proxy class exposes methods for managing everything inside Reporting Services, including the following:

Authorization: Creating, editing, or deleting roles, permissions, and policies.

Data sources and connections: Managing data sources and connections stored on the server.

Linked reports: Listing, creating, and setting linked reports.

Namespace management: Managing report jobs, listing items on the server (reports, jobs, events, etc.), and changing system properties.

Rendering and execution: Setting caching and execution options, rendering a report, and managing the reporting cache.

Report history: Managing the report history and options.

Report parameters: Getting and setting parameters for a report.

Scheduling: Exposing the full capabilities of scheduling reports. With these methods (CreateSchedule(), ListSchedules(), and SetScheduleProperties()), you can create report schedules and assign them to reports.

Subscription and delivery: Creating and managing subscription and delivery methods. The most interesting function here is the ability to create data-driven subscriptions. In the realm of BI, this is a great API to have.

URL-Based Commands

Every report can be delivered via IIS, and every Report Manager option can be driven via URL. (In fact, the reports displayed in the Report Manager window are URL driven if you look at the source for the page.) What this means to the developer is that it's painfully easy to leverage Reporting Services in *any* web-based application—simply create a window, panel, or IFrame on your web page and use the URL to drive the report behavior you want.

■**Note** URL access is fully documented at http://msdn2.microsoft.com/en-us/library/ ms153586.aspx.

An example of a report URL looks like this:

```
http://server/reportserver?/Sales/Northwest/Employee Sales Report
&rs:Command=Render&EmployeeID=1234
```

Here's another example, which will render the report as a PDF:

```
http://servername/reportserver?/Sales/YearlySalesSummary
&rs:Format=PDF&rs:Command=Render
```

Note that the URL to the report server is followed by a parameter for the report path and name, the report server command to render the report, and finally the parameter value for the employee ID.

Report Definition Language

Every report in Reporting Services is represented by an XML-based language called Report Definition Language (RDL). RDL is fully documented by Microsoft, and since it's XML-based, it's relatively straightforward to produce using any XML tool. The main benefit here is that it's possible to write code to generate report definitions—you can even write your own report authoring tools targeting specific special uses.

Semantic Model Definition Language

Semantic Model Definition Language (SMDL) is an XML-based language used by the models produced for use by Report Builder. The opportunity here is to automate building of models. For example, you may want to code an extension in Visual Studio to produce a report model from a particular UML design, or you might want to write code for Visio to produce a report model from an architectural diagram.

Summary

I hope this quick-and-dirty overview of the Reporting Services architecture helps give you a basic idea of how Reporting Services runs. It is a very critical part of any BI solution (despite the gentle derision of transactional reports in Chapter 5, reports are still a cornerstone of understanding and tracking a business).

Now let's crawl out from under the chassis and take a look at how to build and leverage reports in SQL Server Reporting Services.

Creating Reports

Having Reporting Services running is great, but it doesn't do us a lot of good without some reports to run. Let's quickly run through creating and publishing a few reports to get a feel for what we can do with Reporting Services. We'll create a basic relational report and a matrix report from our Texas Analysis Services cube, add a chart, and discuss some third-party add-ins of note.

Table and Matrix Reports

Reporting Services offers two basic styles of report: tables (straight tabular data—Figure 6-9) and matrices (pivot table style, aggregating data along one axis—Figure 6-10). You choose which type of report to create when you work through the Report wizard. Of course, the wizard simply lays out the fundamentals of a report—a single data source, title, and either table or matrix.

Patients by County

Geography	Patients	Avg Age
Anderson County	1,974	40
Andrews County	448	41
Angelina County	2,871	41
Aransas County	829	42
Archer County	315	41
Armstrong County	070	41
Atascosa County	1,373	40
Austin County	885	42
Bailey County	242	40
Bandera County	646	40

Figure 6-9. *A tabular report*

Texas BW Region Matrix

	April 2002	April 2003	August 2002	August 2003	December 2002	December 2003
Region 1	815	1,131	1,249	908	913	1,205
Region 11	1,858	2,388	2,903	2,081	1,988	2,700
Region 2/3	6,367	8,277	9,707	7,148	6,953	9,684
Region 4/5	1,406	1,912	2,256	1,512	1,542	2,186
Region 6/5	5,445	7,022	8,608	6,207	6,069	8,261
Region 7	2,405	3,211	3,746	2,631	2,550	3,671
Region 8	2,222	2,907	3,498	2,449	2,469	3,402
Region 9/10	1,269	1,729	2,139	1,432	1,385	1,971

Figure 6-10. *A matrix report*

You can always add additional data sources to a report, and additional tables, matrices, charts, subreports, or other components to create a more complex report. (Of course, any components you add you'll have to set up by hand.)

Reporting Services 2008: Tablix

As I mentioned earlier, Reporting Services 2008 introduces a new concept called tablix, which overcomes the limitations of dealing with either tables or matrices. Tablix data regions are covered at http://technet.microsoft.com/en-us/library/bb934258(SQL.100).aspx.

Tablix makes designing data regions simultaneously more powerful and easier to understand, since it is driven by dragging tables and matrices to the design surface and nesting them as necessary. You can then merge cells (the Reporting Services engine will even merge cells on the fly).

Figure 6-11 shows a tablix region being built in BIDS, with the user dragging a table over to nest into a data cell in a table nested inside a matrix.

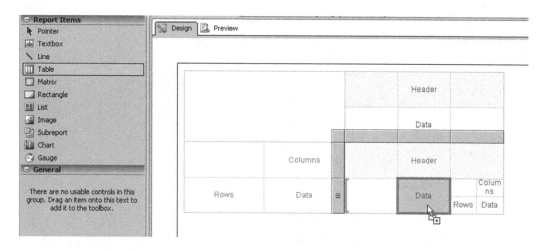

Figure 6-11. *A tablix data region in Reporting Services 2008*

Exercise 6-1 will walk through creating a basic report from the AdventureWorks sample database.

Exercise 6-1. Creating a Basic Report

1. Open BIDS and create a new project.

2. Select Business Intelligence Projects from the Project Types pane, and then select Report Server Project Wizard. Name the project AdventureWorks Product Reports (see Figure 6-12).

3. Click OK. If you get the Welcome to the Report Wizard page, click Next.

4. On the Select the Data Source page, the "New data source" radio button should be selected, since this solution doesn't have any shared data sources. Give the data source a name, and select Microsoft SQL Server from the Type drop-down.

5. You can either type a connection string into the text box or click the Edit button to open the Connection Properties dialog. Enter your server, and then select the AdventureWorks database.

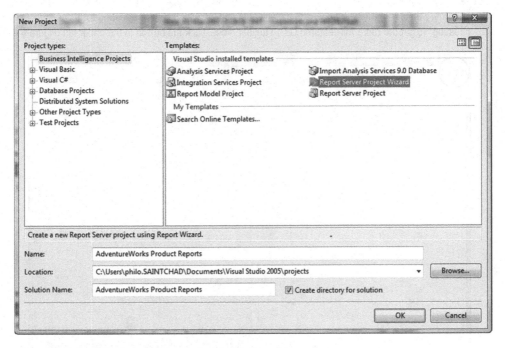

Figure 6-12. *Creating a new Reporting Services project*

6. Check the "Make this a shared data source" box (Figure 6-13), and then click Next.

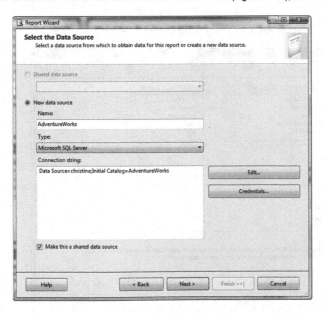

Figure 6-13. *The Select the Data Source page of the Report wizard*

7. On the Design the Query page, you can enter a query directly or use the Query Builder. We'll use the builder—click the Query Builder button.

8. The Query Builder is tricky—it opens to a blank query editor, which is a bit daunting for those of us used to cheating. To get the more full-featured Query Builder mode, click the button in the upper left (Figure 6-14).

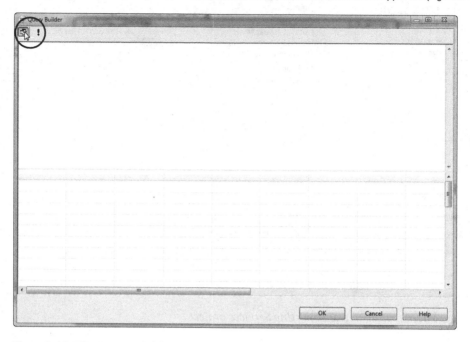

Figure 6-14. *The Query Builder in text mode*

Clicking the button in the top left opens the Query Builder in design mode (Figure 6-15).

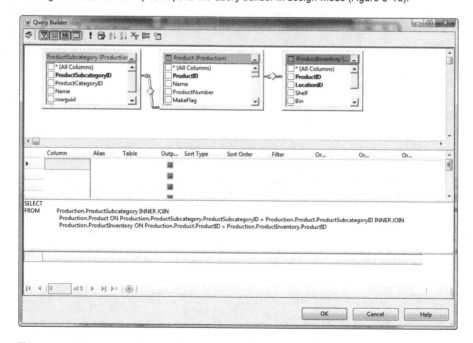

Figure 6-15. *The Query Builder in design mode*

9. In the Query Builder, right-click in the top area and select Add Table.

10. Add the ProductSubcategory table, the Product table, and the ProductInventory table. Note that the relationships are automatically added as well.

11. Check the boxes next to the following fields to add them to the output, and add aliases as shown in the following table.

Adding Fields to the Query Design

Column	Alias	Table
Name	Subcategory	ProductSubcategory
ProductID		Product
Name	ProductName	Product
StandardCost		Product
ListPrice		Product
SellEndDate		Product
Quantity		ProductInventory

12. Add a the following filter for the ProductSubcategory.Name field (alias Subcategory): =@Subcategory. This will add a parameter to the report to allow filtering the report based on the subcategory. (We'll use this when we put the report in a dashboard.)

13. Right-click the design canvas and select Add Group By.

14. Note the addition of the Group By column and the default of "Group By" on each column.

15. Change the "Group By" for Quantity to **Sum**.

16. Change the new alias (Expr1) to **Inventory Qty**.

17. You can click the Run button (Figure 6-16) to view the output of the query. When prompted for a subcategory, enter **Road Bikes**.

Figure 6-16. *The Run button in the Query Builder*

18. When you've finished, click OK. You'll be taken back to the Design the Query page with your SQL in the "Query string" text box.

19. Click the Next button, and you'll be taken to the Select the Report Type page. On this page, select Tabular, and then click Next.

20. On the Design the Table page, add the ProductName, StandardCost, ListPrice, SellEndDate, and Inventory_Qty fields to the Details area (see Figure 6-17).

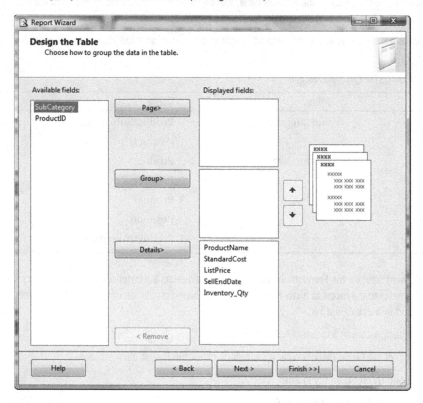

Figure 6-17. *Selecting fields for the report*

21. Click Next. On the Choose the Table Style page, select Slate, and click Next. You'll be taken to the Choose the Deployment Location page (Figure 6-18), which allows you to enter the URL of the report server or Share-Point server (if running in integrated mode), and the folder to deploy the reports to.

22. Click Next. On the final page, you'll see a summary of the wizard actions. Name the report Product List, and click Finish.

23. In Report Designer, click the Preview tab. Enter **Road Bikes** for the subcategory, and click the View Report button. You should see a report similar to Figure 6-19.

24. Let's fix the formatting—click the Layout tab at the top of the designer again to open the report layout.

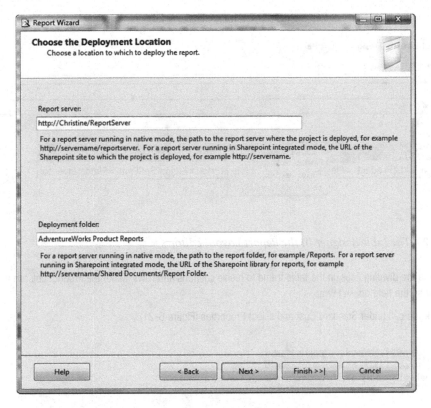

Figure 6-18. *Entering the deployment location for the reports*

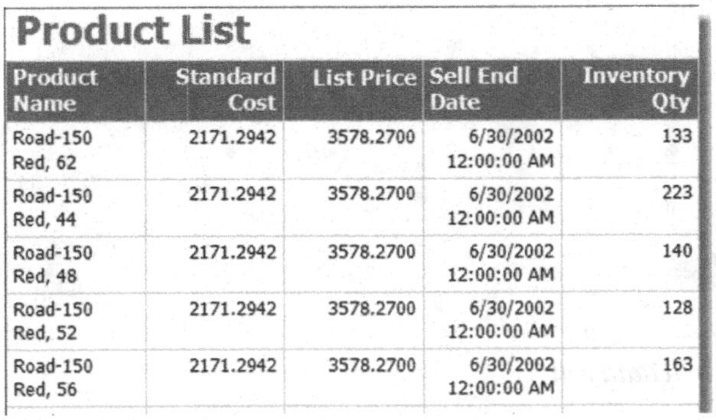

Product List

Product Name	Standard Cost	List Price	Sell End Date	Inventory Qty
Road-150 Red, 62	2171.2942	3578.2700	6/30/2002 12:00:00 AM	133
Road-150 Red, 44	2171.2942	3578.2700	6/30/2002 12:00:00 AM	223
Road-150 Red, 48	2171.2942	3578.2700	6/30/2002 12:00:00 AM	140
Road-150 Red, 52	2171.2942	3578.2700	6/30/2002 12:00:00 AM	128
Road-150 Red, 56	2171.2942	3578.2700	6/30/2002 12:00:00 AM	163

Figure 6-19. *The Product List report*

25. If you click in the table, you'll pop up the table layout frame (Figure 6-20).

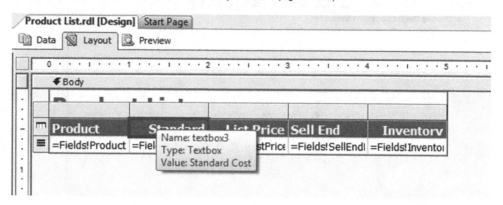

Figure 6-20. *The table designer in the Report Layout editor*

26. You can use the dividing lines on the table frame to resize columns and rows. Make the Product column a little wider so the field doesn't wrap.

27. Right-click the cell under Standard Cost and select Properties (Figure 6-21).

Figure 6-21. *Setting properties on a data cell*

28. In the Properties dialog, select the Format tab. You can either use the Builder button (...) or simply enter **C** (for "currency") in the "Format code" field (Figure 6-22).

29. Click OK to close the Properties dialog, and do the same for the List Price text box.

30. Set the format code for the Sell End Date text box to "d" for the mm/dd/yy format. You can also open up the columns a bit so the column headers are all on a single line.

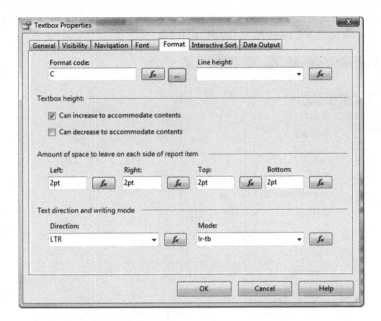

Figure 6-22. *Setting the currency format*

31. To view the report, select the Preview tab and enter **Road Bikes** for the parameter. Your report should end up looking like Figure 6-23.

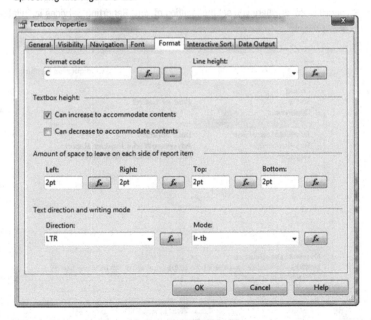

Figure 6-23. *The final report*

32. To deploy the report, you may have to set the report server location—to do so, right-click the Project name in the Solution Explorer on the right, and select Properties (Figure 6-24).

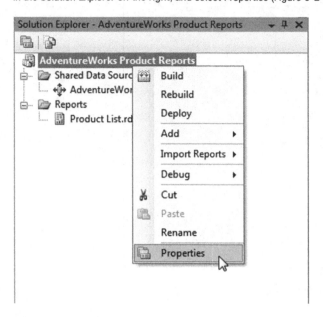

Figure 6-24. *Opening the project properties to set the deployment location*

33. The Solution Property page (Figure 6-25) is where you set the location of your Reporting Services installation.

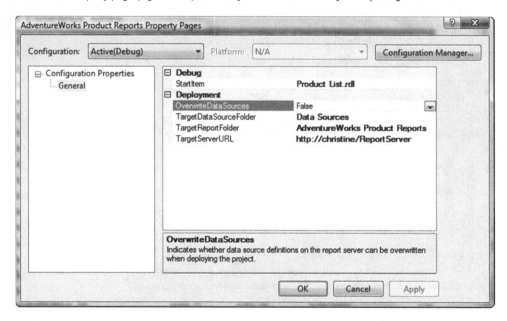

Figure 6-25. *Report Solution Property page*

34. For Reporting Services native installation, TargetServerURL will be the Reporting Services location, ending in /ReportServer, while the Data Source and Report folders will be relative folders on the report server.

35. For SharePoint integrated mode, the Data Source and Report folders will be absolute URLs, while TargetServerURL will be the root URL of the SharePoint server (Figure 6-26).

⊟ Deployment	
OverwriteDataSources	True
TargetDataSourceFolder	http://bi-vpc/Reports/ReportsLibrary
TargetReportFolder	http://bi-vpc/Reports/ReportsLibrary
TargetServerURL	http://bi-vpc/

Figure 6-26. *Folder locations for a SharePoint Integrated deployment*

Hopefully you can already see the usefulness of Reporting Services, even for generating basic tabular reports. This is only the beginning—next we'll take a look at leveraging the cube we built in Chapter 5 to create a matrix report, and we'll add a chart to it—still very introductory stuff, but starting to show off how powerful Reporting Services can be in a BI solution.

Multidimensional Reports

This book is about getting value out of large volumes of transactional data—the ability to take thousands or millions of records and reduce them to a straightforward visual report of some form. Reporting Services is the first step in visualizing our data and delivering it to end users. Tabular data answers some questions our users may have, but matrix reports help a lot more to analyze the data; they are similar to pivot tables in Excel—aggregating data to display summary information.

Figure 6-27 shows transactional data (in Excel). We're showing individual records of parts ordered in the AdventureWorks database (88,000 records). Even with the table tools in Excel, there are various ways we'd want to aggregate this data to get some use out of it.

	Name	PurchaseOrderID	OrderDate	SubTotal	TotalDue	Status	UnitPrice	LineTotal	OrderQty	ItemName
2	Litware, Inc.	1	5/17/2001 0:00	201.04	222.1492	4	50.26	201.04	4	Adjustable Race
3	Advanced Bicycles	2	5/17/2001 0:00	272.1015	300.6721	1	45.12	135.36	3	Thin-Jam Hex Nut 9
4	Advanced Bicycles	2	5/17/2001 0:00	272.1015	300.6721	1	45.5805	136.7415	3	Thin-Jam Hex Nut 10
5	Allenson Cycles	3	5/17/2001 0:00	8847.3	9776.2665	4	16.086	8847.3	550	Seat Post
6	American Bicycles and Wheels	4	5/17/2001 0:00	171.0765	189.0395	3	57.0255	171.0765	3	Headset Ball Bearings
7	American Bikes	5	5/31/2001 0:00	20397.3	22539.0165	4	37.086	20397.3	550	HL Road Rim
8	Anderson's Custom Bikes	6	5/31/2001 0:00	14628.075	16164.0229	4	26.5965	14628.075	550	Touring Rim
9	Proseware, Inc.	7	5/31/2001 0:00	58685.55	64847.5328	4	27.0585	14882.175	550	LL Crankarm
10	Proseware, Inc.	7	5/31/2001 0:00	58685.55	64847.5328	4	33.579	18468.45	550	ML Crankarm
11	Proseware, Inc.	7	5/31/2001 0:00	58685.55	64847.5328	4	46.0635	25334.925	550	HL Crankarm
12	Aurora Bike Center	8	5/31/2001 0:00	693.378	766.1827	4	47.4705	142.4115	3	External Lock Washer 3
13	Aurora Bike Center	8	5/31/2001 0:00	693.378	766.1827	4	45.3705	136.1115	3	External Lock Washer 4
14	Aurora Bike Center	8	5/31/2001 0:00	693.378	766.1827	4	49.644	148.932	3	External Lock Washer 9
15	Aurora Bike Center	8	5/31/2001 0:00	693.378	766.1827	4	45.3705	136.1115	3	External Lock Washer 5
16	Aurora Bike Center	8	5/31/2001 0:00	693.378	766.1827	4	43.2705	129.8115	3	External Lock Washer 7
17	Australia Bike Retailer	9	1/14/2002 0:00	694.1655	767.0528	4	47.523	142.569	3	Thin-Jam Lock Nut 9
18	Australia Bike Retailer	9	1/14/2002 0:00	694.1655	767.0528	4	45.423	136.269	3	Thin-Jam Lock Nut 10
19	Australia Bike Retailer	9	1/14/2002 0:00	694.1655	767.0528	4	49.6965	149.0895	3	Thin-Jam Lock Nut 1
20	Australia Bike Retailer	9	1/14/2002 0:00	694.1655	767.0528	4	45.423	136.269	3	Thin-Jam Lock Nut 2
21	Australia Bike Retailer	9	1/14/2002 0:00	694.1655	767.0528	4	43.323	129.969	3	Thin-Jam Lock Nut 15
22	Beaumont Bikes	10	1/14/2002 0:00	1796.0355	1984.6192	4	47.4705	142.4115	3	Chainring Bolts
23	Beaumont Bikes	10	1/14/2002 0:00	1796.0355	1984.6192	4	42.798	128.394	3	Chainring Nut
24	Beaumont Bikes	10	1/14/2002 0:00	1796.0355	1984.6192	4	25.4205	1525.23	60	Chainring

Figure 6-27. *Transactional records from the AdventureWorks database*

Figure 6-28 shows the records in a pivot table in Excel 2007. Notice the configuration panel on the right—what I've done is set the item names down the left-hand side and the status codes across the columns. Then, the values in the LineTotal column are "pivoted" into the data area—grouped together and summed. The Excel interface allows us to group by different values.

Sum of LineTotal	Column Labels				
Row Labels	1	3	4	Grand Total	
Adjustable Race	301.581	150.7905	7288.1935	7740.565	
Bearing Ball	251.496	125.748	5910.156	6287.4	
Chain	1888.74	944.37	44385.39	47218.5	
Chainring	7936.11		191689.47	199625.58	
Chainring Bolts	705.978	142.4115	16956.009	17804.3985	
Chainring Nut	632.6775	128.394	15182.0235	15943.095	
Cone-Shaped Race	397.9395	132.6465	6101.739	6632.325	
Crown Race	452.3715	150.7905	7087.1535	7690.3155	
Cup-Shaped Race	438.858	146.286	6875.442	7460.586	
Decal 1	787.5	525	11812.5	13125	
Decal 2	787.5	525	11812.5	13125	
External Lock Washer 1	247.2435		5011.965	5259.2085	
External Lock Washer 2	104.6115		2545.767	2650.3785	
External Lock Washer 3	414.6345	278.523	5373.774	6066.9315	
External Lock Washer 4	433.9755	285.0435	5400.5175	6119.5365	
External Lock Washer 5	525.7665		5263.965	5789.7315	
External Lock Washer 6	240.723	129.8115	5014.674	5385.2085	
External Lock Washer 7	532.287	142.632	5167.4175	5842.3365	
External Lock Washer 8	110.9115		2467.7415	2578.653	
External Lock Washer 9	538.3665		5396.4855	5934.852	

Figure 6-28. *Pivot table in Excel 2007*

The matrix control in Reporting Services works the same way (Figure 6-29)—we select a field for the vertical axis, another field for the horizontal axis, and a field to be grouped in the body area. You can see the Sum function in Figure 6-29—if you're not using a dimensional source, then Reporting Services will add an aggregation function. You can change this if you need to (Count, Average, Max, Min, etc.).

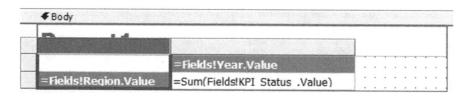

Figure 6-29. *The matrix control on a report*

Note When you run the wizard to create a new report, after you select the data source, you have the option to select "tabular" or "matrix"—this is where you select whether to put a table control or a matrix control on the report page.

The problem with matrix reports and pivot tables is that the data is aggregated on the fly, which can be problematic for large datasets. This type of work is why we want to use Analysis Services—the OLAP engine is designed to optimize aggregation of quantities of data. As an example, I ran the report we're going to design in Exercise 6-2 using Analysis Services and built the same report from the relational database. The relational report ran for about 5 minutes before running out of memory, while the Analysis Services report rendered almost instantly.

In Exercise 6-2, we're going to use our Texas dataset to create a matrix report, showing how straightforward it can be to deliver reports to our users.

Exercise 6-2. Creating a Multidimensional Report

1. In a Reporting Services solution in BIDS, right-click the Reports folder, and then click Add New Report (Figure 6-30) to open the Report wizard.

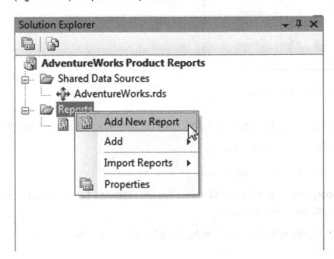

Figure 6-30. *Creating a new report*

2. If the Welcome to the Report Wizard page opens, click Next.

3. On the Select the Data Source page, select "New data source." Name it AdventureWorks DW, and select Microsoft SQL Server Analysis Services under Type.

4. Click the Edit button next to the connection string box. This will open the Analysis Services Connection Properties dialog (Figure 6-31).

Figure 6-31. *The Connection Properties dialog*

5. Enter your server name, and then select the Adventure Works DW cube from the drop-down box. Click OK.

6. Check "Make this a shared data source," and then click Next.

7. On the Design the Query page, click the Query Builder button.

    Note that this Query Builder is more advanced and oriented toward Analysis Services, listing measures, KPIs, and our dimensions in the Metadata pane (Figure 6-32).

8. Open up the Measures group in the Metadata pane, and then open the Reseller Sales folder and drag Reseller Sales Amount to the designer.

9. Next, open the Geography dimension and drag the Country member to the designer.

10. Finally, open the Date dimension and drag the Calendar Year member between Country and Reseller Sales Amount. Again, you'll see all the members populate (Figure 6-33).

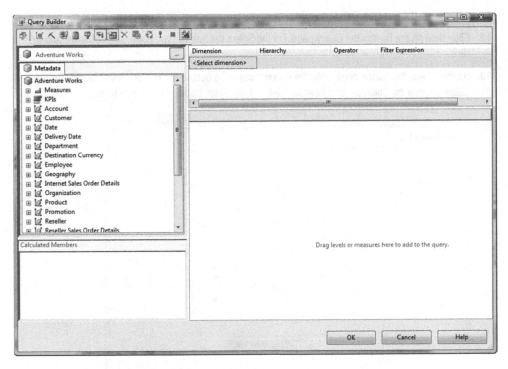

Figure 6-32. *The Analysis Services Query Builder*

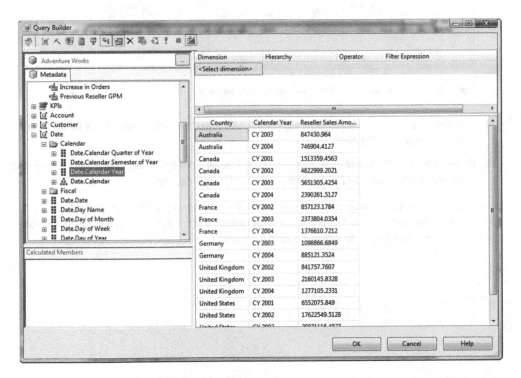

Figure 6-33. *The completed dimensional query*

11. Click OK on the Query Builder to see BIDS generate the necessary MDX and write it into the wizard.

12. Click Next on the Design the Query page. On the Select the Report Type page, select Matrix, and then click Next.

13. On the Design the Matrix page, note the various ways of grouping the report. Move Country for Rows, Calendar_Year for Columns, and Reseller_Sales_Amount for Details (see Figure 6-34).

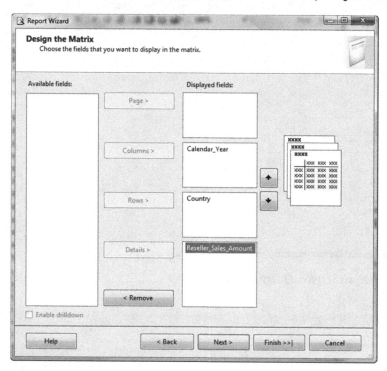

Figure 6-34. *The matrix designer in the Report wizard*

14. Click Next. The Choose the Matrix Style page simply allows you to select a color scheme for the report. Leave it as Slate, and click Next.

15. On the Completing the Wizard page, name the report Reseller Sales By Country, check the "Preview report" check box, and then click the Finish button to return to the BIDS designer.

Figure 6-35 shows what you should see in the report. Note that once again you'll have to do some resizing of columns and set the format for the data cell. If you're not inclined to worry about seeing the pennies on multi-million-dollar sales figures, then use a custom format of $#,###.

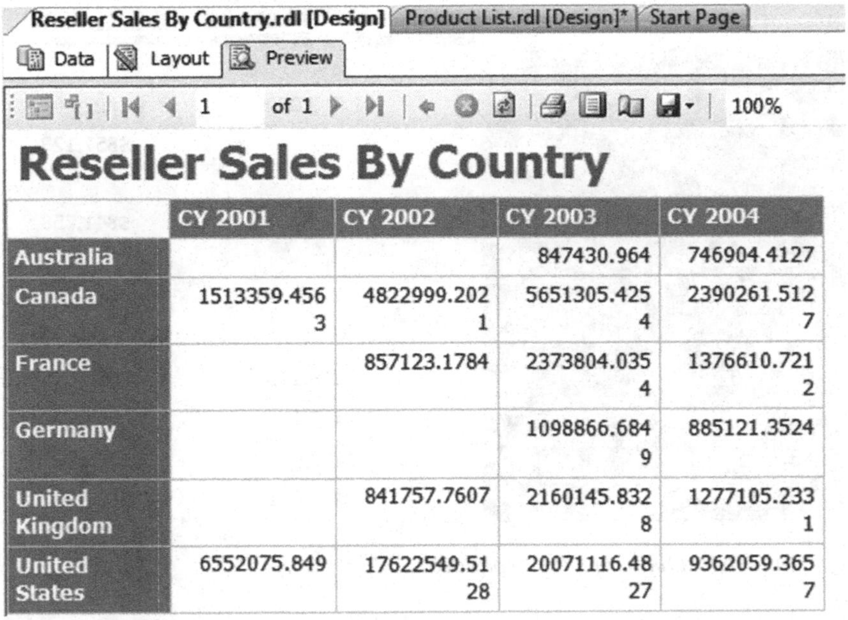

Reseller Sales By Country

	CY 2001	CY 2002	CY 2003	CY 2004
Australia			847430.964	746904.4127
Canada	1513359.4563	4822999.2021	5651305.4254	2390261.5127
France		857123.1784	2373804.0354	1376610.7212
Germany			1098866.6849	885121.3524
United Kingdom		841757.7607	2160145.8328	1277105.2331
United States	6552075.849	17622549.5128	20071116.4827	9362059.3657

Figure 6-35. *The resulting matrix report*

The matrix represents an aggregation of the Reseller Sales by country and by calendar year.

From here, you can enhance the report by setting up a hierarchy in the dimensions. Reporting Services provides a way to drill down into a hierarchy, collapsing subordinate rows as necessary (Figures 6-36 and 6-37).

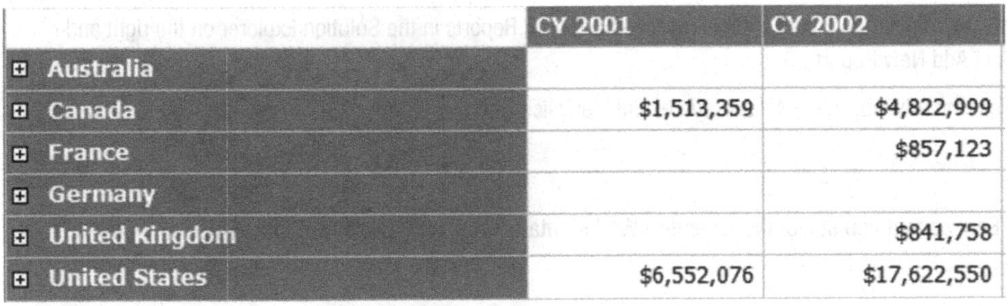

	CY 2001	CY 2002
⊞ Australia		
⊞ Canada	$1,513,359	$4,822,999
⊞ France		$857,123
⊞ Germany		
⊞ United Kingdom		$841,758
⊞ United States	$6,552,076	$17,622,550

Figure 6-36. *A report with a drill-down hierarchy collapsed*

			CY 2001	CY 2002
⊞ Australia				
⊞ Canada			$1,513,359	$4,822,999
⊞ France				$857,123
⊞ Germany				
⊞ United Kingdom				$841,758
⊟ United States	⊟ Alabama	Birmingham		$209
		Florence		$1,124
		Huntsville		$1,777
	⊞ Arizona		$18,133	$259,845
	⊞ California		$1,172,119	$3,394,072
	⊞ Colorado		$133,446	$729,937
	⊞ Connecticut		$90,821	$372,947

Figure 6-37. *The same report with a region expanded*

You can also surface Analysis Services actions into a report—enabling additional drill-down or linking from report details to subreports, web pages, maps, and so on. Let's take a look at how to create a subreport in Exercise 6-3.

Exercise 6-3. Using Subreports

We have a few steps to work through to build our subreport—I've broken them up in this exercise.

Creating a Detail Report

1. First, we're going to create a detail report—right-click Reports in the Solution Explorer on the right and select Add New Report.

2. Select the AdventureWorks data source, and then click Next.

■**Note** Ensure that you select the AdventureWorks data source, not AdventureWorks DW.

---

3. Open the Query Builder, and then add the Product, ProductProductPhoto, and ProductPhoto tables.

4. Select ProductID, Name, ProductNumber, Color, StandardCost, ListPrice, and SellEndDate from the Product table. Select LargePhoto from the ProductPhoto table (Figure 6-38).

5. Add a Filter of =@ProductID for the Product ID.

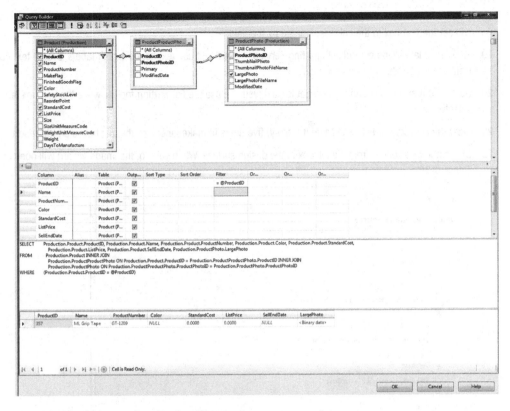

Figure 6-38. *The query for our detail report*

6. Click OK to close the Query Builder, and then click Next on the Design the Query page.

7. Leave the report type as Tabular.

8. Move all the available fields into the Details section, and then click Next.

9. Leave the default table style of Slate, and click Next.

10. Name the report Product Details, and click Finish.

11. Delete the Product Details header and the table area so that you have a blank report.

12. Open the toolbox if it isn't already open (Ctrl+Alt+X or View ➤ Toolbox).

13. Drag a List control to the report surface and resize it to occupy the entire report.

14. Open the Datasets pane (View ➤ Datasets).

15. Drag the Name, Product Number, Color, Standard Cost, ListPrice, and Sell End Date fields to the design surface. Note that as you drag the fields, each creates a text box mapped to the data field.

16. Right-click the StandardCost and ListPrice text boxes, open the Properties dialog, and set the format to C (currency).

17. Set the format of the SellEndDate text box to "d" (short date).

18. Click the Color text box. In the Properties pane, set the BackgroundColor to =Fields!Color.Value. This will set the text box to the color designated by the field.

19. There's no label-type control in Reporting Services—we'll just use text boxes for our labels. Drag a text box from the toolbox to the design surface.

20. Set the font size to 11pt and the weight to bold (you can use the Formatting toolbar while the text box is selected).

21. Copy the text box (Ctrl+C) and paste it (Ctrl+V) five times to make labels for the text boxes on the report.

22. Drag an image control from the toolbox to the design surface. When you do, the Image wizard will open (see Figure 6-39).

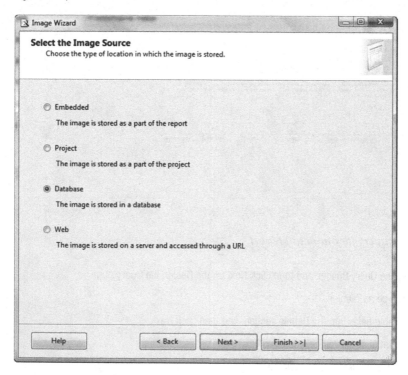

Figure 6-39. *The Image wizard*

23. Select Database, and then click Next.

24. On the Specify the Image Field page, select the AdventureWorks dataset, set the Image field to LargePhoto, and leave the MIME type as the default, "image/bmp." Click Next.

25. On the final page, review the settings, and then click Finish.

26. Resize the image control to suit. The report layout should look like Figure 6-40.

Product:	=Fields!Name.Value	
Number:	=Fields!Product	
Standard Cost:	=Fields!Standar	
List Price:	=Fields!ListPric	
Sell End Date:	=Fields!SellEnd	
Color:	=Fields!Color.V	

Figure 6-40. *The product detail report layout*

27. You can preview the report—use Product ID 753.

Adding the Subreport

1. Open the Product List report.

2. Click in the table to show the table border, and then right-click the detail row and select Insert Row Below (Figure 6-41).

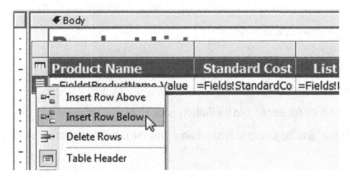

Figure 6-41. *Adding a row to the report*

3. Click and drag to select the five cells in the new row. Right-click and select Merge Cells.

4. Drag the Product Details.rdl report from the Solution Explorer on the right into the row you've just added. It will show up as a dark gray area. This is the subreport.

5. Right-click the subreport and select Properties.

6. Click the Parameters tab. We're going to map the detail parameter (ProductID) to the value in the report.

7. For the parameter name, click the drop-down and select ProductID; for the parameter value, select =Fields!ProductID.Value (see Figure 6-42).

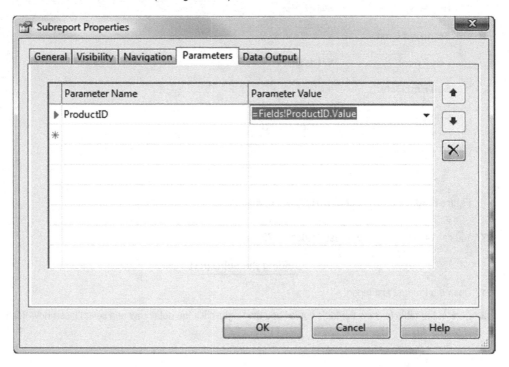

Figure 6-42. *Mapping parameters in a subreport*

8. Click the OK button in the Subreport Properties dialog.

9. Click the row header to select the row.

10. In the Properties pane (press F4 if it's not visible), find the Visibility node.

11. Open the node. Set Hidden to True, and ToggleItem to ProductName. This will hide the row until you click the product name in the report.

12. Preview the report, using Road Bikes as the subcategory. You'll see the list of products, but now the product name will have a small + icon next to it. Click this icon to show the detail report (Figure 6-43).

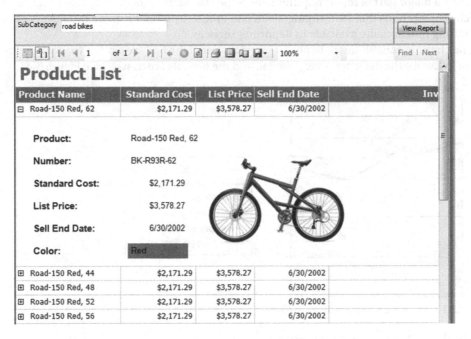

Figure 6-43. *Report with embedded subreport for product detail*

13. Save the solution and deploy the reports.

Subreports provide a reusable way of creating more complex reports and drill-down capabilities. You can also use subreports to build a type of dashboard—putting multiple subreports on a single page bound to the parameters.

■Note Subreports in Reporting Services 2005 also provide a way to create more complex reports with merging and summary data. Some of this functionality, however, will be better served using the Tablix control in Reporting Services 2008.

Charts and Graphs

Of course, a major part of report requirements is the visualization of data. Before we get into the rich visualizations that PerformancePoint and ProClarity offer, I'll give a brief overview of the charting functionality available in Reporting Services.

The charting capabilities in Reporting Services out of the box are similar to what you're used to in Excel—the designer is very similar, and the outputs are as well (see Figure 6-44).

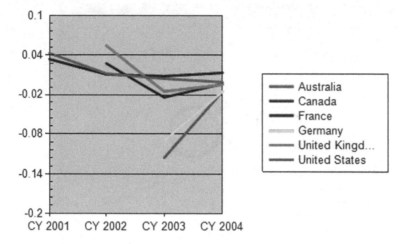

Figure 6-44. *A line chart in Reporting Services*

Reporting Services offers the following:

- Line charts

- Column charts

- Bar charts

- Area charts (filled in under the line)

- Pie charts (an old favorite)

- Doughnut charts

- Scatter charts (also known as X-Y charts)

- Bubble charts (similar to scatter charts, but the size of the bubble indicates a third axis)

- Stock charts (where a candlestick line indicates the range of values in a day)

These charts are fairly configurable, and can show multiple datasets. However, they can be tricky to configure, and managing multiple datasets in a report requires some arcane data alignments to the point where it's not really practical. Also, and perhaps the biggest problem—the charts often simply aren't sexy enough.

Luckily, Reporting Services is extremely extensible, and there are third-party controls that are easy to add in for use in reports. The two major software packages to create charts in Reporting Services are the following:

- Dundas Reports, by Dundas Data Visualization (www.dundas.com/)

- ChartFX, by SoftwareFX (www.softwarefx.com/)

These packages offer additional flexibility and configuration for charting, as well as other types of controls such as gauges and mapping components. They are equivalent packages, and it's worth investigating both if you are interested in a richer reporting strategy.

Exercise 6-4. Creating a Chart

1. We're going to add another report. Right-click Reports in the Solution Explorer, and select Add New Report.

2. Choose the AdventureWorks DW data source, and then click Next.

3. Click the Query Builder button.

4. Drag Reseller Sales Amount from Measures to the plot area.

5. Drag Country from the Geography node over.

6. Open the Date node, and then open the Calendar node. Drag Calendar Quarter of Year and Calendar Year over.

7. From the Product node, drag Category up to the Filters area and drop it, and then under Filter Expression, select {All Products} (see Figure 6-45).

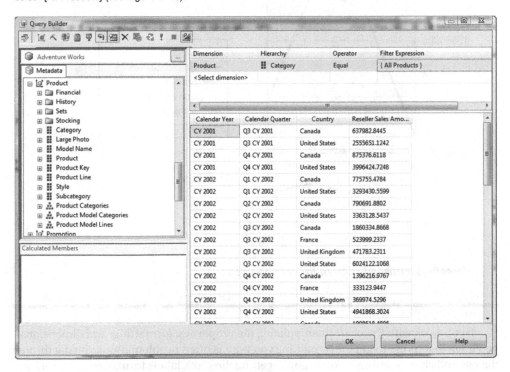

Figure 6-45. *Building the MDX query*

8. Click the OK button in the Query Builder, and then click Next.

9. Select Tabular, and then click Next.

10. Leave the defaults on the Design the Table page, and click Next.

11. Leave the default format, and click Next.

12. Name the report Reseller Sales Chart, and click Finish.

13. In Report Designer, delete the table and label to get a blank design surface.

14. Drag a chart from the toolbox to the design surface, and resize it to fill the chart area.

15. Open the Datasets pane (View ➤ Datasets).

16. Drag Reseller_Sales_Amount to the "Drop data fields here" area at the top of the chart area.

17. Drag Country to the "Drop series fields here" area at the right.

18. Drag Calendar_Year to the "Drop category fields here" area at the bottom.

19. Right-click the chart, select Chart Type, then select Line, and then select Simple Line.

20. You can preview the chart—it should look like Figure 6-46.

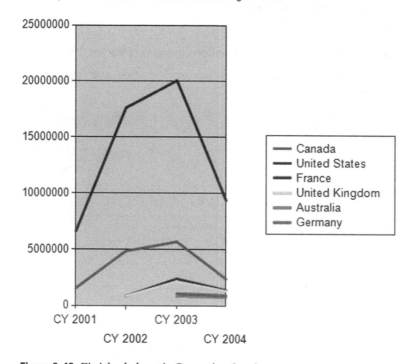

Figure 6-46. *Finished chart in Reporting Services*

If you work with the chart (manipulating the properties, formatting, and dimensions), you'll see that trying to get the formatting you want is often problematic as you dig through dialogs and change settings. For example, getting the y axis labels formatted as currency means figuring out that "Format code" on the Y Axis page is where you put the format code, which you need to know.

Reporting Services 2008 has a vastly improved charting engine—besides offering additional chart types, its formatting is much easier, since it is usually a matter of right-clicking the area of the chart you want to format and using a more intuitive dialog (see Figure 6-47).

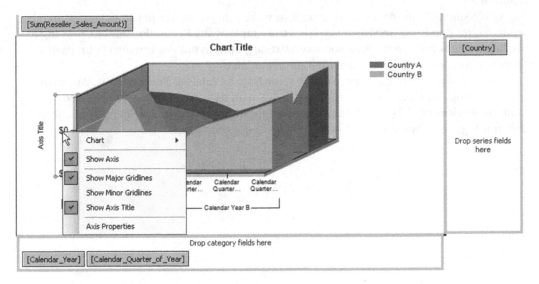

Figure 6-47. *Reporting Services 2008 charting control*

SharePoint Integration

A new feature in SQL Server 2005 SP2 and Microsoft Office SharePoint Server (also known as MOSS) 2007 is the ability to integrate Reporting Services with SharePoint, leveraging SharePoint security and making it easier to deploy Reporting Services reports to SharePoint dashboards.

In SharePoint integrated mode, BIDS deploys reports to a SharePoint document library. This adds the features of a document library—automatic versioning, publishing workflow, and alerts—to your reports.

In addition, security is governed by SharePoint, including any authentication providers you may be using. You can also use the SharePoint topology to render and deploy Reporting Services reports outside the firewall. The Report Manager page is also replaced by a SharePoint site for managing content, schedules, data sources, and so on.

■Note Once you change a Reporting Services server to SharePoint integrated mode, you cannot change it back without reinstalling the server. In addition, note that data-driven subscriptions are not available in SharePoint integrated mode, so think carefully before trying this out.

Conclusion

That's our high-speed run around SQL Server Reporting Services. It provides a powerful way to deliver data from either transactional or dimensional data sources. Remember that Reporting Services is not limited to reporting on data in SQL Server—any ODBC data source can be reported on.

While some of the advanced visualizations we're going to look at in a few chapters may seem to blow Reporting Services away, it is a true staple of any BI solution, and we're going to use Reporting Services reports for some contextual graphs in our PerformancePoint dashboards, so you're going to have to learn it sooner or later.

Now let's look at another way to derive value from an Analysis Services cube. We've covered reporting, which we use to verify answers we're pretty sure we know. We've looked at Analysis Services models, which help us answer questions we know. Now let's take a look at data mining, where we often don't even know what question to ask.

CHAPTER 7

■ ■ ■

Data Mining

Data mining is yet another way we have to get value out of large amounts of data. So far, we've looked at pulling data together, modeling it, and creating reports. However, we haven't really delved into how to get real value from new perspectives on our data.

Data mining is a process of evaluating large volumes of data to identify patterns and relationships. It's the very fact of having a large amount of data that enables us to identify patterns. Relationships and connections in small quantities of data are not reliable—just because five other shoppers bought breakfast cereal when they bought milk doesn't mean you would be interested in a pitch for breakfast cereal when you buy milk. However, if 95 percent of shoppers from several hundred thousand records picked up a box of breakfast cereal when they bought a gallon of milk, then it is most definitely worth putting a rack of cereal near the milk stock.

Data mining can help analyze patterns to help with cross-selling, risk management, fraud detection, customer segmentation, customer retention, and even payoff ratios in casino games. Some real-world examples of data mining include

- Mining the web site visits of an Audi dealership to show that customers who use the Audi nomenclature for colors in the comments box tend to purchase an Audi vehicle[1]

- Identifying patients at risk for health deterioration by mining vital sign and demographic data of the patients[2]

- Discovering for the first time that blood pressure is seasonal[3]

- Identifying crime patterns from past reports and 911 calls to better allocate police forces[4]

---

1. Autobeat Daily, "Data Mining," June 26, 2002 (www.urbanscience.com/pdf/AB_viewpoint_2006-26-02.pdf).

2. Microsoft, "Clalit Health Services: Microsoft SQL Server 2005 Data Mining Helps Clalit Preserve Health and Save Lives," November 3, 2005 (www.microsoft.com/casestudies/casestudy.aspx?casestudyid=49173).

3. Robert Kolodner, MD et al., "Large VA Study Finds Seasonal Differences in Blood Pressure," *American Heart Association News*, November 5, 2007 (www.americanheart.org/presenter.jhtml?identifier=3050865).

4. Steve Lohr, "Reaping Results: Data Mining Goes Mainstream," *New York Times*, May 20, 2007 (www.nytimes.com/2007/05/20/business/yourmoney/20compute.html).

Note As indicated here, data mining results generally don't yield yes/no answers—the results from data mining analysis are generally stated in terms of probabilities.

THE BONFERRONI CORRECTION

A danger when beginning statistical analysis of data is finding false positives—identifying trends or relationships that aren't really there. An example would be watching people order food at a fast-food restaurant. If you are simply looking for any relationship at all, you may notice that customers in red shirts tend to order cheeseburgers and cola drinks together. You could, as a result, create new employee training or a new mass-market program to drive a cheeseburger and cola drink combo targeted at people in red shirts.

But if you analyze the data a different way, you may find that what you've actually identified is that most of your restaurants are next to pizza places, employees at pizza places usually wear red shirts, and the cheeseburger/cola drink combo is simply your most popular combination (i.e., everyone orders that combo, but no other group is as prevalent as your red-shirt customers).

The Bonferroni Correction is one way of treating statistical results to reduce the possibility of multiple tests "creating" a relationship that doesn't actually exist. While I won't pick apart Bonferroni methods, I wanted to bring the concept up as a caution against leaping to conclusions with any relationship that data mining may produce, especially those that are a surprise or counterintuitive.

To learn more about Bonferroni and other statistical methods, I recommend starting with *Statistics for People Who (Think They) Hate Statistics*, by Neil Salkind (Sage Publications, 2003).

SQL Server Implementation

Microsoft has implemented data mining structures in SQL Server (starting with SQL Server 2000) in an attempt to make data mining more accessible to developers and power users.

The main interface for working with data mining is our old friend Business Intelligence Development Studio (BIDS). You can either create data mining models as part of a cube solution, or simply build them on a data source view with no underlying cube (Figure 7-1). This approach will use SQL Server Analysis Services for the data mining, but no cube is necessary.

Note The screenshots and discussion in this chapter are drawn from the Data Mining tutorials at http://msdn.microsoft.com/en-us/library/ms167488.aspx.

Data mining can be somewhat tricky to get into. If you go to create a new data mining structure, after selecting your data source, the first question is "What data mining model do you want to use?" Since there are a significant number of data mining algorithms, and each needs to be understood on its own merits, this is a nontrivial question. My goal in this chapter is to simply review data mining and the value of running a data mining solution, and try to cover some of those data mining algorithms so you can make a more informed decision.

Tip To learn a *lot* more about data mining in SQL Server, I highly recommend *Data Mining with SQL Server 2005*, by ZhaoHui Tang and Jamie MacLennan (Wiley, 2005).

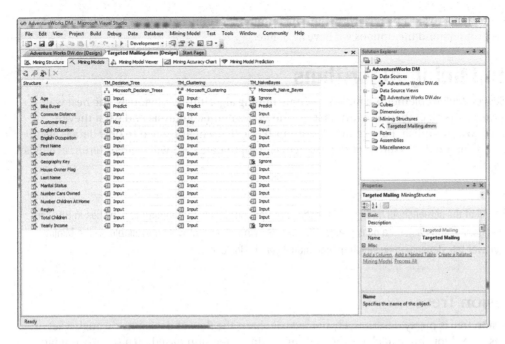

Figure 7-1. *Designing data mining models in BIDS*

To begin with, you can both design and execute data mining models in BIDS (Figure 7-2). The samples in this chapter rely on the AdventureWorks DW database, included as a sample on the SQL Server media, and the data mining tutorial in SQL Server Books Online.

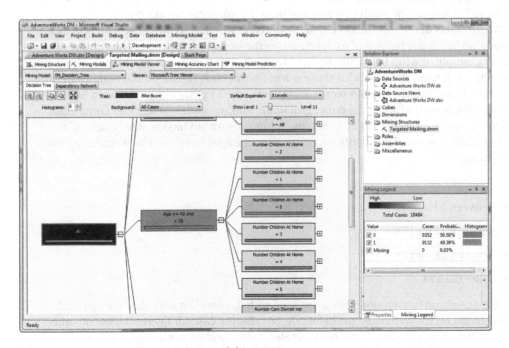

Figure 7-2. *Running a data mining model in BIDS*

We're going to start by reviewing the data mining algorithms in SQL Server 2005 in order to better understand the options we have available.

Data Mining Algorithms

SQL Server 2005 implements a number of data mining algorithms. Obviously, the best way to get the most out of them is to understand the basics of their analysis and what they're intended to accomplish. Each of the algorithms has a different approach to how data is aggregated and analyzed, has different requirements for input data, and will yield different avenues of analysis.

■**Note** All of the screenshots through this section are from BIDS. The data mining capabilities in BIDS are quite staggering, and each data mining algorithm has its own viewer that will be available on the Mining Model Viewer tab, depending on which mining model you are looking at.

Decision Trees

A decision tree is pretty descriptively named—it charts the flow of decisions through a set of options. The algorithm calculates the odds of making a decision based on a set of input factors. For example, in a given set of customer purchase data, you may find that a single female making more than $75,000 a year is 80 percent likely to buy a premium stereo system in her car, but only 25 percent likely to buy a sunroof. Given that, when you have a customer matching that profile, you can focus more energy on selling the advantages of the upgraded stereo system as opposed to the sunroof add-on.

Figure 7-3 shows a decision tree running from the AdventureWorks cube.

The first level in the tree breaks down the decision whether to purchase a bicycle by age. The decision bar at the bottom of each box shows the weighting that factor has on the decision. For example, the top box reads Age >= 74, and the bar is split into two colors. The legend for the chart will show the values for those colors (in this case, the larger bar equates to False for the Bike Buyer value—in other words, customers over 74 years old are not very likely to buy a bicycle). Note that while the data input to the mining model for age was continuous (discrete numbers ranging from 27 to 88), the mining algorithm has created "buckets" for ages that show clusters of probabilities. In this case, the ages have been broken down into the following:

- Younger than 34

- Between 34 and 42

- Between 42 and 58

- Between 58 and 74

- Older than 74

Each age group has a probability associated with it. However, note that the age bucket isn't just based on the individual probabilities, but also the cascading odds based on other factors (in this case, number of cars owned, sales region, and commute distance of the buyer). Now note the breakdown in Figure 7-4.

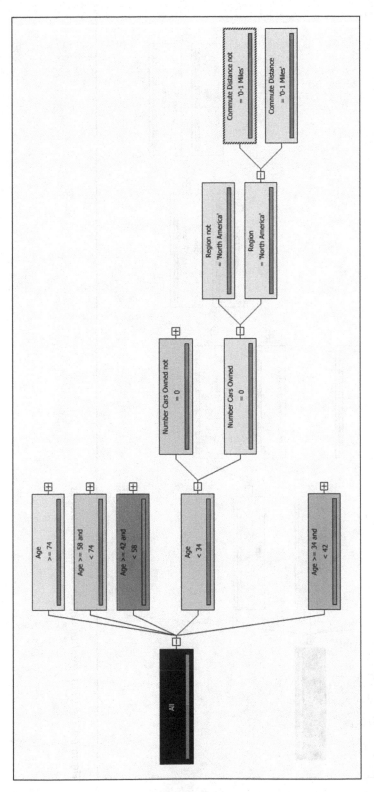

Figure 7-3. *A decision tree result*

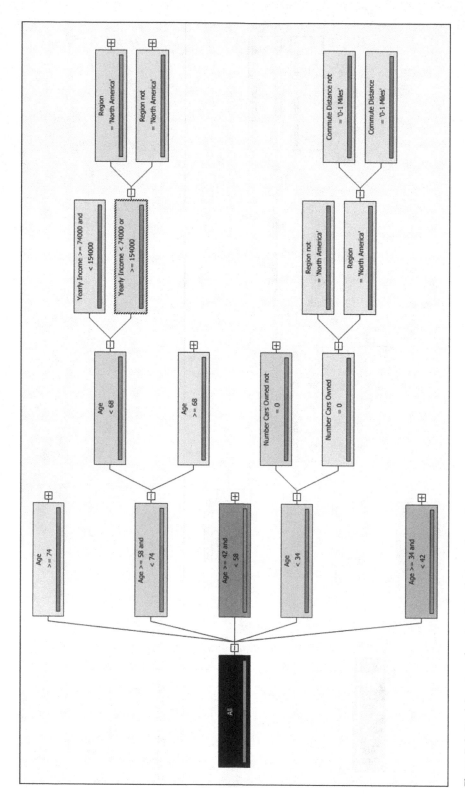

Figure 7-4. *Decision tree showing two decision branches*

Here we see that the breakdown under the 58-to-74 age bracket has a second breakdown by age at the 68-year-old level, and then goes to yearly income. The mining algorithm has determined that for this set of buyers there are more factors and has broken them down appropriately.

Going back to the first branch we opened in Figure 7-3, let's go to the end of the branch (see Figure 7-5).

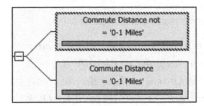

Figure 7-5. *Decision tree leaf nodes*

Here we're at the end of "Customers younger than 34 who don't own a car and who live in North America," and we see the deciding factor is commute distance. For `Commute Distance not = '0-1 Miles'`, the legend looks like Figure 7-6.

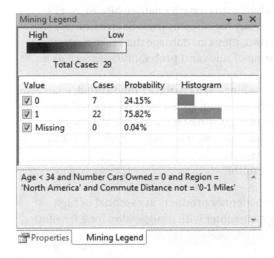

Figure 7-6. *The mining legend for our selected node*

The legend shows us that we have 29 cases matching this set of criteria. We are measuring the "Bike Buyer" attribute, where 0 equals "did not buy a bicycle" and 1 equals "did buy a bicycle." So given these criteria (younger than 34, doesn't own a car, lives in North America, and has to commute more than a mile to work), there is a 76 percent chance they will buy a bicycle. We can now use this information in targeted advertising, cross-selling, upselling, and so on.

> ## UNDERSTANDING YOUR DATA
>
> Data mining results should never be accepted on faith. While there may be the occasional surprise, for the most part one would expect that a subject matter expert in the business would look at the results of a data mining exercise as refining their knowledge of the business and adding objectivity. For example, in our decision tree in the accompanying text, it's not a huge surprise that younger buyers who don't own a car and live more than a mile from work are likely to buy a bicycle.
>
>   Consider an example of a company that likely accepted a data mining result without a sanity check:
>
> *A few weeks after eZiba.com sends out its winter catalog, the call center's pin-drop silence begins to worry execs. As it turns out, a bug in a program designed to identify the best prospects on eZiba's mailing list led to the catalog instead being sent to those deemed least likely to respond. "Sadly, our probability estimates were correct," says eZiba founder Dick Sabot. On Jan. 14, eZiba suspends operations while seeking new investors to cover its cash shortfall. Overstock.com later buys the retailer's assets for $500,000.*[5]

Association Rules

Association rule algorithms are used to identify when items have a relationship. We might be looking at products in a catalog that consumers buy together, or parts in an assembly that often fail together (when your brake pads wear down, they can damage the brake rotors). The *Association Rules engine* generates both a listing of rules and probabilities, as well as a dependency network (Figure 7-7).

   Association rules are used primarily for cross-selling—if a customer buys cereal, what else are they likely to buy? The human process here is to ask when someone buys a can of paint if they need paint brushes. A more intelligent data mining approach could look at a shopping cart full of painting supplies and recognizes that many people who buy a lot of paint, drop cloths, and roller sleeves usually buy paint rollers as well.

   "Did you remember to buy a paint roller, Mr. Smith?"

   "Oh my, no I didn't—thank you."

   Richer data mining implementations may also identify products as essential or high margin, thus keeping the cashier from bothering a customer with a suggestion for a frivolous two-dollar item.

Naive Bayes

Naive Bayes is an algorithm that generates probabilities of a result based on independent variables. While, for example, the decision tree contemplates a series of metrics to estimate a probability (location, car ownership, income, distance to work, etc.), naive Bayes simply considers each variable and its resulting probability (e.g., commuting distance in and of itself can be an excellent predictor of bicycle purchases).

---

5.   Adam Horowitz et al., "101 Dumbest Moments in Business: 2005's Shenanigans, Skulduggery and Just Plain Stupidity," *Business 2.0*, February 1, 2006 (http://money.cnn.com/magazines/business2/101dumbest/full_list/).

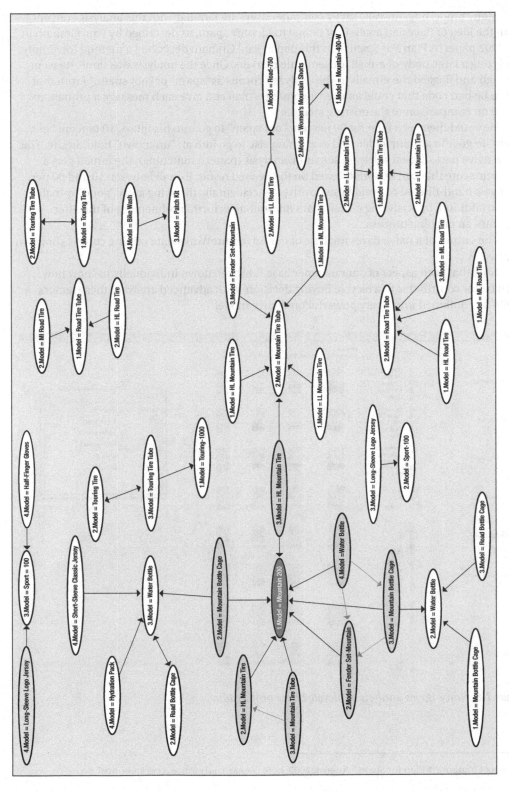

Figure 7-7. *A dependency network generated on the AdventureWorks data mining cube*

Many modern technically savvy computer users are familiar with this analysis concept from the idea of Bayesian analysis of e-mail to identify spam, as described by Paul Graham in his 2002 paper "A Plan For Spam."[6] In this paper, Paul Graham described a method for simply analyzing a large body of e-mail for semantic markers. Once the analysis was done, he went through and flagged the e-mails in the analyzed corpus as "spam" or "not spam." From that point, he had code that could analyze incoming e-mail and give each message a probability based on comparison to the existing analysis.

He could then set a filter for 90 percent "not spam" to go into his inbox, 10 percent "not spam" to go into a spam folder, and everything else to go into an "unknown" holding site. This is the naive part—based solely on semantic analysis (pattern matching), the e-mail gets a numeric score that can be sorted based on the desired result. E-mail between 10 and 90 percent gets hand-filtered to avoid false positives—accidentally throwing away "good" e-mail.

In addition, by analyzing e-mail that's questionable, further refinement of the filter becomes an ongoing process.

The output of a naive Bayes analysis of our AdventureWorks data mining cube is shown in Figure 7-8.

Note that each aspect of our customer base is broken down individually to show how each factor contributes to a bicycle buying decision. With advanced analysis, these factors could be combined into a very powerful predictive model.

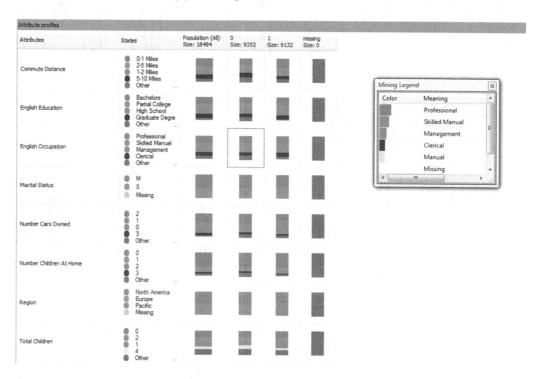

Figure 7-8. *Naive Bayes analysis of bicycle buyer profile data*

---

6.   Paul Graham, "A Plan for Spam," August, 2002, http://www.paulgraham.com/spam.html.

Clustering

The clustering algorithm takes the various inputs and identifies common groups of attributes. In our current example, we have various things like number of children, age, income, marital status, and so on. The clustering algorithm will identify groups of people with common criteria—married folks between 25 and 35 with no children and who make more than $50,000, for example.

Of course, once those clusters are identified, then we also want to determine the probability that a cluster will perform the action we're interested in. Figure 7-9 shows one output of a cluster model.

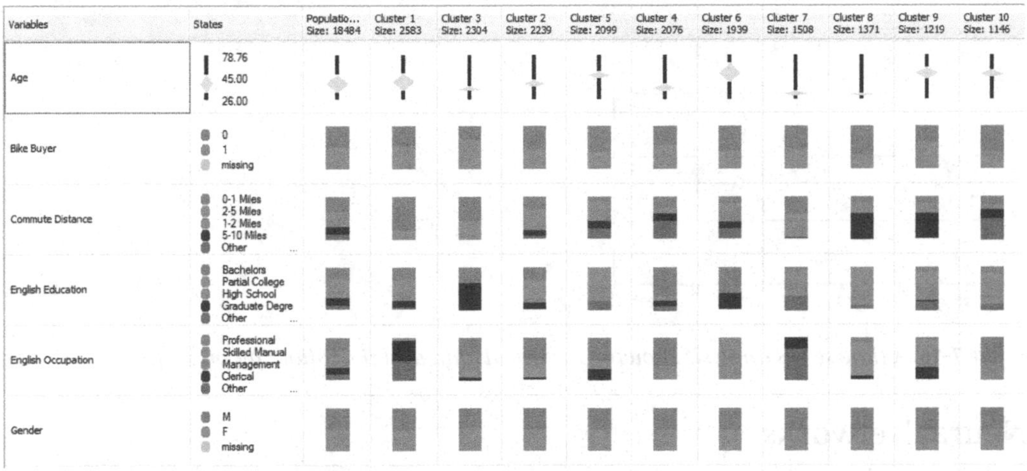

Figure 7-9. *Cluster profiles from the clustering algorithm*

Each column is a cluster of similar attributes that define the group. The first row is an indicator that shows the age and spread of the age group. The second row is the one we're interested in—the probability that a group is a bike-buying group. The following rows show breakdowns of commuting distance, education and occupation, and gender.

So we can use this model to perform predictive analysis—if we had a list of potential customer records, we could run them through this model and create a list of our best potential customers.

Sequence Clustering

Sequence clustering is related to simple clustering, with the exception that the analysis includes some kind of order or precedence. A classic example would be click paths through a web site. While a simple cluster analysis may show that a given customer clicked on the welcome page, a few ads, and certain stories, and then placed an order, a sequence cluster analysis identifies the *order* in which the customer did these things.

Sequence clustering analysis can help optimize paths as well as enable you to identify how to move or rearrange content to best help customers identify products and place orders.

Time Series

Time series analyzes a set of data based on historical data, taking into account various patterns that may occur over time. For example, analysis of flu cases in a hospital can identify seasonality and expected patient loads to best predict how much flu vaccine to order.

Time series analysis will take a collection of historical data along with a time dimension and predict values out using existing data (see Figure 7-10).

Understanding time series is very important, as it is leveraged in forecast graphs in PerformancePoint dashboards.

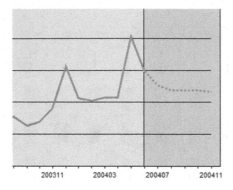

Figure 7-10. *A time series analysis showing historical data and the following prediction*

Neural Networks

Neural networks are similar to decision trees, with the exception that they take a number of inputs simultaneously to provide an output matrix (see Figure 7-11).

Neural networks analyze input data iteratively, refining the model until further iterations yield improvements below a specified margin. The model is built up as a series of weighting and decision nodes—each of a series of inputs leads to another network of nodes (or *neurons*), through a number of hidden layers, until a probabilistic output is indicated.

In Figure 7-11, you can see the inputs at the top of the viewer. In this example, I selected a customer profile where the gender is female, and the customer owns two cars and has a yearly income in a specified bracket (determined by the neural network algorithm). Given those inputs, you can see the probabilities of a customer being a bike buyer or not based on the other potential input values.

THE VALUE OF NEURAL NETWORKS

A.K. Dewdney criticized neural networks in his book *Yes, We Have No Neutrons: An Eye-Opening Tour Through the Twists and Turns of Bad Science* (Wiley, 1998), saying "Although neural nets do solve a few toy problems, their powers of computation are so limited that I am surprised anyone takes them seriously as a general problem-solving tool."

However, several computer scientists reject Dewdney's characterization and analysis. Dewdney's major concern may simply be the overuse of the analogy of the human brain in the neural network concept, which is surely an overstatement of the algorithm. The best resource to counter Dewdney's criticism is Warren S. Sarle's "Bad Science Writing," a review of Dewdney' book (see http://mu.dmt.ibaraki.ac.jp/yanai/neu/faq/badscience.html, which includes a full bibliography).

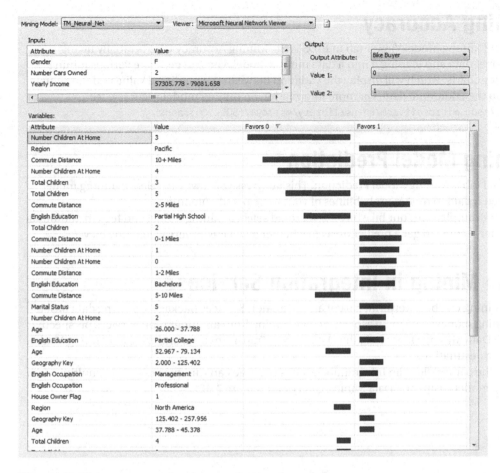

Figure 7-11. *The output matrix of a neural network analysis*

Choosing an Algorithm

While it will really take research and practice to truly have a feel for which data mining algorithm to use when, Table 7-1 should provide some initial guidance.

Table 7-1. *Selecting a Data Mining Algorithm*

Goal	Decision Tree	Clustering	Naive Bayes	Association	Sequence Cluster	Time Series	Neural Network
Predict a continuous value	X					X	
Predict a discrete value	X	X	X				X
Find groups of common items	X			X			
Find groups of similar items		X			X		
Predict a sequence					X		

Mining Accuracy

After the Mining Model Viewer tab in BIDS is the Mining Accuracy Charts tab. By taking additional data and loading it into a data mining model, you can generate various mining accuracy charts, which will display the variation between the predicted value and the actual value in the additional data. For more information on mining model accuracy, see http://msdn.microsoft.com/en-us/library/ms174947(SQL.100).aspx.

Mining Model Prediction

The final tab is Mining Model Prediction. This tab gives you a way to select a mining model and feed it data to render probabilities of your anticipated outcome.

For example, with our bike buyers, we could select a mining model and feed in additional customer records to get a prediction as to whether given customers would buy bicycles.

Data Mining in Integration Services

Data mining can be a powerful part of an Integration Services package, directing data based on mining models. The main aspects of data mining from an Integration Services perspective are the Data Mining Query task, the Data Mining Transform task, and the Data Mining Model Training destination.

In the control flow, an Integration Services package can run queries against multiple data mining models using the Data Mining Query task (Figure 7-12).

Figure 7-12. *The Data Mining Query Task Editor*

The Data Mining Query task saves its results to a table (if a table already exists, the results can overwrite or append the existing table). From there, you can leverage the results from other tasks or within a data flow (e.g., you may use a current customer analysis to evaluate how many coupons to send out this week).

The Data Mining Transformation task takes a number of input columns and runs them against a data mining model to determine the predictive output, which it sends to the output of the component. The most obvious use of this task is to create ranking values for records as they are processed. For example, processing customer data imports, you can run a decision tree algorithm on the customer data and retrieve a probability that the customer will buy based on your weekly flyer, and then route the data as appropriate.

The Data Mining Model Training destination component allows you to process and send data to train an existing data mining model. A good use for this would be to pull customer data from your point-of-sale system and feed it back into the model to update your customer profiles.

Two other transformation components of interest are the Fuzzy Lookup and Fuzzy Grouping tasks. While these are not strictly data mining–related, they are in the same spirit of nondeterministic outcomes.

The Fuzzy Lookup task provides a way of attempting to match text to reference text that may not match exactly. For example, just about anyone can look at 115 Bayrige Ave and reconcile it with 115 Bay Ridge Avenue. However, any kind of straight computer lookup would fail. The Fuzzy Lookup task allows you to map input columns to reference columns in a data source using a data source connection (see Figure 7-13).

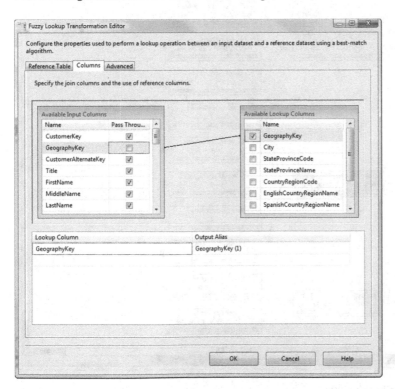

Figure 7-13. *Matching reference columns to input columns in the Fuzzy Lookup component*

The Fuzzy Lookup replaces the matched value with the authoritative value, rendering cleaner data.

SQL Server 2005 SP2 Excel Add-Ins

All the work we've done so far has been in BIDS. While this is great for us, it does tend to keep the data mining tools out of the hands of the analysts we want to do the real grunt work with data mining models and algorithms.

With SQL Server 2005 SP2, Microsoft also provided a free download for Excel 2007 that enabled Excel to act as a front end for the data mining models, as well as powerful data cleaning and analysis tools (see Figure 7-14). You can download the add-ins at www.microsoft.com/sql/technologies/dm/addins.mspx.

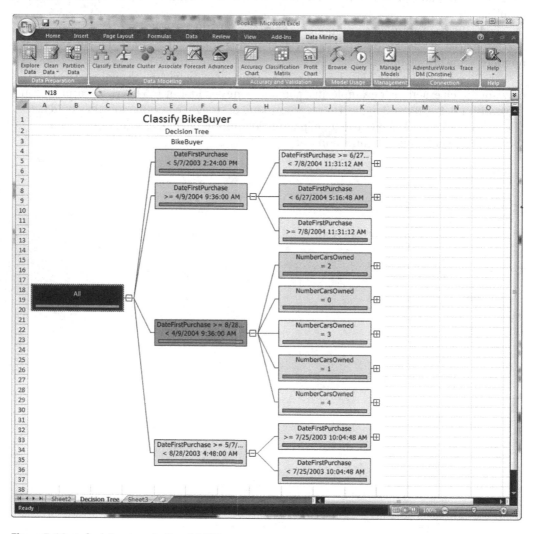

Figure 7-14. *A decision tree in Excel 2007*

Once the add-in is installed, you'll see a new Data Mining tab in the ribbon, which shows all the new data mining tools (see Figure 7-15).

Figure 7-15. *The Data Mining tab in Excel 2007*

■Note All the data mining tools use SQL Server 2005 Analysis Services to perform their magic, even if the data you're working with is wholly contained in Excel. So, to use the tools, you will need access to an instance of Analysis Services.

Table Analysis

We'll start by looking at a table of data in Excel. I've pulled in our customer data view from AdventureWorks using a data connection. The first aspect of the ribbon that opens is the Analyze tab under Table Tools (Figure 7-16). These table tools use the Analysis Services data mining engine against data in an Excel spreadsheet without having to build mining models.

■Tip You will only see the Table Tools tabs when your cursor is actually in the table.

Figure 7-16. *The Table Analysis ribbon in Excel 2007*

The Analyze Key Influencers tool allows you to select a column in a table of data, and will run a naive Bayes analysis on the table, and then publish the analysis report back to Excel (see Figure 7-17). The power here is that a user doesn't have to understand data mining or algorithms, or have ever heard of naive Bayes—they simply select the column they're interested in identifying patterns from, and the wizard does the rest.

The Detect Categories tool also uses naive Bayes to identify categories in the data, similar to classification or clustering.

The Fill From Example tool is used to fill a column that is only partially filled in. From a table in Excel, select the Fill From Example tool—it will prompt you for a column you wish to flesh out. From there, it analyzes the influencers and categories on the data for which there are values, and then uses that model to predict the values for the column where it's empty. Again, it's a very simple tool—the user needs only select one column!

	A	B	C	D	E
1		**Key Influencers Report for 'BikeBuyer'**			
2					
3		Key Influencers and their impact over the values of 'BikeBuyer'			
4	Filter by 'Column' or 'Favors' to see how various columns influence 'BikeBuyer'				
5	Column ▼	Value ▼	Favors ▼	Relative Impact ▼	
6	DateFirstPurchase	10/25/2002 4:22:20 PM - 7/23/2003 9:21:00 PM	1		
7	DateFirstPurchase	3/9/2002 2:02:16 PM - 10/25/2002 4:22:20 PM	1		
8	DateFirstPurchase	< 3/9/2002 2:02:16 PM	1		
9	NumberCarsOwned	0	1		
10	TotalChildren	1	1		
11	Region	Pacific	1		
12	BirthDate	2/29/1960 5:35:25 AM - 12/31/1969 4:28:10 PM	1		
13	Age	38 - 48	1		
14	CommuteDistance	0-1 Miles	1		
15	SpanishEducation	Licenciatura	1		
16	FrenchEducation	Bac + 4	1		
17	EnglishEducation	Bachelors	1		
28	DateFirstPurchase	7/23/2003 9:21:00 PM - 1/17/2004 12:11:31 AM	0		
29	DateFirstPurchase	>= 1/17/2004 12:11:31 AM	0		
30	NumberCarsOwned	2	0		
31	SpanishEducation	Educación secundaria (en curso)	0		
32	EnglishEducation	Partial High School	0		
33	FrenchEducation	Niveau bac	0		
34	TotalChildren	5	0		
35	Age	>= 69	0		
36	CommuteDistance	10+ Miles	0		
37	BirthDate	< 11/2/1943 6:00:05 AM	0		
38	Region	North America	0		
39	NumberChildrenAtHome	4	0		
40	TotalChildren	4	0		
41	Age	59 - 69	0		
42	BirthDate	11/2/1943 6:00:05 AM - 4/9/1950 3:08:06 AM	0		
43	CommuteDistance	5-10 Miles	0		
44	NumberChildrenAtHome	3	0		
56					

Figure 7-17. *A key influencers report in Excel 2007*

The Forecast tool uses the time series algorithm to use existing data to predict future values. The results here are the same as for time series forecasting—a chart showing the value over time historically followed by a predictive analysis.

Highlight Exceptions will run a clustering analysis on the data in the table you select, and then highlight values that fall outside the main clusters determined by the algorithm.

Data Preparation (Data Mining Tab)

On the Data Mining tab, the first segment of the ribbon is Data Preparation—this gives your users tools to review the data they're working with, clean it, and partition a data table (into training and testing groups).

The Explore Data tool allows you to select a column and analyze the values in the column—showing the distribution and breakdown of the contents of the data column (see Figure 7-18).

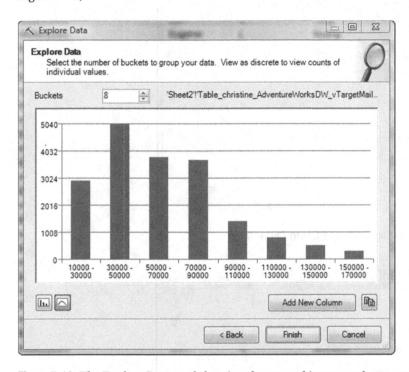

Figure 7-18. *The Explore Data tool showing the annual income column analysis*

The Clean Data tool helps a user work with both discrete and continuous data types.

For continuous data, the tool helps identify and remove outliers in data. Figure 7-19 shows a plot of the income field in our bike purchasers table.

Once we have the data laid out, we may look at the data points to the right and decide the sample size for those customers is too small to work with, and we want to cull that data out. So we drag the Maximum value slider to the point where we want to cut off our data. Next we have an option as to what to do with the outlying values (Figure 7-20).

What you do here simply depends on your data and the circumstances—whether you leave the fields blank, change them to the mean or limit, or simply delete the entire record. The next step allows you to either replace the values in place or add the "adjusted" column as a new column.

For discrete values, the Clean Data tool makes it very straightforward to simply change labels, either to change an existing label to a wholly new value or merge labels into a single value.

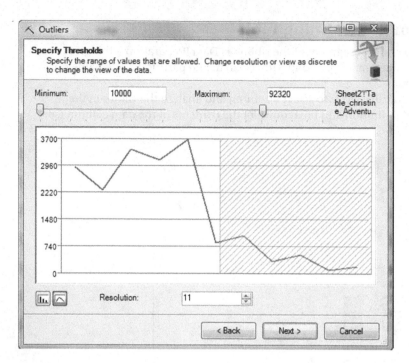

Figure 7-19. *Identifying outliers with the Clean Data tool*

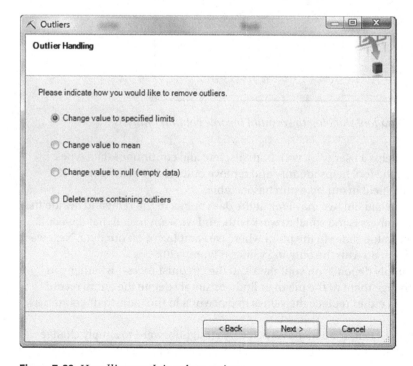

Figure 7-20. *Handling outlying data points*

Data Mining Tools

The data mining tools enable an end user to perform data mining on data in Excel (which may have been linked or imported from another data source).

Running a data mining analysis is as easy as clicking the button for the mining model you want to use, and then walking through the wizard. After the mining model is built and trained, you will get back an interface that shows the results (see Figure 7-21).

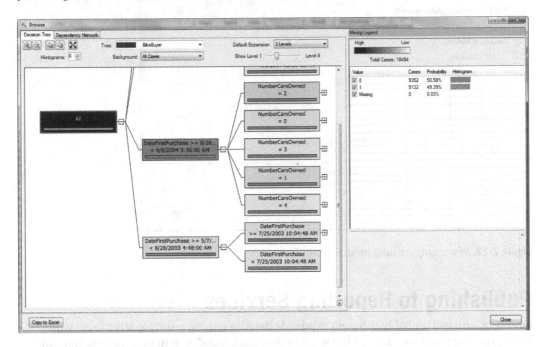

Figure 7-21. *The mining model output interface*

From here, you can investigate the generated model and dependency network, expand the tree as necessary, and finally copy the decision tree to Excel.

The toolbar will also let you create a mining model based on a table or range of data in Excel, and then publish the model back to Analysis Services. There is an interface for managing mining models in Analysis Services (Figure 7-22), browsing models, running DMX (Data Mining Extensions) queries against existing models, verifying model accuracy, and so on.

Before this year, access to data mining meant having a copy of the SQL Server client installed and climbing a fairly steep learning curve to even know where to start. Thanks to bringing the power of data mining into Excel, now analysts and power users can work with data mining models based on data in Excel without having to get their hands dirty in the database.

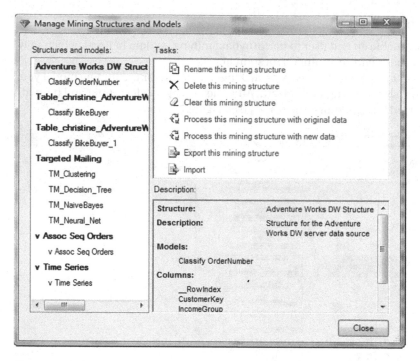

Figure 7-22. *Managing mining models from Excel 2007*

Publishing to Reporting Services

Of course, you will probably also want to provide the data mining results to other users who need to get the predictive analysis but won't be messing around with mining models. You can use DMX to query a data mining model, or use the data mining as a dimension in a SQL Server Analysis Services cube, and represent the data in any tool that can connect to Analysis Services.

Another alternative is to use SQL Server Reporting Services. In addition to the Analysis Services approach mentioned previously, Reporting Services understands how to connect to a data mining model for reporting purposes.

When you create a new report, choose Analysis Services as the data source. If you then choose a data source that has data mining models, the query builder will allow you to switch to DMX editing, where you can select a data mining model and a related input table, and map values between them (Figure 7-23).

This will yield a report with probability values, depending on what mining model you use and how you query it. To render something snazzier, you'll have to hand-code color coding on the records based on the probability, sort and group by probability, and so on.

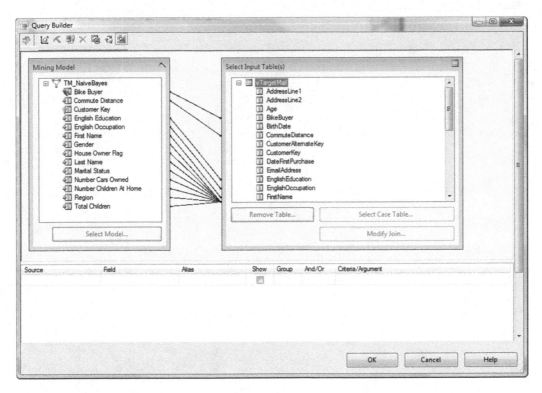

Figure 7-23. *Creating a report based on a mining model*

Conclusion

This has been another high-speed overview. Hopefully this will demystify data mining enough and entice you to learn about this powerful toolset sitting inside SQL Server. Next, we're going to look at what Microsoft Office SharePoint Server 2007 offers us in terms of BI and how we can leverage a very powerful collaboration tool.

CHAPTER 8

■■■

Business Intelligence in Excel and SharePoint

We've laid a lot of groundwork, but you may be wondering when we're going to get to the actual BI and PerformancePoint stuff. Well, we're at the doorstep.

When Business Scorecard Manager (BSM) was launched in 2005, life was simple for BI in the Microsoft platform—if you wanted a scorecard, you used BSM. If you wanted reports, you used SQL Server Reporting Services, and you could do some cube analysis in Excel with the Excel OLAP plug-in. That was pretty much it.

Since that time, we've seen the acquisition of ProClarity, the launch of Office 2007 and SharePoint 2007, and the launch of PerformancePoint 2007. It's become something of an embarrassment of riches in Microsoft BI land, which can be very confusing. My goal in this book, and especially in the chapters that follow, is to familiarize you with the capabilities and limitations of each platform. There is no right answer for what to use—we have a collection of tools in a toolbox that we can use to build what we need.

So let's start by looking at our fundamental BI tools—the analytics built into Excel 2007 and SharePoint Enterprise Edition 2007.

Note This chapter expects a certain basic level of familiarity with SharePoint, preferably SharePoint 2007. In addition, the "Excel Services" section of the chapter has some significant setup hurdles that require administrative access to the server as well as systems administration expertise to get the connection security working properly. If you have worked with SharePoint 2003 but not 2007, the administrative infrastructure has changed a *lot*. A good book to introduce you to SharePoint 2007 is *SharePoint 2007 User's Guide*, by Seth Bates and Tony Smith (Apress, 2007). For understanding SharePoint administration, I recommend *Beginning SharePoint 2007 Administration*, by Goran Husman (Wrox, 2007).

Business Intelligence in Office

With Office 2007, Microsoft started embracing BI by adding features in Excel and SharePoint—specifically Microsoft Office SharePoint Server (a.k.a. MOSS). Excel has new charting and data connection features (Figure 8-1), and SharePoint (enterprise version) adds KPI lists, selectors, data connection libraries (DCLs), and Excel Services.

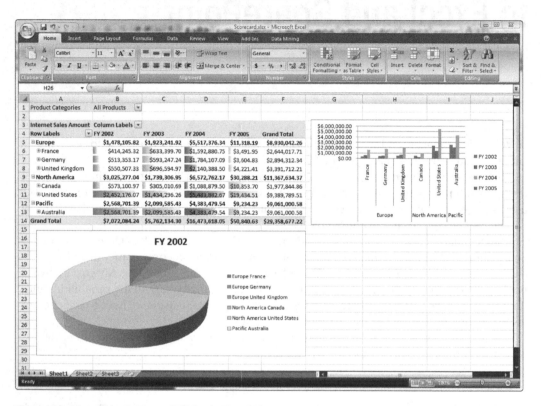

Figure 8-1. *New charting capabilities in Excel 2007*

SharePoint Server also adds a dashboard-building capability through its report libraries (Figure 8-2). This is to enable groups to build lightweight dashboards, or for entry-level BI. As we dig into building a dashboard, I'll note some of the shortcomings to be addressed with PerformancePoint Server.

In this chapter, we're going to use Excel 2007 and SharePoint Server 2007 to create some ad hoc data analysis charts, graphs, and dashboards. We'll start with pulling data into Excel pivot tables and pivot charts, and then we'll quickly go over Excel Services and publish our Excel content to Excel Services in SharePoint. Once we've done that, we'll finally set up a dashboard in SharePoint, review SharePoint's KPI capabilities, and hook everything together with a filter web part.

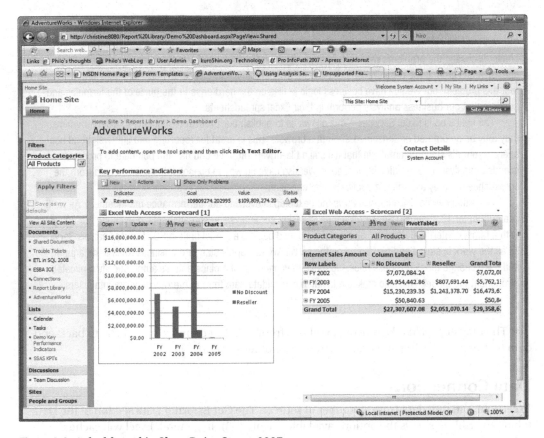

Figure 8-2. *A dashboard in SharePoint Server 2007*

Excel 2007

Most BI work today is performed in Excel. Whatever the front end may be, or wherever back end data is stored, it always seems to end up cut and pasted into Excel for analysts and regular users to manipulate, analyze, and share.

The problem is when Excel is used for data storage instead of just data analysis. Once an analyst has created a spreadsheet he uses for making decisions, often that spreadsheet becomes a "golden tablet"—the sole source of whatever BI may come out of it. Not only is it now locked to the analyst's hard drive, but there's the additional problem that actual data may be recorded in the spreadsheet (key performance data, percentages, numbers for what-if scenarios, etc.).

This data should be kept on a server—raw data in a relational database and/or OLAP system, and analysis and visualization data in OLAP, reporting, or BI systems. This improves the security and reliability of the information, as well as making it more accessible and avoiding the analyst being a single point of failure for an important business system.

EXCEL VS. PERFORMANCEPOINT

I have discussed the problems with performing analysis in Excel by itself—most notably that scattering spreadsheets around the organization is asking for trouble. Connecting Excel to back-end data starts to correct this problem, but we still have business logic in files on the hard drive in the guise of the formulas and analysis that our business analysts perform in their Excel spreadsheets.

The next step is Excel Services—this allows us to publish our Excel spreadsheets to a server where they may be automated or consumed through a browser. This is great for reporting and lightweight ad hoc analysis, but it's still problematic in that it's still a file-driven interface and has the potential to produce islands of analysis in unpredictable locations. We also have no way to consolidate business data from the spreadsheets—they are solely a publication mechanism.

PerformancePoint Planning Server is the next step in evolving our performance management. As we'll see in Chapter 13, Planning Server allows us to design our analysis in spreadsheets, presenting our analysts with a familiar interface. However, all the data is bound back to a model built in SQL Server Analysis Services, so all the work is stored and performed on the server. We can apply standard business rules to data input, and if we change those business rules, we make the change in one place and it's automatically replicated throughout the model. This also makes it trivial to consolidate data from numerous departmental users.

The first step we'll take is using Excel as a front end, but connecting directly to back-end data (instead of copying and pasting from some other system).

Data Connections

Excel 2007 can pull data from a number of sources. The Get External Data section of the Data tab on the ribbon shows the options available (Figure 8-3). In general, Excel will cache the data, and you can refresh the connection to refresh the data in the workbook. When you connect to a data source, you will be prompted whether to import the data as a table, pivot table, or pivot chart (for Analysis Services connections, the table option won't be available).

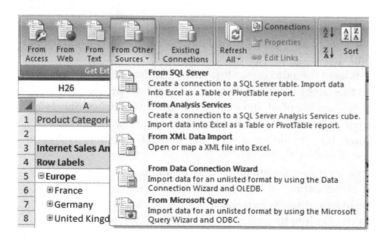

Figure 8-3. *Bringing external data into Excel 2007*

How the data is refreshed is all managed through the Connection Properties dialog (Figure 8-4). Note that from here you can set up a connection (and its represented data) to be automatically refreshed, refreshed (or not) when the file is opened, and so on. Also in this dialog you can specify what aspects of formatting from the OLAP server to automatically pull in.

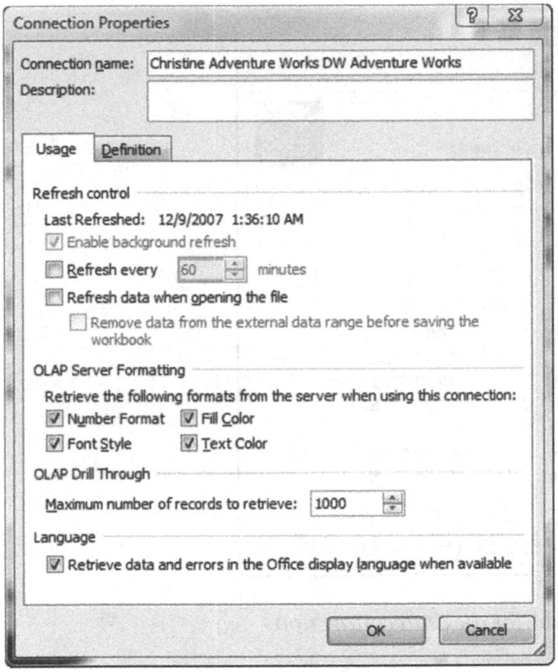

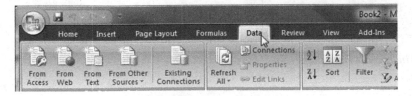

Figure 8-4. *The Connection Properties dialog*

Data from a database data connection is pulled in and formatted as an Excel table, which enables you to set properties, sort, filter, and use the data mining tools for table analysis. (Note that text and web connection data are not automatically formatted as a table.)

Exercise 8-1 shows you how to pull some data from the AdventureWorks cube into a spreadsheet.

Exercise 8-1. Pulling OLAP Data into an Excel Spreadsheet

1. Open Excel 2007.

2. Click the Data tab on the ribbon (Figure 8-5).

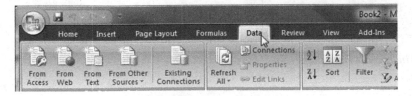

Figure 8-5. *Opening the Data tab of the ribbon in Excel 2007*

3. In the Get External Data section, click From Other Sources and select From Analysis Services.

4. In the Data Connection wizard, enter the name of the server where your AdventureWorks cube is located. Leave Use Windows Authentication selected for "Log on credentials."

5. Click the Next button. On the Select Database and Table page, select the AdventureWorks DW database, and then the AdventureWorks cube (Figure 8-6).

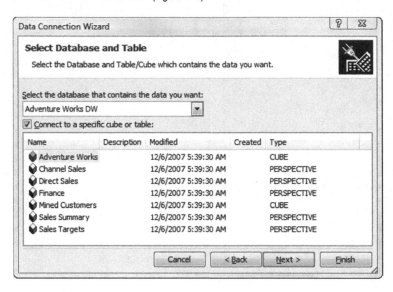

Figure 8-6. *Selecting the database and cube for the data connection*

6. Click Next. On the final page, note that the data connection file will be saved as an *.odc file in your My Data Sources folder. You can add a description and search keywords if you like. Click the Finish button.

7. The Import Data page opens next (see Figure 8-7). Select PivotChart and PivotTable Report, and click the OK button.

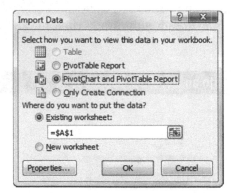

Figure 8-7. *The Import Data page*

8. The sheet you inserted the chart and table into will now have the pivot table builder and a pivot chart object, and the PivotTable Field List will be open on the right (Figure 8-8). In addition, the ribbon will have switched to the Design tab in the PivotChart Tools section.

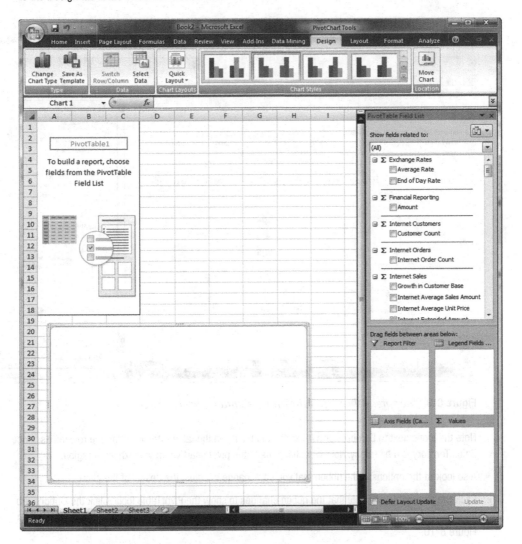

Figure 8-8. *Excel with the PivotTable and PivotChart tools open*

9. Look through the fields to see that you've pulled your measures, KPIs, and dimensions from the cube. The measures have a sigma symbol (Σ), KPIs have a stoplight, and the dimensions have a small table icon.

10. You can experiment with dragging various items to the fields in the areas at the bottom of the task pane. Measures must go in the Values box, while the other three boxes (Legend Fields, Axis Fields, and Report Filters) are for dimensions.

11. For the report we're going to create, let's put Internet Sales Amount from the Internet Sales table into Values, Fiscal Year from the Date table into Legend Fields, and Sales Territory into Axis Fields. Pull Product Categories into the Report Filter box. The final result should look like Figure 8-9.

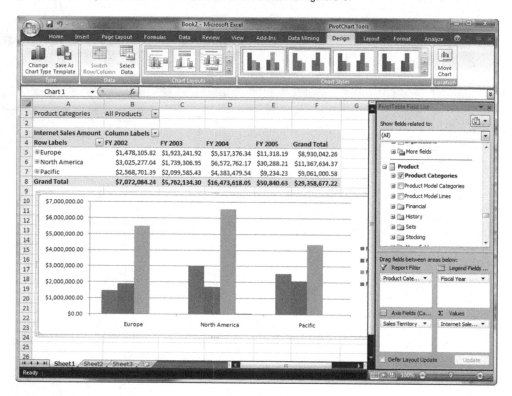

Figure 8-9. *The spreadsheet after the dimensional report is designed*

Note the icons next to Europe, North America, and Pacific in the table—they expand the row labels, since Sales Territory is a hierarchy. Note what happens to the pivot chart when you expand a region.

Also look at the options in the ribbon that you can change to adjust the design of the chart.

12. Click the pivot table and note that the ribbon changes to show the PivotTable tools. Click the Options tab under PivotTable Tools and change the name of the pivot table to Internet Sales by Territory, as shown in Figure 8-10.

Figure 8-10. *Renaming the pivot table*

13. Click the pivot chart, select the Layout tab, and rename the chart to Internet Sales Chart.

14. Finally, click cell B1—where it currently says All Products. Type *ProductCategory* in the name box just above the A column—we'll use this as a parameter in Excel Services. (Make sure you type "ProductCategory" as all one word—no spaces!)

    Now we have a data-driven report that's fully interactive—we can use the numbers in the chart to drive other calculations or analyses. We can also set the data connection to refresh automatically, refresh when the sheet is opened, or only refresh on demand.

15. Save the spreadsheet in a location where you can find it later.

However, we still have the problem that this report is going to reside on someone's desktop—other people can't use it unless it's e-mailed around, and then maintenance becomes problematic. This is where Excel Services comes in.

Excel Services

Excel Services was introduced as part of Microsoft Office SharePoint Server 2007. Excel Services is part of the enterprise configuration of SharePoint (along with InfoPath Forms Services and Business Data Catalog).

The goals of Excel Services are to provide a server-based Excel capability and to blur the line between Excel as a client (desktop-based, easy to use, doesn't scale) and a relational database or application server (server-based, complex to program, scales).

Why Excel Services?

There are three main use cases Excel Services targets—publishing spreadsheets via the Web, executing complex spreadsheets on a server, and providing Excel capabilities via web services or code.

Publishing Spreadsheets

Often you want to share the contents of a spreadsheet with others. Usually it's a simple a matter of e-mailing the file to the recipient. However, there are times when this is impractical. There may be proprietary formulas or calculations in the spreadsheet that you don't wish to share. The spreadsheet may be an ongoing effort, and you may fear the recipients will refer to old data (or forward the spreadsheet on to others). Or perhaps you can't rely on the target audience having Excel!

With Excel Services, you can publish an Excel spreadsheet so that it can be viewed in a browser (Figure 8-11). You can also set spreadsheets so that users can download a "snapshot" of the spreadsheet—they will get the cell values, but none of the underlying formulas or data connections.

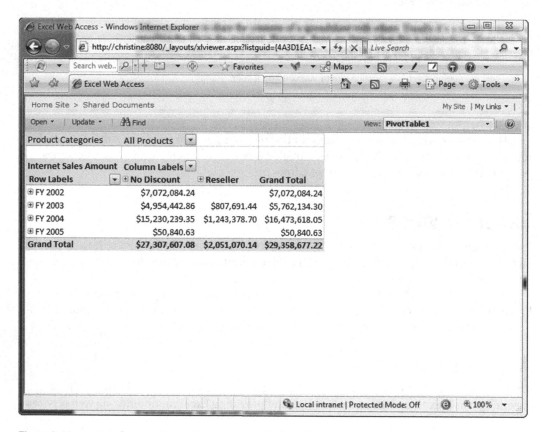

Figure 8-11. *An Excel spreadsheet in a browser via Excel Services*

It's important to note that the browser-based spreadsheet is not a fully functional spreadsheet—it is read-only with interactive drill down (you can expand the hierarchies just as you could in Excel). Browser-based spreadsheets can also be parameterized—set a parameter in the sheet and an end user can set the parameter to calculate the sheet (an example would be a loan table where the principle value is the input value).

From this page, users can also copy down the spreadsheet with the Open command in the toolbar (Figure 8-12). They can either get a copy of the spreadsheet or just open a "snapshot"—the values in the sheet, but none of the underlying logic or connections. The ability to grab either the full sheet or just a snapshot can also be governed by security settings.

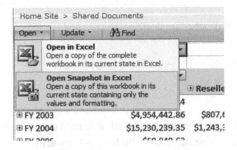

Figure 8-12. *Opening a spreadsheet from Excel Services*

Running Spreadsheets on a Server

Most organizations have an analyst that lives for Excel. They will have some multimegabyte spreadsheet that they've tweaked and tuned over years to perform some critical business analysis. Often they will have a desktop as powerful as a server, and hang a "Do not power off" sign on it while their spreadsheet crunches overnight.

Of course, there are a myriad of problems with this situation—the analyst's desktop is a single point of failure; the need to leave the desktop alone means it is probably not being patched properly, making it vulnerable. Critical business processes should not depend on the cleaning staff not unplugging a desktop. And so on.

Excel Services allows the analyst to publish the spreadsheet to SharePoint on a server. This means the spreadsheet is running on proper server hardware, protected by an uninterruptible power supply and failover clusters. The spreadsheet runs as a service, so it does not require a user to be logged in. The process can even be farmed among several servers if necessary. In addition, as you'll see in the next section, this critical business process can be accessed via code for reuse in other aspects of the business.

In general, running a spreadsheet on a server is pretty straightforward—publish the spreadsheet to Excel Services, and then open the sheet in a browser and run a recalculation.

Note For more information about this, start at the MSDN section on Excel Services: http://msdn2.microsoft.com/en-us/library/ms546204.aspx.

Providing Excel Functions via Code

Finally, a developer can take a complex spreadsheet created by an analyst and publish it into Excel Services such that the calculations are available via Web Services. For example, let's say an analyst creates a probability matrix based on parameters in a database and other input values. Instead of trying to massage the matrix math and Excel worksheets into code, you can add parameters to the Excel spreadsheet, publish it to Excel Services, and then call the spreadsheet functions via code.

■**Note** For more information about using Excel Web Services to develop applications, see `http://msdn2.microsoft.com/en-us/library/ms572330.aspx`.

Configuring Excel Services

Configuring Excel Services properly and publishing an Excel spreadsheet with external data connections to SharePoint are nontrivial exercises. Due to the nature of the technology and the potential vulnerabilities they could open (web-based access to back-end business systems), the security infrastructure is very robust. As a result, to configure it properly, you need to understand SharePoint architecture, active domain security, delegation and single sign-on, and other aspects of authentication.

In consideration of this, the exercises in this chapter are almost more of a roadmap than a how-to. They do go through configuration and deployment step by step, but depending on the architecture of your SharePoint installation and the data you want to display, you may have additional research to do on how to configure those products to get everything working properly. I just want to set expectations that this is tricky, and not something you might rip through in half an hour.

To make sure Excel Services is configured properly, you need a trusted location for your files, you need to configure single sign-on in SharePoint, and you need a trusted DCL.

■**Note** We're going to blaze through the security aspects in get-it-working mode. For a proper enterprise architecture including Excel Services, you will need to understand and plan out the data connection security for Excel spreadsheets. A good place to start is the TechNet article "Plan external data connections for Excel Services," at `http://technet2.microsoft.com/Office/en-us/library/7e6ce086-57b6-4ef2-8117-e725de18f2401033.mspx?mfr=true`.

Exercise 8-2 will walk you through getting SharePoint configured for Excel Services.

Exercise 8-2. Configuring Excel Services

1. On the SharePoint server, open the Central Administration console by clicking Start ➤ All Programs ➤ Microsoft Office Server ➤ SharePoint 3.0 Central Administration.

2. First, ensure that Excel Services is enabled. Go to the Operations tab, and in the Upgrade and Migration section, make sure that Enable Enterprise Features is checked.

■**Note** You must have the enterprise version of SharePoint to enable the enterprise features.

---

3. Once enabled, you may also have to enable features on existing sites on the Operations tab, in the Upgrade and Migration section. Check "Enable all sites in this installation to use the following set of Features: Office SharePoint Server Enterprise Features," and click OK.

Now we're going to add a trusted file location.

4. In SharePoint Central Administration, click the link to the shared services provider on the left (the default name is SharedServices1).

5. On the Shared Services Administration page, under the Excel Services Settings section, click the link "Trusted file locations," as shown in Figure 8-13.

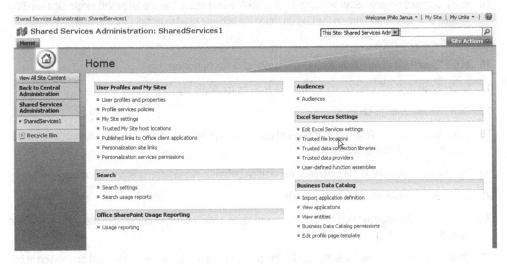

Figure 8-13. *Opening the "trusted file locations" page*

6. Click the Add Trusted File Location link in the menu bar.

We're going to use a SharePoint document library for the trusted file location. Since SharePoint document libraries are URL addressable, the URL for the document library will work here.

7. Fill in the address, but do not include a trailing slash (e.g., `http://servername:8080/sites/document%20library`).

8. Check "Children trusted" if you want all sites and lists subordinate to the link to be trusted.

9. Scroll down to External Data. For Allow External Data, select "Trusted data connection libraries and embedded."

10. Click OK to add the trusted location.

Now let's set a trusted DCL.

Tip For more information about DCLs, see `http://technet.microsoft.com/en-us/library/cc262739.aspx`.

---

11. From the Shared Services page, in the Excel Services section, click "Trusted data connection libraries."

12. Click Add Trusted Data Connection Library.

13. Enter the URL of a DCL in the site, and then click OK.

The next step is configuring single sign-on in SharePoint.

■**Note** For additional information about single sign-on in SharePoint, see the TechNet article "Configure single sign-on (Office SharePoint Server)," at `http://technet.microsoft.com/en-us/library/cc262932(TechNet.10).aspx`.

14. In the Services console (Start ➤ Administrative Tools ➤ Services), find the Microsoft single sign-on (SSO) service and set the account on the Log On tab to the account used to install Office SharePoint Server.

15. Start the SSO service.

16. In the SharePoint Central Administration console, click the Operations tab.

17. Under Security Configuration, click "Manage settings for single sign-on."

18. Click "Manage server settings."

19. In the Single Sign-On Administrator account text box, enter the same account name (domain\user name) that you entered for the SSO service.

20. Use the same account in the Enterprise Application Definition Administrator account text box.

21. Leave all other settings as-is, and click OK.

22. Back on the "Manage settings for single sign-on" page, click "Manage settings for enterprise application definitions," and then click New Item.

23. On the Create Enterprise Application Definition page, enter a unique name for this SSO application in both the Display Name and Application Name fields. (Use ExcelService if you can't think of anything else.)

24. Enter your e-mail address for the contact e-mail address.

25. Leave Group as the account type.

26. Check the box for "Windows authentication."

27. Under Logon Account Information Field 1: Display Name, enter *Username and Mask = No*.

28. In Field 2: Display Name, enter *Password* and *Mask = Yes*.

29. Click OK. Navigate back to the "Manage settings for single sign-on" page and click Manage Account Information for an Enterprise Application Definition.

30. Ensure that the unique ID you chose in step 23 is selected in the drop-down list.

31. For "Group account name," enter *<Domain>\Domain Users*.

■**Caution** This is a fairly broad permission set. Again, this is simply a walkthrough for demonstration purposes. To implement Excel Services in production, make sure you understand the security implications of SSO and restrict permissions appropriately.

32. Click the Set button.

33. Enter the domain\username and password of an account that has access to the data sources you will be using.

34. Click OK, and then click Done.

That's it—we've got Excel Services ready to publish our spreadsheet!

Publishing to Excel Services

After all the configuration, actually publishing objects to Excel Services can be very straightforward. You'll want to name the ranges and objects in your workbook that you may want to work with on the server. The quickest and easiest way to learn this is to walk through it, so let's go!

Exercise 8-3. Publishing a Spreadsheet to Excel Services

1. Open the spreadsheet from Exercise 8-1.

2. Before you can publish this spreadsheet to Excel Services, you need to adjust the connection. Click the Data tab on the ribbon.

3. In the Connections section, click the Connections button to open the Workbook Connections dialog.

4. Select the connection and click the Properties button to open the Connection Properties dialog.

5. Click the Definition tab.

6. At the bottom of the dialog, click the Authentication Settings button.

7. In the Excel Services Authentication Settings dialog, select the SSO radio button, and then enter the ID for the SSO you created in Exercise 8-2 (ExcelService). Click OK.

8. Click OK and acknowledge the warning, and then click Close.

9. Click the Office button in the top left of Excel (Figure 8-14).

Figure 8-14. *The Office button*

10. From the Office button menu, select Publish, and then select Excel Services. This opens the Save As dialog (Figure 8-15).

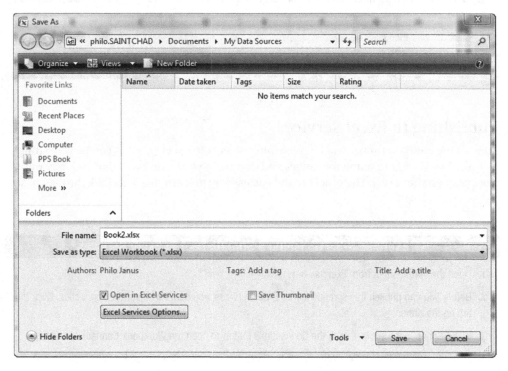

Figure 8-15. *The Save As dialog for publishing to Excel Services*

11. Click the Excel Services Options button to open the corresponding dialog (Figure 8-16).

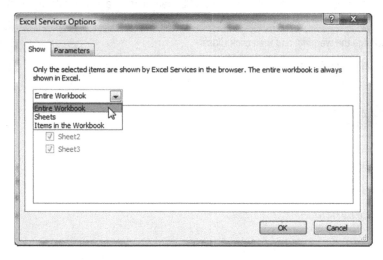

Figure 8-16. *The Excel Services Options dialog*

12. On the Show tab, ensure that Entire Workbook is selected. Note that you have other options for selecting what is published to the server.

13. Click the Parameters tab, and then click the Add button.

14. Check the box next to ProductCategory, and then click OK.

15. Click OK. Enter the URL of the SharePoint document library you want to upload the Excel workbook to in the "File name" box, and then press the Enter key—this should open the document library in the dialog box (Figure 8-17). You can then give your spreadsheet a unique name and click Save.

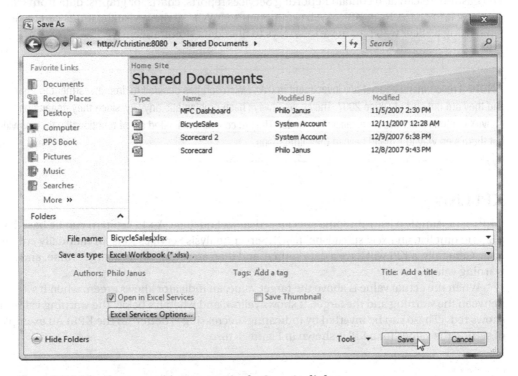

Figure 8-17. *The document library open in the Save As dialog*

Once you've clicked Save, the spreadsheet should open in a browser. If you've configured everything right, you should be able to open each of the regions (Europe, North America, Pacific) by clicking the small plus icon to the left of them. Note that when you open a region, the chart redraws to show the subordinate countries.

You can also filter by product category (with the option at the top of the chart), or use the table tools by clicking the down arrow buttons next to Row Labels or Column Labels.

Voila—a functional spreadsheet in a browser! In the next section, we'll see how this can play into SharePoint BI.

MOSS Business Intelligence

As I've mentioned several times, SharePoint is the framework for any BI work we're going to do. However, with the enterprise edition of MOSS, the new Report Library list type also gives us a dashboard page model to work with. The heart of a SharePoint dashboard is the KPI list—a list of KPIs that can draw data from Excel, SharePoint lists, Analysis Services, or manually entered data.

We can then take those KPIs and use them as the central perspective of our dashboard. The dashboard can also contain Reporting Services reports, charts, or graphs; data from Excel Services; and charts from Office Web Components (OWC). All these visualizations can be filtered using a Slicer web part in various ways to filter data simultaneously.

■**Note** I recommend against any investment in OWC. Microsoft has decided to drop investment in them, and they are not part of Office 2007. They have always been problematic anyway, since they depend on ActiveX controls and have no extensibility model. They're cool for the limited set of functionality they provide, but there's no way to expand beyond their limitations.

KPI Lists

A KPI list is simply a list with some specialized views and logic. A KPI list item can be based on a SharePoint list, an Excel spreadsheet, SQL Server Analysis Services KPIs, or manually entered data. Generally, a KPI will have a data source, and then an actual value, a target value, and a warning value.

When the actual value is above the target value, an indicator shows green; when it's between the warning and the target, it shows yellow; and when it's below the warning value, it shows red. (These can be inverted by indicating "decreasing is better" in the KPI.) An example of setting the values for a KPI is shown in Figure 8-18.

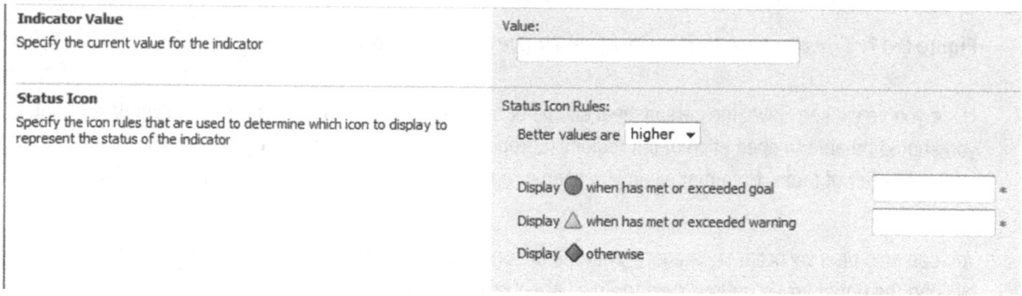

Figure 8-18. *Setting the values for a manual KPI*

There are significant limitations to SharePoint KPI lists and dashboards, but I will dig into those more in Chapter 10 by contrasting SharePoint dashboards to PerformancePoint dashboards.

Dashboards

SharePoint Server dashboards can be a bit tricky to find. You can create them from the New command in a Report Library list type. (Of course, in a more general sense, any web part page could be configured as a "dashboard." Here we're talking about the specific SharePoint dashboard functionality.)

Again, the easiest way to understand how a SharePoint dashboard works is to walk through building one.

Exercise 8-4. Building a SharePoint Dashboard

1. Create or open a report library in a SharePoint site (SharePoint Server, not WSS).

2. Click New, and then click Dashboard Page (Figure 8-19).

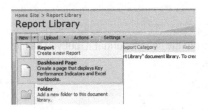

Figure 8-19. *Creating a new dashboard page*

3. On the New Dashboard page, make the file name MOSS Dashboard and the page title My Demo Dashboard.

4. Leave the other defaults as-is, and then click OK. This will create the dashboard page and navigate to it, as shown in Figure 8-20. Note the empty KPI list and Excel Web Access web parts.

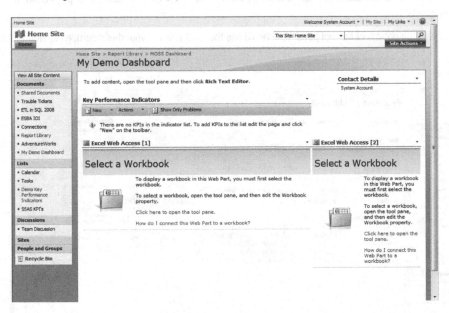

Figure 8-20. *Newly created dashboard page in SharePoint*

5. In the KPI list, click New, and then click Indicator from SQL Server Analysis Services.

6. In the Data Connection box, click the browse (...) button to the right, and select the AdventureWorks DW connection. Note the warning that the data connection is not encrypted. If you don't have a connection listed, create an odc connection to the AdventureWorks cube (see `http://msdn.microsoft.com/en-us/library/ms771995.aspx`).

7. In the KPI List list box, select Revenue (this is a list of the KPIs defined in the AdventureWorks cube).

8. Name the KPI Bicycle Revenue and click OK (Figure 8-21).

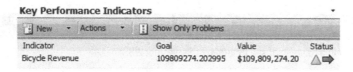

Figure 8-21. *The KPI in your KPI list*

■**Note** The Goal value will not be formatted. You can go back into the cube to format it, but you cannot change it here. This is one of the limitations of SharePoint KPIs.

Now we're going to map the Excel Web Access web parts to our spreadsheet.

9. In the web part titled Excel Web Access [1], click "Click here to open the tool pane."

10. In the tool pane on the right, click the browse button next to Workbook.

11. Open the shared documents library and select the `BicycleSales.xlsx` workbook.

12. In the Named Item text box, type *Internet Sales by Territory* (or whatever you named your pivot chart in Exercise 8-1).

13. Click OK at the bottom of the tool pane. You should see the pivot chart in your dashboard, as in Figure 8-22.

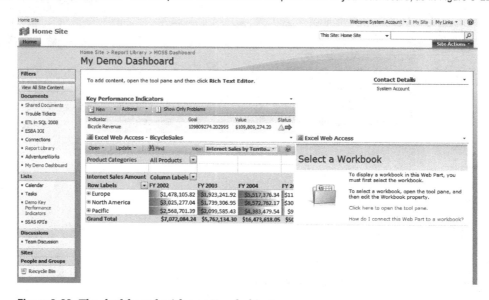

Figure 8-22. *The dashboard with one Excel object*

14. Repeat steps 9 through 13 for the same spreadsheet, but select Internet Sales Chart to bring that pivot chart into the dashboard.

    Now you have a dashboard showing a KPI, pivot chart, and pivot table of data. Next, you'll want to be able to slice your data.

15. Click the Site Actions button in the top right of the page, and then click Edit Page.

16. Note the filter zone that now appears in the top of the left-hand navigation bar (Figure 8-23).

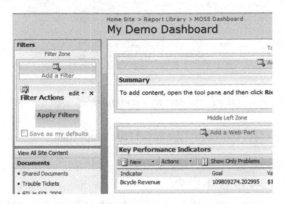

Figure 8-23. *The filter zone on a dashboard page*

17. Click Add a Filter.

18. Check the box next to SQL Server 2005 Analysis Services Filter, and then click the Add button.

19. Click "Open the tool pane" to open the tool pane on the right.

20. For Filter Name, enter *Categories*.

21. The Filter web part should have picked up the data connection—leave that as selected.

22. Under Dimension, select Product.

23. After the page refreshes, under Hierarchy select Product Categories. Click OK.

    Now you'll see the filter in the filter zone. It should have already connected to the KPI list and thus read "Sending values to: Key Performance Indicators."

24. Note the current value in the Bicycle Revenue KPI—it should be about $109 million.

25. Click the Filter button next to the filter box to open the filter selector, which draws its list from the hierarchy in the cube. Check the box next to Components, and then click OK.

26. Click the Apply Filters link.

27. Note that bicycle revenue is now $11 million.

28. Now let's connect the filter to our Excel pivot table. On the filter, click the "edit" drop-down menu.

29. Select Connections, then Send Filter Values To, and then Excel Web Access – BicycleSales [1]. This sets up the web part connection between the filter web part and the Excel Services web part (Figure 8-24).

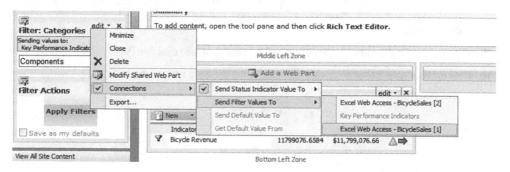

Figure 8-24. *Connecting the filter web part to the Excel Services web part*

30. This will open the Choose Connection dialog. Leave Connection Type as Get Filter Values From.

31. Click the Configure button.

32. Leave Filtered Parameter as ProductCategory, and then click Finish.

33. Now note that when you change the product category and click Apply Filters, both the KPI and the pivot table change values. (The KPI shows total revenue and the pivot table shows internet sales.)

I'll leave connecting the pivot chart as an exercise for you.

Now we have a dashboard that shows various values from our AdventureWorks sales cube. We could fold in other values, also filtered by the slicer in the Filter box. We could show Reporting Services reports, add KPIs, and so on.

Conclusion

While this is a great ad hoc way to build some dashboards, it does lack some complexity that most organizations will need in any full-featured BI solution. In the next chapter, we're going to look at using ProClarity to build advanced visualizations and publish them to a web-based environment, and then we'll look at how we can use PerformancePoint to bring together all the concepts introduced so far.

CHAPTER 9

■ ■ ■

ProClarity Analytics Server

Microsoft acquired the ProClarity Corporation in June of 2006. ProClarity made its name with tools that made it easy for end users to create interactive visualizations (charts and graphs) from SQL Server Analysis Services cubes and perform the analysis that OLAP promises. ProClarity Analytics Server (PAS) is a server-based tool that enables design and publication of various web-based views of Analysis Services OLAP data. Currently, PerformancePoint Server is focused on scorecards and dashboards, and it leverages PAS and SQL Server Reporting Services for drill-down analytic reporting. PerformancePoint Server has some charting capabilities, but expect to see more of the PAS functionality moved into it over the next few versions.

ProClarity Analytics Server Overview

PAS sits between Analysis Services and the user. The benefit is that it sits in the data center on a fast link with the OLAP server. This makes it easy to optimize reports—design a report to draw the minimum amount of data necessary, format it, and deliver the report down to the client.

■Note ProClarity had several products: PAS, ProClarity Dashboard Server, Business Logic Server, and Desktop Professional. The latter three are somewhat in limbo, and we'll be focusing on PAS, so from here on out I'll be using "ProClarity" to refer to PAS.

ProClarity basically has two interfaces: Web Standard and Web Professional. Web Standard is a web-based interface that provides users access to charts published to the server. It's a fairly interactive interface, but targeted toward consumption of existing analysis. The Web Standard interface is shown in Figure 9-1.

Web Professional is the designer interface—oriented toward actual analysis, creating charts, and publishing them. Think of Web Professional like Excel—a tool to build pivot tables and pivot charts, except the pivoting has already been done by Analysis Services, so all you have to do is design the charts themselves. The Web Professional interface is shown in Figure 9-2.

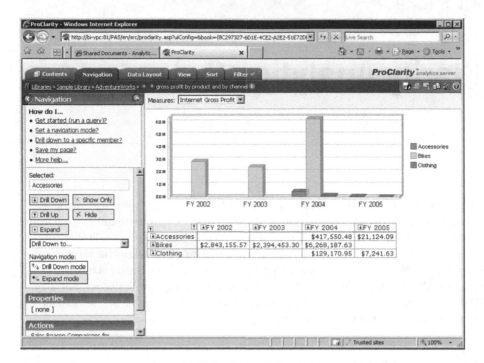

Figure 9-1. *ProClarity Web Standard interface*

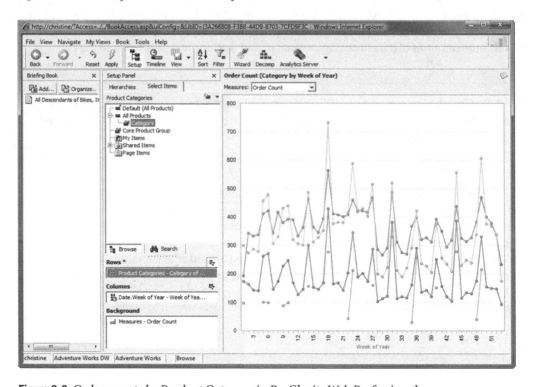

Figure 9-2. *Order counts by Product Category in ProClarity Web Professional*

Once charts are designed and published, they can also be consumed—PAS is web addressable so that charts can be embedded in any web page. In addition, there is a ProClarity SharePoint web part so that ProClarity views can be displayed on SharePoint pages. Finally (and the main reason we're here), ProClarity charts can be consumed as report views in a PerformancePoint dashboard (Figure 9-3).

We'll take a quick look at each of the types of ProClarity visualizations, and then we're going to tour the interfaces of the Web Standard and Web Professional clients, doing exercises to get our hands dirty. We'll take a look at how ProClarity can integrate with SharePoint, and in the last section of the chapter, we'll walk through how to install ProClarity.

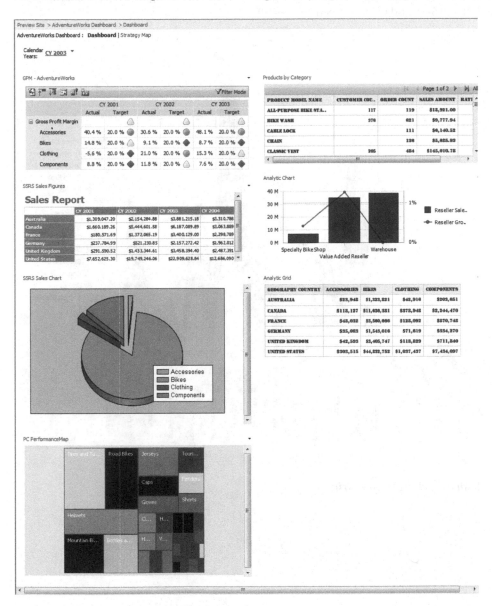

Figure 9-3. *PerformancePoint dashboard with ProClarity charts*

ProClarity Charts

ProClarity offers a number of chart styles—broken down into *business charts* and *advanced analysis tools*. The advanced analysis tools are the decomposition tree, perspective view, and performance map. Let's take a quick look at each of these.

Business Charts

The business charts are your standard reporting chart styles—specifically, area charts (Figure 9-4), bar charts (Figure 9-5), horizontal bar charts (Figure 9-6), line charts (Figure 9-7), pie charts (Figures 9-8 and 9-9), and point charts (Figure 9-10).

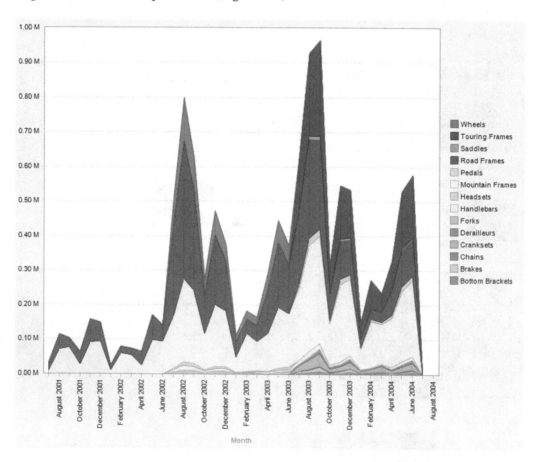

Figure 9-4. *An area chart in ProClarity*

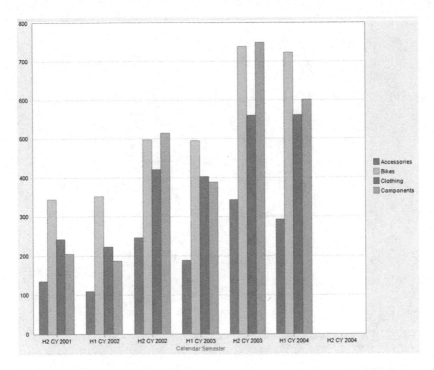

Figure 9-5. *A bar chart in ProClarity*

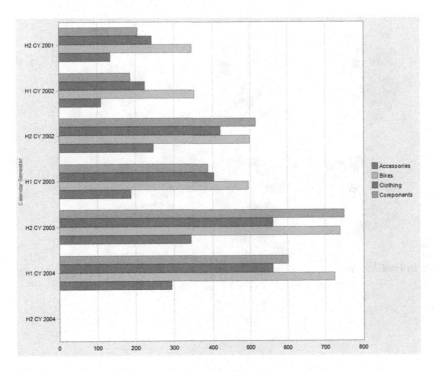

Figure 9-6. *A horizontal bar chart in ProClarity*

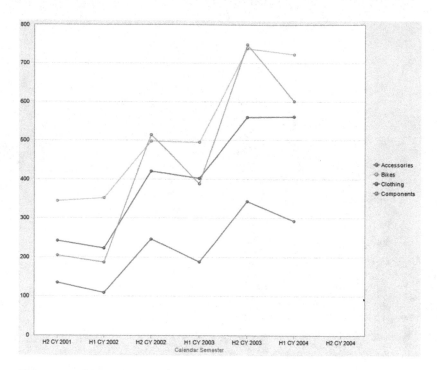

Figure 9-7. *A line chart in ProClarity*

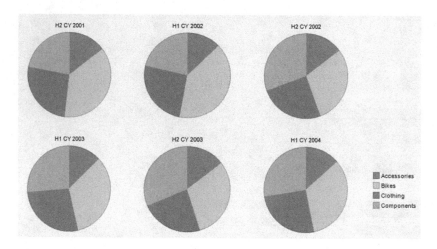

Figure 9-8. *Pie charts in ProClarity*

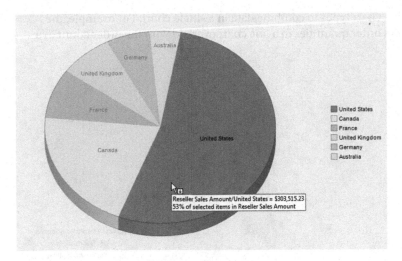

Figure 9-9. *Another view of a pie chart in ProClarity*

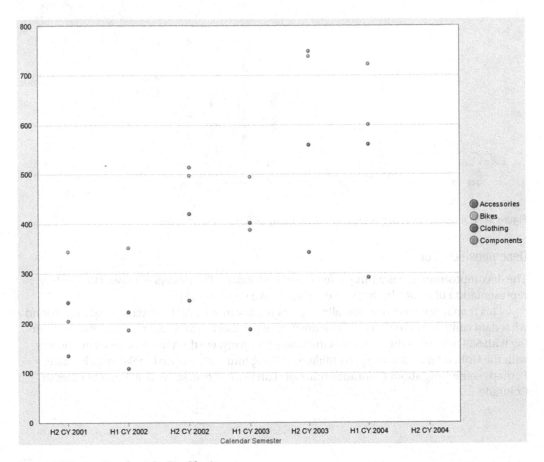

Figure 9-10. *A point chart in ProClarity*

You can also combine chart types to combine data in a single chart. For example, the chart in Figure 9-11 shows order quantities in a line chart overlaid with the order count in a bar chart.

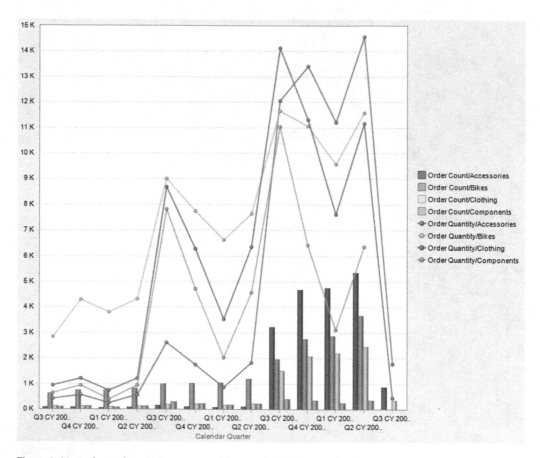

Figure 9-11. *A chart showing two sets of data using different chart types*

Decomposition Tree

The decomposition tree is a unique feature of ProClarity—I've always felt it was the perfect representation of what "drilling into data" looks like (Figure 9-12).

This is an interactive tree that allows users to click into OLAP hierarchies and understand what data contributes to a value. In Figure 9-12, we're looking at reseller sales amounts. Starting with $80 million at the top across the whole company, we then break it down by country, with the United States showing $54 million. Drilling into that, we see breakdowns by state. Perhaps something about Colorado's numbers catches our eye, so we drill into the cities in Colorado.

Then we want to learn more about the $816,000 in sales in Loveland, CO, so we look at the breakdown of sales by product category. Finally, we want to understand the historical numbers behind the clothing sales, so we look at those numbers by calendar year.

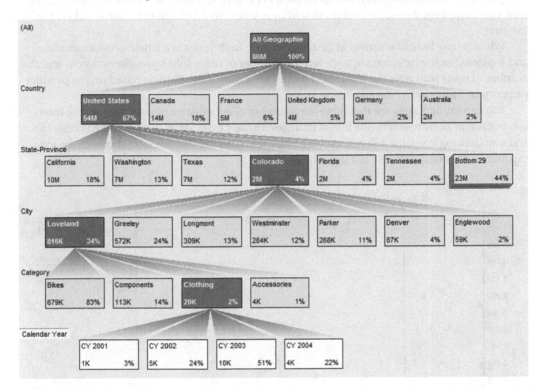

Figure 9-12. *A ProClarity decomposition tree*

All of this is performed via a point-and-click interface that is very intuitive, enabling our users to really dive into the data and analysis provided by an OLAP cube. (Each of the levels is a level of a hierarchy in a cube dimension, and the reseller sales amount is a dimension—see how these concepts keep coming back?)

Perspective View

The perspective view is a way to identify relationships and trends in large amounts of data by comparing two dimensions against each other. For example, Figure 9-13 shows a perspective view that compares the number of units sold by resellers to the number of units sold via the Internet.

While it may look like a mess at first, look closer. Each point is a single product model, and is plotted at the intersection between the number of units sold by resellers (x axis) and the number of units sold over the Internet (y axis). The shape of the point is based on the product category, as indicated in the legend.

You can immediately see that there are a number of accessories that sell well on the Internet, but not at all by resellers (the line of triangles up the y axis). We also have some accessories and one clothing item that sell well via both channels. (Drilling into the data shows us the logo cap and 30 oz water bottle are our big-selling items.)

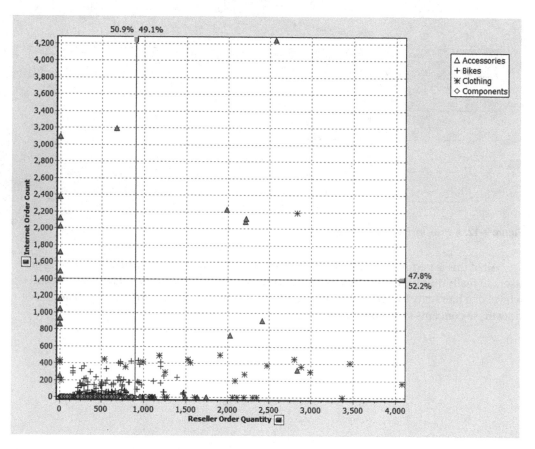

Figure 9-13. *A ProClarity perspective view*

Well, we're not going to get too excited over a $5 water bottle or $2 logo cap—where can we see some big money? If we do some additional analysis, we can compare gross profit margin to total sales (Figure 9-14), and start to identify areas to focus our energy. Couple this chart with the previous one and we can differentiate our efforts between Internet sales activities and reseller activities. We're using our business data to plan our marketing efforts.

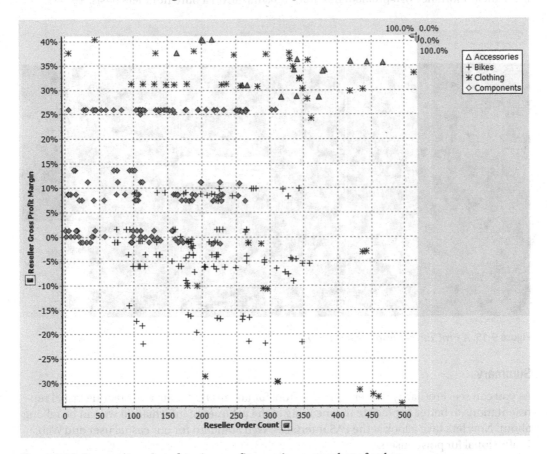

Figure 9-14. *Perspecitve view showing profit margin vs. number of orders*

Performance Map

ProClarity's performance map is simply a heat map (Figure 9-15). Again, it compares two measures—in this case, using the size of the square to indicate the relative magnitude of one value and the color of the square for the other value. This can be a quick visual way to determine the importance of a problem that may look drastic on a pure numbers basis.

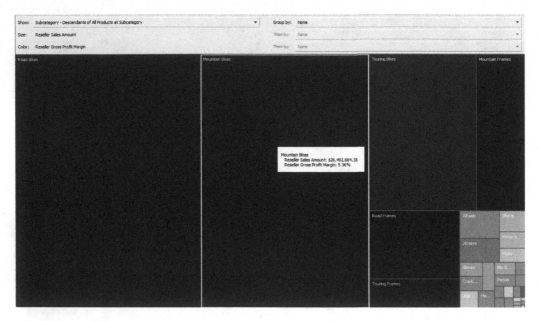

Figure 9-15. *A ProClarity performance map*

Summary

As you can see, ProClarity is a very powerful tool for taking OLAP data and creating visual representations to better appreciate the meaning of the volumes of information we can be talking about. Now let's take a look at the PAS interfaces: Web Standard for our casual user and Web Professional for power users.

Web Standard

The interface for most users into ProClarity briefing books will be ProClarity Web Standard—this is a "pure thin" web client that gives an interactive graphical view. Power users can use the Web Professional interface to design reports and publish them to Analytics Server, and other users can use the Web Standard interface to view and interact with the reports. The Web Standard interface is shown in Figure 9-16.

The Analytic Chart and Data Grid are data displays—users can generally click regions of the chart to drill down, drill up, drill to detail, analyze the data in a decomposition tree, and so on. Mouseover hints give detail data such as the label and value of a given area. Users can also use the Actions panel at the left for navigation.

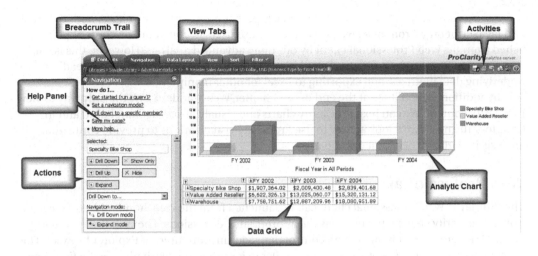

Figure 9-16. *ProClarity Web Standard interface*

When a user opens the Web Standard interface, they'll see something similar to Figure 9-17. For a standard user, all the content that's available to them will be listed here. Content is organized into collections called *briefing books*. A briefing book is the unit that users can check out to edit, and will contain one or more of the charts shown in this chapter.

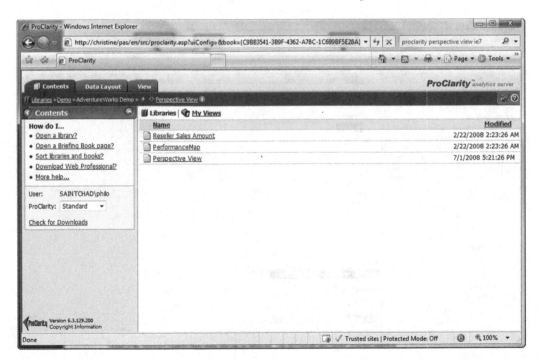

Figure 9-17. *Opening the ProClarity Web Standard interface*

As mentioned, the Web Standard interface is pure thin—it's browser-based, and it's HTML and JavaScript only. From here, we expect most of our users to consume the content published from the Web Professional client by our more advanced analysts. However, this is still a very powerful interface, allowing manipulation of charts, drilling down into data, reading underlying data matrixes, and exporting to Excel for other manipulation.

In addition, as you'll see at the end of this chapter, Web Standard isn't the only way to view ProClarity content. We can host ProClarity charts and visualizations in SharePoint, and in Chapters 10 and 11 we'll look at how to use ProClarity visualizations to provide contextual analysis in PerformancePoint dashboards.

Web Professional

The ProClarity Web Professional client can be launched from the Web Standard interface (or from a ProClarity chart) if the user has the appropriate permissions. The Web Professional (a.k.a. "Web Pro") client is an ActiveX control that loads into an Internet Explorer browser. The download and install are pretty painless—similar to installing the Flash plug-in the first time, if you've ever done that.

The Web Professional client (Figure 9-18) provides all the tools necessary for a power user or advanced analyst to create charts, graphs, and advanced visualizations from SQL Server Analysis Services data. Next to the browser component in BIDS, I have found ProClarity to be the best tool for learning how to consume Analysis Services data, and for best positioning OLAP information for consumption by nontechnical users.

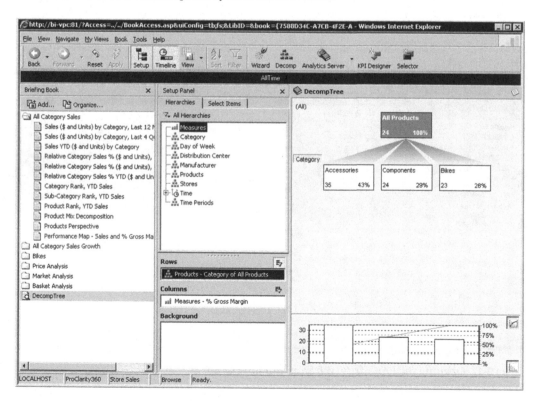

Figure 9-18. *The ProClarity Web Professional (Web Pro) client*

The ProClarity client also helps to understand why perspectives are important in cubes—as you scroll back and forth through a myriad of dimensions, members, and measures, you will come to appreciate the idea of more targeted lists provided by a perspective.

In this chapter, we're going to walk through installing PAS, and then we'll walk through using the Web Professional and Web Standard clients, as well as publishing ProClarity visualizations to SharePoint.

Architecture

PAS runs as a server application. It stores its configuration data and reports in a SQL Server database and uses SQL Server Analysis Services as the data source for its reports. The user interface is web-based (both for publishers and consumers), and the administrative interface (user accounts and permissions) is through a client-side application. Figure 9-19 shows the basic architecture.

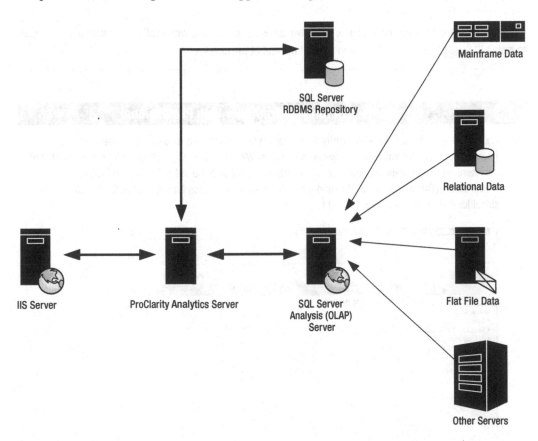

Figure 9-19. *PAS architecture*

Note that PAS can only display data from SQL Server Analysis Services. However, remember what we've covered to date—in a mature business intelligence solution, you're going to want some form of OLAP cube as an aggregation point to consolidate your business data to business constructs. Using that OLAP cube as a marshaling point allows you to represent data from any number of back-end systems.

■Tip We're going to install PAS in an "all-in-one" architecture—on the same machine with Analysis Services and IIS. To scale for production use, you'll want to install PAS on a different machine from Analysis Services, and probably separate from the web server. To use integrated authentication in this architecture, you're going to need to implement Kerberos so that the user credentials can be forwarded.

As mentioned, PAS has two styles of interface: Web Professional and Web Standard. The professional mode is for ad hoc analytics, and designing and publishing reports. Reports are stored in collections called briefing books on the server and can be accessed by users through the Web Standard version, or (and this is the part we care about) consumed in SharePoint or by other applications.

■Note The following exercises assume you have access to a machine with ProClarity installed. If you need to install PAS, see Exercises 9-8 through 9-11 at the end of the chapter.

Exercise 9-1. Setting Up ProClarity Web Professional

1. Go to Start ➤ All Programs ➤ ProClarity ➤ ProClarity Web (or open a browser and navigate to http://[server]/pas). This will open a browser to ProClarity Web Standard (Figure 9-20). Since you're just starting, there are no libraries or briefing books available—you have to be in ProClarity Web Professional to create those. (That's why we need to add the Web Professional access for our user and set up Web Professional for download – see Exercise 9-11.)

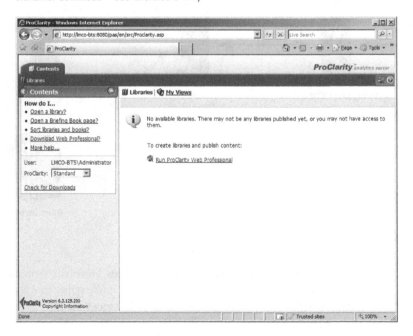

Figure 9-20. *ProClarity Web Standard*

2. Click the link on the left that says Check for Downloads. This will open the Download Components dialog (Figure 9-21).

3. Check the box next to ProClarity Web Professional 6.3.

4. Click the Download Now button.

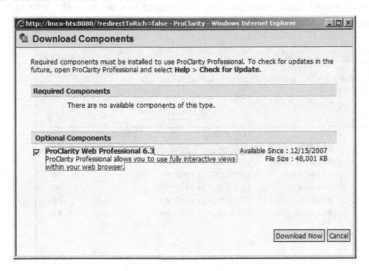

Figure 9-21. *Downloading Web Professional*

5. When the security dialog prompts you to run or save, click Run.

6. When the installation completes, click the Continue button.

7. After the installer completes, click Cancel to close the Download Components dialog.

8. Next, click the Run ProClarity Web Professional link in the right pane of Web Standard (Figure 9-22)—this will open a new window with Web Professional.

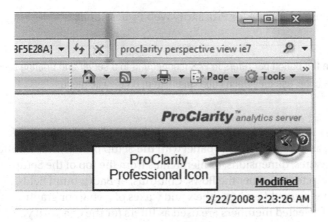

Figure 9-22. *Opening ProClarity Web Professional from Web Standard*

Using ProClarity Web Professional

Web Professional opens in a browser, but it is an ActiveX-based application (Internet Explorer 6+ only). Once you connect it to an Analysis Services cube (Figure 9-23), you can select the type of visualization and what members to use (dimensions and measures). The decomposition tree and perspective view both have wizards; the other charts just open in the interface, and it's up to you to design them.

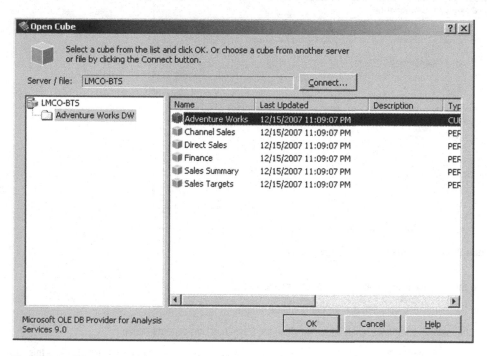

Figure 9-23. *The Open Cube dialog in Web Professional*

Figure 9-24 is a guide to the user interface for ProClarity Web Professional.

■**Tip** The Analytics Server button on the button bar refers to PAS (connecting to a server and briefing book activities). If you want to connect to a cube, use the "Open cube" menu item on the File menu.

You will do most of your work in the Setup panel in the center, where the cube members and chart design areas are. (You can show or hide this panel with the Setup button on the button bar.) Generally, you just drag measures, dimensions, or hierarchies from the top of the Setup panel (with the Hierarchies tab selected) to either the Rows, Columns, or Background fields.

Rows and columns are what you would expect—the x and y axes of a chart or graph.

Background hierarchies and selected members are used as filters for the chart—if you select Calendar Year and then CY2007, only data from 2007 will be displayed in the chart. If you select multiple members from a dimension or hierarchy, ProClarity creates a *slicer*—a filter that allows you to select each of the members individually.

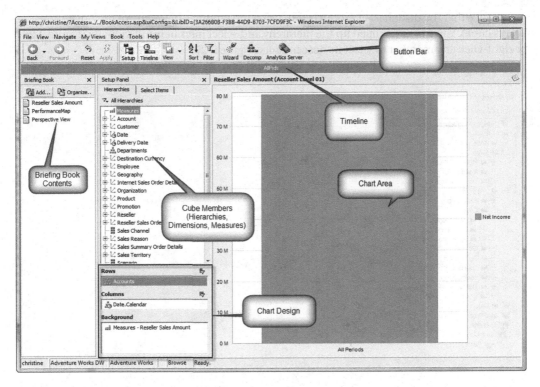

Figure 9-24. *Guide to the ProClarity Web Professional user interface*

When you select a dimension for a chart, ProClarity will use the default member. This often results in the big, blue box shown in Figure 9-24—the total measure for all dimensions. Boring, eh? The trick is to select the dimension in the Rows or Columns entry of the chart designer, and then either click the Select Items tab at the top of the cube members panel, or just double-click the dimension. Then you'll be presented with something like the panel in Figure 9-25.

Figure 9-25. *Selecting members for a dimension in ProClarity Web Professional*

Notice that the default is All Products (I'm using the Products hierarchy of the Adventure-Works cube). You can either open up the hierarchy and select members individually (Figure 9-26) or right-click any member to select its descendants (Figure 9-27).

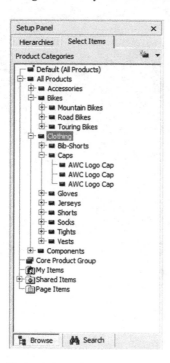

Figure 9-26. *Selecting members individually*

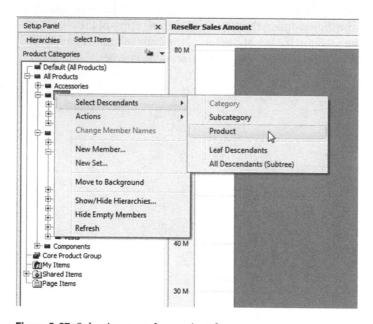

Figure 9-27. *Selecting members using the context menu*

After making changes, you'll need to click the Apply button to, well, apply them. So let's build a few charts and publish them using Web Professional to see how this works.

Exercise 9-2. Creating Charts in ProClarity Web Professional

1. Open ProClarity Web Professional. See Exercise 9-1 if you need help.

2. Let's connect to the AdventureWorks cube—click the File menu and then Open Cube to show the Open Cube dialog (Figure 9-28).

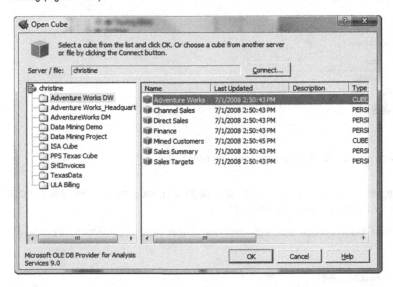

Figure 9-28. *Connecting to a SQL Server Analysis Services cube*

3. Select Adventure Works DW on the left, then select the Adventure Works cube, and then click the OK button.

4. Next, you'll see the dialog for selecting a visualization (Figure 9-29). On this dialog, click Chart View.

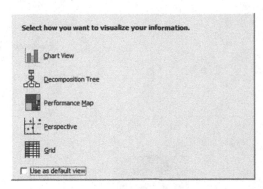

Figure 9-29. *Selecting a visualization*

5. The default selection (based on default members in the cube) is the Reseller Sales Amount, in the Net Income Account, for all the calendar periods in the cube (a big, blue box).

6. In the Rows area of the Setup panel (click the Setup button in the button bar if it's not visible), click and drag the Accounts dimension off to one side until you see an X—then drop to delete it.

7. Click and drag the Product dimension down to the Rows area (where it will appear as Product Model Categories).

8. Double-click Product Model Categories to open the member selector. Note that Default (All Products) is selected.

9. Right-click All Products (don't click the default value; click under it, where All Products has an expansion symbol next to it, as in Figure 9-30).

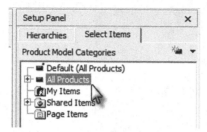

Figure 9-30. *Selecting members from the Products hierarchy*

10. After right-clicking, select Select Descendants from the context menu, and then Category. Note that Category is now under the All Products node and selected.

11. Click the Apply button. You should now have a bar chart with reseller sales amounts for each category (Figure 9-31).

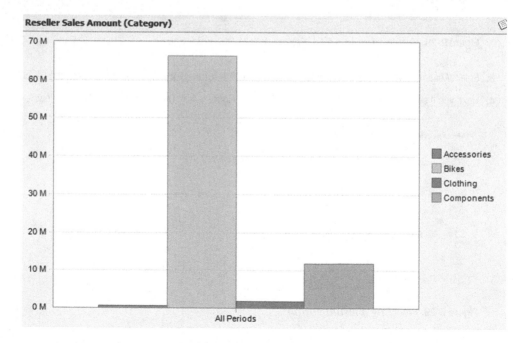

Figure 9-31. *The chart shown after selecting the category descendants of the Products hierarchy*

12. Now double-click the Date.Calendar entry under Columns in the Setup panel.

13. Right-click All Periods, then Select Descendants, and then Calendar Year.

14. Click the Apply button. Now you'll have a bar chart showing product category breakdowns by year.

15. This would probably make more sense as a line chart—right-click the chart, select Chart Type, and then select Line Chart to change this to a line chart (Figure 9-32).

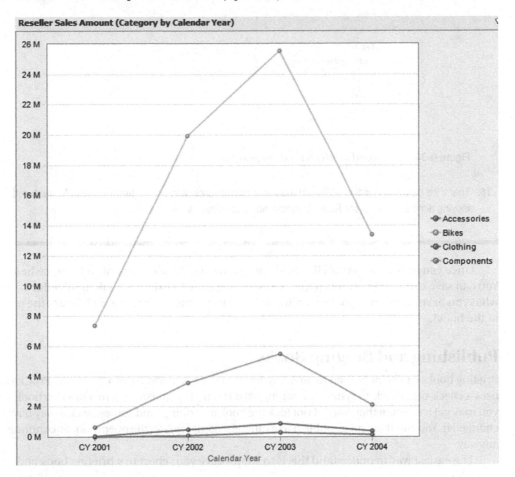

Figure 9-32. *Showing a line chart*

16. Mouse over a point to see the detail about that data point (Figure 9-33).

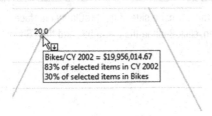

Figure 9-33. *Mouseover text box showing detail for a data point*

17. You can also right-click to drill into the data or analyze it in different ways (Figure 9-34).

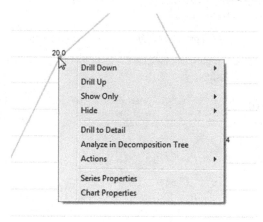

Figure 9-34. *Additional analysis on data points*

18. That's the basics. Try adding additional measures (double-click Measures – Reseller Sales Amount) and moving dimensions between Rows, Columns, and Background to see the effects.

Once you have a chart you'd like to share, you need to be able to publish it somewhere. You can save various views and charts in a collection called a briefing book (that's effectively what you have open when you're working in ProClarity—the pane to the far left lists the pages in the book).

Publishing and Briefing Books

Briefing books can be published to an Analytics server or saved locally as a *.bbk file. ProClarity uses a check-out/check-in system for editing, so if you try to publish back to a briefing book, you may get a warning that you did not lock the book for editing, and someone else may have changed it. You can then either publish to a different name, cancel the operation, or continue anyway.

The easiest way to understand this is to simply save your chart to a briefing book and publish it.

Exercise 9-3. Publishing a Briefing Book

1. Using the chart from Exercise 9-2, click the Add button on the left-hand side of the ProClarity interface (Figure 9-35). If you don't have the Briefing Book pane open, click Book in the menu bar, and then Show Briefing Book.

2. Name the page Sales by Category, and then click OK.

3. Now you can change the chart and save additional charts, or click the Sales by Category page at any time to return to this view.

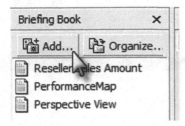

Figure 9-35. *Adding a page to the briefing book*

4. To publish the book, click File ➤ Analytics Server ➤ Publish Book.

5. You'll get the Publish Book dialog (Figure 9-36). If you don't have any libraries, you'll have to create one (by clicking the New Library button).

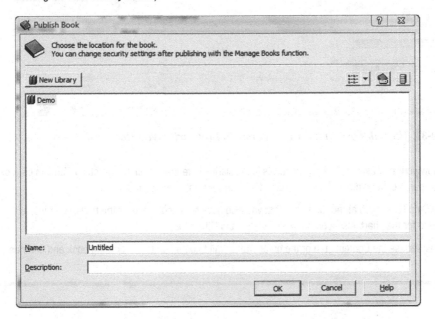

Figure 9-36. *Publishing a briefing book*

6. Name the book PPS Book and click OK.

7. That's it! Now open ProClarity Web Standard by opening a new browser and navigating to `http://[server]/pas`.

8. Click the library you created the briefing book in, and then open PPS Book.

9. You should see your Sales by Category page listed—click it to open it (Figure 9-37).

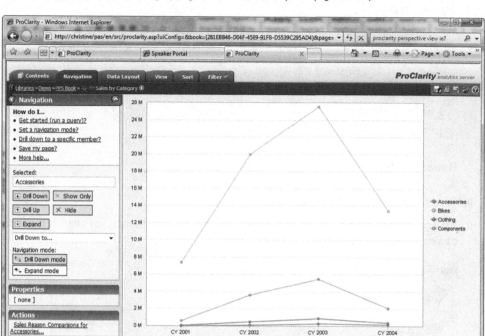

Figure 9-37. *The Sales by Category chart open in ProClarity Web Standard*

10. This is how your end users will see your charts in ProClarity (note that it's still interactive). You can click data points to open a context menu (left-click), drill down, analyze data points, and so on.

11. Click the Data Layout tab at the top to see that you also have some control over the rows, columns, and background for the chart. Also look at the View, Sort, and Filter tabs.

12. You can either use the Contents tab or the breadcrumb trail to get back to the briefing book and libraries.

Advanced Visualizations

Earlier in the chapter I showed you several of the advanced visualizations for analyzing information available in ProClarity. In the following exercises, I'll walk you through creating each one: a decomposition tree, perspective view, and performance map. In Exercise 9-4 you'll create a decomposition tree to drill down on reseller sales by time and by geography. In Exercise 9-5, I'll show you how to create a perspective view to look at possible relationships and patterns by comparing gross profit to total sales. Finally, in Exercise 9-6, you'll create a performance map (heat map) for evaluating profit margin against sales amounts, to identify the best areas to focus attention for maximum return.

Exercise 9-4. Creating a Decomposition Tree

1. Open the Sales by Category chart in Web Professional.

2. Click the Decomp button in the toolbar to open the Decomposition Tree wizard (Figure 9-38).

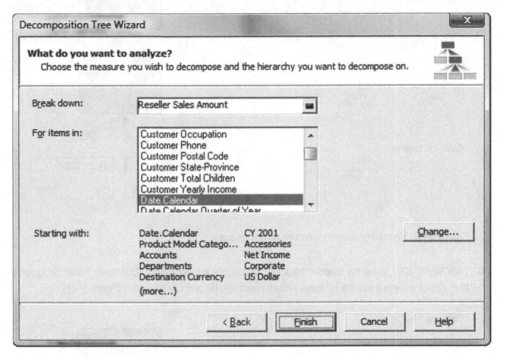

Figure 9-38. *The Decomposition Tree wizard*

3. Note the "Starting with" filters—you can click the Change button and scroll down to select the filter levels for any dimension. We'll leave it as-is for now. Click the Finish button.

4. You'll start with a single block: the reseller sales amount for the Accessories member of the Product Categories hierarchy in CY 2001, as the title indicates (Figure 9-39).

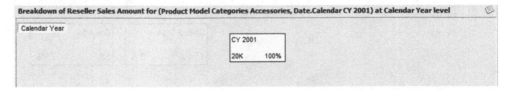

Figure 9-39. *Initial view of a decomposition tree*

5. If you click the block, you'll get H2 CY 2001 (we have no data for H1). Click H2 and you'll see Q3 and Q4 CY 2001 (Figure 9-40).

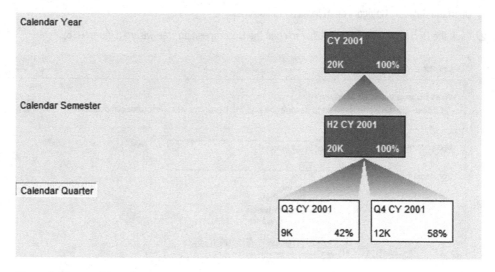

Figure 9-40. *Breaking down a decomposition tree*

6. Click H2 CY 2001 to roll the quarters back up. Then right-click and select "Drill down," then Geography, and then Country—you'll see the H2 sales broken down into US and Canada sales (Figure 9-41).

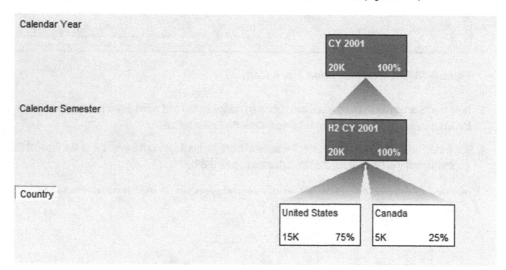

Figure 9-41. *Breaking down sales geographically*

7. You can also use the Rows, Columns, and Background dimensions to change choices—double-clicking any of these dimensions will bring you to the familiar Select Items tree.

8. Finally, you can publish a Decomposition tree to a briefing book for publishing or review later.

Exercise 9-5. Creating a Perspective View

1. Click the View menu ➤ Advanced Analysis Tools ➤ Perspective to open the Perspective wizard.

2. Click Next to bypass the first information page.

3. On the "Select the items you wish to analyze" page, scroll down—if any dimension has a selection, select it, click the Change Selection button, and then select Default.

4. Select Product Categories and click the Change Selection button. Right-click Product to open the context menu, and then select Select Descendants and click Product.

5. Click OK, and then check again that the only entry in the Selected Items column is Product of All Products. Click Next.

6. Set the y axis to Reseller Gross Profit and ensure that the x axis is set to Reseller Sales Amount.

7. Click Finish. You should see a chart as in Figure 9-42.

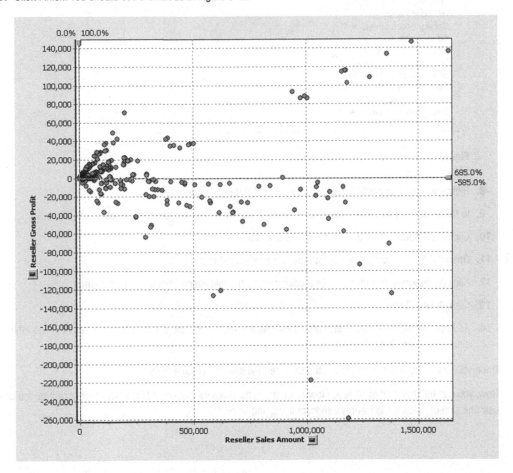

Figure 9-42. *A perspective view of reseller sales*

This shows a layout of gross profit vs. sales amount for each product sold by a reseller. We can now identify products that produce a good profit for resellers, as well as products that sell well. If a product produces a negative gross profit for a reseller, but we still wish to sell it, we can couple it with something above the line that has a higher profit and sells well. To identify what each dot represents, mouse over the marker (Figure 9-43).

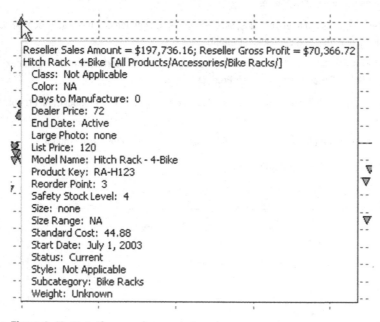

Figure 9-43. *Details on a data point*

8. Right-click the perspective chart, and then select Data Point Attributes.

9. In the Data Point Attributes dialog, open Product, and then click Product Categories.

10. Click the Select Items tab at the top of the selector.

11. Open the All Products node and note the four product categories.

12. Click Accessories, and then choose a color and the triangle shape from the center column.

13. Click the Add button.

14. Add each of the three remaining categories with a distinct color and shape, which will result in something similar to Figure 9-44. Click OK.

Once you've clicked OK, you should see the chart redraw similar to Figure 9-45.

Now, you can tell that a lot of bikes are low-profit items for resellers, but some bikes have higher profits. You can use this kind of guidance to identify trends, outliers, and so on.

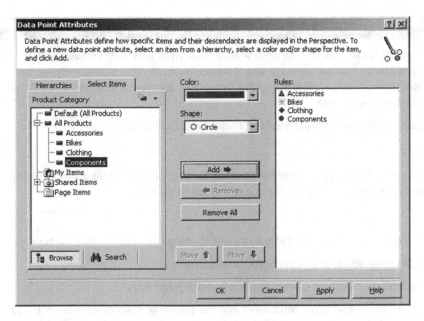

Figure 9-44. *Setting the data point attributes for the product categories*

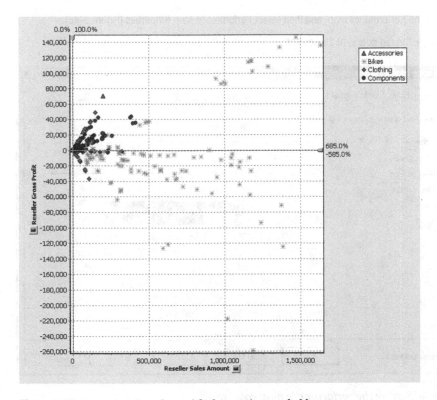

Figure 9-45. *A perspective view with data points coded by category*

Exercise 9-6. Creating a Performance Map

1. From your perspective view, click the View menu ➤ Advanced Analysis Tools ➤ Performance Map. The perspective view will switch to a heat map–style view of the data we've laid out. You can already see some interesting things here as certain values pop out (the Touring 1000 is losing our resellers a mint!). But let's shift to look at something different.

2. Under All Measures, click Sales Amount, and then Ctrl-click Gross Profit Margin.

Note You select your measures by selecting one measure, and then Ctrl-clicking the second. The first measure you select will be the size of the regions; the second will be the color.

---

3. Click the Apply button. You've now switched to a view of profit margin vs. sales, but this is too busy.

4. Double-click the Rows text box to open the Product dimension selector.

5. Right-click All Products, click Select Descendants, and then click Subcategory.

6. Click the Apply button. Now we have a performance map, but it looks like all our products are in the red, which can't be good. However, mousing over the various regions shows a lot of positive profit margins. The scale is probably off, so let's fix it.

7. Right-click the performance map, and then select Performance Map Properties (Figure 9-46).

   Sure enough, the red cuts in at 25 percent.

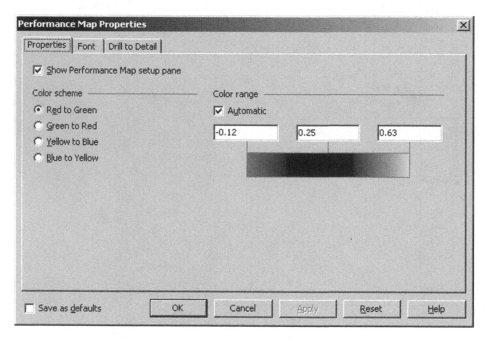

Figure 9-46. *Setting the performance map color range*

8. Set the center point to 0.0 so that green is positive and red is negative. Click OK.

Now we have a great chart that shows us what categories have high sales and good profit margins, and where we might be able to focus efforts with maximum effect. For example, while mountain bikes have $35 million in sales and a 16 percent profit margin, road bikes have $43 million in sales, but only a 10 percent profit margin—perhaps we can get the head of the road bike group to talk to the mountain bike group and increase his margins?

Also, we now see one area of bright red—Jerseys (Figure 9-47). With three quarters of a million in sales, we face a 12 percent loss on every jersey sold. It's worth investigating if we absolutely have to carry this product line (perhaps a bike store that doesn't sell jerseys loses business?), and if maybe we should pair jerseys with a high-profit product to offset the loss.

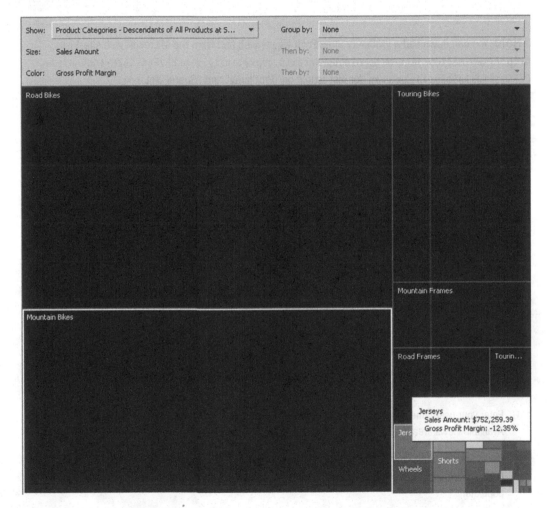

Figure 9-47. *Underperforming category in the product line*

But to reiterate the main theme again, this one performance map represents millions of lines of sales data—yet with a single glance, we can identify new initiatives to improve our business.

ProClarity and SharePoint

Now that we've created these views, we want to share them. I often say "business intelligence doesn't exist in a vacuum"—by hosting ProClarity business intelligence charts on interactive SharePoint pages, you enable users to add unstructured content around the chart—action items, amplifying documentation in document libraries, threaded discussions, points of contact, and so on.

We have Web Standard for users to view reports when they choose to, and we'll look at PerformancePoint to integrate ProClarity views into dashboards. However, there are also ways to display ProClarity visualizations in SharePoint natively.

■**Note** You can download a ProClarity SharePoint viewer web part from the Microsoft web site. Visit http://www.microsoft.com/downloads/details.aspx?familyid=A6EE7F46-D625-4A49-B717-CEFC11F1232A&displaylang=en (or just search on "ProClarity" and "SharePoint").

Exercise 9-7. Using ProClarity with SharePoint

1. Download and unzip the package. The (rather arcane) installation instructions are included in a PDF.

■**Note** This exercise is just a thumbnail sketch of adding a web part here. If you need help understanding using SharePoint, I recommend *SharePoint 2007 User's Guide*, by Seth Bates and Tony Smith (Apress, 2007).

---

2. To add the web part to a SharePoint page (WSS 3.0 or MOSS 2007), click the Site Actions tab on the site, and then click Edit Page.

3. Click the Add a Web Part bar, check the box for ProClarity Web Part, and then click the Add button.

4. Open the tool pane, which will look like Figure 9-48.

5. Enter the URL for PAS. (If you've done the single-machine install from this chapter's walkthrough, then http://localhost:8080/PAS should work.)

6. Enter your username and password, and then click the Login button. Your demo library should now be in the Available views area.

7. Click the library, and then click the Briefing Book. You can choose any of the views you've created.

8. Once you've selected a view, click Apply at the bottom of the tool pane, and you should see the view populate.

9. Open the ProClarity View Options for some additional options to control the view (such as interactivity).

10. Click OK to close the tool pane. Now you've got a ProClarity view on your SharePoint page (Figure 9-49).

Figure 9-48. *Configuring the ProClarity web part in SharePoint*

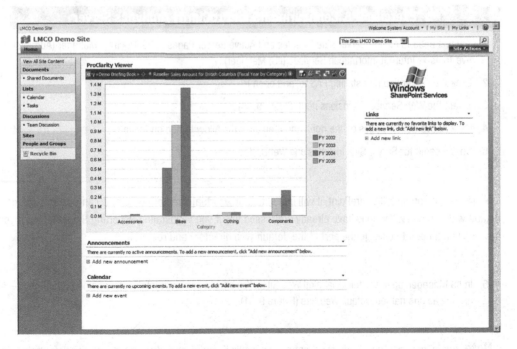

Figure 9-49. *A ProClarity view on a SharePoint site*

Installing ProClarity Analytics Server

Our base machine is Windows Server 2003, SP 2, with the .NET Framework 2.0 installed. You will need access to SQL Server 2008 or 2005 SP 2 as a relational store, as well as Analysis Services and Reporting Services. Finally, we'll use Microsoft Office SharePoint Server 2007 (although WSS 3.0 would be fine) for SharePoint integration, although it's not used otherwise.

Caution Beware installing PAS on a 64-bit (x64) machine. PAS requires IIS to be in 32-bit mode, and on Windows Server 2003, IIS can only be in one mode for the entire server (in Windows 2008 x64, IIS can run separate application pools as either 32 bit or 64 bit). So if you have installed SharePoint, SQL Server Reporting Services, or any other web application in 64-bit mode, and then you install PAS on the same box, it will force IIS into 32-bit mode (after a warning prompt), and your other applications will cease working. If you have a 64-bit environment, this more than anything is a good reason to install PAS on its own box.

In Exercise 9-8, you'll set up IIS for PAS. You'll have to be sure you've configured a few settings correctly for the installation to succeed. Then in Exercise 9-9, you ensure SQL Server is configured correctly (most notably that it must be in mixed mode authentication for PAS to install correctly). Exercise 9-10 covers the actual installation of PAS, and finally, in Exercise 9-11, you'll run the PAS administration console to configure PAS for your first use. By the time you finish all four exercises, you'll have everything you need to start building charts on PAS!

Exercise 9-8. Configuring IIS for ProClarity Analytics Server

1. You will need to enable Server Side Includes and Active Server Pages in IIS. Open IIS Manager (Administrative Tools ➤ Internet Information Services (IIS) Manager).

2. Click the server you're installing PAS to, and open it.

3. Select the Web Service Extensions item (Figure 9-50).

4. Click Active Server Pages on the right, and then click the Allow button on the left.

5. Do the same for Server Side Includes and WebDAV.

Note When you install SharePoint, it will install to a new virtual directory on port 80 and disable the default web directory. You may have already addressed this if you've installed Reporting Services, but if you haven't, you'll need to change the port of the default web directory and restart it.

---

6. In IIS Manager, open the folder labeled Web Sites. You should see a virtual directory named SharePoint – 80, as well as one named Default Web Site (Figure 9-51).

Note Again, you may have a different setup, especially if you've already worked with the default directory to enable Reporting Services.

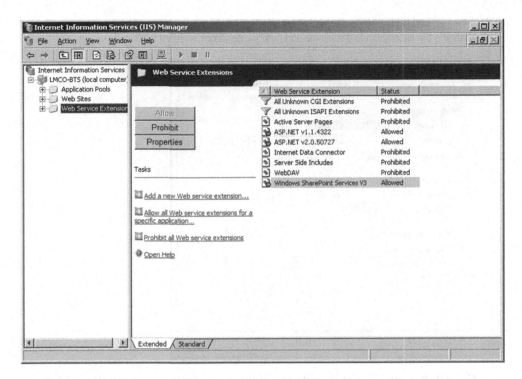

Figure 9-50. *Opening IIS Manager*

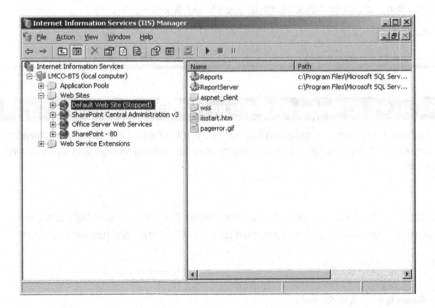

Figure 9-51. *Web sites in IIS*

7. Right-click Default Web Site, and then click Properties.

8. If the TCP port is 80, change it to something else (I generally use 81, 8080, or 8100). I also recommend changing the description to display the port number, as shown in Figure 9-52.

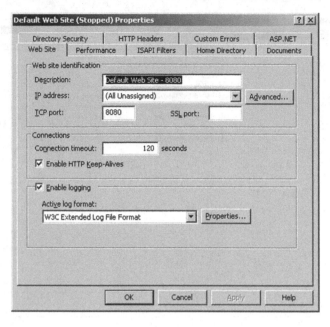

Figure 9-52. *Reconfiguring the default web site properties*

9. Click the OK button, and then right-click the default web site and click Start.

10. Close IIS Manager.

Exercise 9-9. Configuring SQL Server for ProClarity Analytics Server

The only thing you have to worry about in configuring SQL Server is that it is running in mixed-mode authentication. If this conflicts with your standards for SQL Server security, use a separate server or at least a new instance of SQL Server for PAS.

■**Note** *Do not* change this setting on a production database server if you're not sure what you are doing. Mixed-mode authentication enables username/password access to SQL Server and has serious security ramifications.

---

1. Open SQL Server Management Studio.

2. Right-click the server you wish to configure, and then click Properties.

3. In the Server Properties dialog, select Security from the left-hand selector (Figure 9-53).

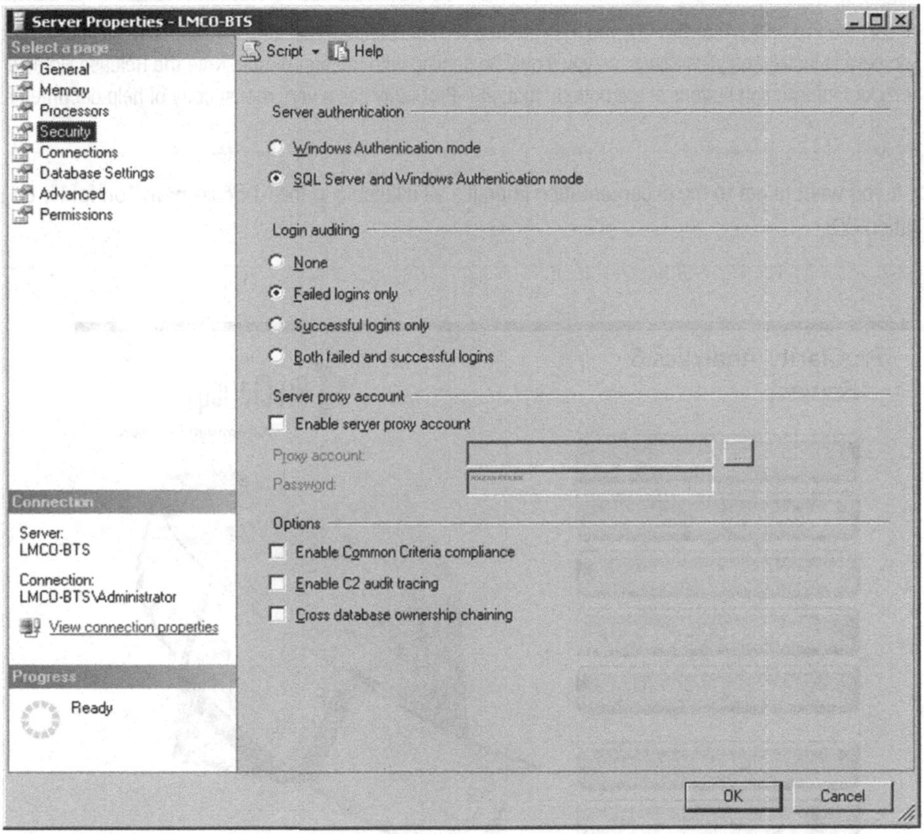

Figure 9-53. *Configuring SQL Server for mixed-mode authentication*

4. Under "Server authentication," select "SQL Server and Windows Authentication mode," and then click OK.

   Now you need to enable the sa user and set the password. (If you have already enabled the sa user and know the password, you can skip down to Exercise 9-10.)

5. Open the tree for the server you just configured, and then the Security node, and finally "Logins."

6. Find the sa user, right-click the user, and click Properties.

7. Assign a password and verify the password. (Use strong password conventions: longer than eight characters, mixed case, and at least one digit and one symbol.)

8. Uncheck "Enforce password policy." (I'm not sure why, but I've generally had problems installing PAS when this check box was checked. So I uncheck it.)

9. Finally, click the Status page for the login. Select "Grant" for "Permission to connect to database engine" and "Enabled" for "Login." Click OK.

10. If you need to restart SQL Server due to changing the authentication type, do it now.

Exercise 9-10. Installing ProClarity Analytics Server

1. Insert the ProClarity Analytics CD; you'll be greeted with the welcome screen (Figure 9-54). All you're going to do here is install Analytics Server, so you'll only be dealing with the first button. Note the Release Notes and Product Information buttons at the bottom, though—ProClarity has a very robust body of help documents.

Tip If you want to get to the documentation later, it's all available in the \Documentation folder on the installation CD.

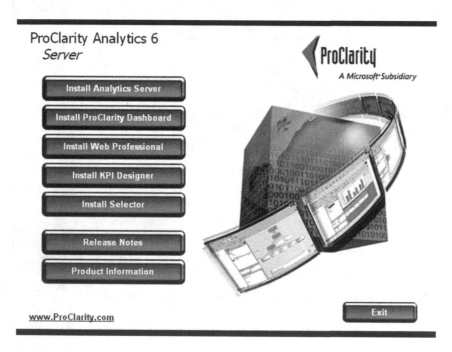

Figure 9-54. *PAS welcome screen*

2. Click the Install Analytics Server button to start the installation routine.

3. The first screen in the installer is the licensing agreement; read the agreement, and if you agree to it, click Next.

4. The next screen (Figure 9-55) offers the options of installing the full Analytics server or just the administration tool (you may want to install the admin tool on a workstation later). Select "Full product," and then click Next.

5. The next page allows you to name the virtual directory: accept the default name of PAS, and then click Next.

6. The following page provides for selecting the location of the install files. Again, I recommend accepting the default and clicking Next.

7. The next page allows you to select the database server and instance for the PAS configuration database (where briefing books and credentials will be stored—not where the data for analysis is located). You also enter the sa password here. Click Next.

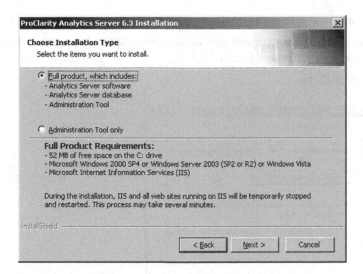

Figure 9-55. *Selecting the installation type*

■Tip If you run into issues here, ensure that SQL Server is in mixed mode and you have the correct password for the sa user.

---

8. The next page (Figure 9-56) allows you to set up the Analytics Server database. You can create a new database and name it (I recommend the default here), and you also have the options of setting up an additional Analytics server for use with an existing database.

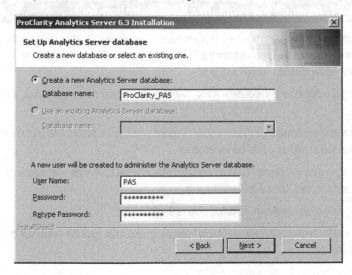

Figure 9-56. *Setting up the Analytics Server database*

9. The PAS installer also creates a user and adds the user to the database. Set the username and password here, and click Next.

10. Finally, you'll be presented with a screen to review the installation options. Click the Install button to proceed.

11. If everything has gone well up to this point, you should get a success screen (Figure 9-57). Your next step is to run the administration tool to set up users and security.

12. Click the Run Administration Tool button.

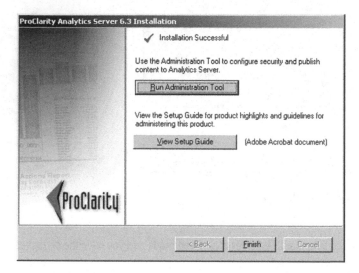

Figure 9-57. *Successfully completing the Analytics Server installation*

Exercise 9-11. Running the ProClarity Administration Tool

1. Open the ProClarity Analytics Server Administration tool. This will happen automatically after you click the Run Administration Tool button. You can also open it from the Start menu by choosing All Programs ➤ ProClarity ➤ Analytics Server Administration Tool (Figure 9-58).

2. You may be prompted for login credentials immediately; if not, then click the server name, right-click, and click Refresh.

3. The login credentials are the user credentials you were logged in under when you installed PAS (*not* the PAS username and password that you set up as a SQL Server account).

4. Browse around the folders. Note that you already have an Administrator role set up—your user account is set up in the Users folder and mapped to the Administrator role.

5. Double-click your user to open the user preferences dialog (Figure 9-59).

6. Check the boxes labeled Allow Professional Access and Allow Publishing, and then click OK—this will give you access to Web Professional.

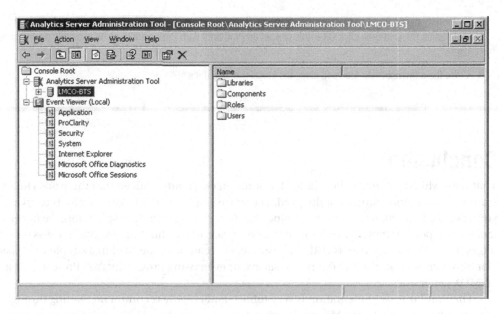

Figure 9-58. *The ProClarity Analytics Server Administration tool*

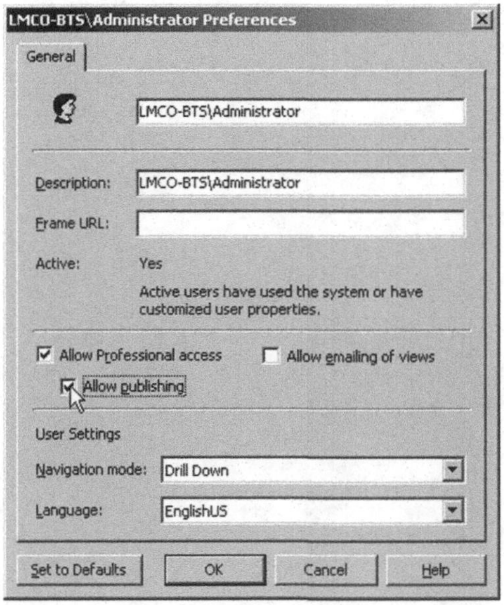

Figure 9-59. *Setting user permissions*

The other thing you want to do here is add Web Professional for download.

7. Right-click the components folder, and then click New Component.

8. In the new dialog that opens, browse to \Install\WebProfessional\WebProfessional.xml on the installation CD, and then click OK—this will set up ProClarity Web Professional as an available download for users.

9. Close the administration tool, and close the installer dialog if it's still open.

Conclusion

That's our whirlwind tour of ProClarity. I'm sure you've already noticed that there are a lot of features, nooks, and crannies in the product that we just blew by. My goal, again, is to give you a simple familiarization and a running start to really dig into the application. We haven't looked at exporting ProClarity charts to Reporting Services or hosting ProClarity views on web pages (every ProClarity view is URL addressable, so it can be embedded in a simple web page). Nor have I covered ProClarity filters and slicers, or even using ProClarity Web Professional as an MDX generator.

The ProClarity documentation is very robust, and I highly recommend reading through it, as well as the content on the Microsoft web site.

Now let's take a look at where all this has been leading us—scorecards, dashboards, and pervasive business intelligence. We're going to start with the dashboard capabilities of PerformancePoint Server in Chapter 10.

■ ■ ■

CHAPTER 10

PerformancePoint Monitoring

$\mathbf{A}$nd now we come to the big show . . . We've pulled our data together, put it into a cube, mined it, twisted it, reported on it, printed it, folded, spindled, mutilated . . .

The question is, how do we get value out of all this information? Reports are great, but when we're talking about gigabytes of data, we can't peruse all the reports necessary to understand what's going on.

So we use a scorecard.

Scorecards

A lot of organizations today have scorecards, but they track them in Excel (Figure 10-1) or PowerPoint. While the organizational move toward keeping a scorecard is a plus, the effort required to keep the scorecard up-to-date can often be daunting. (I know of organizations that spend literally ten or more man-days per month keeping their scorecards updated.)

Consider that such an organization usually has to

- Get reports submitted from various departments (via e-mail)

- Comb through the reports, make sure they're all received, and contact folks who are tardy with their reports

- Validate the reported data

- Copy the data from the reported format to some input format (usually an input spreadsheet), manipulating it as necessary

- Get the reporting values for the scorecard

- Put the scorecard report together for presentation to an executive board

You'll note that these first steps pretty much align with the BI services we've talked about in SQL Server (get data, clean data, aggregate data, process data). We can obviate much of the manual process by setting up ETL jobs in Integration Services, loading the data into cubes, and producing reports.

All we're missing is the all-up executive summary view, a view generally represented by a scorecard, an example of which is shown in Figure 10-2. Here we get an overview of the gross profit margin for resellers over four quarters in several states. While just looking at the numbers for these 17 states (just imagine looking at 50) over four quarters or longer would make it difficult to pull out the underperforming districts, this scorecard quickly and easily shows us that we need to focus on California and Colorado, while keeping an eye on Connecticut and South Dakota.

This still may look fairly simplistic, and prompt the question as to why you can't just get a "worst five" report or something similar. You could, but individual transactional reports still don't give a situational awareness of the organization. In the preceding scorecard, you can tell at a glance not only which states aren't performing, but that most states *are* performing. You can also see trends over time.

And that's just for 17 states. What about a more complex geography? Figure 10-3 shows four countries, and Figure 10-4 shows the countries opened up to show their subordinate regions.

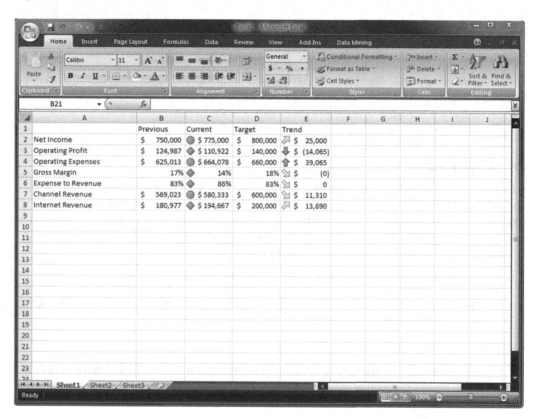

Figure 10-1. *A scorecard in Excel*

	Q1 FY 2003		Q2 FY 2003		Q3 FY 2003		Q4 FY 2003	
	Actual	Target	Actual	Target	Actual	Target	Actual	Target
⊟ Gross Profit Margin								
Arizona	11.42%	4.00%	10.77%	4.00%	10.67%	4.00%	10.87%	4.00%
California	2.59%	4.00%	3.87%	4.00%	2.69%	4.00%	3.58%	4.00%
Colorado	2.32%	4.00%	3.67%	4.00%	2.45%	4.00%	3.62%	4.00%
Connecticut	3.95%	4.00%	5.55%	4.00%	3.92%	4.00%	6.41%	4.00%
Florida	3.16%	4.00%	6.66%	4.00%	4.73%	4.00%	6.88%	4.00%
Georgia	10.74%	4.00%	10.56%	4.00%	10.36%	4.00%	11.20%	4.00%
Kentucky	13.05%	4.00%	12.96%	4.00%	13.17%	4.00%	20.71%	4.00%
Maine	0.76%	4.00%	6.72%	4.00%	7.84%	4.00%	7.79%	4.00%
Michigan	4.06%	4.00%	5.68%	4.00%	4.74%	4.00%	4.43%	4.00%
Mississippi	11.65%	4.00%	12.84%	4.00%	11.80%	4.00%	10.90%	4.00%
Nevada	10.71%	4.00%	9.17%	4.00%	7.12%	4.00%	8.67%	4.00%
New York	6.33%	4.00%	6.71%	4.00%	6.55%	4.00%	6.52%	4.00%
Oregon	7.27%	4.00%	7.45%	4.00%	5.51%	4.00%	6.49%	4.00%
South Carolina	11.87%	4.00%	10.72%	4.00%	10.63%	4.00%	10.87%	4.00%
South Dakota	7.50%	4.00%	11.31%	4.00%	1.30%	4.00%	8.61%	4.00%
Utah	9.71%	4.00%	9.97%	4.00%	8.41%	4.00%	9.99%	4.00%
Wyoming	9.80%	4.00%	10.42%	4.00%	9.41%	4.00%	10.09%	4.00%

Figure 10-2. *A scorecard to show profit margin at a glance*

	Q1 FY 2003		Q2 FY 2003		Q3 FY 2003		Q4 FY 2003	
	Actual	Target	Actual	Target	Actual	Target	Actual	Target
⊟ Gross Profit Margin								
⊞ Canada	4.06%	4.00%	4.79%	4.00%	3.76%	4.00%	4.34%	4.00%
⊞ France	1.64%	4.00%	4.54%	4.00%	4.75%	4.00%	4.69%	4.00%
⊞ United Kingdom	5.33%	4.00%	5.63%	4.00%	4.59%	4.00%	5.68%	4.00%
⊞ United States	3.79%	4.00%	4.48%	4.00%	3.51%	4.00%	4.36%	4.00%

Figure 10-3. *A scorecard showing multiple countries*

	Q1 FY 2003		Q2 FY 2003		Q3 FY 2003		Q4 FY 2003	
	Actual	Target	Actual	Target	Actual	Target	Actual	Target
⊟ Gross Profit Margin								
⊟ Canada	4.06%	4.00%	4.79%	4.00%	3.76%	4.00%	4.34%	4.00%
Alberta	11.56%	4.00%	10.93%	4.00%	10.61%	4.00%	11.32%	4.00%
British Columbia	1.12%	4.00%	4.31%	4.00%	3.79%	4.00%	3.88%	4.00%
Ontario	4.12%	4.00%	4.33%	4.00%	3.05%	4.00%	3.44%	4.00%
⊟ France	1.64%	4.00%	4.54%	4.00%	4.75%	4.00%	4.69%	4.00%
Essonne	4.10%	4.00%	7.50%	4.00%	-0.90%	4.00%	26.00%	4.00%
Hauts de Seine	-1.20%	4.00%	3.92%	4.00%	9.88%	4.00%	8.26%	4.00%
Loiret	6.29%	4.00%	6.57%	4.00%	7.02%	4.00%	7.39%	4.00%
⊟ United Kingdom	5.33%	4.00%	5.63%	4.00%	4.59%	4.00%	5.68%	4.00%
England	5.33%	4.00%	5.63%	4.00%	4.59%	4.00%	5.68%	4.00%
⊞ United States	3.79%	4.00%	4.48%	4.00%	3.51%	4.00%	4.36%	4.00%

Figure 10-4. *Opening up the scorecard to show subordinate regions*

Now we can drill down into countries to see how their reseller regions are doing. If you start to multiply this out, it comes to dozens of countries and hundreds of regions, but it's still very easy to visually assess overall performance and identify underperforming regions.

Figure 10-5 shows a different way of breaking down a scorecard—instead of focusing on trends over time, we're comparing a metric (gross product margin, or GPM) across product categories and geographic areas.

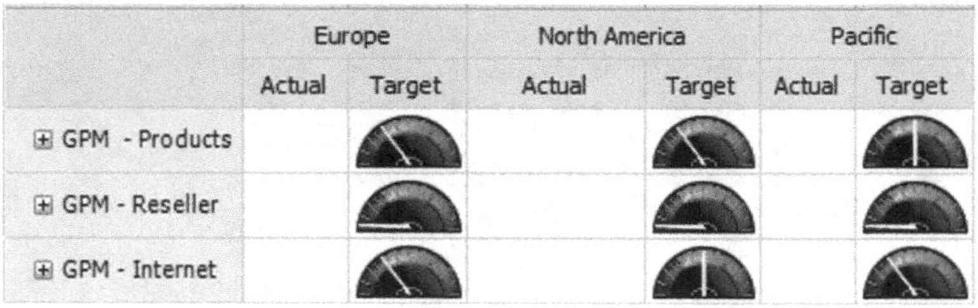

	Europe		North America		Pacific	
	Actual	Target	Actual	Target	Actual	Target
⊞ GPM - Products		🎚		🎚		🎚
⊞ GPM - Reseller		🎚		🎚		🎚
⊞ GPM - Internet		🎚		🎚		🎚

Figure 10-5. *A gauge-style scorecard showing product margins*

Note Previously, I dismissed the use of gauges as visual indicators. Here I'm simply using them to show a general degree—the gauges are just five-position graphics, as opposed to any attempt to show an actual value. They could be any other graphic that gives a general visual cue as to a qualitative value—stoplights, smiley faces, and so on.

Again, we can choose to drill into an area simply by clicking the plus sign next to it (Figure 10-6).

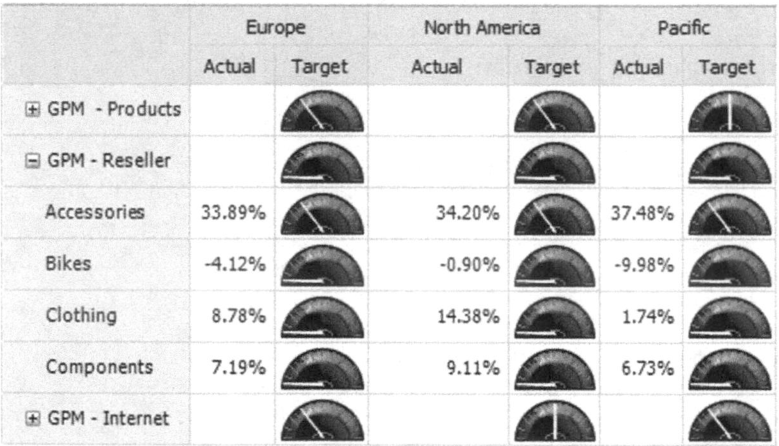

	Europe		North America		Pacific	
	Actual	Target	Actual	Target	Actual	Target
⊞ GPM - Products		🎚		🎚		🎚
⊟ GPM - Reseller		🎚		🎚		🎚
Accessories	33.89%	🎚	34.20%	🎚	37.48%	🎚
Bikes	-4.12%	🎚	-0.90%	🎚	-9.98%	🎚
Clothing	8.78%	🎚	14.38%	🎚	1.74%	🎚
Components	7.19%	🎚	9.11%	🎚	6.73%	🎚
⊞ GPM - Internet		🎚		🎚		🎚

Figure 10-6. *Opening up the GPM – Reseller area to see detail by product category*

And we can scan to see the areas where our product margin is underperforming. From here, we could drill further into individual products, looking at performance over time; identifying problems by region, country, and district; and so on.

We've stepped back from transactional reports to aggregating information in cubes, and then representing that information in scorecards that can be evaluated at a glance. However, this is all moving from the data outward—showing us what's happening in our organization. We want to drive what happens in our company; we have a strategy that we use to manage investment into the various areas that these indicators represent.

So how do we map that strategy to the KPIs?

Strategy Maps

Strategy maps were created by Robert Kaplan and David Norton (who created the balanced scorecard) as a way of mapping the KPIs, objectives, and perspectives in a scorecard to actual business strategy. They recognized that business strategy in business terms doesn't always map directly to the desired results indicated in a balanced scorecard; in addition, the actions needed to achieve performance in various perspectives may be contradictory (as a simplistic example, you could raise employee morale by giving everyone six months vacation a year, but then productivity would suffer).

The goal of a strategy map (Figure 10-7) is to show how business strategies can affect the perspectives and objectives in the scorecard. Note the arrows indicating interrelationships—factors that a manager must take into account before making significant changes in an organization's direction.

A cool feature of PerformancePoint is that if you draw your strategy map in Visio, you can import it as an associated report for a scorecard and even connect the strategy map shapes to related KPIs (Figure 10-8).

Last (but by no means least) is PerformancePoint's ability to associate report views with a scorecard. This dashboarding capability is the most exciting feature in PerformancePoint, because you can show contextual information to accompany a scorecard, hopefully empowering users to better understand the contents of the scorecard and get a feel for what is going on with a KPI aside from a simple score and icon (see Figure 10-9).

In this chapter, we're going to walk through installing PerformancePoint Monitoring Server, and then through building a scorecard. In Chapter 11, we'll look at some more advanced data-driven scorecards. In Chapter 12, we'll look at analytic reporting capabilities and building dashboards.

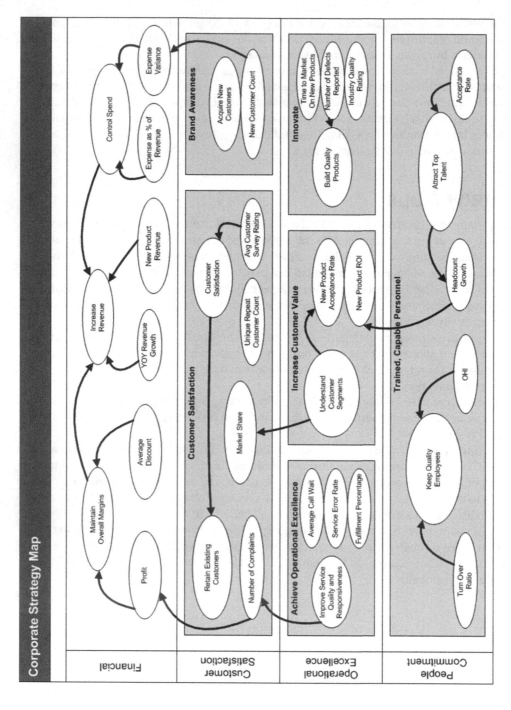

Figure 10-7. *A strategy map*

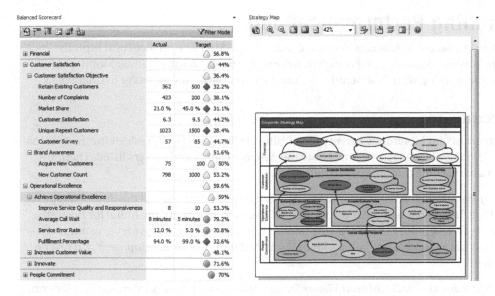

Figure 10-8. *A balanced scorecard with associated strategy map*

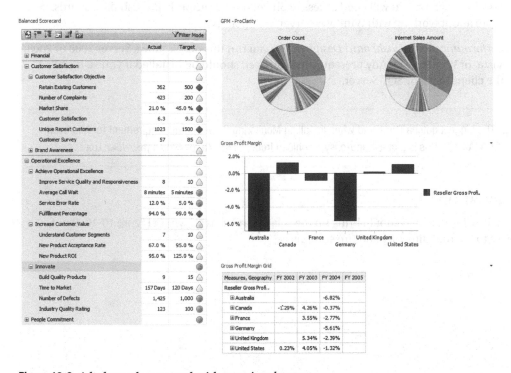

Figure 10-9. *A balanced scorecard with associated reports*

Installing PerformancePoint

Unlike its predecessor, Business Scorecard Manager (BSM), PerformancePoint is pretty straightforward to install. In this chapter, we're going to talk about installing Monitoring Server and working with Dashboard Designer. I'll cover the planning server in Chapter 13.

Prerequisites

PerformancePoint Monitoring Server prerequisites are listed at `http://technet.microsoft.com/en-us/library/bb821191.aspx`. You'll note the different clients and servers listed. There are three main machine roles to keep in mind:

PerformancePoint Monitoring Server: This is the server that does all the dashboard heavy lifting. It's the repository for the scorecards and dashboards, it's the home for the web services, and it does the processing necessary to display them. This server can run on Windows Server 2003, Windows XP, or Vista (the latter two for development and testing only).

PerformancePoint Dashboard Viewer for SharePoint: Our primary interface for Monitoring Server dashboards is SharePoint (either Microsoft Office SharePoint Server or WSS 3.0), so you will need a SharePoint server to view your dashboards. Since SharePoint only runs on Windows Server, you will need access to SharePoint to properly publish dashboards. (See more about working with Windows Server in Appendix A.)

PerformancePoint Dashboard Designer: You can run this on Windows Server 2003 or 2008, Vista, or Windows XP. Any prerequisites you need should be installed if you've installed the client tools for SQL Server.

Tip The biggest gotcha I've found when installing Monitoring Server is the requirement for Microsoft ASP.NET AJAX 1.0. This is a quick-and-easy download from `http://asp.net/ajax/downloads/`.

Installation

Insert the CD—Autorun should bring up the splash screen, as shown in Figure 10-10. If not, browse to the root directory and run `setup.hta`.

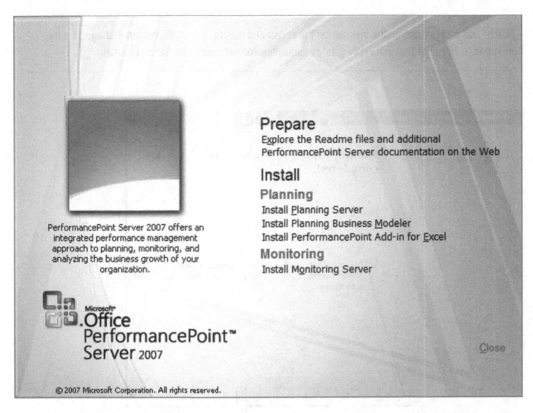

Figure 10-10. *The PerformancePoint splash screen*

Click Install Monitoring Server. Read the licensing terms and, if you agree, check the box for "I accept the license terms," and click Next. If you do not accept the terms, click the Cancel button and skip to Chapter 13.

The next screen is a standard directory selection screen. Choose a directory or accept the default, and click Next. Then click the Install button. The Monitoring Server installer will run, and then finish with the final screen (shown in Figure 10-11). Leave the Configuration Manager Wizard check box checked, and click Finish.

Note This part just stores the installer on the server and sets up the Configuration Manager. It's the Configuration Manager that will verify your prerequisites and get everything up and running.

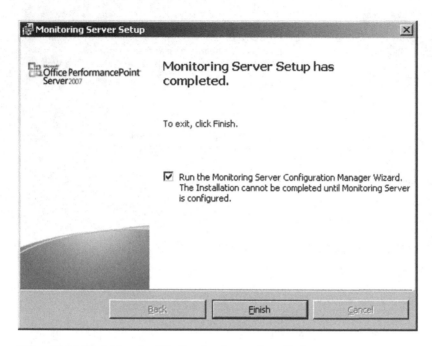

Figure 10-11. *Finishing the Monitoring Server installation*

The Monitoring Server Configuration Manager (Figure 10-12) walks through actually installing and configuring the server. To start, click the Next button.

The Configuration Manager will then verify the prerequisites for installing Monitoring Server. If a prerequisite is missing, you will see a report like Figure 10-13.

If you get an error on a prerequisite, you'll have to cancel out of the Configuration Manager, deal with the missing prerequisite, and rerun it. (Pressing Previous and then Next won't rerun the verifier.) You'll find the Configuration Manager on the Start Menu under Microsoft Office PerformancePoint Server 2007. Once you get a list of green check marks, click the Next button.

On the Installation Options page (Figure 10-14), you can select which components to install on the current server. We're going to walk through a single-server installation, so just select the "Standalone configuration" radio button, and click Next.

The next page (Figure 10-15) is where you set up the connection for the database store Monitoring Server will use for the scorecard and dashboard metadata. You can select a SQL Server instance from the drop-down or enter the server name. (Remember to use server\ instance if you're not using the default instance.) Give the database name, and then select whether you want the Configuration Manager to create the database or use an existing one to provision the tables and objects. After you've set this up, click Next.

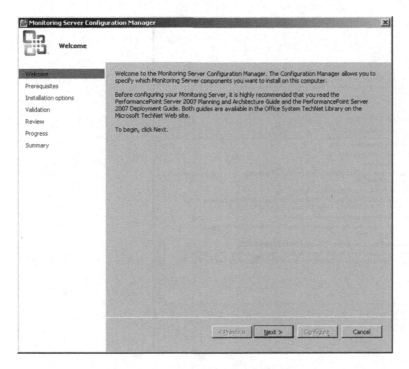

Figure 10-12. *Starting the Monitoring Server Configuration Manager*

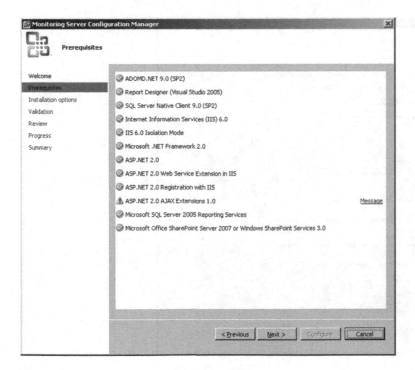

Figure 10-13. *Error report on the Prerequisites page*

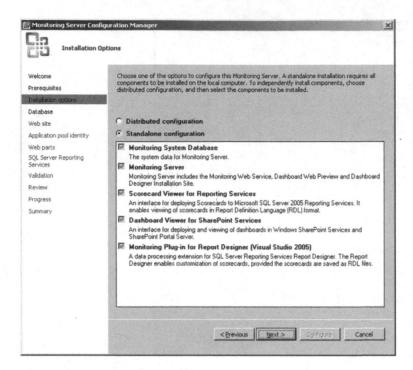

Figure 10-14. *Selecting which components to install*

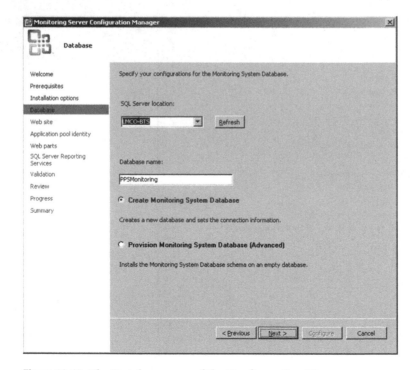

Figure 10-15. *The Database page of the Configuration Manager*

The next page (Figure 10-16) provisions the site for the Monitoring Server web site and web services. For the demo, we won't need SSL, so you can uncheck the "Require SSL connections to Monitoring Web site" check box, but I do recommend SSL for production use, and no way should you run PerformancePoint Server on a server exposed to the Internet over anything but SSL. The default unsecured port is 40000—accept that and leave the IP address as All Unassigned unless you already have a site or service on the IP address and port. Click Next when you've finished here.

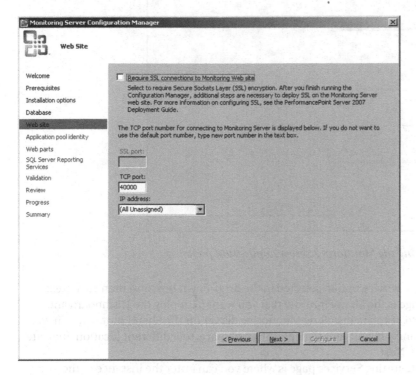

Figure 10-16. *Configuring the Monitoring Server web site*

The Application Pool Identity page (Figure 10-17) indicates which credentials the Monitoring Server application pool should use. This is critical, since this is the identity that will be used to communicate to SharePoint for publishing dashboards, and may be the identity used to connect to data sources.

■**Tip** For more information about application pools, read "Configuring Application Pools in IIS 6.0 (IIS 6.0)" on Microsoft TechNet. Considering the amount of interprocess and intermachine communication necessary in PerformancePoint, understanding application pools is critical.

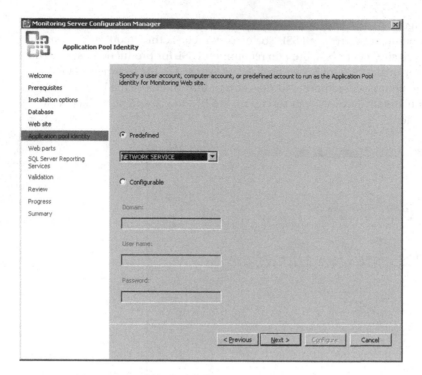

Figure 10-17. *Configuring the Monitoring Server application pool*

Leave the Network Service option selected in the drop-down box, and then click Next.

The Web Parts page is the SharePoint site that you want to deploy the Dashboard and Scorecard web parts to. If you're installing Monitoring Server on the SharePoint server, it will pick up the local instance. If you want to deploy the web parts to a different location, indicate so here, and then click Next.

The SQL Server Reporting Services page is where you can enter the instance of the Reporting Services server you want to deploy the Monitoring Server viewer to. Leave this as the default, and then click Next.

The Validation page (Figure 10-18) will verify all the settings you've entered and note any errors or warnings for you to deal with. If you have straight green checks, then click Next. Otherwise, review any errors—you may have to exit the Configuration Manager to correct them.

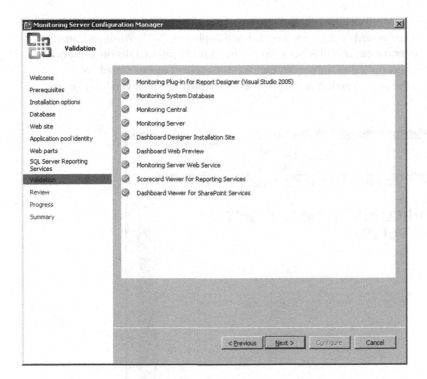

Figure 10-18. *Validating the settings for Monitoring Server*

The Review Options page shows all the actions that will take place when you click to the next page. Review all the parameters and ensure that everything looks satisfactory, and then click the Configure button. The Configuration Manager will run through all the configuration steps until you get an error or it's complete. Once you see the message "Configuration completed successfully," you can click Close.

Running Dashboard Designer

Once you have Monitoring Server installed, you will need to open Dashboard Designer. There are two ways to do this that pretty much accomplish the same thing:

- Open the Monitoring Central site under Start ➤ All Programs ➤ Microsoft Office PerformancePoint Server ➤ Monitoring Central.

- Open a browser and navigate to `http://server:40000/`, which will redirect to the Monitoring Central page.

Once you've opened Monitoring Central (Figure 10-19), click the Run button to open Dashboard Designer. Dashboard Designer is a click-once deployed .NET Windows Forms application. This means no local install is necessary—the application installs on demand. In addition, when a patch is applied to the server, the next time a user opens Dashboard Designer, they will get the latest version without having to deploy the new version to every desktop.

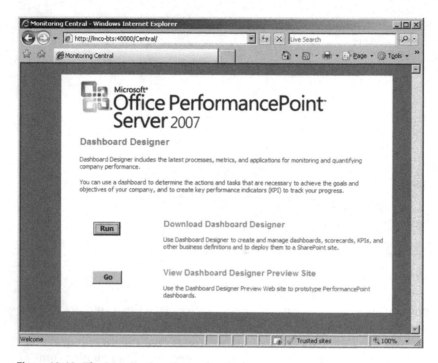

Figure 10-19. *The Monitoring Central web site*

Once you click Run, you may get a security warning like that shown in Figure 10-20. Click Run.

Figure 10-20. *The click-once installer security dialog*

This will download and install Dashboard Designer (13 MB), create a Start menu shortcut, and launch the designer (Figure 10-21). In the future, you can open the designer directly from the PerformancePoint menu.

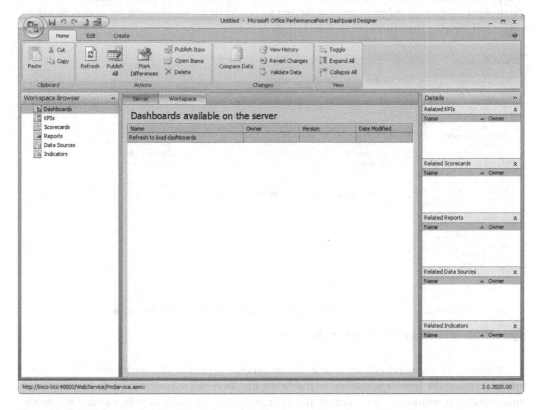

Figure 10-21. *PerformancePoint Dashboard Designer*

When you create data sources, scorecards, report views, or dashboards in the designer, you can save the workspace locally (as a BSWX file) and/or publish the contents to the server. BSWX files can be used to manage dev/test/production scenarios.

■**Tip** If you have used BSM 2005 previously and have BSW files from other projects, you can download a tool to migrate those scorecards to PerformancePoint from http://technet.microsoft.com/en-us/library/bb838761.aspx.

Tour of Dashboard Designer

First, we'll go over Dashboard Designer, and then we'll dig into KPIs, indicators, and score-cards, and how they interact.

Server vs. Workspace

Dashboard Designer is the editor for a dashboard workspace (saved as a BSWX file), and also provides an interface into the objects in the server repository (Figure 10-22). When the designer is connected to a server, selecting an object in the Workspace Browser offers the options of viewing the objects in the workspace or on the server.

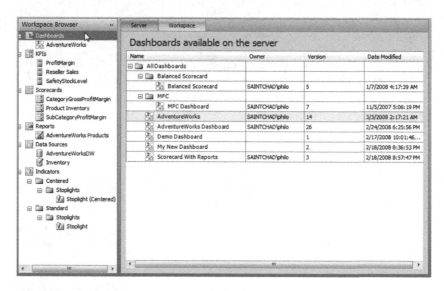

Figure 10-22. *Browsing dashboards on the server*

When you create and edit an item in the designer, it is part of the workspace. If you save the workspace, the item is just saved in the BSWX file. To make it available on the server, you must publish it, either by right-clicking the item and selecting Publish or by using the Publish All command.

The Fluent User Interface

Dashboard Designer uses the Fluent (or "ribbon") user interface introduced with Microsoft Office 2007. The tabs at the top break functionality down into broad areas, and the application changes tabs based on the context of what you're doing (e.g., switching to the Edit tab after you create a new dashboard item).

The Home tab (Figure 10-23) is pretty consistent across the various items you may have open. Some commands in the Home tab may be disabled if they are not appropriate for the current selection.

Figure 10-23. *The Home tab in Dashboard Designer*

Some of the commands on the Home tab include

Refresh: Synchronizes the server list in the designer with what is stored on the server.

Publish All: Publishes all changed items from the workspace to the server.

Mark Differences: Flags all items in the workspace that don't match (or aren't present on) the server.

Open Items: Opens an item in the workspace when you select an item. Open Items is only enabled in the Server view.

Compare Data: Opens a dialog showing the differences between the selected item in the workspace and the item on the server. Compare Data is only enabled when an item is selected in the Workspace Browser.

The contents of the Edit tab (Figures 10-24 and 10-25) vary depending on the type of object selected.

Figure 10-24. *The Edit tab for a scorecard*

Figure 10-25. *The Edit tab for a dashboard*

As you can see, when a scorecard is selected in the Workspace Browser, there are sections for formatting and for working with the editor. The Properties button will be active when an item is selected in the editor that has a properties dialog. The Update button is used to update the WYSIWYG view when editing the scorecard or underlying KPIs. And the SQL Server Reporting Services button opens a wizard to publish the scorecard to Reporting Services.

In the Edit tab for a dashboard, the two most notable buttons are Preview (for opening a preview of the dashboard rendered by Monitoring Server) and SharePoint Site (which opens a wizard to publish the dashboard to SharePoint).

Connecting to a Monitoring Server

The designer must be connected to a monitoring server to render WYSIWYG views of score-cards and to publish workspace items or dashboards. To connect to a monitoring server, click the Office button in the top left of the designer (Figure 10-26) to open a File menu.

Figure 10-26. *The Office button in Dashboard Designer*

Once you open the File menu, click the Options button at the bottom of the menu to open the Options dialog (Figure 10-27).

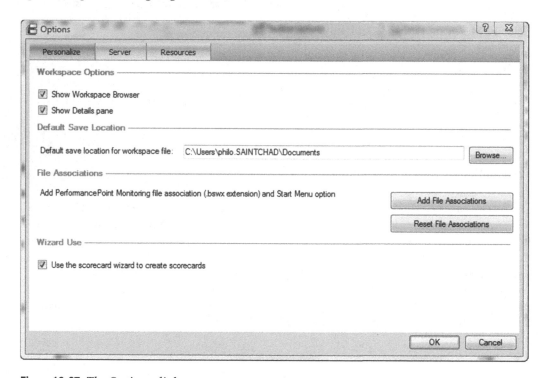

Figure 10-27. *The Options dialog*

The options on the Personalize tab are pretty straightforward. We're interested in the Server tab (Figure 10-28).

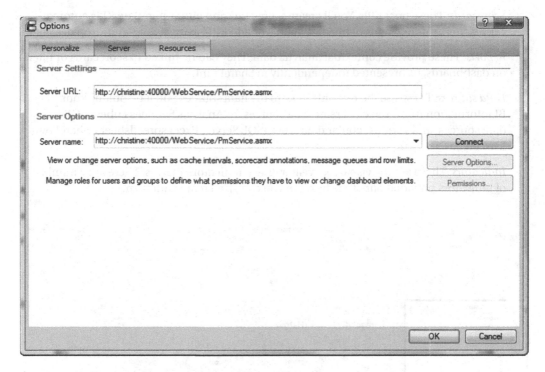

Figure 10-28. *The Server tab in the Designer Options dialog*

The server URL on this page is the server associated with the workspace. If you save a BSWX file and copy it to another network (e.g., to move from development to test), you'll have to change the setting here to point to the new monitoring server.

Under Server Options, you can enter the URL of a monitoring server, connect to it, and set various server options. In the Server Options dialog, you can set various settings and defaults. The most important setting to note here is the Microsoft Analysis Services Server name—until that's set, Trend Analysis reports won't work (they use the data mining engine in Analysis Services to perform the predictive analysis).

The Workspace Browser

The Workspace Browser is on the left-hand side of Dashboard Designer (see Figure 10-29). This shows all the items in the current workspace.

In the Workspace Browser, you'll see the items in a dashboard, which are described in the following list:

Dashboards: These are the main containers for PerformancePoint Monitoring Server. Dashboards are rendered as web part pages in SharePoint, containing scorecards, filters, and reports. Dashboards also allow linking filters to scorecards and reports, as well as linking scorecards to reports.

KPIs: These are, as mentioned previously, where the data meets the business. These are the items you'll use to define metrics, targets, and how they relate.

Scorecards: These host KPIs. You'll create scorecards and either populate KPIs automatically from the dimensions of the data source or add KPIs using a drag-and-drop designer.

Reports: These provide contextual analytic data. They can be linked to scorecards or filters on dashboards, or presented independently in SharePoint.

Data sources: These are the reusable links to the data sources you'll be pulling your BI information from. You can create data sources for Analysis Services cubes, ODBC data sources, and various tabular data types (SQL Server, Excel spreadsheets, SharePoint lists, etc.).

Indicators: These are the visual red/yellow/green indicators in KPIs. There are a number of indicators provided out of the box, but you can also create your own.

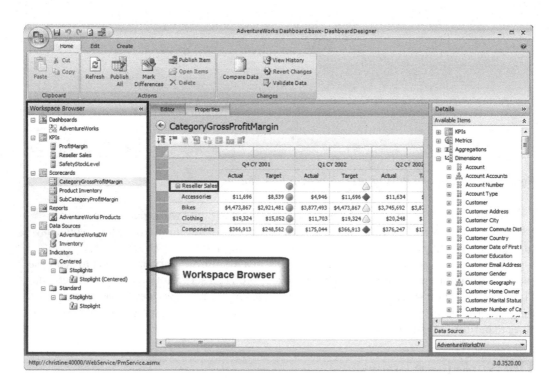

Figure 10-29. *The Workspace Browser in Dashboard Designer*

Editor and Properties

In the center area of Dashboard Designer are the Editor and Properties tabs. The Editor tab (Figure 10-30) is where you'll do most of your work building KPIs, reports, and dashboards. The Editor tab changes depending on what item you're working on—I'll cover those in more depth later in the chapter.

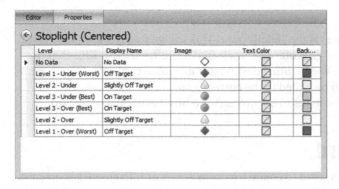

Figure 10-30. *The Editor tab in Dashboard Designer*

The Properties tab (Figure 10-31) is where you can set metadata and security permissions for the various dashboard items. If you want to change the name of an item, you can change it here (you can't rename items in the Workspace Browser). The Description and Person Responsible fields are basically informative, but can be displayed in the scorecard (more on this later).

The Custom Properties section allows you to create and maintain custom properties for the items in the workspace. However, only the custom properties for a KPI can be displayed in a dashboard without custom code. You can create a new custom property with the New Property button, and select from text, decimal, date, or hyperlink properties.

In the Permissions section, you can enter either users or domain security groups. The designer does verify the user name (although it doesn't provide any kind of lookup interface). Once you've entered a user or group, you can select either Editor or Reader for the role.

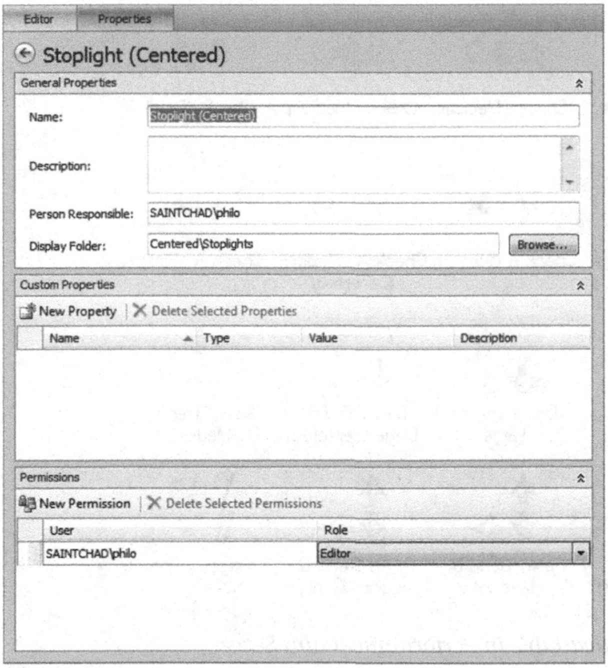

Figure 10-31. *The Properties tab in Dashboard Designer*

The Details Pane

On the right-hand side of the designer is the Details pane. This will generally show either a list of items related to the current item (e.g., scorecards a selected KPI is used in, or KPIs that use the currently selected data source). When editing dashboards and scorecards, the Details pane lists items in the workspace that can be added to the current item.

Now let's take a closer look at the items in a scorecard and build a manual scorecard.

Creating a Scorecard

Now we'll walk through the items required to create a manual scorecard. To create a scorecard, you need to import indicators, create one or more KPIs, and then create the scorecard. We'll go over data sources in Chapter 11, and building and publishing a dashboard in Chapter 12.

The scorecard we build here will also be used in Chapter 12 to illustrate connecting a scorecard to a strategy map.

Indicators

PerformancePoint comes with a library of sample indicators you can use in your scorecard (Figure 10-32). Alternatively, you can also create your own (perhaps some corporate branding or, as one executive I worked with wanted, a little skull and crossbones for "severely below target").

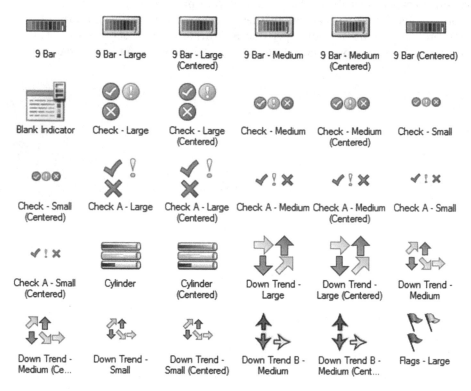

Figure 10-32. *Just some of the indicators available in PerformancePoint Server*

The three main types of indicators are the following:

Blank indicators: As their name implies, these are simple frames for creating your own indicators.

Centered indicators: These are indicators where the "green," or target, value is a specific value—either higher or lower is bad. For example, when considering spending to budget, spending either over or under the budget is off target.

Standard indicators: Standard indicators are the basic "one direction is good, the other direction is bad," red/yellow/green stoplights. The same indicator can be used for both "increasing is better" and "decreasing is better."

Under each of these categories, you'll find various types of indicators, from two-light stoplights to ten-segment progress bars. The only practical difference is being able to set thresholds for each option (two lights, three lights, ten segments, etc.). You'll also find indicators for trend arrows, which are just a special type of indicator.

Exercise 10-1 will walk you through the steps of adding an indicator.

Exercise 10-1. Adding an Indicator

1. Right-click the Indicators item in the Workspace Browser (on the left), and then select New Indicator from the context menu. This will open the Select an Indicator Template dialog (Figure 10-33).

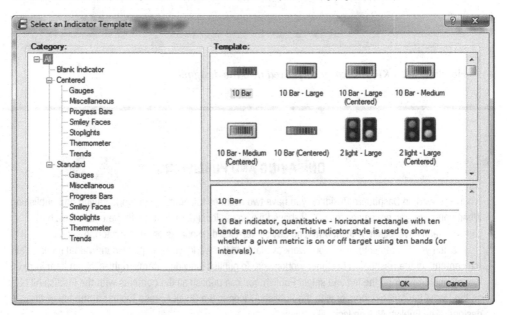

Figure 10-33. *Adding an indicator set to a workspace*

2. Under Standard, select Stoplights, and choose Stoplight from the Template pane on the right.

3. Click OK. This imports the indicator into the designer and shows the indicator levels in the editor (Figure 10-34). You can edit the display name by clicking and typing, and change the indicator image, text color, or background color by double-clicking.

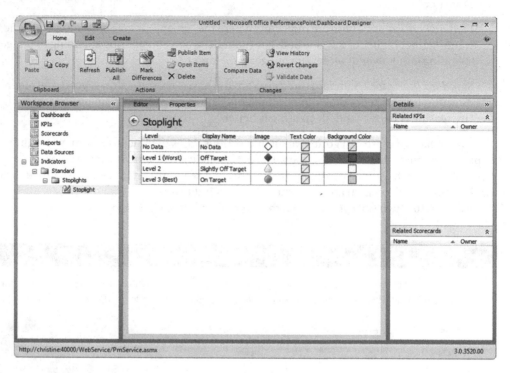

Figure 10-34. *A KPI indicator imported into the designer*

ON SAVING AND PUBLISHING

When you work in Dashboard Designer, you have two avenues to commit your work: saving and publishing. When you save, you are saving to an XML-based file on the local hard drive (with the extension .bswx). You can work and save locally without affecting any server-based resources on the monitoring server.

When you are ready to make your work available to the world, you can publish individual items or all the contents of the Dashboard Designer workspace. To publish individual items, right-click an item in the Workspace Browser on the left and select Publish. You can publish all the contents with the Publish All button on the Home tab of the ribbon, or with the Publish All icon in the Quick Access Toolbar at the top of the designer. The Publish All icon looks like this:

BSWX files also provide a good way to manage moving a scorecard from development to test and production—manage the file and publish to the appropriate server.

Alternatively, if you don't have access to the BSWX file, you can load a dashboard, scorecard, and other elements directly from the server—click Scorecards (for example) in the Workspace Browser and ensure that the Server tab is selected in the middle work area. Refresh the designer to get a list of the scorecards on the server. Double-click a scorecard to pull the scorecard, its KPIs, reports, data sources, and indicators into the current workspace.

Now that we have an indicator, let's look at what we can do with it.

KPIs

Of course, the KPI is the most important part of this whole exercise. The KPI is where the data of the business interfaces with the metrics and objectives of the business. KPIs in PerformancePoint Server scorecards have a single actual value and one or more target values. Figure 10-35 shows a KPI with an actual value ($25,000), a target value ($100,000), a target value indicator (the diamond shape, showing performance of the actual against the target), and a second target value indicator being used to indicate trending over time (the downward arrow).

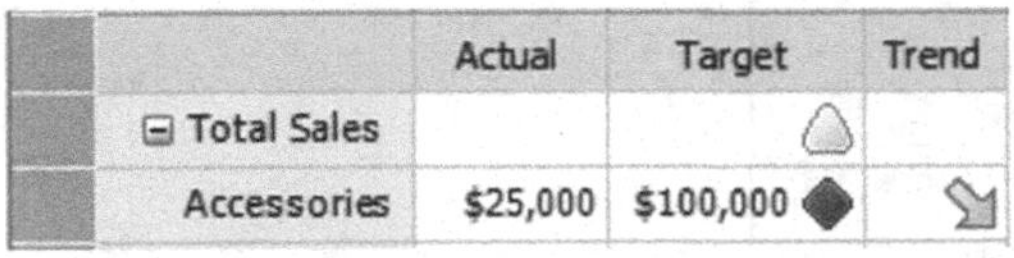

	Actual	Target	Trend
⊟ Total Sales		△	
Accessories	$25,000	$100,000 ◆	⬊

Figure 10-35. *A KPI in PerformancePoint Monitoring Server*

Actual values and target values can be data-driven or entered manually. The target value indicator can be driven by an algorithm measuring actual value against performance, or can be directly data-driven or manually set. Since the KPI is the most important part of our BI monitoring efforts, let's dig more deeply into the indicators.

Actual Values

The actual value for a KPI is fairly straightforward—it's simply a manually entered or data-driven numeric value. Figure 10-36 shows the designer for actuals and targets. For the actual value, you can format the number, set the data mapping (or enter a hand-keyed value), and indicate the rollup calculation.

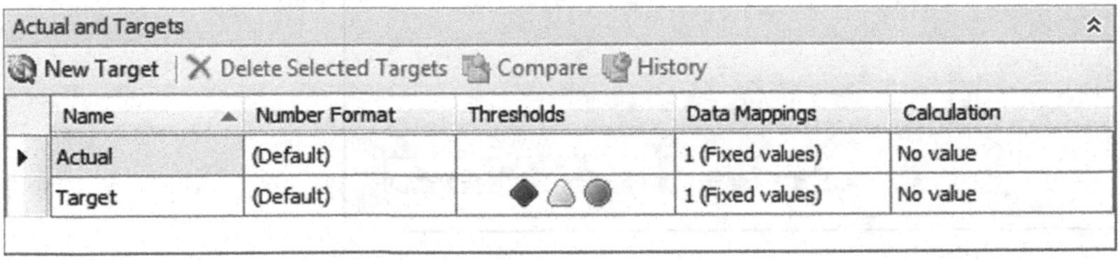

Actual and Targets   ⌃

🔲 New Target | ✕ Delete Selected Targets 🔲 Compare 🔲 History

	Name ▲	Number Format	Thresholds	Data Mappings	Calculation
▶	Actual	(Default)		1 (Fixed values)	No value
	Target	(Default)	◆ △ ⬤	1 (Fixed values)	No value

Figure 10-36. *Designing actual and target values in a KPI*

Dashboard Designer offers some basic formatting capabilities. Figure 10-37 shows the Format Numbers dialog. Here you can set the number of decimal places, indicate how to display negative numbers (–1 or (1)), indicate how to show zero, and indicate what tooltip to display. You can also put in a multiplier (mostly used for percentage) so that, for example, .75 would be displayed as 75 but still compare properly with targets. The Symbols options allow you to add any text to a display—for example, a currency sign on the left, and perhaps other units on the right (a percent sign, gallons/mile, loss per week, etc.).

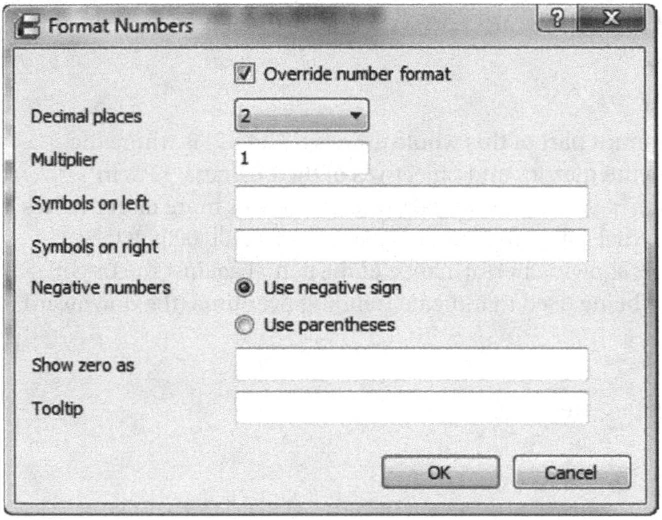

Figure 10-37. *The Format Numbers dialog*

The entries in the Data Mappings column indicate that both the actual value and the target value are manually entered (fixed values). The dialog box for this setting is shown in Figure 10-38. Here a user can enter the manual value for either the actual or target values. In addition, you can change the data mapping by clicking the button at the bottom of the dialog. (I'll cover data sources and data-driven KPIs in Chapter 11.)

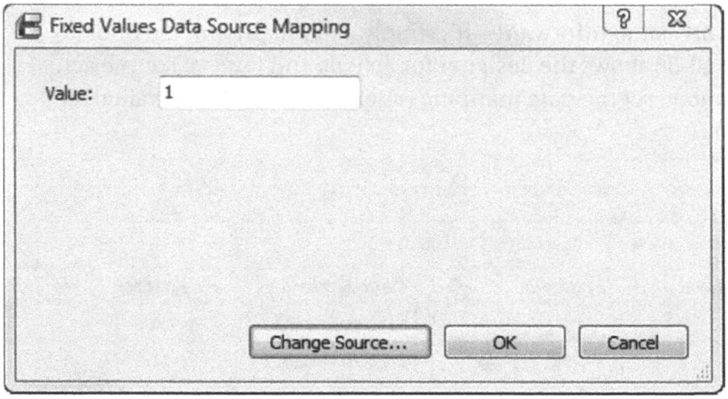

Figure 10-38. *Setting a fixed value*

That's pretty much it for actual values—they're just a readout of the current value of a KPI. The real scorecard work is done in targets, which map what the numbers are to what you want them to be.

Calculations

The final column is the Calculation column, which reflects how the values of child indicators can be rolled up into the current indicator (Figure 10-39).

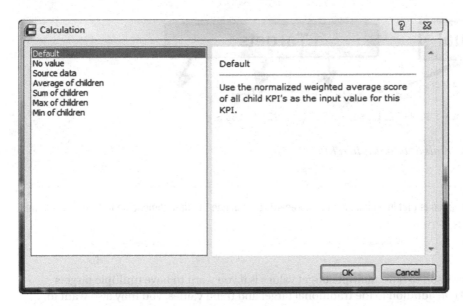

Figure 10-39. *Child calculations for actuals and targets*

These are used to determine how to roll child values up into a parent. KPIs in Performance-Point can be either parent or child, simply depending on how they are laid out in the scorecard. So when a KPI is put in position as a parent, this setting determines how the actual scores are rolled up.

The default option is that child values will be rolled up as a weighted average. In other words, if you just took a collection of KPIs, and put one as a parent and the rest as children underneath, the actual value you entered into the parent KPI would be "overlaid" by the weighted average of the actual values of the children.

■**Note** We'll explore weighting the values of KPIs when we return to our scorecard later in this chapter.

The next option, "No value," is useful if you have a motley collection of KPIs (e.g., one measures days, another percentages, and a third one cars per hour). Since you can't average those values, you would just blank the actual value of the parent. If instead you wanted to present the data-driven value as you entered/connected it, you could select "Source data." The rest of the calculation options are pretty much as they sound.

Targets

While a KPI in PerformancePoint can only have one actual value, it can have many targets. If you want to show the previous period's value, you can use a target and map it to the previous period's value (see Figure 10-40).

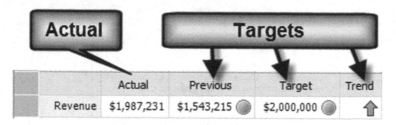

	Actual	Previous	Target	Trend
Revenue	$1,987,231	$1,543,215 ●	$2,000,000 ●	⬆

Figure 10-40. *Actuals and targets in a KPI*

■**Tip** One exception is that in a dimensional scorecard you can use the time dimension to show current and previous periods.

Another reason to have multiple target values is if you want to have multiple targets (Figure 10-41). In addition to the traditional target and trend values, you may also want to have short-term and long-term goals. For example, when a scorecard is implemented, the target may be 95 percent while the current value is 45 percent. Given this situation, the indicator will be red for a long time, which can lead to people simply ignoring it. To remedy this, you could add a short-term target of, say, 65 percent, which puts the indicator in the yellow. Once customer satisfaction is solidly green, you can move the target slowly quarter by quarter until the short-term target matches the corporate goal.

	Actual	FY 08 Target	Long Term Target	Trend
Revenue	$1,987,231	$2,000,000 △	$2,500,000 ◆	⬈

Figure 10-41. *A KPI showing multiple targets*

You add targets by clicking the New Target button at the top of the editor. The value of the target can again be either fixed or mapped to a data source—the "number" part of the target works just as it does for the actual value. You'll need to add an indicator if you want that stoplight or arrow.

Scoring Pattern and Indicator

What works differently is the indicator part of a target (the red/yellow/green light, the trend arrow, the gauge indicator, etc.). This is driven by the scoring pattern, the indicator, and the thresholds. Understanding this is key to understanding how your scorecard will work.

You configure the threshold values by selecting the box in the Thresholds column for the target; the Thresholds editing area at the bottom of the editor will show a "Set scoring pattern and Indicator" button, and may show your threshold selector if you've chosen one or one was selected by default (see Figure 10-42).

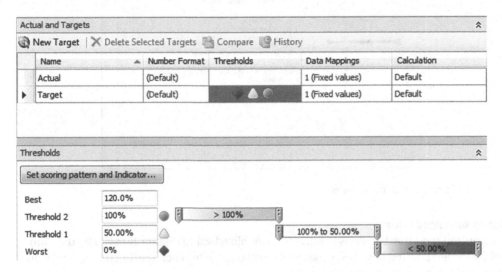

Figure 10-42. *Setting up a new target*

The indicator is configured by clicking the "Set scoring pattern and Indicator" button to open the Edit Banding Settings dialog (Figure 10-43). On the first page, you can select the scoring pattern. This sets up whether the indicator goes green when the actual value is greater than the target (Increasing is Better), when it is less than the target (Decreasing is Better), or when it gets closer to the target value (Closer to Target is Better).

■**Note** No, you can't change pages in the wizard by clicking the steps on the left; you have to use the Previous and Next buttons.

Recall that when we were looking at indicators to import, we had a choice between standard and centered. This is where that factors in—if you select either Increasing is Better or Decreasing is Better, you will only be able to choose from standard indicators in the workspace in the next step; if you select Closer to Target is Better, then you will only be able to select from centered indicators.

You will also select the banding method from the options of normalized value, numeric value of actual, and stated score. This is the lynchpin of the whole scorecard, and is critical to designing your KPIs correctly.

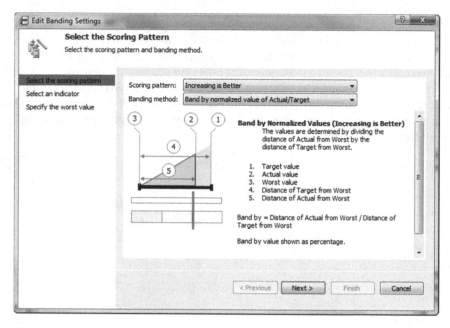

Figure 10-43. *Editing banding settings*

Banding by Normalized Value

The first option (and the default) is to band by normalized value (Figure 10-44). The diagram is critical for understanding how this works, and it will change for each scoring pattern. I'll walk through the Increasing is Better case.

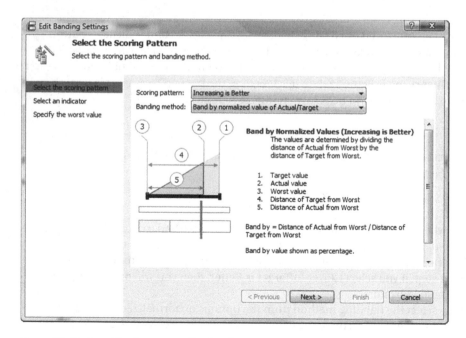

Figure 10-44. *Banding by normalized value*

Let's also look at the thresholds on a three-light indicator, as displayed in Figure 10-45 (the default values are shown).

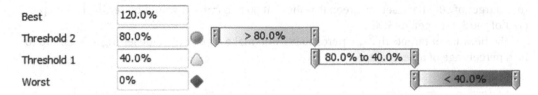

Figure 10-45. *Setting thresholds on an indicator*

So, any actual value over 80 percent will be green, but what does this mean? We have to evaluate the thresholds in conjunction with the banding method to see where our values will change. Let's look at an example, assuming a KPI with an actual value of 75 percent (0.75).

We set the target value to 80 percent (.80), and leave all the indicator defaults (Increasing is Better, banding by normalized values, and a worst value of 0). Then we figure we want anything below 80 percent to be yellow, so we change our thresholds as shown in Figure 10-46.

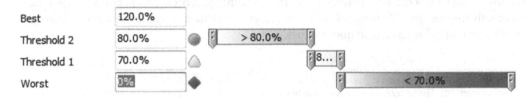

Figure 10-46. *Setting the thresholds*

OK, so we've set our target to 80 percent, our actual value to 75 percent, and our banding threshold so that anything between 70 and 80 percent is yellow. So if we looked at this indicator in a scorecard, it would be yellow, right? Let's see (the KPI is shown in Figure 10-47).

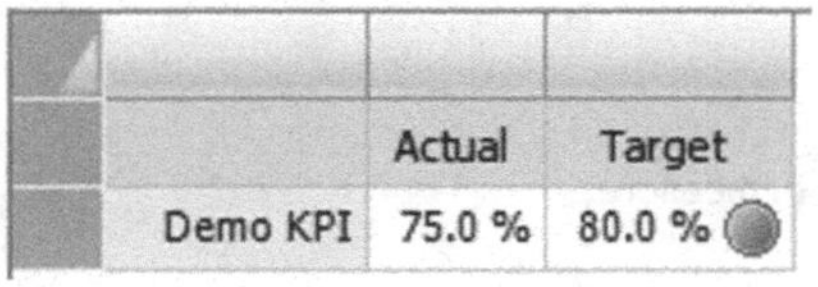

	Actual	Target
Demo KPI	75.0 %	80.0 % ⬤

Figure 10-47. *The KPI in a scorecard*

It's green? How did that happen?

The trick is to realize the meaning of "target value." We're tempted to think that out of 100 percent, our target is 80 percent (that's where it will be green). But by setting the target value to 80 percent, we've made that value the maximum point to shoot for. Also, our threshold at 80 percent refers to 80 percent of the target value of 80 percent, making the boundary between yellow and green at 64 percent.

Confused? Let's try it again with different units.

This time, assume a revenue measurement for which any amount over $80 can be considered "in the green." So we set the target value to 80. Now when we look at our threshold, it makes more sense—we want our teams to be in the green when they are over 100 percent of their target of $80. If we set the green threshold at 80 percent, we would be setting it at 80 percent of the $80 target, or $64.

So be wary of targets that are percentages and make sure you're not setting a threshold to be a percentage of a percentage.

Note Scoring gets even stranger once the KPI is in the scorecard and you have to average multiple KPIs together. PerformancePoint does some serious magic to normalize the scores such that they can be properly averaged together. For more details, see Nick Barclay's blog entry at `http://nickbarclay.blogspot.com/2006/02/business-scorecard-manager-whats-score.html`.

Banding by Numeric Value

Another approach is to band by numeric value (Figure 10-48). This allows you to simply enter the threshold values directly, instead of entering percentage scores. This is best when you have externally defined specific values. For example, if you were measuring revenue, you might set your threshold values based on quota values.

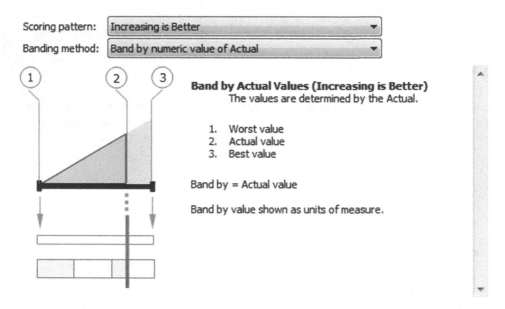

Figure 10-48. *Banding by numeric value*

What you'll also notice is that if you choose to band by numeric value, you won't have to enter a worst value, as it no longer applies.

Banding by Stated Score

Banding by stated score (Figure 10-49) severs the indicator from the target and actual values. Using this method, you design the indicator to change based on a data-driven value. So, you'll have an actual value and a target value, and the indicator will change based on its own logic.

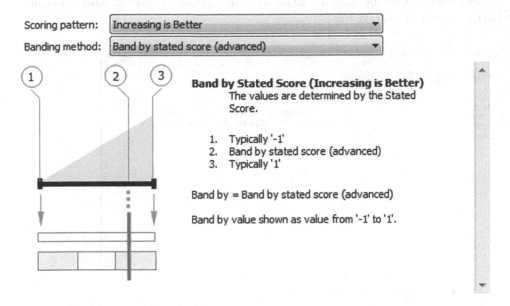

Figure 10-49. *Banding by stated score*

When you step through the wizard with "Band by stated score," the final page will have a button allowing you to map the indicator to a data source. Then the indicator will have a value, and you can set the thresholds to reflect what you want the indicator to do relative to the value.

■ **Note** This is most often used for trend arrows, where the data mapping will map to previous values to identify a trend direction.

Calculations

Calculations for targets are almost identical to actual value calculations, with one notable exception (see Figure 10-50). Note the check box at the bottom labeled "Use calculated values of actual and target to compute score."

Again, this requires you to realize that there are actually two values involved in a target. First, you have the target value, which you've mapped in the Data Mapping column. However, there is also a score calculated for the indicator. Checking this box (the default state) means that the score will be calculated normally from the actual and target values and thresholds. If you uncheck this box, then the score will be the weighted average of the child scores (no matter what the actual and target values are).

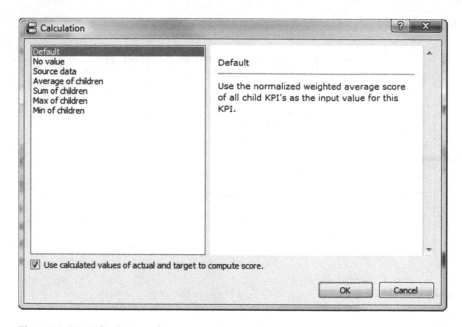

Figure 10-50. *Calculations for target values*

Next, in Exercise 10-2, we're going to create some KPIs. In Exercise 10-3, we'll use the KPIs to build a scorecard, which is going to look like the scorecard in Figure 10-51. In Chapter 12, we'll connect the scorecard to a strategy map and publish it to a dashboard.

	Actual	Target	
⊟ Total Sales			△
Accessories	$25,000	$100,000	◆
Bikes	$75,000	$100,000	△
Clothing	$50,000	$100,000	△
Components	$100,000	$100,000	⬤
⊟ Customer Service			△
Repeat Visitors	12.0 %	30.0 %	◆
Complaints	27	25	⬤

Figure 10-51. *A basic scorecard*

Exercise 10-2. Creating a KPI

1. Right-click KPIs in the Workspace Browser, or click KPI on the Create tab in the ribbon.

2. Select Objective and click OK.

3. Name the KPI Total Sales, and then click Finish. You'll get a default KPI, as shown in Figure 10-52.

Figure 10-52. *A new KPI*

Since this is an objective (parent) KPI, note that the Calculation column is set to "No value."

4. Click the Properties tab at the top.

5. We're going to add a custom property to our objectives. In the Custom Properties section, click New Property.

6. From the Property Type Selector (Figure 10-53), select Text and click OK.

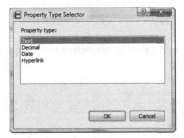

Figure 10-53. *Selecting the data type for a custom property*

7. After you click OK, the cursor will be in the Value field, and if you try to click out without an entry, you'll get an error, so type your name in.

8. Click where it says New Property and type **Stakeholder** as the new name.

9. Click back on the Editor tab.

10. Now right-click the Total Sales KPI in the Workspace Browser and select Copy.

11. Right-click KPIs and select Paste to paste a copy of your objective. You should now have two objectives, the new one named Copy of Total Sales.

12. Select the Copy of Total Sales KPI and click the Properties tab. Change the name to Customer Service, as shown in Figure 10-54.

Figure 10-54. *Renaming the new objective KPI*

13. Click the Editor tab again.

14. Right-click KPIs in the Workspace Browser again and select New KPI.

15. Select Blank KPI and click OK.

16. Name the KPI Accessories, and then click Finish.

17. With the Actual row selected, select the Edit tab in the ribbon (if it isn't already selected) and click the $ format button (Figure 10-55).

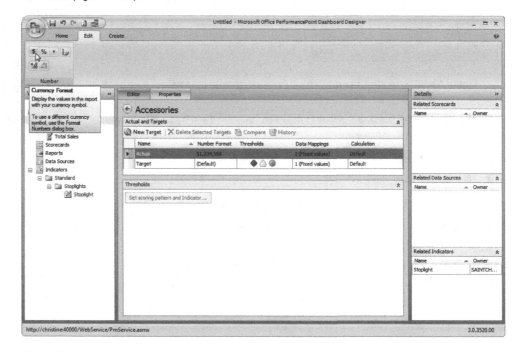

Figure 10-55. *Selecting the currency format for the actual value*

18. Do the same for the target value.

19. Click "1 (Fixed values)" in the Target value row to set the value of the target.

20. In the Fixed Values Data Source Mapping dialog, set the value to 25000, as shown in Figure 10-56.

Figure 10-56. *Setting the target value for the KPI*

21. Click OK, and follow steps 10 through 12 to make three more copies of the Accessories KPI.

22. Rename the new KPIs Bikes, Clothing, and Components.

23. Click each KPI, click "1 (Fixed values)" for the actual value, and set the actual value for each KPI as shown in the following table.

KPI Values for Demo Scorecard

KPI	Actual Value	Target Value (Already Set)
Accessories	26000	25000
Bikes	18000	25000
Clothing	24000	25000
Components	12000	25000

24. Create two more KPIs—Repeat Visitors and Complaints—using the properties shown in the following table.

Additional KPI Values

Name	Format	Actual Value	Target Value
Repeat Visitors	Percentage	0.12	0.30
Complaints	(Default)	27	25

25. For the Complaints KPI, click the target in the editor.

26. In the Thresholds section, click the "Set scoring pattern and Indicator" button, as shown in Figure 10-57.

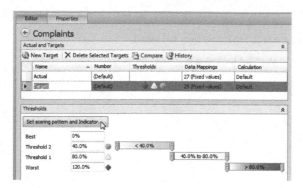

Figure 10-57. *Setting the scoring pattern*

27. In the Edit Banding Settings dialog, change the scoring pattern to Decreasing is Better.

28. Click Next, Next, and then Finish to close the dialog.

29. You now have all the KPIs you need for your scorecard. Be sure to save the workspace!

Now that we have some KPIs, let's put them into a scorecard! Not a lot of theory here—mostly learning by doing and trial and error.

Scorecards

You have several options when creating a scorecard (see Figure 10-58). We're only going to look in depth at the standard/blank scorecard here, but we'll dig into the other scorecard types in Chapter 11.

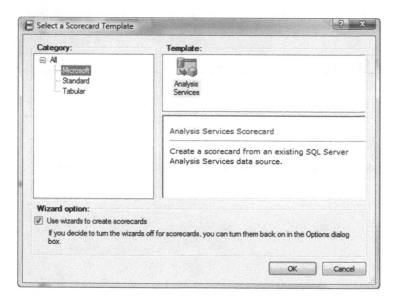

Figure 10-58. *Creating a scorecard*

Microsoft Scorecards

The only entry under the Microsoft category is Analysis Services, which lets you create a score-card based on KPIs built into an Analysis Services cube, or using your own KPI and selecting dimensions and members from a cube.

Standard Scorecards

The standard scorecards basically give you a plain scorecard to start with—whether you want to wire it to a collection of data sources or just enter a group of manual KPIs.

Blank: Simply creates an empty scorecard. Everything else is up to you.

Fixed values: Similar to an empty scorecard, but the wizard provides an easy-to-use inter-face for entering a number of new KPIs.

Tabular Scorecards

Tabular scorecards offer various ways of getting a running start with a data-driven scorecard:

Excel 2007: Creates a scorecard by importing KPI labels, targets, and actual values from an Excel 2007 spreadsheet (XLSX). This is a very straightforward way to type in a bunch of KPI labels and values, and then build a scorecard from them.

Excel Services: Similar to the Excel 2007 scorecard, except the labels and values are stored in Excel Services.

SharePoint list: Lets you create a scorecard based on a SharePoint data source. These are an important addition to Microsoft's scorecarding capabilities. Previously, with BSM, the best solution for creating an early ad hoc data-driven scorecard was to connect it to an Excel spreadsheet. However, this had severe scalability implications.

SQL tabular: Creates a scorecard based on a SQL table drawn from a SQL data connection. Again, this is a quick-and-easy way to build a scorecard from a structured data source.

Tip You can also create your own scorecard templates. See `http://msdn2.microsoft.com/en-us/library/bb833104.aspx` for a bare-bones how-to and code sample.

Next, in Exercise 10-3, we're going to create a scorecard using our KPIs.

Exercise 10-3. Creating a Scorecard

1. Right-click Scorecards, and then New Scorecard. (You can also select the Create tab at the top, and then select Scorecard in the Objects pane.)

2. In the Select a Scorecard Template dialog, choose Standard, then choose Blank Scorecard, and then click OK (Figure 10-59).

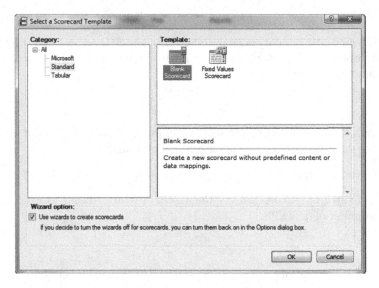

Figure 10-59. *Creating a blank scorecard*

3. You will see the Create a Blank Scorecard dialog. Name the scorecard Strategy Map Scorecard, and then click Finish.

4. You'll now have the scorecard open in the editor, as shown in Figure 10-60.

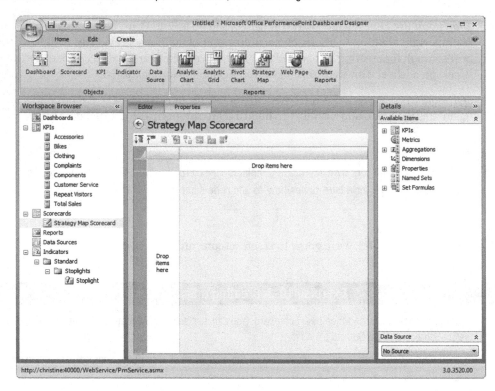

Figure 10-60. *A blank scorecard in the Scorecard editor*

5. Now let's add our KPIs. In the Details pane on the right, open the KPIs node.

6. Drag the Total Sales KPI from the Details pane to the left-hand column labeled "Drop items here" (Figure 10-61).

■**Note** We're working with the list in the Details pane on the *right*. You cannot drag KPIs from the Workspace Browser on the *left*.

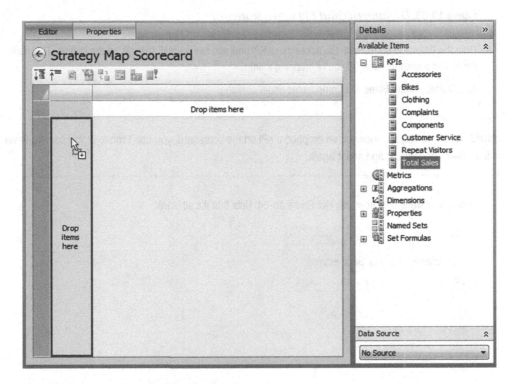

Figure 10-61. *Dragging the Total Sales KPI*

Note that in addition to the Total Sales KPI, the Actual and Target columns are now displayed (see Figure 10-62).

Figure 10-62. *The Total Sales KPI*

7. Now drag the Accessories KPI from the Details pane to the right side of the Total Sales label until you see the small arrow (look closely at Figure 10-63). This adds the KPI as a child of the KPI you're dropping it onto.

Figure 10-63. *Dropping a child KPI into a scorecard*

8. Drag the Bikes KPI underneath the Accessories KPI until you see a small triangle on the bottom. This adds the KPI as a sibling of the KPI you're dropping it onto.

9. Add Clothing under Bikes and Components under Clothing.

■**Note** As far as I know, once you've dropped a KPI on the scorecard, you can't move it. You can, however, undo (Ctrl+Z), or delete it and add it again.

Your scorecard should now look like Figure 10-64. Note that it's all blank.

Figure 10-64. *The scorecard with the first set of KPIs*

10. Select the Edit tab in the ribbon, and then click Update. This will populate the KPIs (see Figure 10-65).

	Actual	Target
⊟ Total Sales		△
Accessories	$26,000	$25,000 ●
Bikes	$18,000	$25,000 △
Clothing	$24,000	$25,000 △
Components	$12,000	$25,000 ◆

Figure 10-65. *The populated KPIs*

■**Note** The Total Sales KPI was our objective—the objective KPI creates a KPI with no values of its own, so it purely inherits the aggregated score from its children KPIs.

11. Now drag the Customer Service KPI to the bottom of the Total Sales KPI to add it as a sibling (see Figure 10-66).

	Actual	Target
⊟ Total Sales		△
Accessories	$26,000	$25,000 ●
Bikes	$18,000	$25,000 △
Clothing	$24,000	$25,000 △
Components	$12,000	$25,000 ◆

Figure 10-66. *Adding the Customer Service KPI as a sibling of the Total Sales KPI*

12. Delete the four new KPIs by clicking the label and pressing Delete.

13. Now drag the Repeat Visitors KPI over as a child of the Customer Service KPI (drop it on the right-hand border as in step 10).

14. Add Complaints as a sibling of Repeat Visitors.

15. Click the Update button to populate the KPIs. You should see something similar to Figure 10-67.

Figure 10-67. *The finished scorecard*

16. Right-click a KPI name and select Properties from the context menu to open the KPI View Settings dialog (Figure 10-68).

Remember the mention of "weighted averaging" earlier in the chapter? This is where you can set the weighting for individual KPIs. Since the weighting is set here in the scorecard, a KPI can be weighted differently depending on how it's used. The name override is simply a way to relabel a KPI without changing the KPI itself.

Figure 10-68. *The KPI View Settings dialog*

17. Right-click the Target header in the scorecard, and select Properties from the context menu to open the Target Settings dialog (Figure 10-69).

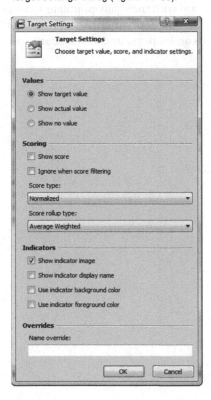

Figure 10-69. *Options for the Target column in the scorecard*

18. There are a number of options here that will affect the whole scorecard. You can display the calculated score, choose whether to normalize the score, select rollups (a common request is "Show worst child"; e.g., if 20 KPIs are green and one is red, this option will show the parent as red).

Conclusion

That's the quick-and-dirty tour of how to build a scorecard with manually populated values. In Chapter 11, we'll look at data-driven KPIs and scorecards, and in Chapter 12, you're going to learn how to create analytic reports and load scorecards and reports into a dashboard and publish them to SharePoint.

CHAPTER 11

Advanced Scorecarding

Now that you've learned how to build a basic KPI and a basic manual scorecard, let's go through some more advanced scorecarding concepts. In this chapter, we'll create a more complex balanced scorecard, an OLAP scorecard, and scorecards from Excel and SharePoint sources. We'll also dig into annotations and export our scorecard to SQL Server Reporting Services.

Hooking KPIs to Data

In Chapter 10, we built a manual scorecard—this is a great way to get a scorecard published so that people can start taking advantage of it. However, our goal through this whole exercise has been to drive our scorecards with actual data from live systems. So let's walk through each of the options for connecting individual KPIs to back-end data. We'll use various resources to show how to connect a KPI to an ODBC data source (using an Access database), an Excel spreadsheet, a list stored in MS SharePoint, a table in SQL Server, and data from SQL Server Analysis Services, connecting directly and consuming a KPI defined in a cube.

Connecting a KPI to each of these sources is as much about setting up the data source as the KPI, but for each of these, we'll look at both together.

ODBC (Access Database File)

The ODBC connection provides a method for connecting to any ODBC data source—this is the "connection of last resort." The biggest downside to using ODBC connections is that you have to write the query for every single data point—targets, actuals, trend arrows, and so on.

The data source provides the connection credentials, while the KPI is where you indicate the query to pull the data necessary for the KPI. The KPI will simply read the first row in the first column of the returned dataset. Given this, the query you write for the KPI should trim the returned results as much as possible, and ensure that you explicitly call the column you want to read the data from. In other words, don't ever use SELECT * in a KPI query.

The data connection is made from the server running the monitoring service with the credentials of the monitoring service application pool. Keep this in mind when designing ODBC connections.

Exercise 11-1 will walk you through creating an ODBC-based KPI.

Exercise 11-1. Connecting a KPI to an Access Database

1. For this exercise, we're going to use the Access Northwind database (nwind.mdb). You can download this from the Office Download Center (go to www.microsoft.com/downloads/ and search for nwind.mdb).

2. Copy the file to C:\northwind\nwind.mdb on the server where you are running Monitoring Server.

3. Open Dashboard Designer. Either open the BSWX file you created in Chapter 10 or import the indicators for a new file.

4. Right-click Data Sources, and then click New Data Source.

5. In the Select a Data Source Template dialog, select Standard Queries, and then select ODBC (see Figure 11-1).

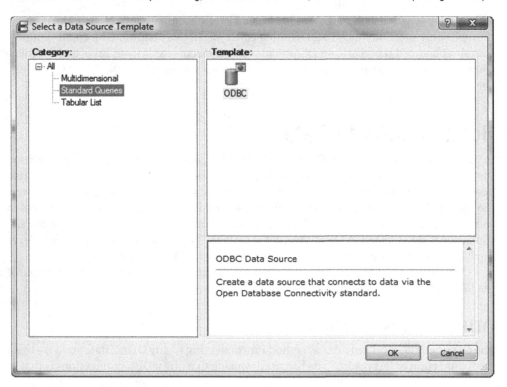

Figure 11-1. *Selecting the data source template*

6. Click the OK button. In the Create a Data Source dialog, give the data source a name (I'm using "Access Data Source"), and then click the Finish button. This opens the ODBC data source editor, which is pretty much just a text box for a connection string (see Figure 11-2).

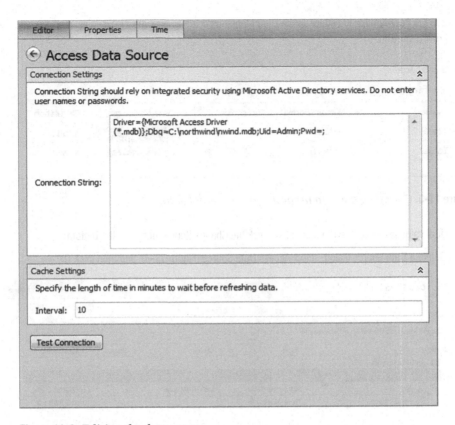

Figure 11-2. *Editing the data source*

7. Get a connection string from www.connectionstrings.com and edit it to suit.

8. Click Test Connection to test the connection. There are a couple of possible trouble spots here. Namely, you need to make sure that the IIS application pool has rights to the directory, and that the file is on Monitoring Server and in the right directory.

   Once you've successfully connected, you can create a KPI to use the data.

9. Right-click KPIs, and then click New KPI.

10. From the Select a KPI Template dialog, select Blank KPI, and then click OK.

11. Name the KPI Northwind Sales, and click Finish.

12. You'll see the now-familiar KPI editor. In the Data Mappings column, click the "1 (Fixed values)" entry in the Actual row (Figure 11-3).

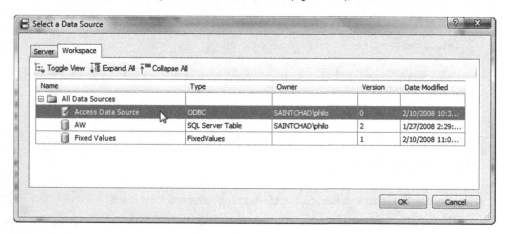

Figure 11-3. *Changing the data mapping for the actual value*

13. The actual value is currently set to manual, so click the Change Source button at the bottom.

14. In the Select a Data Source dialog, select Access Data Source (Figure 11-4), and then click OK.

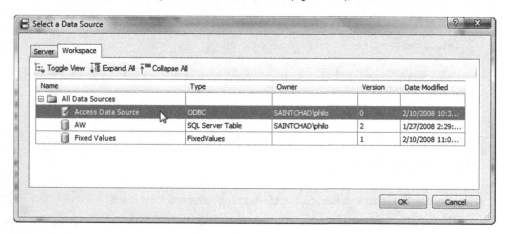

Figure 11-4. *Selecting the data source*

■Note Our data source is now a text box for a query. Since the ODBC connector is for any ODBC data source, it would be difficult to use a query builder here. Remember that the value will be the first column of the first row returned by the query.

---

15. Enter this query into the editor:

```
SELECT Sum([UnitPrice]*[Quantity]) AS LineTotal, Employees.LastName
FROM Employees INNER JOIN (Orders INNER JOIN [Order Details]
ON Orders.OrderID = [Order Details].OrderID)
INNER JOIN [Employees]
ON Employees.EmployeeID = Orders.EmployeeID
GROUP BY Employees.LastName
HAVING (((Employees.LastName)='Fuller'));
```

Note If you create the query in the Access query editor, it will put double quotes around `Fuller`, which will throw an error in the scorecard. You must use single quotes. (ODBC errors will show up in the Event Log on the Monitoring Server.)

---

16. With the actual value selected, click the $ format button on the Edit tab in the ribbon.

17. Right-click the Northwind Sales KPI in the Workspace Browser (on the left) and select Publish.

18. If you do not have a scorecard in the workspace, create a blank scorecard using the directions in Chapter 10.

19. Drag the Northwind Sales KPI to the scorecard—you should see it as in Figure 11-5.

	Actual	Target
Northwind Sales	$177,749	1 ◯

Figure 11-5. *The scorecard showing Access data*

20. You can either enter a value for the target or write another query.

As you can see, driving a scorecard in this manner can get tedious—every single KPI actual and target value requires its own query. One change in a data schema and you may have to edit every data connection in your scorecard. However, it does offer the ultimate in flexibility—as a last resort, scorecard data points can be data driven this way.

Excel 2007 Spreadsheets

Using Excel as the repository for scorecard data was a very popular option in BSM 2005, the predecessor to PerformancePoint Monitoring Server. However, there were a number of problems with using an Excel file as a data source, most notably locking problems when someone opened the spreadsheet to edit it.

In PerformancePoint Server 2007, you can use Excel spreadsheet data to drive a scorecard, but Dashboard Designer caches the data into Monitoring Server, so you don't have a file-locking problem. The downside here is that you have to use Dashboard Designer to edit the values in the spreadsheet.

Note Dashboard Designer automates Excel to import the spreadsheet, so you must have Excel 2007 installed to import a spreadsheet. However, you can import either XLSX (2007) or XLS (2003) format.

When you create a data connection to an Excel spreadsheet, you have the option to import a spreadsheet from an XLSX, XLS, or XLSB file, or to create a new (blank) spreadsheet. When you select a spreadsheet, Dashboard Designer will pick up on any table defined in the spreadsheet and import that. Once you've imported the data, you need to identify the structure of the data in the View tab, as well as any time dimension considerations (see Figure 11-6).

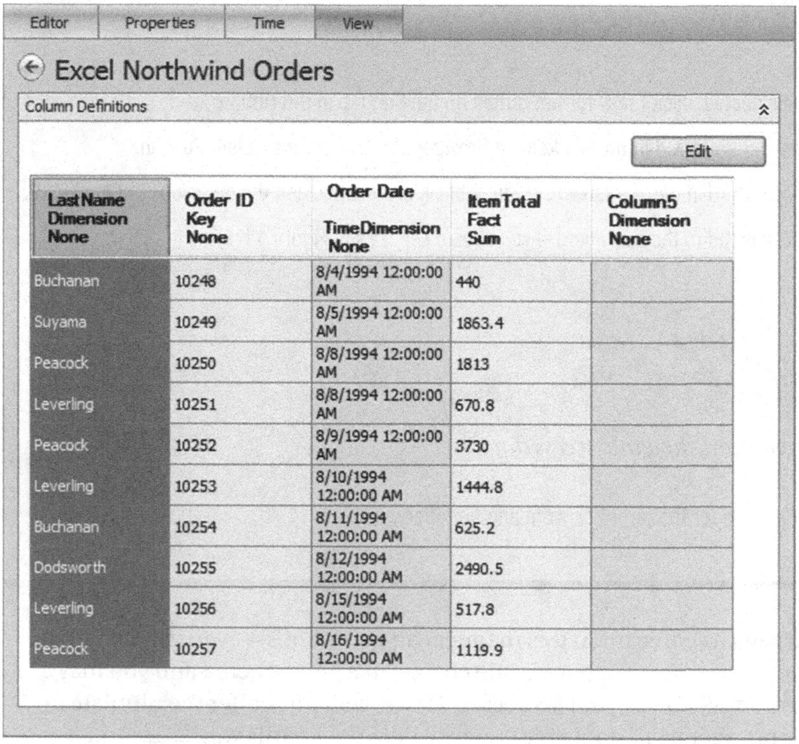

Editor	Properties	Time	View

⊖ Excel Northwind Orders

Column Definitions   ⌄

[Edit]

Last Name Dimension None	Order ID Key None	Order Date TimeDimension None	Item Total Fact Sum	Column5 Dimension None
Buchanan	10248	8/4/1994 12:00:00 AM	440	
Suyama	10249	8/5/1994 12:00:00 AM	1863.4	
Peacock	10250	8/8/1994 12:00:00 AM	1813	
Leverling	10251	8/8/1994 12:00:00 AM	670.8	
Peacock	10252	8/9/1994 12:00:00 AM	3730	
Leverling	10253	8/10/1994 12:00:00 AM	1444.8	
Buchanan	10254	8/11/1994 12:00:00 AM	625.2	
Dodsworth	10255	8/12/1994 12:00:00 AM	2490.5	
Leverling	10256	8/15/1994 12:00:00 AM	517.8	
Peacock	10257	8/16/1994 12:00:00 AM	1119.9	

Figure 11-6. *Defining columns in an Excel data connection*

For each column, you can define the contents from the Details pane on the right (Figure 11-7). Dashboard Designer does a pretty good job of selecting the options, but you may want to adjust them.

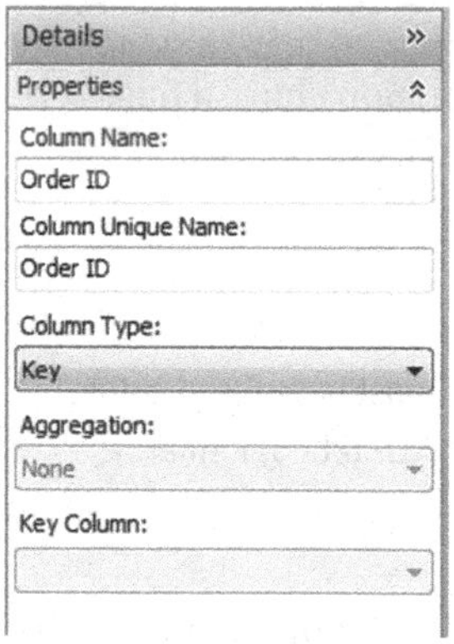

Details	»
Properties	⌃

Column Name:
Order ID

Column Unique Name:
Order ID

Column Type:
Key ▼

Aggregation:
None ▼

Key Column:
▼

Figure 11-7. *Setting the properties for an Excel column*

The properties are as follows:

Column Name: This is the text that will be displayed for the column.

Column Unique Name: Like an ID value, this is used internally by PerformancePoint when linking items in a dashboard (see Chapter 12).

Column Type: This sets the way you want PerformancePoint to treat the contents of the column (see the following list).

Aggregation: For fact columns, this is how you want PerformancePoint to aggregate the values together (generally a sum, but you may want a count, maximum, or standard deviation, for example).

Key Column: The key column is used in scenarios where you have to slice across different data sources—if the key value in, say, a cube doesn't match the key value in your table, then you can't slice across both at the same time (e.g., if the cube provides the actual value and the table provides the target). However, you can create a column in your tabular source as a map to match members in the tabular source to the members in the cube, and use that column as the key column.

Following are the column types for you to select from:

Dimension: Just like dimensions in OLAP, these are values (generally text values) that you will use to group the fact values, such as sales region, store, product, and so on.

Fact: These are numerical values that you will use to measure performance (dollars, days, counts, etc.). These are the numbers that will end up as actual values or targets.

Ignore: This allows you to ignore a column you don't plan to use.

Key: This is a unique identifier for the records in the table.

Time Dimension: Selecting a time dimension allows you to use time intelligence in the scorecard. Most notably, values can be indicated as "last six months" so you don't have to constantly edit the KPI to display current values.

TIME INTELLIGENCE IN THE DASHBOARD

Time intelligence is a PerformancePoint monitoring feature that allows you to set up a KPI to measure, for example, sales over the last two months, and PerformancePoint Server will recalculate the KPI as the date changes to keep it current. In addition, using time intelligence provides a way of mapping KPIs from different data sources to a uniform calendar. This uniform calendar, an internal construct for Monitoring Server, is called the *master time dimension*.

To configure a time dimension, select one or more of the columns in the tabular data source as a time dimension. Then go to the Time tab in the designer and select the check box for the dimension you want to act as the master time dimension. You can also check the boxes underneath to indicate what periods you want the data aggregated for.

Exercise 11-2 will walk you through connecting a KPI to an Excel spreadsheet.

Exercise 11-2. Connecting a KPI to an Excel Spreadsheet

In this exercise, we're going to use an Excel spreadsheet generated from the Access Northwind database with this query:

```
SELECT Orders.OrderID, Orders.OrderDate, Orders.ShipCountry,
Employees.LastName,
Sum([UnitPrice]*[Quantity]) AS OrderTotal
FROM (Employees INNER JOIN Orders
ON Employees.EmployeeID = Orders.EmployeeID)
INNER JOIN [Order Details] ON Orders.OrderID = [Order Details].OrderID
GROUP BY Orders.OrderID, Orders.OrderDate,
Orders.ShipCountry, Employees.LastName;
```

1. Save the spreadsheet on the system you will be running Dashboard Designer from.

2. In Dashboard Designer, create a new data connection. Select Tabular List and then Import from Excel 2007 Workbook.

3. Name the connection Excel Northwind Data and click Finish.

4. When the connection editor opens, it should open to the Editor tab, but since it remembers the last tab you were on, it may not. Click the Editor tab to open the editor (Figure 11-8).

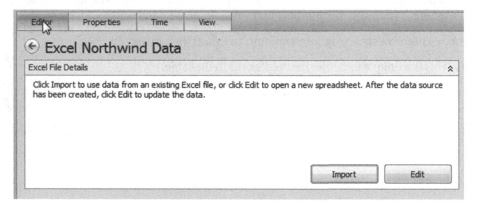

Figure 11-8. *Opening the Editor tab*

5. If you click the Edit button, you'll get a blank Excel spreadsheet you can type values into, and you can run the whole spreadsheet manually. Instead, click the Import button.

6. You'll get the File Open dialog—browse to your Northwind.xlsx spreadsheet and open it.

7. Excel will open the spreadsheet, and you'll get the "Edit data in Excel" dialog (Figure 11-9). Make sure Headers on First Row is checked, and then click the "Accept changes" button.

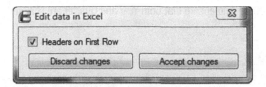

Figure 11-9. *Importing a spreadsheet*

Dashboard Designer will import the data and show a sample of the data on the View tab (Figure 11-10).

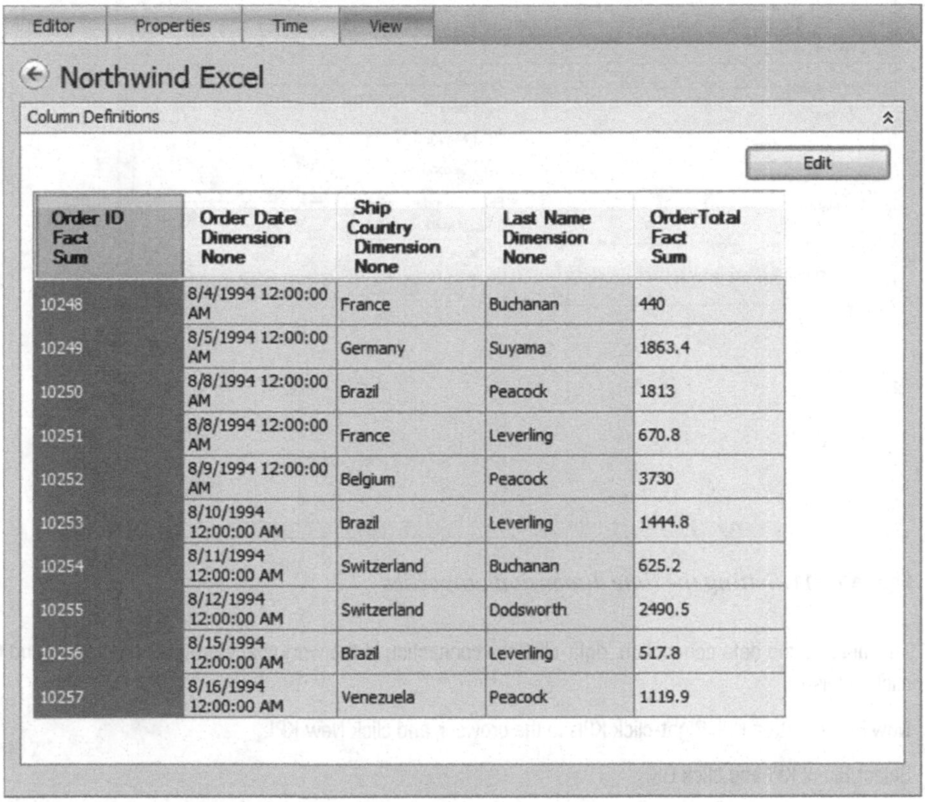

Editor	Properties	Time	View

⬅ Northwind Excel

Column Definitions   ⌃

Edit

Order ID Fact Sum	Order Date Dimension None	Ship Country Dimension None	Last Name Dimension None	OrderTotal Fact Sum
10248	8/4/1994 12:00:00 AM	France	Buchanan	440
10249	8/5/1994 12:00:00 AM	Germany	Suyama	1863.4
10250	8/8/1994 12:00:00 AM	Brazil	Peacock	1813
10251	8/8/1994 12:00:00 AM	France	Leverling	670.8
10252	8/9/1994 12:00:00 AM	Belgium	Peacock	3730
10253	8/10/1994 12:00:00 AM	Brazil	Leverling	1444.8
10254	8/11/1994 12:00:00 AM	Switzerland	Buchanan	625.2
10255	8/12/1994 12:00:00 AM	Switzerland	Dodsworth	2490.5
10256	8/15/1994 12:00:00 AM	Brazil	Leverling	517.8
10257	8/16/1994 12:00:00 AM	Venezuela	Peacock	1119.9

Figure 11-10. *The Excel data on the View tab*

Note that you can click each column to change the definition in the Details pane.

8. Change OrderID to Column Type: Key.

9. Change OrderDate to Column Type: TimeDimension.

10. Leave ShipCountry, LastName, and OrderTotal with their defaults.

11. Click the Time tab. Check the box next to OrderDate, and ensure that both Year and Quarter are selected under Time Period Levels (Figure 11-11).

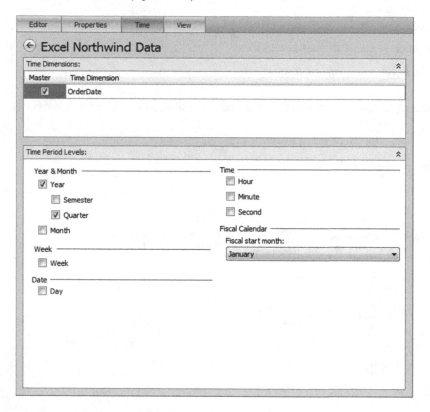

Figure 11-11. *Setting the time dimension properties*

12. This finishes the data connection; right-click the connection in the workspace browser on the left, and then click Publish.

13. Now let's create a KPI. Right-click KPIs in the browser, and click New KPI.

14. Select Blank KPI and click OK.

15. Name the KPI Excel Northwind Sales and click Finish.

16. In the KPI designer, click the Actual row, and then click the $ button in the Number pane of the Edit tab in the ribbon.

17. Under Data Mappings, click the "1 (Fixed values)" in the Actual row to open the Data Source Mapping dialog.

18. Click the Change Source button at the bottom of the dialog.

19. Select the Excel Northwind Data data source from the Select a Data Source dialog (Figure 11-12).

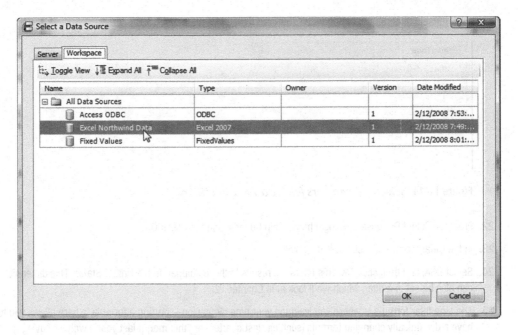

Figure 11-12. *Selecting the Excel data source*

20. Click OK. In the Dimensional Data Source Mapping dialog (Figure 11-13), select OrderTotal for the measure.

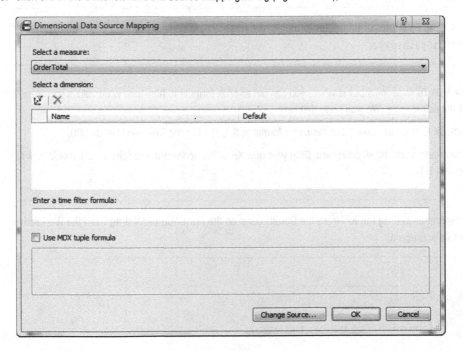

Figure 11-13. *Mapping a dimensional data source*

21. Click the Select Members button under "Select a dimension" (Figure 11-14).

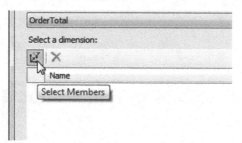

Figure 11-14. *Selecting members for the dimension filter*

22. From the Select Dimension dialog, choose Ship Country, and then click OK.

23. In the Default column, click the Default link.

24. Select USA, and then click OK. This filters the results to those shipped to the United States. This dimension can also be set in a filter, which we'll look at in Chapter 12.

25. The time filter formula is where you leverage your time dimension—putting a formula in here allows you to have a dynamically changing formula (such as "last quarter" or "this month last year") without having to constantly edit the filter. For the Northwind data, you can try Year-13, which would filter the data in 1995 (2008 – 13).

Tip For more examples of time filter formulas, see http://office.microsoft.com/en-us/help/ HA102411381033.aspx#2.

The MDX Tuple formula box is where you can put an MDX formula to fine-tune what values you are selecting for the actual value. We won't use that here.

26. Click OK to close the dialog. Set the target format to $, and enter the fixed value of 20,000.

27. Now create a new blank scorecard. Drag your new KPI to the scorecard and refresh it. It should look like Figure 11-15.

Tip Remember to drag the KPI from the Details pane on the right. You can't drag from the Workspace Browser to a scorecard.

	Actual	Target
Excel Northwind Sales	$127,615	$20,000 ⬤

Figure 11-15. *An Excel KPI*

Excel 2007 Scorecards

You should already see that this is better than writing a query for every data point in a scorecard. However, you still have to manually configure every KPI. Consider the configuration necessary to display the scorecard in Figure 11-16. PerformancePoint also has a way to build a whole scorecard from a data source all at once.

	1995 Q1		1995 Q2		1995 Q3		1995 Q4	
	Actual	Target	Actual	Target	Actual	Target	Actual	Target
⊟ Excel Northwind Sales		△		△		△		●
Buchanan	$13,228	$20,000 △	$7,762	$20,000 ◆	$13,237	$20,000 △	$10,967	$20,000 △
Callahan	$21,077	$20,000 ●	$10,399	$20,000 △	$11,357	$20,000 △	$18,827	$20,000 △
Davolio	$19,393	$20,000 △	$14,902	$20,000 △	$31,230	$20,000 ●	$25,488	$20,000 ●
Dodsworth	$1,375	$20,000 ◆	$2,522	$20,000 ◆	$5,718	$20,000 ◆	$18,188	$20,000 △
Fuller	$11,143	$20,000 △	$21,514	$20,000 ●	$17,436	$20,000 △	$23,440	$20,000 ●
King	$17,594	$20,000 △	$15,616	$20,000 △	$16,080	$20,000 △	$16,471	$20,000 △
Leverling	$20,818	$20,000 ●	$40,537	$20,000 ●	$12,863	$20,000 △	$21,836	$20,000 ●
Peacock	$45,591	$20,000 ●	$27,551	$20,000 ●	$27,104	$20,000 ●	$26,829	$20,000 ●
Suyama	$8,634	$20,000 ◆	$11,701	$20,000 △	$9,512	$20,000 ◆	$13,928	$20,000 △

Figure 11-16. *A scorecard with 36 KPI indicators*

Note again that this is one more option; it's not necessarily meant to be the way to do things. If you want to build a scorecard from a single source of data, this is a great way to assemble it quickly. However, you may instead need to create a scorecard that aggregates data from numerous multiple data points. In that case, you can create individual KPIs from the various data sources.

Tabular-based scorecards in PerformancePoint leverage the dimension-style model created in the data source to enable columns, rows, and filters based on the dimensions (in Figure 11-10, the date, last name, and country columns).

When you create a tabular-based scorecard, Dashboard Designer will only show data sources based on the same type of data (Excel 2007, Excel Services, SharePoint, and SQL Server). You have the option to either use an existing KPI or create a KPI based on measures in the data source (Figure 11-17).

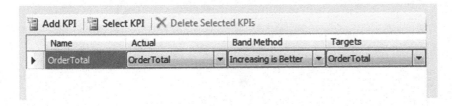

Figure 11-17. *Adding a new KPI to a scorecard*

You can then select the data for the actual and target values. (Once the wizard is complete, it creates the KPI and you can tweak it as necessary.) You can also add multiple KPIs here.

The next step (Figure 11-18) allows you to add filters to the scorecard to narrow down the data reported—this is also something you can tweak later or use to add a filter. You can select a dimension for the filter and the members to use for both the actual and target values. On this page, you can also add time filters using the formulas mentioned previously.

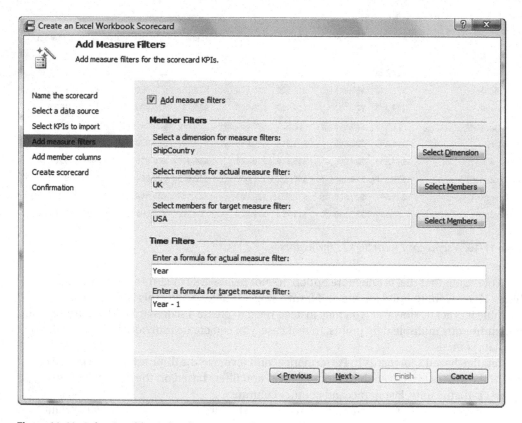

Figure 11-18. *Selecting filters for the scorecard*

The final page (Figure 11-19) allows you to choose members for creating columns in the scorecard (again, this can all be edited once the scorecard is created). If you don't add member columns, then a single column for actual values and targets will be created for the aggregates as filtered. If you add member columns, you'll be able to select a dimension, and then one or more members of that dimension, to create the columns.

After you finish this page, the wizard will generate the KPI(s), indicators, and scorecard to reflect what you've designed, and leave the scorecard open for you to edit. Exercise 11-3 walks you through creating a scorecard from the Excel data source created previously.

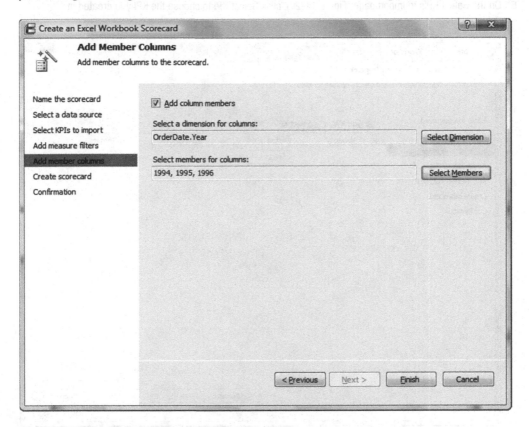

Figure 11-19. *Creating columns for the scorecard*

Exercise 11-3. Creating a Tabular Scorecard from an Excel Spreadsheet

1. Right-click the Scorecards node in the Workspace Browser, and then click New Scorecard.

2. Select Tabular, and then Excel 2007, and then click OK.

3. Name the scorecard Excel Northwind Scorecard, and then click Next.

4. Select the Excel Northwind Data data source, and then click Next.

5. On the Select KPIs to Import page (Figure 11-20), click Select KPI to choose the KPI you created in Exercise 11-2.

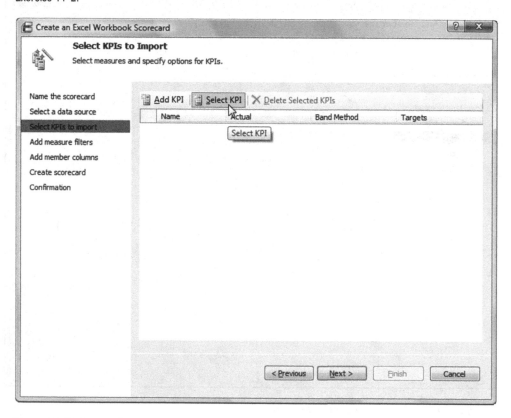

Figure 11-20. *Importing a KPI*

6. Select the Excel Northwind Sales KPI, and then click OK. Note that the KPI is brought in but the options are grayed out. Also, if you chose to, you could import additional KPIs.

7. Click Next. We won't add any measure filters, so click Next again.

8. Check the check box for "Add column members."

9. Click the Select Dimension button, and then select OrderDate.Quarter (Figure 11-21).

Figure 11-21. *Selecting the dimension for column members*

10. Click the Select Members button.

11. Select Q1 through Q4 in 1995, and then click OK (Figure 11-22).

Figure 11-22. *Selecting the members for the additional columns*

12. Click Finish to generate the scorecard. You should get something similar to Figure 11-23.

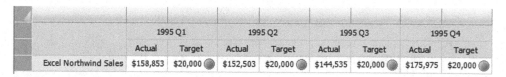

	1995 Q1		1995 Q2		1995 Q3		1995 Q4	
	Actual	Target	Actual	Target	Actual	Target	Actual	Target
Excel Northwind Sales	$158,853	$20,000 ●	$152,503	$20,000 ●	$144,535	$20,000 ●	$175,975	$20,000 ●

Figure 11-23. *The Excel scorecard*

On the right side, in the Details pane, are the dimensions we created for the scorecard data source.

13. As one final touch, click LastName and drag it to the scorecard, as shown in Figure 11-24.

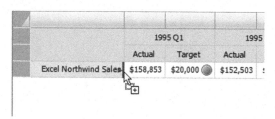

Figure 11-24. *Adding a dimension to the scorecard*

14. Note where to drop the dimension. Dragging it to the right-hand side of the cell with Excel Northwind Sales creates the dimension as a child to the KPI.

15. You'll get a dialog to select the members to use in the scorecard. Check all the names or right-click and select Check Children, and then click OK.

16. Update the scorecard (click the Update button on the Edit tab on the ribbon). The result should look like Figure 11-25.

	1995 Q1		1995 Q2		1995 Q3		1995 Q4	
	Actual	Target	Actual	Target	Actual	Target	Actual	Target
⊟ Excel Northwind Sales		△		△		△		●
Buchanan	$13,228	$20,000 △	$7,762	$20,000 ◆	$13,237	$20,000 △	$10,967	$20,000 △
Callahan	$21,077	$20,000 ●	$10,399	$20,000 △	$11,357	$20,000 △	$18,827	$20,000 △
Davolio	$19,393	$20,000 △	$14,902	$20,000 △	$31,230	$20,000 ●	$25,488	$20,000 ●
Dodsworth	$1,375	$20,000 ◆	$2,522	$20,000 ◆	$5,718	$20,000 ◆	$18,188	$20,000 △
Fuller	$11,143	$20,000 △	$21,514	$20,000 ●	$17,436	$20,000 △	$23,440	$20,000 ●
King	$17,594	$20,000 △	$15,616	$20,000 △	$16,080	$20,000 △	$16,471	$20,000 △
Leverling	$20,818	$20,000 ●	$40,537	$20,000 ●	$12,863	$20,000 △	$21,836	$20,000 ●
Peacock	$45,591	$20,000 ●	$27,551	$20,000 ●	$27,104	$20,000 ●	$26,829	$20,000 ●
Suyama	$8,634	$20,000 ◆	$11,701	$20,000 △	$9,512	$20,000 ◆	$13,928	$20,000 △

Figure 11-25. *The completed scorecard*

As you can see, this is far less painful than having to write a query for every single data point. This is a great way to create a visual display for tabular data. The methods we covered are very similar for Excel Services (where the spreadsheet stays in Excel Services on the server instead of being cached in Monitoring Server), SharePoint Lists (using the web-based SharePoint interface instead of an Excel spreadsheet), and SQL Server tables.

Now let's take a look at how pulling data and KPIs from Analysis Services is somewhat different than working with our tabular data sources, but also how using the dimensional model keeps a lot of the concepts similar.

Analysis Services

Hooking KPIs and scorecards to SQL Server Analysis Services is where PerformancePoint really shines—Monitoring Server is practically a native front end for an Analysis Services cube. A lot of what's been covered so far (the use of dimensions and measures) will resonate in this section, and it will relate back to what was covered in Chapter 5.

We're going to walk through building a scorecard in two ways. First, we'll connect a KPI to Analysis Services by hand and create a dimensional scorecard using that KPI. In the second exercise, we'll create an Analysis Services scorecard in one step; but we'll import a KPI from Analysis Services to do it. (You have the option of importing a KPI, using an existing KPI in the workspace, or creating a new KPI along with the scorecard.)

Note When you import a KPI, it is a one-way trip; subsequent changes to the KPI won't be reflected in the KPI in PerformancePoint Server.

ON MDX

I have mentioned Multidimensional Expressions (MDX) throughout the book. Using Analysis Services as a data source for a scorecard is where you may finally have to really confront MDX to accomplish some of the more advanced scorecard scenarios.

One of the first times you'll run into a need for MDX is when using trend arrows. PerformancePoint Server does not have a "point-and-click" solution for creating trend arrows. A *trend arrow* is simply an indicator— when the value is at a certain amount, the arrow points down; at a different amount, it's flat; and at a higher amount, it points up. Generally the way to accomplish this is to create an MDX formula similar to the following:

```
(([Time].[Calendar].CurrentMember, [Measures].[Units])-
([Time].[Calendar].CurrentMember.PrevMember,[Measures].[Units]))/
([Time].[Calendar].CurrentMember.PrevMember, [Measures].[Units])
```

This equation takes the current value in the measure, subtracts the previous value (using the MDX PrevMember statement), and divides by the previous value, creating a normalized value between −1 and 1. You then set the mapping on your arrow to point in the appropriate direction based on the value. (Another solution you may see uses CASE statements and comparison operators.)

You may also use MDX in targets—for example, you may want a revenue target to be the previous year's target plus 10 percent. You can set that value using MDX.

We're now going to build two scorecards—we'll use these in Chapter 12 to build our dashboard. First, we'll build a KPI and add it to a scorecard; then we'll create an OLAP scorecard directly. On the dashboard, we'll connect them together to create a "drill down" style approach.

Our first scorecard (Exercise 11-4) will show the reseller sales for each category in the AdventureWorks bicycle company. Our basic goal is to have increasing sales, so our revenue target each quarter is simply to beat the revenue of the quarter before. We'll write MDX for the target value to make the target for a given calendar quarter equal to the revenue of the quarter before. Then, in Exercise 11-5, we'll create a scorecard to display the gross profit margin for the subcategories of each product against a fixed target of 20 percent.

In Chapter 12, we'll use the first scorecard to filter the second so that it only shows the subcategories of the selected category; then we'll add our reports from Chapter 6 to display product detail reports when a subcategory is selected in this scorecard.

Exercise 11-4. Connecting a KPI to Analysis Services

This exercise will show you how to configure a KPI in a scorecard to reflect dimensional data from an Analysis Services cube.

Creating the Data Connection

1. Right-click Data Sources in the Workspace Browser and click New Data Source.

2. Select Multidimensional and then Analysis Services.

3. Click OK. Name the Data Source Analysis Services AW (for "AdventureWorks").

4. Click Finish. Enter the Server Name in the data source editor.

5. Drop down the selector for Database and select AdventureWorks DW.

Note If you cannot connect here, you will need to check permissions. In IIS Manager, check the account that the Monitoring Service application pool is running under; then ensure that account has permissions on the AdventureWorks cube. You can set this by connecting SQL Server Management Studio to Analysis Services, creating a role, and granting the Application Pool account read permissions on the Adventure-Works cube.

---

6. Leave Roles blank. For Cube, select Adventure Works (Figure 11-26).

7. Publish the data connection (right-click the connection in the Workspace Browser and select Publish).

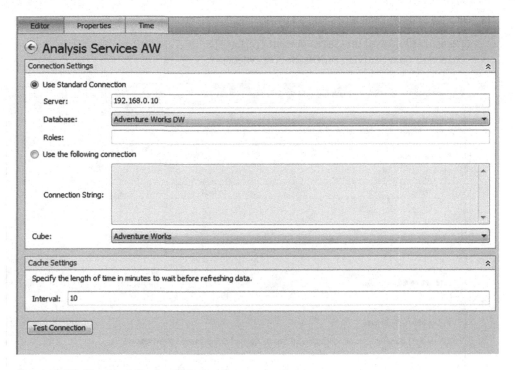

Figure 11-26. *Creating the Analysis Services connection*

Creating the KPI

1. Right-click KPIs in the Workspace Browser and click New KPI.

2. Select Blank KPI and click OK.

3. Name the KPI Reseller Sales and click Finish.

4. Set both the actual and target values to $ format (on the Edit tab in the ribbon).

5. Click "1 (Fixed values)" for the actual data mapping.

6. Click the Change Source button on the Fixed Values Data Source Mapping dialog.

7. Select the Analysis Services AW data source created earlier, and then click OK.

8. Select the Reseller Sales Amount measure.

9. Click OK. Click "1 (Fixed values)" for the target data mapping.

10. Click the Change Source button.

11. Select the Analysis Services AW data source, and then click OK.

12. Check the box next to "Use MDX tuple formula"—note that this disables the other entry controls.

13. Enter the following formula (see Figure 11-27):

```
([Measures].[Reseller Sales Amount], [Date].
[Calendar Quarter].CurrentMember.PrevMember)
```

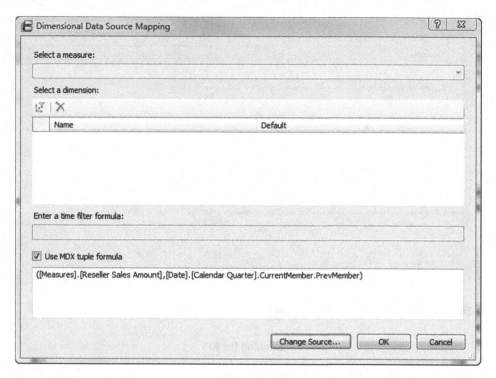

Figure 11-27. *An MDX-based target value*

■**Note** This *tuple*, combined with filters and dimensions on the scorecard, will define a unique value. A tuple is defined as an ordered collection of one or more members from different hierarchies (creating an intersection set). In this case, we are selecting the Reseller Sales Amount from the Measures group, and then the Calendar Quarter from the Date dimension. Finally, we are indicating to take the current member of the Calendar Quarter (defined by the column definitions in the scorecard) and select the previous member in the set (the previous quarter).

---

14. Click OK.

Publishing the Reseller Sales KPI

1. Create a new, blank scorecard. Name it Reseller Sales by Category.

2. Drag the Reseller Sales KPI from the Details pane on the right.

■Note If you update this, the target will be blank, as you can't select the calendar period before all the data that is in the data set.

3. Open up the dimensions in the Details pane.

4. Drag Date Date.Calendar to the line above the actual/target indicators (Figure 11-28).

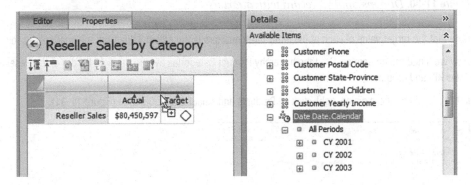

Figure 11-28. *Dragging the date dimension over*

5. When you drop the dimension, you will get a chooser—open up CY 2002, and then H1 and H2, and select the four quarters in CY 2002 (Figure 11-29).

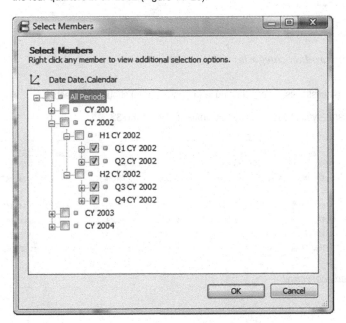

Figure 11-29. *Selecting the four quarters in CY 2002 for the date dimension*

6. Click OK. You'll now have four quarters across the columns. You can update this scorecard to see the results (Figure 11-30).

	Q1 CY 2002		Q2 CY 2002		Q3 CY 2002		Q4 CY 2002	
	Actual	Target	Actual	Target	Actual	Target	Actual	Target
Reseller Sales	$4,069,186	$4,871,801 △	$4,153,820	$4,069,186 ●	$8,880,239	$4,153,820 ●	$7,041,184	$8,880,239 △

Figure 11-30. *Dimensional scorecard with quarters*

7. Note that the target value of each of the latter three quarters is the actual value from the quarter preceding.

8. Now we'll add the categories. Drag the hierarchy Product Categories over to the right border of the Reseller Sales KPI and drop it.

9. In the Select Members dialog, right-click All Products and select Check Children (Figure 11-31).

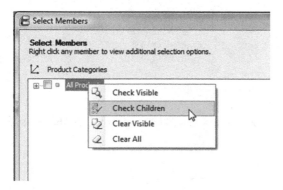

Figure 11-31. *Selecting the product categories*

10. The four product categories (Accessories, Bikes, Clothing, and Components) should be selected.

11. Click OK. Update the scorecard—you should see a result similar to Figure 11-32.

	Q1 CY 2002		Q2 CY 2002		Q3 CY 2002		Q4 CY 2002	
	Actual	Target	Actual	Target	Actual	Target	Actual	Target
⊟ Reseller Sales		△		●		●		△
Accessories	$4,946	$11,696 ◆	$11,634	$4,946 ●	$44,359	$11,634 ●	$31,797	$44,359 △
Bikes	$3,877,493	$4,473,867 △	$3,745,692	$3,877,493 △	$6,638,294	$3,745,692 ●	$5,694,536	$6,638,294 △
Clothing	$11,703	$19,324 △	$20,248	$11,703 ●	$262,533	$20,248 ●	$191,103	$262,533 △
Components	$175,044	$366,913 ◆	$376,247	$175,044 ●	$1,935,053	$376,247 ●	$1,123,749	$1,935,053 △

Figure 11-32. *The finished scorecard*

12. Publish the scorecard.

Creating an OLAP Scorecard

Our final exercise will be to create an OLAP scorecard using the wizard and import the KPI from Analysis Services. The process is fairly similar to what we did in Exercise 11-4.

Exercise 11-5. Creating an OLAP Scorecard

We're going to use the Analysis Services connection we created in Exercise 11-4, so if you skipped that exercise, go back and do it now.

1. Right-click Scorecards in the Workspace Browser, and then click New Scorecard.

2. Select Microsoft and then Analysis Services, and then click OK.

3. Name the scorecard Profit Margin by Subcategory, and click Next.

4. In the Select a Data Source page, select the Analysis Services AW data source, and click Next.

   The Select a KPI Source offers two options, as shown in Figure 11-33.

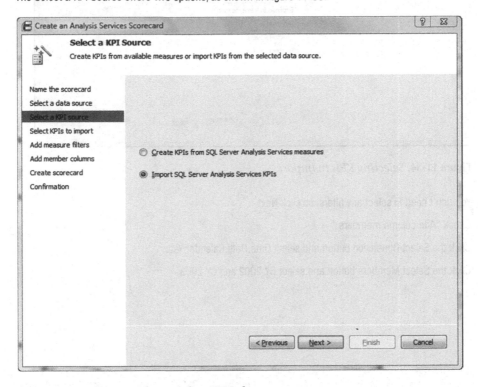

Figure 11-33. *Selecting where to draw KPIs from*

5. "Create KPIs from SQL Server Analysis Services measures" will open a page similar to what we saw in our tabular scorecard, where we could either select KPIs that already exist in the workspace or create KPIs on the fly. However, here you're going to select Import SQL Server Analysis Services KPIs.

6. Click Next. The next page (Figure 11-34) will connect to the Analysis Services server, fetch a list of KPIs from the cube you selected in the data source, and list them. Note that you can select multiple KPIs to import. Check Product4 Gross Profit Margin, and click Next.

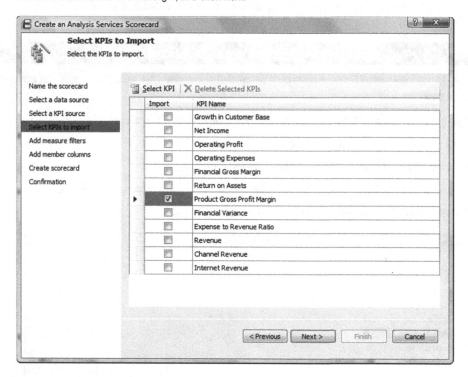

Figure 11-34. *Selecting KPIs to import*

7. You don't need to select any filters, so click Next.

8. Check "Add column members."

9. Click the Select Dimension button and select Date.Date.Calendar Year.

10. Click the Select Members button and select CY 2002 and CY 2003.

11. Click OK to close the Select Members dialog, and then click Finish. The designer generates the necessary objects and shows a status page (Figure 11-35).

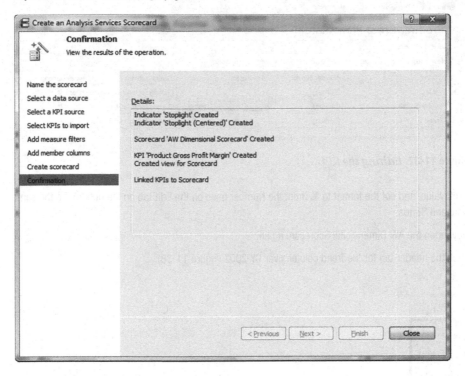

Figure 11-35. *The setup confirmation page*

12. Click the Close button. You'll have a scorecard showing Value, Goal and Status, and Trend, as created in the Analysis Services KPI (see Figure 11-36).

	CY 2002			CY 2003		
	Value	Goal and Status	Trend	Value	Goal and Status	Trend
Product Gross Profit Margin	9.68304451065213E-02	0.12	0	9.29704366528024E-02	0.12	0

Figure 11-36. *The scorecard from the wizard*

13. Let's clean it up a bit. Open the Product Gross Profit Margin KPI that the wizard created (Figure 11-37).

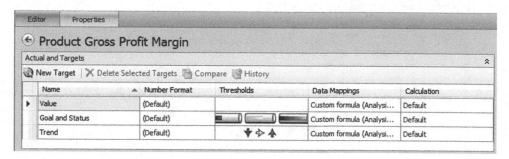

Figure 11-37. *Editing the KPI*

14. Click Value, and set the format to % (from the Number pane on the Edit tab on the ribbon). Do the same for Goal and Status.

15. Now open the AW Dimensional Scorecard again.

16. Click the header tab for the Trend column over CY 2002 (Figure 11-38).

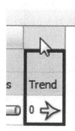

Figure 11-38. *Selecting the Trend column*

17. To open the Target Settings dialog (Figure 11-39), either right-click and select Properties or click the Properties button in the ribbon.

18. Under Values, select Show No Value, and then click OK. Do the same for the other Trend column.

19. From the dimensions in the Details pane on the right, drag Product Subcategories to the right side of Product Gross Profit Margin (Figure 11-40).

20. Right-click All Products, click Check Children from the Select Members dialog, and then click OK.

21. Click the Update button to refresh the view of the scorecard, which should look like Figure 11-41.

Target Settings
Target Settings
Choose target value, score, and indicator settings.
Values
Show target value
Show actual value
Show no value
Scoring
Show score
Ignore when score filtering
Score type:
Normalized
Score rollup type:
Average Weighted
Indicators
Show indicator image
Show indicator display name
Use indicator background color
Use indicator foreground color
Overrides
Name override:
OK
Cancel

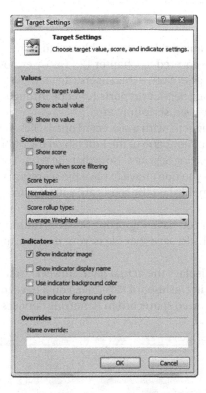

Figure 11-39. *The properties dialog for the Trend column*

CY 2002
Value
Product Gross Profit Margin
9.7 %
12.0 %

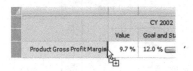

Figure 11-40. *Adding the Product Categories dimension*

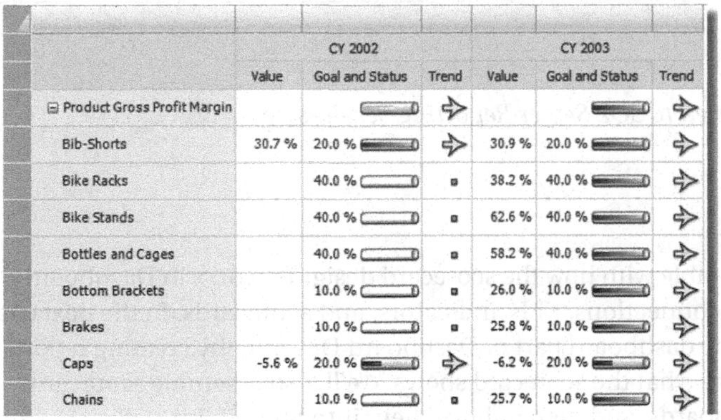

CY 2002
CY 2003
Value
Goal and Status
Trend
Value
Goal and Status
Trend
Product Gross Profit Margin
Bib-Shorts 30.7 % 20.0 % 30.9 % 20.0 %
Bike Racks 40.0 % 38.2 % 40.0 %
Bike Stands 40.0 % 62.6 % 40.0 %
Bottles and Cages 40.0 % 58.2 % 40.0 %
Bottom Brackets 10.0 % 26.0 % 10.0 %
Brakes 10.0 % 25.8 % 10.0 %
Caps -5.6 % 20.0 % -6.2 % 20.0 %
Chains 10.0 % 25.7 % 10.0 %

Figure 11-41. *The finished dimensional scorecard*

Reporting Services

Generally, you have to put a scorecard in a dashboard and publish the dashboard to Share-Point for users to consume the scorecard. (This will be covered in Chapter 12.) However, you can export a scorecard directly to SQL Server Reporting Services—then users can view the scorecard in the same ways that they can view Reporting Services reports (directly through the report manager, embedded in another web page, via subscription, etc.).

You can export the scorecard from Dashboard Designer—with a scorecard open, click the SQL Server Reporting Services button in the Scorecard Editor pane of the Edit tab on the ribbon. This will start a wizard for exporting a scorecard to Reporting Services. Note that the wizard will show a list of scorecards on the server to select from, so you don't have to have the scorecard you want to export open, but you do have to ensure you've published the scorecard you want to export to the server.

You can export directly to Reporting Services, or if you have Reporting Services running in SharePoint integrated mode, you can export to an RDL file, save that file to your desktop, and then upload it to Report Center in SharePoint.

The scorecard in Reporting Services is "live"—it displays the actual data. However, since it is an export, if you edit the definition of the scorecard in Dashboard Designer, you'll have to export the scorecard again. Figure 11-42 shows an exported scorecard in Reporting Services.

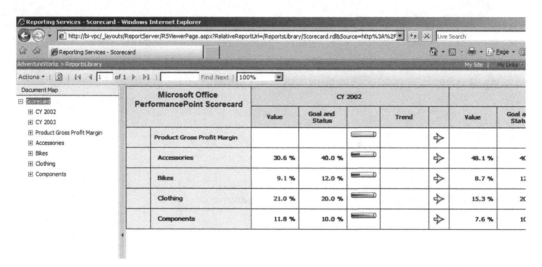

Figure 11-42. *A scorecard exported to SQL Server Reporting Services*

Conclusion

Hopefully you're now comfortable with how the scorecard designer works in Dashboard Designer. We've created data connections, KPIs, indicators, and scorecards. In the next chapter, we're going to finish off the dashboard part of Dashboard Designer by creating report views of data to give context to what the scorecard shows. We'll also assemble scorecards, reports, and filters into dashboards, and then publish them into SharePoint.

CHAPTER 12

■ ■ ■

Dashboards and Reports

We've created KPIs and scorecards, and now we want to share them. So how do we get our scorecards out where people can see them? Now we look at the feature that Dashboard Designer was named for—in this chapter, we're going to explore creating and publishing dashboards, and we're going to examine the types of analytic charts available to put on these dashboards.

Overview of the Dashboard Editor

The Dashboard editor (Figure 12-1) works in a similar manner to the Scorecard editor—a blank canvas with items in the details pane to the right that you can drag and drop into the editor. The items available are scorecards, reports, and filters. Also note the page container—dashboards can have multiple pages and will include the page navigation when published.

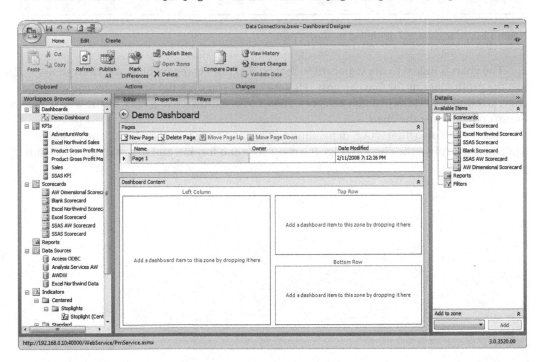

Figure 12-1. *The Dashboard editor*

Figure 12-2 shows a simple scorecard and analytic chart in a dashboard. The scorecard shows gross profit margin, broken down by product category and calendar year, from the AdventureWorks cube. The analytic chart shows gross profit margin, Internet gross profit margin, and reseller gross profit margin over four calendar years for all product categories. This gives us some contextual insight—the scorecard shows how product categories are performing against targets, and the chart shows the contributing factors and trends over time.

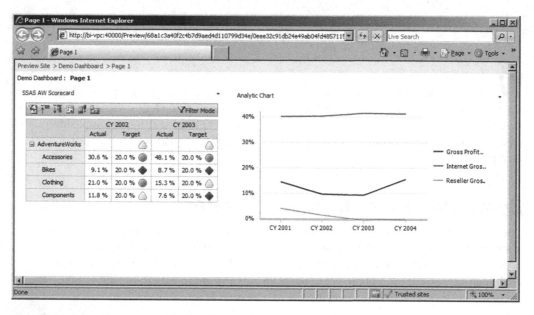

Figure 12-2. *A dashboard deployed to SharePoint*

The chart is linked to the scorecard so that by clicking a category filter, the chart shows just the profit margins for that category (Figure 12-3). If you click the Accessories category, the chart is redrawn to show just that category. The chart is redrawn using Ajax, so the whole page doesn't reload—just the chart.

The chart is also interactive, depending on the chart shown (Figure 12-4). The end user can add filters, pivot the chart, change the chart style and format, and in some cases drill into underlying data.

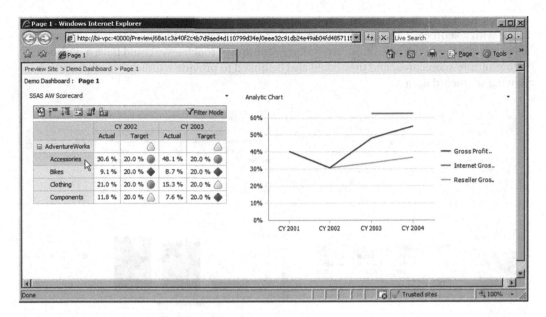

Figure 12-3. *Contextual chart filtered on Accessories*

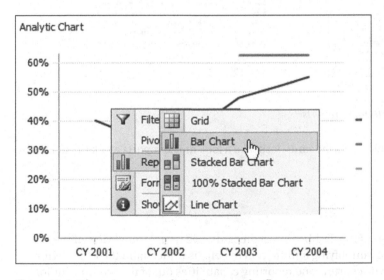

Figure 12-4. *Changing an analytic chart on the fly*

We can make a dashboard as simple or as complex as we desire. Figure 12-5 shows a dashboard with a scorecard and analytic chart, as well as a data grid and other reports. Of course, we're not limited to the one-scorecard-and-its-reports approach—we could have a dashboard with multiple scorecards, and they could also be linked to provide a drill-down approach to viewing scorecard data.

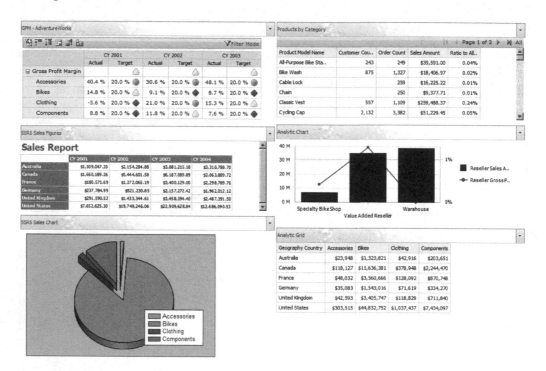

Figure 12-5. *A dashboard with more reports*

Before we dive into building dashboards, let's take a look at the reports available in Dashboard Designer.

Reports

Reports are the analytic part of the dashboard—scorecards give us an overall view of the organization; reports give us amplifying information to help us understand the KPIs. PerformancePoint provides analytic charting and reporting capabilities out of the box. In addition, you can hook to reports from SQL Server Reporting Services, ProClarity Analytics, Excel Services, and web pages. You can also create a report based on a Visio diagram (for strategy mapping). A sample analytic chart report is shown in Figure 12-6.

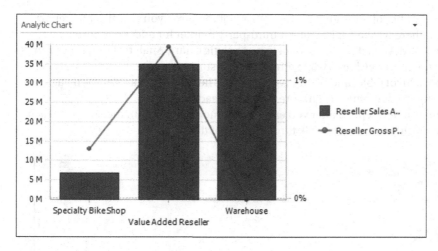

Figure 12-6. *An analytic report*

You create reports in Dashboard Designer, and they can be reused in multiple dashboards. Like all the other items in the workspace, they can be put in folders for easier management. When you create a report, you'll open the Select a Report Template dialog (Figure 12-7).

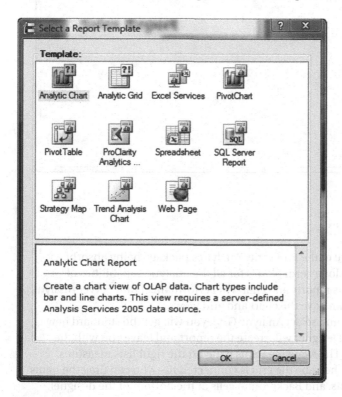

Figure 12-7. *Selecting a report template*

You can see a number of report types available out of the box—you can also add report types (and I expect there will be a fairly robust third-party market for add-on reports). Some of the report types are designed for OLAP data (e.g., Analytic Chart, Analytic Grid, ProClarity Analytics, and Trend Analysis Chart), while others can consume any type of data (e.g., Excel Services, PivotChart, PivotTable, and SQL Server Report). The Strategy Map and Web Page report types are somewhat unique, as I'm sure you can already tell.

When you create a new report, after you enter the name (Figure 12-8), the setup for each of the report types is different, so let's walk through each of them.

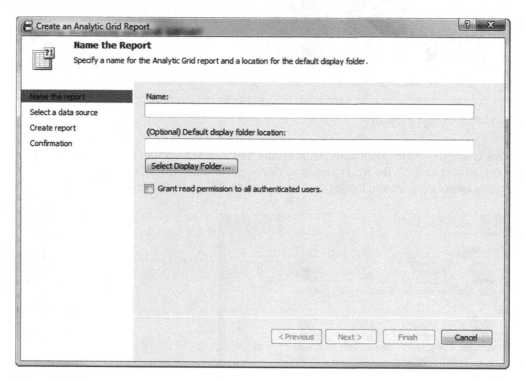

Figure 12-8. *Creating a new report*

Analytic Grids

The analytic grid is the leading edge of the ProClarity Analytics package being absorbed into PerformancePoint Server. The long-term plan is for all the analytic capabilities of ProClarity to be available natively as reports and charts in PerformancePoint Server Analytics. In PerformancePoint Server 2007, we have the chart and grid views.

When you create a new report and select Analytic Grid, you will get the standard new report setup, and then Dashboard Designer will create the report and leave you with the report design screen (Figure 12-9). The Available Items pane on the right lists measures, dimensions, and named sets from the cube the grid is connected to—you can drag the items from the pane to the Rows, Columns, and Background cells at the bottom of the designer.

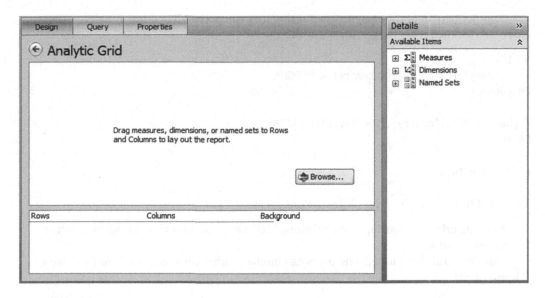

Figure 12-9. *Creating an analytic grid*

As an example, if you're using AdventureWorks, dragging Reseller Sales Amount to Background, Product Category to Columns, and Geography Country to Rows gives you something like Figure 12-10. You could also add Calendar Year to the Background area and select members to filter the view to a particular year.

Analytic Grid

Measures: **Reseller Sales Amount**

Geography Country	Accessories	Bikes	Clothing	Components
Australia	$23,948	$1,323,821	$42,916	$203,651
Canada	$118,127	$11,636,381	$378,948	$2,244,470
France	$48,032	$3,560,666	$128,092	$870,748
Germany	$35,083	$1,543,016	$71,619	$334,270
United Kingdom	$42,593	$3,405,747	$118,829	$711,840
United States	$303,515	$44,832,752	$1,037,437	$7,434,097

Browse...

Rows	Columns	Background
Geography Country ▼ ✕	Product Category ▼ ✕	Reseller Sales Amount ✕

Figure 12-10. *A grid showing sales by category, by country*

Another benefit of the analytic views is that they can act as MDX query builders—the Query tab for the preceding grid shows us this query:

```
SELECT
{ [Product].[Category].[Category].ALLMEMBERS }
ON COLUMNS,

{ [Geography].[Country].[Country].ALLMEMBERS }
ON ROWS

FROM [Adventure Works]

WHERE ( [Measures].[Reseller Sales Amount] )
```

Building grids and looking at the resulting MDX can be a good way to understand how MDX queries work.

Once the grid is published, end users can interact with it via a right-click context menu (Figure 12-11).

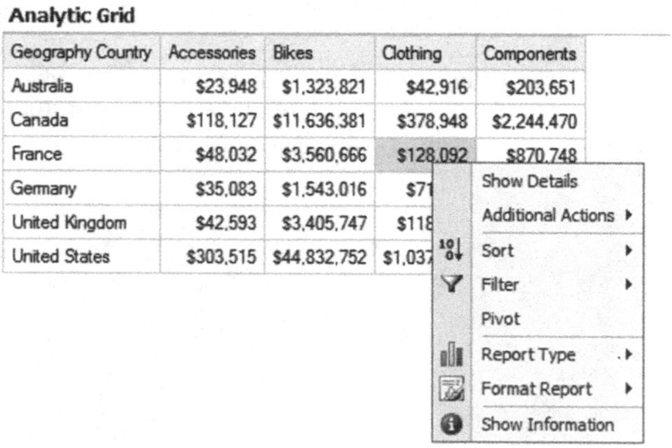

Analytic Grid

Geography Country	Accessories	Bikes	Clothing	Components
Australia	$23,948	$1,323,821	$42,916	$203,651
Canada	$118,127	$11,636,381	$378,948	$2,244,470
France	$48,032	$3,560,666	$128,092	$870,748
Germany	$35,083	$1,543,016	$71	
United Kingdom	$42,593	$3,405,747	$118	
United States	$303,515	$44,832,752	$1,037	

Context menu options:
- Show Details
- Additional Actions ▶
- Sort ▶
- Filter ▶
- Pivot
- Report Type ▸▶
- Format Report ▶
- Show Information

Figure 12-11. *Context menu in an analytic grid*

Show Details will open a window with *drill-through* data—the underlying tabular data from the source of the cube. This option may not be available if drill-through isn't enabled on the cube, if calculated measures are used, or if the user doesn't have permission to drill through on the cube.

Under Additional Actions, you'll find OLAP actions (for more about actions, see http://msdn2.microsoft.com/en-us/library/ms174515.aspx)—specifically URL, drill-through , and Reporting Services. These are attached to cells in the OLAP cube and can perform contextual actions depending on the data selected. (Note that Drillthrough here is the same as Show Details previously.)

The Sort and Filter options are fairly self-explanatory.

Pivot is a command to transpose the rows and columns in the table.

Report Type changes among the analytic report types—you can switch between a grid and the various charts from here.

Format Report switches between a hierarchical tree-type layout and a tabular layout.

Show Information toggles a header that shows background and filter information about the analytic report.

If you right-click a row or column header, you'll notice additional options, as shown in Figure 12-12. Here you can drill down into different dimensions, or drill up (move up to a parent dimension). You can isolate a single member of a dimension or remove it from the grid.

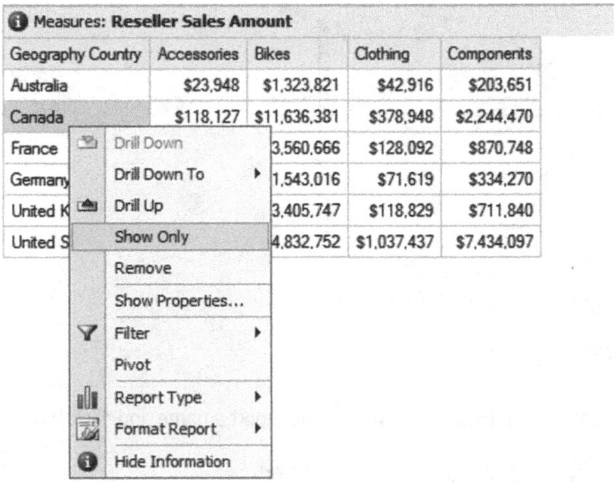

ⓘ Measures: **Reseller Sales Amount**				
Geography Country	Accessories	Bikes	Clothing	Components
Australia	$23,948	$1,323,821	$42,916	$203,651
Canada	$118,127	$11,636,381	$378,948	$2,244,470
France	3,560,666		$128,092	$870,748
Germany	1,543,016		$71,619	$334,270
United K	3,405,747		$118,829	$711,840
United S	4,832,752		$1,037,437	$7,434,097

Context menu items:
- Drill Down
- Drill Down To ▸
- Drill Up
- Show Only
- Remove
- Show Properties...
- Filter ▸
- Pivot
- Report Type ▸
- Format Report ▸
- Hide Information

Figure 12-12. *Contextual actions on a row or column header*

Exercise 12-1. Creating an Analytic Grid

■Tip The Analytic Grid wizard only lets you select data sources from the server, so you must publish any data sources you plan to use before creating this report.

1. Right-click Reports in the Workspace Browser and click New Report.

2. Select Analytic Grid from the Select a Report Template dialog (Figure 12-13).

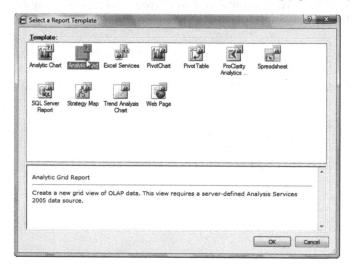

Figure 12-13. *Selecting the report type*

3. Click OK. In the Create an Analytic Grid Report dialog (Figure 12-14), give the report a name and click Next.

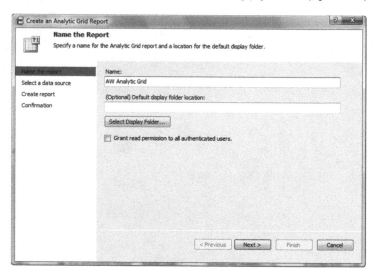

Figure 12-14. *The report creation wizard*

4. The next page lists data sources on the server for you to select from (Figure 12-15). Select an Adventure-Works data source for this report.

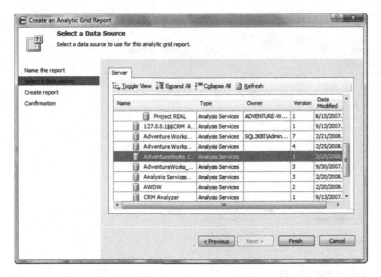

Figure 12-15. *Selecting a data source*

5. Click Finish. The wizard will generate the report.

6. Click Close on the wizard after the report is created. You'll now be looking at the report editor (Figure 12-16).

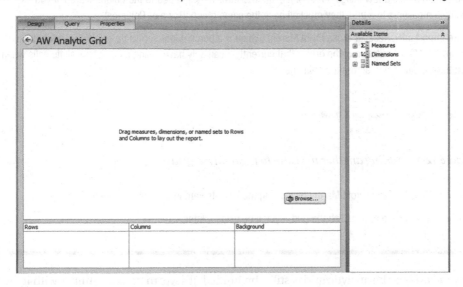

Figure 12-16. *The Analytic Grid report editor*

7. Open up Measures on the right. Scroll down and drag Reseller Sales Amount to the Background area at the bottom of the editor.

8. Now open up Dimensions (you may have to scroll down again—it's under Measures) and drag Geography Country to the Rows area on the editor.

9. Finally, drag Product Category (*not* Product Categories) from the dimension list to the Columns area in the editor.

10. You should end up with a chart like Figure 12-17.

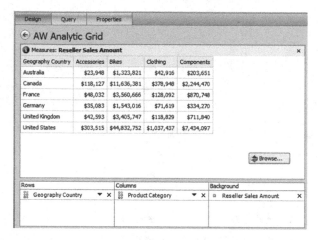

Figure 12-17. *The finished analytic grid*

11. Now go back to Measures in the Details pane—find Reseller Gross Profit Margin and drag it to the Background area under Reseller Sales Amount.

You should notice a few things—first of all, the measures have jumped to the Columns area. If you have multiple measures in a grid, they must all be in the same group (Rows or Columns).

More importantly, Reseller Gross Profit Margin (which is a percentage) shows up as a dollar amount (see Figure 12-18). A limitation of the grid is that currently it can only have a single format for all its cells when you have a dimension across the columns.

	Accessories	
Geography Country	Reseller Sal..	Reseller Gro..
Australia	$23,948	$0

Figure 12-18. *Adding another measure to the analytic grid*

12. Remove Reseller Gross Profit Margin by clicking the X on its item in the Columns area.

13. Make sure you save and publish the grid—you'll be using it later.

As you can see, the analytic grid is still a bit limited. It's worth getting familiar with it, both to understand its uses and limitations, but also because the native reporting capabilities will certainly expand in future versions of the product. For the time being, if your needs for analytic reporting are beyond what the grid can offer, design a grid in ProClarity or Reporting Services, each of which offer much richer formatting and data manipulation capabilities.

Analytic Charts

As I mentioned in the previous section, analytic charts are just chart representations of the data in an analytic grid. Figure 12-19 shows a dual-axis analytic chart. The designer uses the same setup as the grid, now labeled Series, Bottom Axis, and Background.

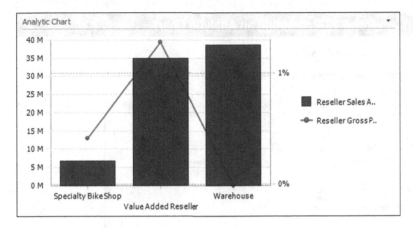

Figure 12-19. *A dual-axis analytic chart*

You can select the type of chart from the Report Type selector in the Format section of the Edit tab on the ribbon (Figure 12-20).

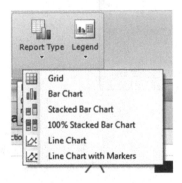

Figure 12-20. *Chart options for an analytic chart*

Pretty basic stuff—bar charts and line charts. Also, it doesn't offer much control over formatting (colors, line styles, axes, etc.). Again, if you want fancier charts, you can either use SQL Server Reporting Services or ProClarity. ProClarity is a powerful choice if your data is in Analysis Services. If you need to report on other transactional data, I recommend using Reporting Services, and if your needs extend beyond what's possible there, I recommend a third-party charting package for Reporting Services (such as Dundas or ChartFX).

Tip To get the dual-axis chart as shown in Figure 12-19, add a second measure to the series in the designer—the second measure will be added as a line chart over the bar chart.

Exercise 12-2. Creating an Analytic Chart

1. Right-click Reports in the Workspace Browser.

2. Click New Report to open the Select a Report Template dialog (Figure 12-21).

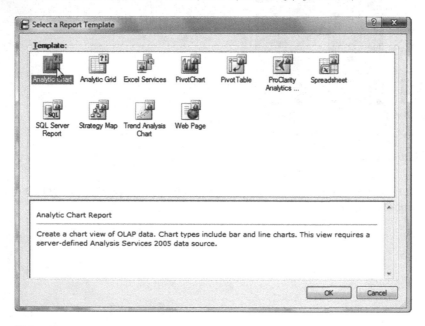

Figure 12-21. *Creating a new analytic chart*

3. Click Analytic Chart and click OK.

4. Name the report AW Analytic Chart and click Next.

5. You'll see the list of data sources on the server again; select an AdventureWorks cube and click Finish.

6. When the report is created, click Close.

   Note that the editor here (Figure 12-22) looks very similar to the editor for the analytic grid.

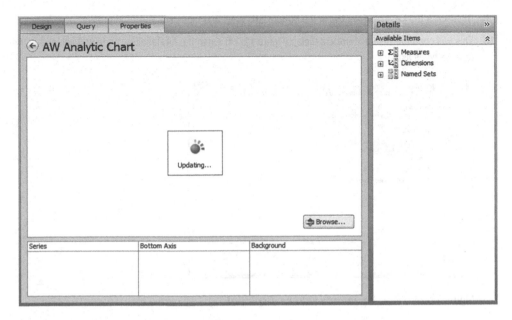

Figure 12-22. *The Analytic Chart editor*

7. Open the Measures group in the Details pane on the right, and drag Reseller Sales Amount and Reseller Gross Profit Margin to the Series area.

8. From the Dimensions group, drag Reseller Type to the Bottom Axis area. You should get the big blue box shown in Figure 12-23.

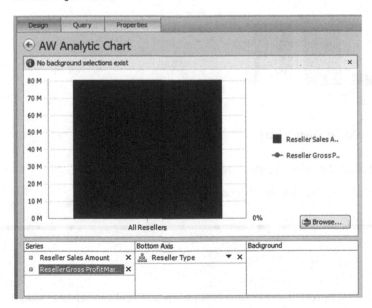

Figure 12-23. *Reseller sales info in an analytic chart*

9. Right-click the Reseller Type bar in the Bottom Axis area, and then click Select Members.

10. This will open the Select Members dialog (Figure 12-24). Open the All Resellers node and select the three reseller types listed.

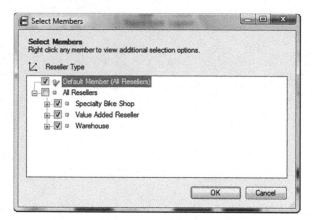

Figure 12-24. *Selecting members to be displayed*

11. When you click OK, you should see a chart like Figure 12-25.

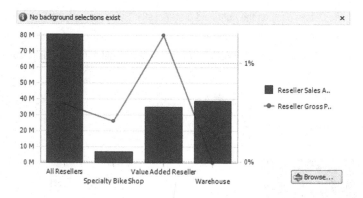

Figure 12-25. *The finished analytic chart*

Note that if you leave Default Member (All Resellers) checked, you'll get that as a column.

12. Save and publish the chart—we'll use it in our dashboard.

Excel Services

An Excel Services report allows presentation of an object from an Excel spreadsheet stored on an Excel Services–enabled SharePoint server. After creating the report, you'll see the Editor tab, where you select the SharePoint site, library, workbook, and item name to be displayed (Figure 12-26).

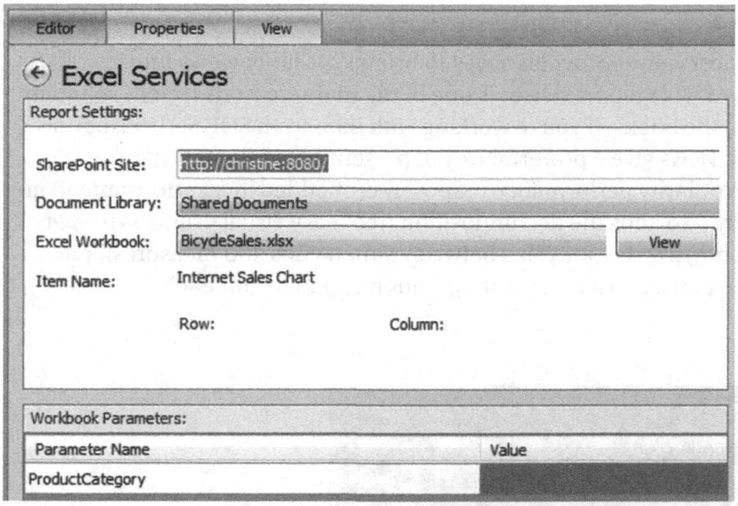

Figure 12-26. *Setting properties for an Excel Services report*

The Properties tab has the standard editor for name, description, custom properties, and so on. The View tab shows a preview of the Excel Services object for the report, including the toolbar. You can configure the viewer in the Edit tab of the ribbon—the view options and toolbar options each bring up dialogs to set the capabilities in the web part.

PivotChart, PivotTable, and Spreadsheet Reports

The PivotChart, PivotTable, and Spreadsheet reports leverage the Office Web Components (OWC). I strongly advise avoiding these report types, for a number of reasons:

- The OWC are being deprecated. They are not even included in Office 2007—if your users have Office 2007 installed, you'll have to deploy the OWC11 package separately.

- OWC leverages an ActiveX control. Apart from not being cross-browser capable, many organizations refuse to allow installation or activation of ActiveX controls in the browser.

- Since the data is selected by the OWC, you have to provide connectivity to your data source from the users' desktops, which is not a best practice.

- The OWC are pretty powerful for what they do, but there is no extensibility whatsoever, so if they don't do what you need, you have to quit and start over with a different report type.

I'm not going to walk through these report types—I very strongly recommend using SQL Server Reporting Services (or Excel Services if you have it available) for any type of presentation for which you're tempted to use these reports.

ProClarity Analytics

The ProClarity Analytics report viewer provides a way to bring ProClarity views into a PerformancePoint dashboard. This report viewer is one of the major reasons I spent so much time on ProClarity earlier in the book—if you're working with data from SQL Server Analysis Services, ProClarity analytic views give a powerful way of presenting contextual data.

Figure 12-27 shows a ProClarity performance map view embedded in a PerformancePoint Server dashboard. ProClarity also adds the decomposition tree (easy visual drill-down), perspective view (for easily identifying relationships between dimensions and measures), pie charts, scatter charts, Pareto plots, and a richer configuration capability for each.

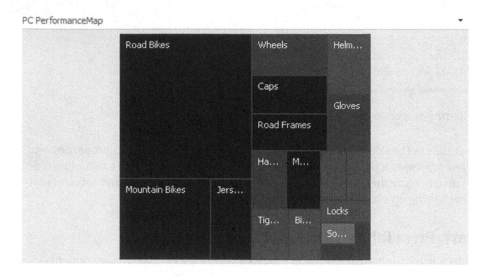

Figure 12-27. *A ProClarity performance map in a PerformancePoint dashboard*

Configuring a ProClarity report is very straightforward (see Figure 12-28). Set the URL of the ProClarity Analytics server (generally the /pas directory of the default IIS location). Clicking the Browse button opens a dialog that allows you to navigate the briefing book structure of the PAS server and select a report to display.

The Configuration Options drop-down offers a few selections, but you can type any ProClarity UI configuration option into the text box. These are detailed in the Analytics Server Administrators Guide (a PDF installed with ProClarity Analytics Server), but here's the full list:

tb: Hides the tabs, logo, and left pane of the ProClarity interface.

dt: Hides the Data Layout tab, preventing the user from changing the selected hierarchies, members, and so on.

st: Disables the actions within a chart, grid, or decomposition tree.

ti: Hides the breadcrumb trail, page title, and toolbar.

fs: Adds a button to the toolbar that allows the user to open the chart in a new window.

vh: Used for debugging; when the user performs an action while this is set, a new window is opened showing the HTML request sent to the server.

ad: Disables the Analyze in Decomposition Tree command.

dd: Disables the Drill to Detail command.

ht: Hides the breadcrumb trail, Contents tab, and previous and next page arrows.

Other than that, the ProClarity report view is very straightforward.

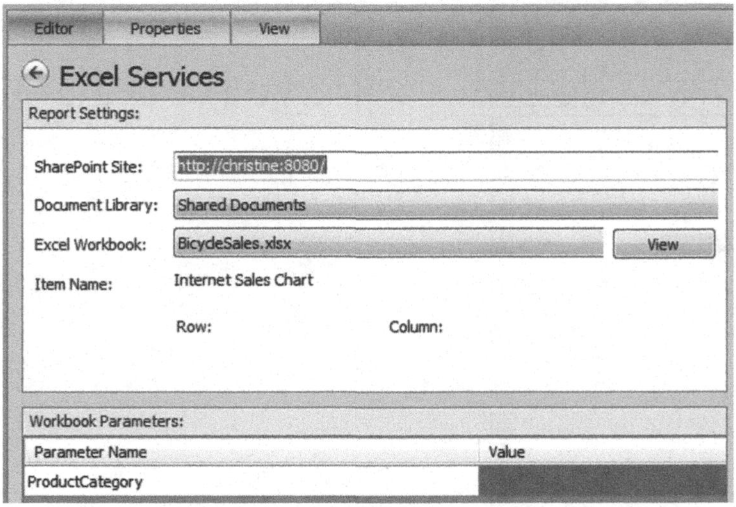

Figure 12-28. *Configuring a ProClarity report view*

Exercise 12-3. Adding a ProClarity Report

1. Right-click Reports in the Workspace Browser and click New Report.

2. Select ProClarity Analytics Server Page and click OK.

3. Name the report AW ProClarity and click Finish.

4. On the confirmation page, click Close.

5. In the editor, enter the URL for the PAS server (Figure 12-29).

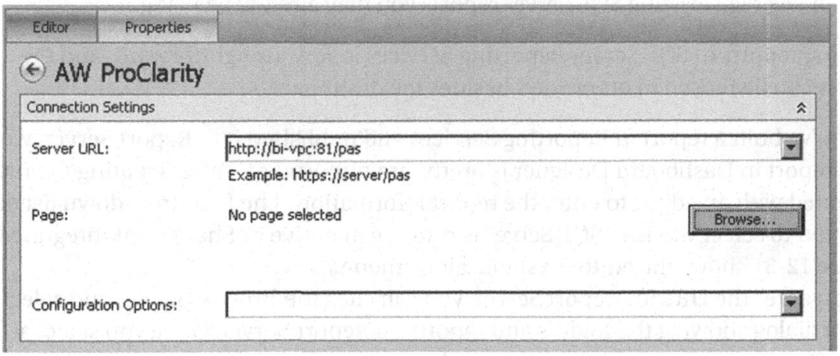

Figure 12-29. *Editing the PAS report*

6. Click the Browse button to open the PAS Browser dialog (Figure 12-30).

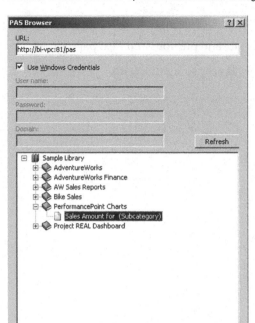

Figure 12-30. *Selecting the ProClarity report*

7. Open up the tree to find the performance map you built in Chapter 9, and then click OK.

8. Publish the report—you're done!

SQL Server Reports

These are very powerful report viewers for two reasons:

- You can leverage existing SQL Server reports you may already be using.

- Building reports in SQL Server Reporting Services is very straightforward, and the reports can be reused in other ways besides the dashboard.

Once you've built a report in Reporting Services and published it to Report Server, working with the report in Dashboard Designer is pretty straightforward—after creating the report, you're presented with an editor to enter the report information. The first drop-down list on the page allows you to select whether SQL Server is running in native or SharePoint integrated mode. (Figure 12-31 shows the editor in stand-alone mode.)

Once you enter the URL for Report Server, you can click the Browse button and select the report from a dialog showing the folders and reports on Report Server. Once you select a report, a preview of the report will show in the editor.

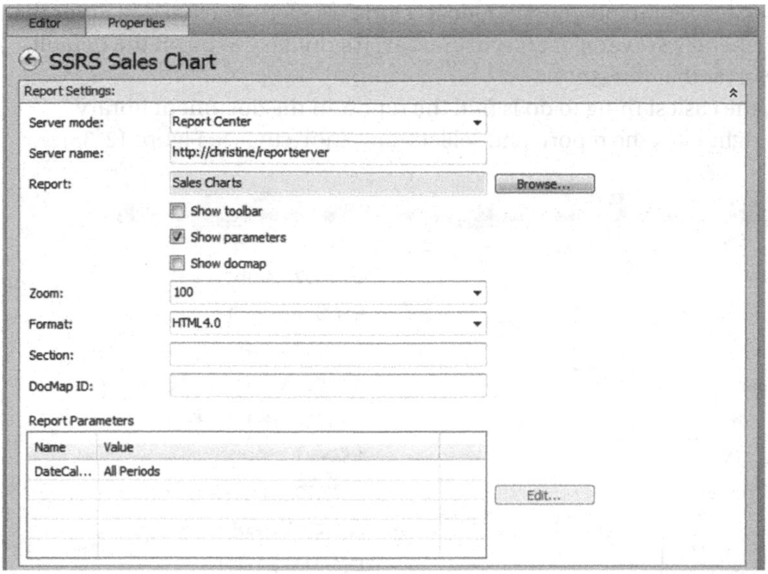

Figure 12-31. *Editing a Reporting Services report in native (Report Center) mode*

The options are fairly self-explanatory—whether you want to show or hide the toolbar, parameter selectors, and docmap for complex reports. The Report Parameters section will also automatically populate with the parameters from the report with the default values. You can select a parameter, click the Edit button, and set a different default value for the report in your dashboard.

Figure 12-32 shows the Reporting Services editor in SharePoint integrated mode.

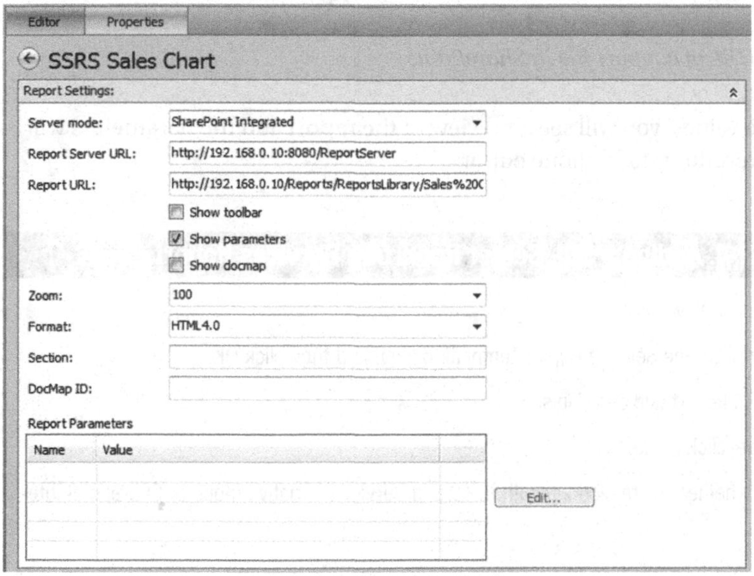

Figure 12-32. *The Reporting Services report editor in SharePoint integrated mode*

Setting up reports in SharePoint integrated mode is a little trickier—you need to enter the URL for Report Server (generally `server:port/ReportServer`; it's unlikely to be on the default port, as SharePoint takes over that directory).

For the report URL, the easiest thing to do is find the report in the document library where it was published, right-click the report, and select Copy Shortcut (see Figure 12-33).

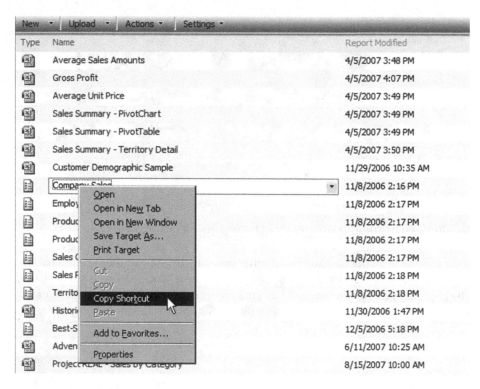

Figure 12-33. *Copying the URL of a report file in SharePoint*

Once you enter these values, you will see a preview of the report and the parameters will populate, just as in the preceding stand-alone editor.

Exercise 12-4. Adding a SQL Server Reporting Services Report

1. Right-click Reports and click New Report.

2. Select SQL Server Report from the Select a Report Template dialog, and then click OK.

3. Name the report AW SSRS Report and click Finish.

4. On the configuration page, click Close.

The next steps will depend on whether you're working with Reporting Services in native mode or SharePoint integrated mode.

5. If you're working in native mode, follow these steps:

   a. Select Report Center for the server mode (Figure 12-34).

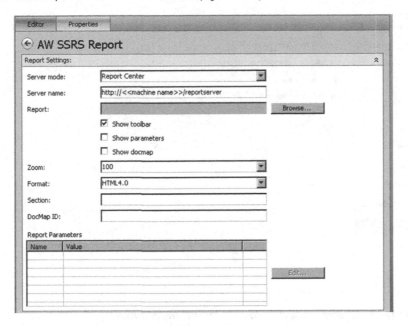

Figure 12-34. *Adding a Reporting Services report in native mode*

   b. Enter the Report Server URL—it may be on a different port if Reporting Services is on the same server as the PerformancePoint server, or in the root if you're using a stand-alone Reporting Services server.

   c. Click the Browse button to open the report selector (Figure 12-35).

Figure 12-35. *Selecting a report from Reporting Services*

6. If you're working in SharePoint integrated mode, follow these steps:

a. Select SharePoint Integrated for the server mode (Figure 12-36).

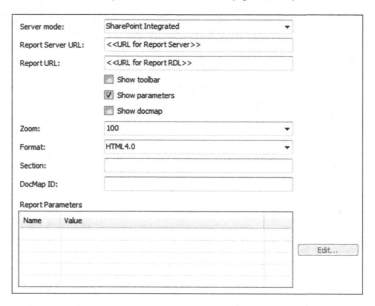

Figure 12-36. *Adding a report in SharePoint integrated mode*

b. For the report server URL, enter the server name with /ReportServer—for example, http://myserver/ReportServer.

c. For the report URL, paste the copied link to the report from the document library where it's published.

Note There's a quirk of the designer here—if you get an error, you might try switching to Report Center mode, and then back to SharePoint integrated mode. Even when you have the URLs correct, you'll often get an error until you do that. (I guess it shakes a cache loose somewhere.)

---

7. Once you've selected a report, you should see the parameters in the Report Parameters box—you can set values or leave the parameters at their defaults. Since you'll be using the parameter to link the report, leave the defaults.

8. That's it—publish the report.

Creating Dashboards

Creating a dashboard follows what you've learned so far—use the Create tab of the ribbon or right-click Dashboards and select New Dashboard to get the Select a Dashboard Page Template dialog (Figure 12-37). The options here give you some basic templates to work from, but all of the layout can also be tweaked from the Dashboard editor.

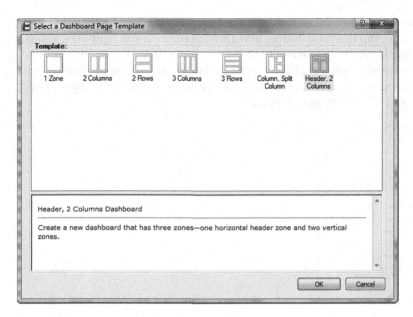

Figure 12-37. *Creating a new dashboard*

After you give it a name, you'll have your new dashboard open in the editor (Figure 12-38). On the left-hand side, dashboard pages are listed at the top, and the current page is open for editing at the bottom (the dashboard in Figure 12-38 has three zones). On the right, in the Details pane, are the items you have available to add to the dashboard—it's simply a matter of dragging and dropping to add them.

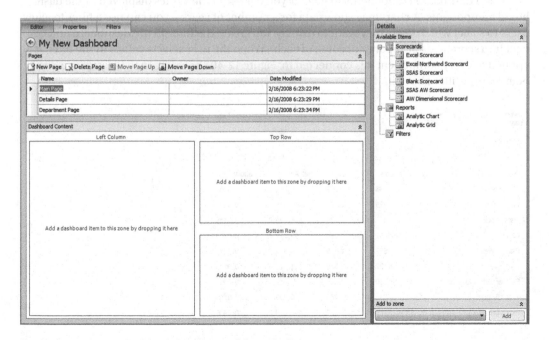

Figure 12-38. *A new dashboard in the Dashboard editor*

As mentioned previously, you can edit the dashboard layout in the Dashboard editor. The areas labeled Left Column, Top Row, and Bottom Row are each zones. If you right-click a zone, you'll get a context menu similar to that in Figure 12-39. As you can see, you can add additional zones, delete the current zone, or split it. Selecting Zone Settings will open a dialog that allows you to change the name of the zone, set how items are arranged within the zone (horizontally or vertically), and change the size of the zone.

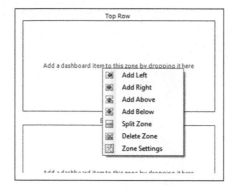

Figure 12-39. *Manipulating zones in the Dashboard editor*

The Properties page of the editor is the same as other properties throughout Dashboard Designer—name, description, person responsible, custom properties, and permissions.

Filters

Filters are dashboard components that allow you to restrict the values displayed in the dashboard components. A chart may show data for a number of years—you can use a filter to allow users to select which years they want to display. You create the filter in the dashboard and connect it to scorecards or reports (or some of each). When the user selects values in the filter, it is applied to every component it is connected to. Figure 12-40 shows an analytic grid on a dashboard with a filter above it.

Calendar Years: **All Periods** ▼

Products by Category   ▼

				⁞⁞ ◄ Page 1 of 2 ► ►⁞ All
Product Model Name	Customer Cou..	Order Count	Sales Amount	Ratio to All..
All-Purpose Bike Sta..	243	249	$39,591.00	0.04%
Bike Wash	875	1,327	$18,406.97	0.02%
Cable Lock		259	$16,225.22	0.01%
Chain		250	$9,377.71	0.01%
Classic Vest	557	1,109	$259,488.37	0.24%
Cycling Cap	2,132	3,382	$51,229.45	0.05%
Fender Set - Mountain	2,110	2,121	$46,619.58	0.04%
Front Brakes		266	$50,299.31	0.05%
Front Derailleur		257	$44,484.27	0.04%

Figure 12-40. *An unfiltered analytic grid*

You can use the filter to select a specific year (other filter options allow multiple selections). Figure 12-41 shows the selection of calendar year 2002.

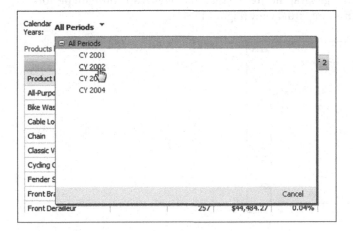

Figure 12-41. *Changing the Calendar Years filter*

After selecting the filter value, the analytic grid automatically refreshes to show the data filtered for 2002 (shown in Figure 12-42—not a lot of sales in 2002).

Product Model Name	Customer Cou..	Order Count	Sales Amount	Ratio to All..	
All-Purpose Bike Sta..					
Bike Wash					
Cable Lock		148	$10,084.70	0.03%	
Chain					
Classic Vest					
Cycling Cap		388	$9,387.61	0.03%	
Fender Set - Mountain					
Front Brakes					
Front Derailleur					

Figure 12-42. *Filtering the analytic grid*

The Filters tab of the editor lists all the connections in the dashboard—for a complex multipage dashboard, it may get tricky keeping track of what's connected to what, so you can work with connections here. More importantly, this is where you can create filters for the dashboard.

For example, considering our AdventureWorks retail sales cube, you might have a page that shows a scorecard and various reports and charts for the organization. You could add a filter that allows drilling down to the geographic area so that managers can compare performance by geography with the same contextual view (Figure 12-43).

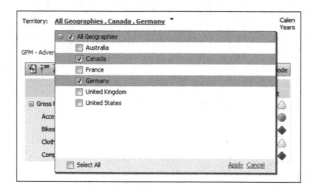

Figure 12-43. *A filter showing various geographies*

The Filters tab shows the filters available in the dashboard and how they're linked to dashboard items. The Filters tab is also where you create new filters (see Figure 12-44). Selecting a filter will show where it's used and linked on the various dashboard pages, and clicking the data source type will allow you to edit the filter. You can create a new filter by clicking the New Filter button.

Name	Data Source Type	Display Method
Named Set Filter	Named Sets	Multi-Select Tree
Tabular Data	Tabular Values	List
Geography	Member Selection	Multi-Select Tree

Dashboard Item	Endpoint	Source Value
⊟ Main Page		
Analytic Chart	[Product].[Product Categories]	DisplayValue
⊟ Details Page		
⊟ Department Page		

Figure 12-44. *The Filters tab of the Dashboard editor*

Figure 12-45 shows the filter templates available. The list of filter templates is extensible, so if you wanted to add a standard filter (e.g., a standard list of corporate departments or projects), you could create and customize that filter, and then add it to the list. For more information on creating custom filters, see http://msdn2.microsoft.com/en-us/library/cc159446.aspx.

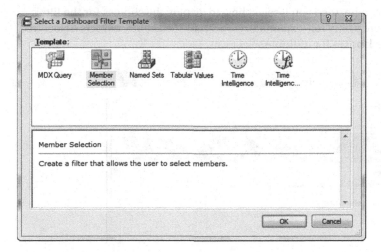

Figure 12-45. *Filter templates in the Dashboard editor*

You can have several filters on a page and reuse them across pages. However, note that filters are dashboard specific; they aren't shared across the dashboards in a workspace. The filters available by default are as follows:

MDX Query: This filter creates a filter list from an MDX query. You select a multidimensional data source, and then you can enter any MDX expression that returns a set.

■**Tip** This filter is somewhat misnamed. You don't use a Select...Where query, but just an MDX expression, such as [Time].[Calendar Year].Children.

Member Selection: Once you select a multidimensional data source, you will get a by now familiar dialog to choose the dimension and members for the filter list.

Named Sets: Again, from a multidimensional data source, you'll get a list of named sets defined in the cube.

Tabular Values: This filter offers a list of tabular data sources defined in the workspace, and then allows you to select the key and display values from the table.

Time Intelligence: This filter allows you to enter a list of time formulas (e.g., this year, last year, previous six months, etc.) that will be presented as the list in the filter.

Time Intelligence Post Formula: This filter allows you to map calendar ranges from the filter to the dashboard items, and map each item differently. For example, you may have a scorecard that shows the last four quarters and a related chart that shows the year before that. You can map a Time Intelligence Post Formula filter to look at four quarters two years ago, and the chart will map to the year before that shown on the scorecard.

Once you select the filter type, then you'll select how to display the choices for the filter (Figure 12-46). The options are pretty self-explanatory—a simple select list, a single-select tree view, or a tree view with check boxes for multiple selections.

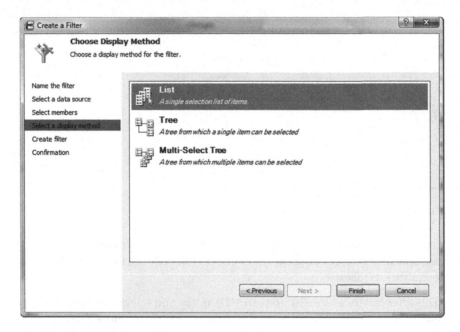

Figure 12-46. *Display options for dashboard filters*

Once you have filters in place, then you'll be able to connect the filters just as you can interconnect other dashboard items. So let's look at connecting items on the dashboard.

Linking Dashboard Items

You can link filters to scorecards, filters to reports, and scorecards to reports in the Dashboard editor. Figure 12-47 shows the available options to connect a scorecard. You can drag any of those endpoints to a report to drive the report.

■**Note** When connecting a scorecard to a report view, don't think of it as a filter, but rather as a contextual connector, since the connection may not filter the report view per se, but rather perform some kind of contextual action.

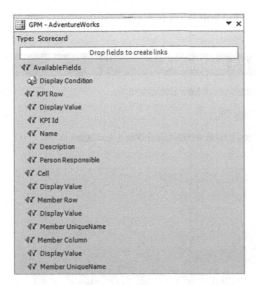

Figure 12-47. *Connecting a scorecard*

The available connectors are as follows:

Display Condition: This one's a bit unique—when you use this to connect to a report item, you'll get a dialog listing the KPIs in the scorecard. You can select various KPIs, and when those KPIs are selected by the user, the report item will display.

KPI Row: The options under KPI Row are the basic properties of a KPI—Display Value, ID (internal monitoring server ID), Name, Description, and so forth. Custom properties of the KPIs will also be surfaced here.

Cell: The display value of a cell passes the number displayed in a cell that the user selects.

Member Row: For a dimensional scorecard, Display Value and Member UniqueName pass the values for members of a selected dimension—the label displayed and a unique key that can be used to map against reports using the same dimension from the same cube.

Member Column: This is similar to Member Row, but works on the column members of a dimensional scorecard.

When you connect a filter, the only options you have are Display Condition, Display Value, and Member UniqueName for the values in the filter.

Publishing Dashboards

We've got scorecards, filters, and reports—finally, we want to tie it all together and make it available for others to view. Publishing a dashboard is very easy—simply a matter of deploying the scorecard to a SharePoint site, where PerformancePoint will build the pages and lay out the web parts for you. You can also preview your dashboard before publishing—this will open a page using web services to mimic a SharePoint site so that you can review the dashboard before publishing it.

Just a quick walkthrough, and then you'll have what you need to start building your own.

Exercise 12-5. Creating a Dashboard

1. Right-click Dashboards in the Workspace Browser, and then select New Dashboard.

2. Select Header, 2 Columns for the dashboard template. Click OK.

3. Name the Dashboard AdventureWorks and click Finish. You'll have a blank Dashboard, as shown in Figure 12-48.

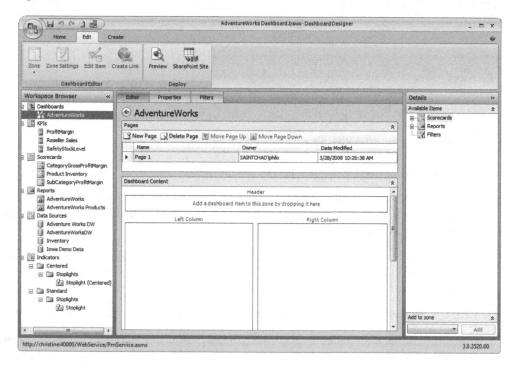

Figure 12-48. *A new blank dashboard*

Note the page list—you can add additional pages and rename pages.

4. Open the Scorecards node in the Available Items list on the right.

5. Drag the Category Sales scorecard to the Left Column zone of the dashboard.

6. Drag Subcategory Profit Margin to the Left Column zone underneath the Category Sales scorecard (see Figure 12-49).

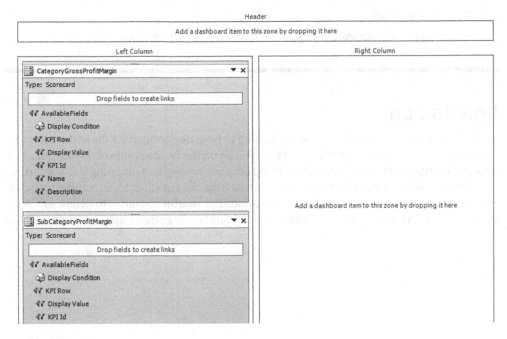

Figure 12-49. *Two scorecards in the dashboard*

7. Drag the AdventureWorks and AdventureWorks Products reports to the Right Column zone (Figure 12-50).

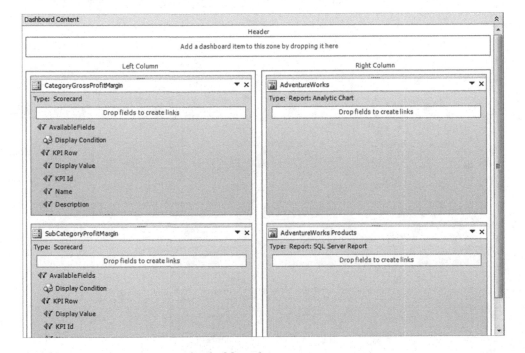

Figure 12-50. *Adding reports to the dashboard*

8. Publish the dashboard.

9. You can preview the dashboard by clicking the Preview button in the ribbon (on the Edit tab).

Conclusion

Most of the work in creating a dashboard is going to be in designing the KPIs and scorecards. One more time—a majority of effort and time will be on the *business* side of the analysis, not the development side, and then on identifying data availability and mapping it to the business.

Now that we have a dashboard, what do we do when an indicator turns red? We probably want to analyze the problem and do some forecasting or what-if scenarios to determine the next steps. And that's where the PerformancePoint Planning Server comes into play. Let's take a look.

CHAPTER 13

■ ■ ■

Planning

Now that we've collected our business data together, aggregated it, built reports, performed analysis and created scorecards, what do we do next?

PerformancePoint Server also offers a planning engine, for modeling, reconciling, consolidating, and forecasting business data. Prior to PerformancePoint, this kind of planning engine was a premium piece of software, and generally limited to the financial planning office. With PerformancePoint Server, it's in the box, so understanding at least the basic capabilities is worth the effort.

Probably the most popular financial planning tool today is Excel—not "Excel with plug-ins" or "Excel as the front end of a multimillion-dollar enterprise planning engine"—just Excel. Dozens or hundreds of spreadsheets filled with custom formulas and years of financial data result in millions of dollars laid out in complex sheets with arcane macros running the whole thing.

I don't have an extensive background in financial planning. However, I know enough to be shocked at what I've seen at the places I've visited. The surprises I've found (which I'm assured by subject matter experts are not unusual) include the following:

- Not only do the offices of financial planning and budget execution seldom talk to each other, they're often in different parts of the organization (imagine having your spouse draw up the household budget for the year, and then give you a checkbook with no balance to pay bills and go shopping).

- Large organizations do not delegate financial planning to subordinate departments. Why? Since all the planning is done by spreadsheet, collecting inputs from, say, two dozen departments means 24 spreadsheets that have to be copied and pasted into a master. It's easier to just get input via e-mail and do all the planning at the top.

- Often, the spreadsheets have grown so complex that nobody is really sure what exactly is happening when they enter numbers.

These are processes that have grown over years or decades, and moving to a new toolset would be a Herculean effort.

What Microsoft hopes to offer in PerformancePoint Planning Server is the easiest possible migration from spreadsheet-based planning to a proper enterprise-class client-server–based approach, where the client is still Microsoft Excel.

■**Note** PerformancePoint Planning is an incredibly intricate subject. My goal here is to provide a basic introduction and demystify the subject. For more in-depth information, I recommend *The Rational Guide To Planning with Microsoft Office PerformancePoint Server 2007*, by Adrian Downes and Nick Barclay (Rational, 2008).

Why Plan?

Why does an enterprise need planning? We've talked a lot about data and aggregations of data throughout this book. Just about everything to date has been historical—out of the past. We've looked for patterns and problems and identified ways to track how our business is performing. But what next? If a KPI on our scorecard turns red, we analyze the data, read our reports, and come up with a plan of action.

Now, we need to be able to predict how our plan will perform based on existing business data. We need to be able to distribute the proposed changes, allow our subordinate organizations to plan around the changes, and consolidate their responses.

This is where PerformancePoint Planning Server comes in. Using SQL Server Analysis Services on the back end, it allows our financial experts to build models (which are built as cubes) and then build input forms and reports on top of those models. After that, the organization can use these models to delegate budget planning, reconcile financial records, and perform what-if analysis on various scenarios (5 percent increase in revenue, 10 percent reduction in personnel, etc.). Most importantly, the front end for entering and working with this financial data is Microsoft Excel (see Figure 13-1).

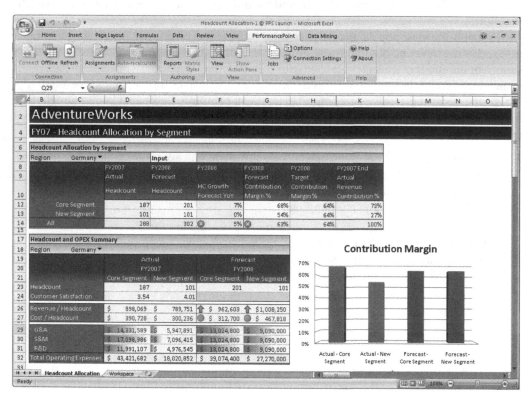

Figure 13-1. *Using Excel 2007 for data entry in PerformancePoint Planning*

■**Note** PerformancePoint Planning 2007 allows you to use both Excel 2003 and 2007 for data entry forms.

Let's take a look at the primary scenarios for using PerformancePoint Planning Server models.

PerformancePoint Planning Server Scenarios

The primary function of PerformancePoint Planning Server is to provide a more accessible user interface for building cubes, for building the architecture for reporting and data entry on those cubes, and for running the aggregations. The ways to take advantage of the Planning engine in PerformancePoint are numerous.

Planning and Budgeting

The ubiquitous term "planning" can cover a lot, but typically in PerformancePoint, it refers to budget planning. This is the simple task of setting up a budget for the future in order to plan for expenses and obligations. Generally, budgets are laid out on paper or in Excel, and often, once written, they're never really looked at again. With PerformancePoint, once the budget is modeled (e.g., accounts laid out, district hierarchies created, forms designed), accountants can work on the budget in Excel forms, and once completed, the data is stored back in the server.

Once stored, you can see how straightforward comparing actual expenditures to planned amounts would be—just two different measures on similar dimensions. You could also use a scorecard: set the budgeted amounts as the targets and use "closer to the target is better" indicators.

Consolidating

Figure 13-2 shows the problem in consolidating budgets. For a company to produce an annual budget, they need input from various departments; a large corporation may need inputs from various districts; and a multinational corporation may get inputs from various countries.

Ideally, we want to get direct input from everyone who has a balance ledger. However, in a world of Excel spreadsheets and Outlook, this means e-mailing Excel files and collecting them back. If you need updates, you either e-mail the file out again or just ask interested parties to send it again. Then you have to take your collection of spreadsheets, go through each one, copy and paste the values into the right places, verify formulas, and save often. Figure in the fact people are still submitting budgets and changes, so you're saving more files, copying more data, pasting, checking . . . It's a formula for making a mistake.

As I mentioned previously, at the large enterprise level, some financial planners don't even ask for submissions for this reason. They simply act on previous years' budgets, capital projects, and requests. Once they get all the allocations figured out, they submit the budget, and every group is told what their allocations are.

With PerformancePoint Planning, the financial planning group at a corporation can design a model for its budget. The planning group includes a dimension representing the organizational hierarchy, and then it can use PerformancePoint to distribute assignments that the subordinate organizations will complete in Excel. Once each departmental budget is completed, that budget officer submits the entries via the Excel plug-in. The plug-in submits the data back to the server, where it's written to the cube.

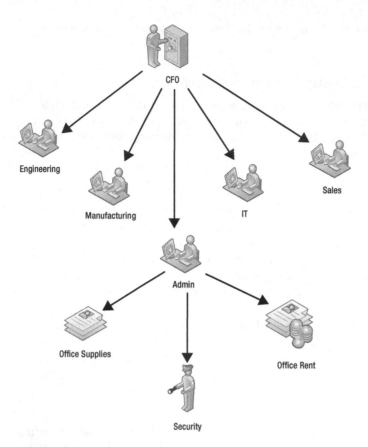

Figure 13-2. *Budget consolidation*

Since all this information is written to the cube, it is automatically aggregated; our financial planning group just has to open up any report that can view OLAP data to view the budget data in any breakdown or create the final report for the rolled-up organization.

What-If Scenarios

Another major abuse of Excel is performing what-if scenarios:

- What if I cut my workforce by 10 percent?

- What if I shift trucks from one district to another?

- What if I reinvest 25 percent of my profits?

- What if my budget is cut 5 percent?

Generally when these situations crop up, we open Excel, copy and paste a bunch of data into it, manipulate the data here and there until we like our answer, and then make the changes and save the Excel file somewhere we can find it later (maybe).

PerformancePoint Planning Server allows you to build a model based on business data, then build a what-if and forecasting form using assumptions and business rules to try various approaches to solving the problem, and seeing how it affects interrelated data. Since it's client-server based, then when we're done with our analysis, we can save the model and our work for review later (what went wrong?) or reuse next year.

Reconciling Ledgers

This may be a bit startling, but when companies or branches interact with each other, they can often make bookkeeping errors. Sometimes a price may be recorded in the wrong currency in one ledger, or the exchange rate may be used from the day before or day afterward. This creates a discrepancy in our company if both entities roll up to the same parent; for example, let's consider a manufacturing unit and a warehouse unit of a bicycle manufacturer.

The manufacturing unit buys 1,280 widgets at $1 a widget from the warehouse unit (executes paperwork and transfers money between accounts). Due to a typo, the manufacturing unit records the transaction as $1,200. Both organizations' books balance, but the parent company just "lost" $80 in their overall accounting ledgers. In the bad old days of manual ledgers (which for some companies was last Tuesday), reconciling accounts would mean going through line by line and finding the discrepancies.

With PerformancePoint Planning, the transaction logs from the two organizations are run through an intercompany reconciliation process: transactions are matched between ledgers, and any mismatch is entered into reconciliation accounts to track the disparities and correct them in one group's account. The tracking account is flagged so it is not rolled up into any corporate consolidation, leaving the corrections to be rolled up, and everything balances out.

For more information about intercompany reconciliation, see http://msdn.microsoft.com/en-us/library/bb839195.aspx.

PerformancePoint Planning Server Architecture

PerformancePoint Planning Server consists of essentially three things:

1. A server-based process accessed via web services

2. A Planning Business Modeler client for designing Planning models and workflows

3. An Excel plug-in for users to interact with Planning Server from Excel (2003 or 2007)

Installation

Installing PerformancePoint planning is fairly straightforward. There are three things to install: Planning Server, the Planning Business Modeler (PBM), and the PerformancePoint add-in for Excel (see Figure 13-5). Install Planning Server on the server dedicated to PerformancePoint Planning Server; you'll need access to SQL Server for metadata and model databases and to Analysis Services for the models.

■**Note** You will need PerformancePoint Service Pack 1 to install PerformancePoint Server on Windows Server 2008. While SP1 will install on SQL Server 2008, installation on SQL Server 2008 won't be supported until SP2.

PerformancePoint, Windows 2008, and 64 Bits

PerformancePoint Server has both 32-bit and 64-bit installers. While a lot of 32-bit applications will run happily on a 64-bit machine, 32-bit PerformancePoint Planning Server will not install on a 64-bit server. The problem is the error code you will get if you try; the installer will complain that it is only supported on Windows Server 2003.

Rest assured this error is solely about trying to install the 32-bit server on a 64-bit server operating system. If you install the 64-bit version, it will install cleanly (Server, Modeler, and add-in).

You will also need the IIS 6 management compatibility role service installed in Windows Server 2008 to enable the Planning web services to run.

Now, those who have been paying attention will realize a problem: if we have ProClarity installed, IIS is running in 32-bit mode, and we can't install 64-bit web services (in fact, the 64-bit installer will complain about this at the end and fail). However, this is where IIS 7 really scores—it can run 32-bit and 64-bit webs side by side.

Before you install Planning Server, open IIS Manager (see Figure 13-3). Select DefaultApp-Pool, and click the Advanced Settings link on the right.

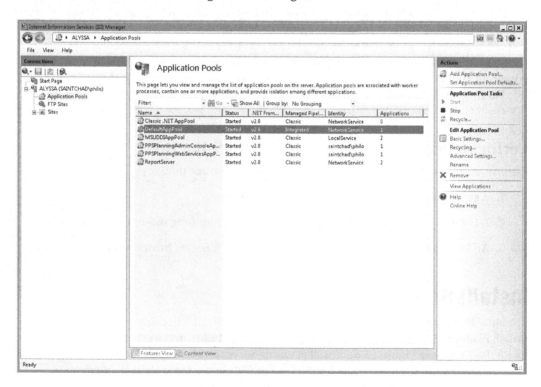

Figure 13-3. *Use Windows Server 2008 IIS Manager to select DefaultAppPool*

In the Advanced Settings dialog (see Figure 13-4) change Enable 32-Bit Applications to False, and click the OK button. Next, click Set Application Pool Defaults, and do the same thing.

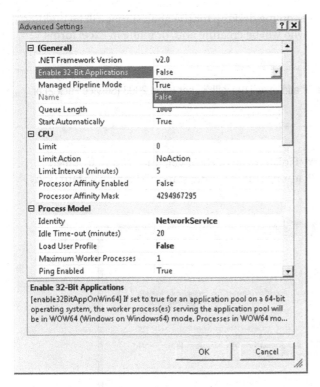

Figure 13-4. *Changing the default AppPool to 64-bit settings*

Once you've set these, you can install PerformancePoint Planning Server in 64-bit mode. I found afterward that my 32-bit applications had been switched to 64-bit ones, but I switched them right back, and everything ran fine.

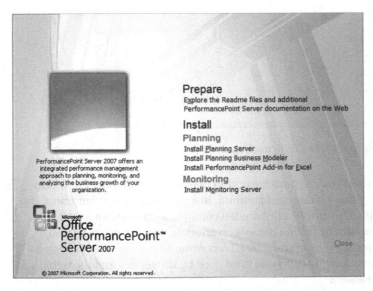

Figure 13-5. *The Installer splash page for PerformancePoint Server*

Install the Planning Business Modeler on the desktop for the analyst that will be building models; the Excel add-in is for the users who will be creating and/or filling in Excel forms.

Note The PerformancePoint Planning Server add-in will run with either Excel 2003 (Service Pack 2) or Excel 2007.

The installers are all basic Next-Next-Finish wizards. However, once you've installed Planning Server, you'll need to run the Planning Server Configuration Manager wizard (see Figure 13-6).

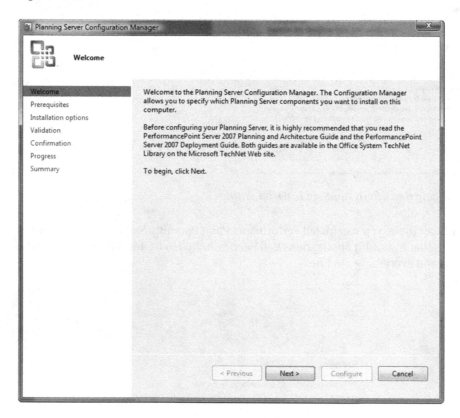

Figure 13-6. *Running the Planning Server Configuration wizard*

After checking prerequisites, you will have the option to install PerformancePoint Planning Server as a distributed or stand-alone configuration. In a stand-alone configuration, you install all services on the same machine. In a distributed configuration, you can install Planning Server on one server, the administration console on another, and the Planning web services on a third machine for the sake of scalability. I recommend the stand-alone installation to start with; then, monitor loading (CPU and RAM used by the service and the web services) and scale out as necessary.

Working with Planning

We'll walk through creating a model from the AdventureWorks database, issuing jobs to two subordinate districts, reviewing and consolidating the results, and performing a what-if scenario analysis.

For the walkthrough, I'll be using the personas in Table 13-1.

Table 13-1. *Setting Up User Roles*

Name	User ID	Office	Role
Administrator	administrator	US	Administrator/modeler
Bethani Chappell	bchappell	US	Financial planner
Ben Burton	ben	Georgia	Financial planner
Dennis Weaver	dweaver	Virginia	Financial planner

First, we'll need to add users to the Planning Server; then, we'll create an application and a model site. Applications are containers that can hold multiple models, forms, and other information. An application maps directly to a single application database and a single staging database in the underlying database server.

A model site is the container for a model, including permissions, business processes, dimensions, and member sets. A model site maps directly to a single database in SQL Server Analysis Services (what you think of as a solution if you usually work in BIDS).

Exercise 13-1. Planning Administration

1. Open a web browser, and navigate to `http://[server]:46788/` where `[server]` is the location of Planning Server. This will open the administration console (see Figure 13-7).

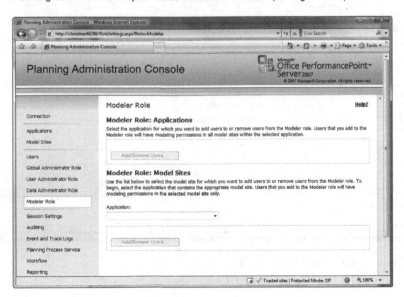

Figure 13-7. *The Planning Administration Console*

2. Click the Connection link on the left.

3. Connect to the planning server (`http://[server]:46787`), and click Connect.

4. Once connected, you should see "Connected to the computer running Planning Server."

5. Now, click the Users link on the left.

6. The Users console (see Figure 13-8) lets you add, import, or delete users from the Planning Server.

   • To list all of the users in the system, click the Find button with nothing in the fields.

   • To enter users individually, click the Add button.

   • Importing users requires a text CSV file with three columns: name (display name), label (domain\user name), and e-mail address.

   • Enter the User ID and the Display name (No, I have no idea why they didn't just look up the username from Active Directory). Click the "Add" button and you're done.

   • Note the roles available: Global Administrator, User Administrator, Data Administrator, and Modeler. The user account that installed the Planning Server should already be the Global Administrator.

Figure 13-8. *The user administration console*

Creating an Application and a Model Site

7. Click the Applications tab on the left.

8. Click the Create button to open the Create Application form (see Figure 13-9).

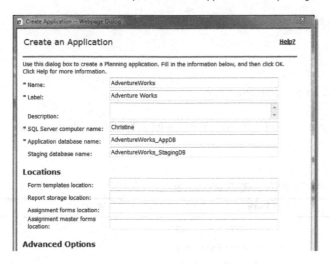

Figure 13-9. *Creating a new application*

9. Enter the information shown in Table 13-2.

Table 13-2. *Fields to create a Planning application*

Field	Value
Name	AdventureWorks
Label	Adventure Works
SQL Server computer name	localhost or the name of your SQL Server
Application database name	AdventureWorks_AppDB
Staging database name	AdventureWorks_StagingDB

10. On the client where you will be using the Modeler, create a folder on a drive named AdvWPPS.

■**Note** When you design forms in Excel, the forms will be saved to the *local directory* indicated in step 12. For collaboration purposes, you could use a network share with appropriate rights for modelers or, for the best solution, use a SharePoint document library with appropriate privileges (document libraries can be addressed using \\server\path UNC syntax).

---

11. In the folder you just created, create four folders: Forms, Reports, Assignments, and AssignmentsMasters (see Figure 13-10).

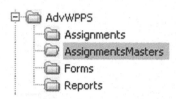

Figure 13-10. *The file repository on Planning Server*

12. In the Locations section of the Create an Application page, enter the full path for each folder; paths are shown in Table 13-3.

Table 13-3. *Paths for the File Locations in the Create an Application Dialog*

Location	Path
Form templates location	`C:\AdvWPPS\Forms`
Report storage location	`C:\AdvWPPS\Reports`
Assignment forms location	`C:\AdvWPPS\Assignments`
Assignment master forms location	`C:\AdvWPPS\AssignmentsMasters`

13. Check the box labeled "Enable native SQL/MDX rules," which allows analysts to write business rules that are written in native SQL or MDX script. The planning engine passes these rules directly to the underlying database, so you can see the vulnerability here. Leave Enable Excel Macro Support unchecked.

■**Note** As the PerformancePoint help file states, when this feature is enabled, it may pose a security risk because users will have more processing capabilities that could affect many database objects. As an added layer of security, before a new or an edited native rule can be run, a database administrator must set its `isActivated` property to `TRUE` in the `RuleSetsOrRules` table in the application database.

---

14. For the default model site, enter **HQPlanning** for "Root site name," **Headquarters Planning** for "Root site label," and the computer name for the server running SQL Server Analysis Services.

15. Click OK.

Editing a Model Site

16. Click the Model Sites tab in the console.

17. Notice that the HQ model site has already been created.

18. Click the User Administrator Role link on the left.

19. Add your current user to the Applications and Model Sites User Administrator roles.

20. Finally, you're ready to create a data source for the model. Click the Data Sources link on the left.

21. Select the AdventureWorks application and the HQPlanning model.

22. Click Add to open the data source connection dialog (see Figure 13-11).

23. Name the connection **AdventureWorks** and type **Adventure Works** in the Label field. The Description field is optional—you can add some descriptive text if you wish.

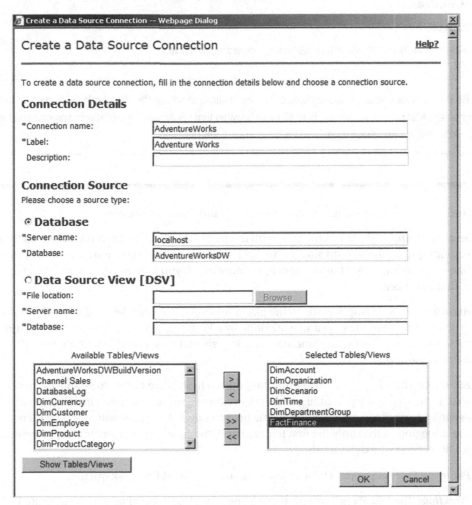

Figure 13-11. *Creating a data source connection for a model*

24. Select the radio button next to Database—we're going to connect to the AdventureWorksDW database. Enter the Server name where you will connect, and "AdventureWorksDW" for the Database as shown in Figure 13-11.

25. Click the Show Tables/Views button on the lower left to list the tables and views in the database.

26. Select the following tables, and move them to the Selected Tables/Views list using the button with the single right-facing arrow (>):

   - DimAccount
   - DimOrganization
   - DimScenario
   - DimTime
   - DimDepartmentGroup
   - FactFinance

27. Click OK.

28. Note that the data connection has been added and is already active.

Note For each role, you can add users to either the Application role or the Model role. Adding users to the role for an application gives them rights to all models within that application. Alternatively, you can add them to the Model role for just those models you want to grant them rights on.

Notice these other settings in the Planning Administration Console:

Session Settings: All communication with the planning server is via web services, so these settings govern the session state for the web services. For the most part, the defaults are fine—as you implement more models for more users, you may need to tweak this to work with users' needs.

Auditing: Tracks changes made to the planning server, both models and data. Given the probable nature of the data and work done by a PerformancePoint Planning installation, robust auditing is necessary, and the audit logs should be secured to a limited set of administrators.

Event and Trace Logs: The most important option here is the ability to enable event consolidation. Given the potential number of events in a robust planning installation, the event and trace logs can quickly become bogged down. Event consolidation restricts event logging so that only the first ten events of the same type are written to the log every 3,600 seconds (the default value).

Planning Process Service: These two settings manage workflow task queues.

Workflow: The OLAP cube refresh interval indicates how long after data is submitted the cube refreshes (this prevents cube thrashing while multiple users are submitting changes). The notifications section is for the e-mail server information for the planning server to e-mail workflow notices.

Reporting: This allows you to enter the URL to a server running SQL Server Reporting Services for publishing operational reports (assignments, workflow status, jobs, etc.) and business reports you design for financial reporting.

Data Sources: This one allows you to list and maintain the data sources used in models.

Now, let's leave the administration console and create a model.

Creating a Model

Most of our work will be done in the Planning Business Modeler (see Figure 13-12). The modeler, once connected, will be where you create models and dimensions. You can associate Excel forms that you create in Excel 2003 or 2007 (with the PerformancePoint Planning add-in), and create workflow.

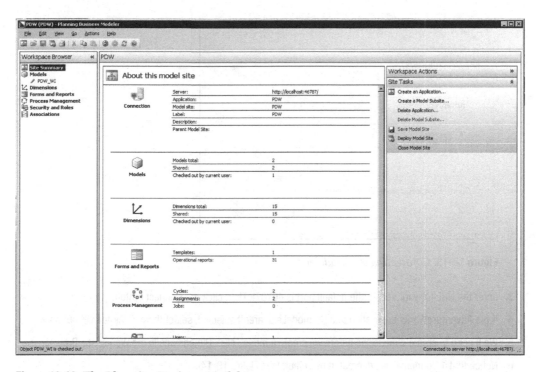

Figure 13-12. *The Planning Business Modeler*

PerformancePoint Planning also has a basic check-in/check-out capability; checking out an object locks it so that other modeler users cannot edit it.

The modeler manages the models and dimensions you build, as well as associated forms (Excel spreadsheets), and the workflow used to push jobs out to other users (for example, the subordinate budget requests for our budget analysts that have to be aggregated again afterward).

The easiest way to understand the modeler is to use it, so let's create a model.

Exercise 13-2. Creating a Model

1. Open the Planning Business Modeler.

Note When you open the Planning Business Modeler, it doesn't do anything. This may seem like an odd note, but we're all so used to Microsoft products opening a wizard when they open, you may find yourself sitting and waiting for something to happen. After opening the modeler, you need to connect to a model—there's no wizard or welcome screen.

2. Connect to the Planning Server by selecting File ➤ Connect to open the Connect dialog box (see Figure 13-13).

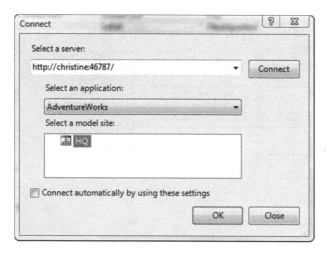

Figure 13-13. *Connecting the modeler*

3. Enter the URL for your server (the default port is 46787). Then click the Connect button.

4. If the AdventureWorks application and HQ model site aren't selected, select them. Click the OK button.

5. We'll need to create dimensions before we create a model; click Dimensions in the Workspace Browser.

6. Notice that 11 dimensions are created by default (see Figure 13-14).

7. We're going to edit the entity dimension to create our organization hierarchy. Click the Entity link to open the entity dimension (entities represent units of our business, like sales districts, branches, or other subdivisions).

8. Click the blue Check Out link on the right to check out the dimension for editing.

Tip If the Check Out link isn't enabled, go back to the administration site and verify the permissions for your user.

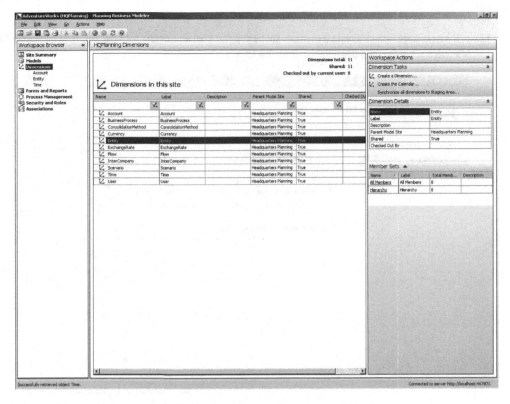

Figure 13-14. *Default dimensions in the Planning Business Modeler*

9. Click the Member Maintenance tab; we're going to add the offices in our organization.

10. Select the No Member default member, and click the "Add sibling" button:

11. In the new member, you can type directly into the fields to add values.

12. Give the member you just created the name **Headquarters** and the label **Headquarters**.

■**Tip** Names are descriptive fields displayed for users; there are no restrictions on the name field. Labels are the primary key for a member and have a number of restrictions on naming. See the help topic "About Names and Labels" for more information.

---

13. Create six more members: Northeast District, Southeast District, Florida, Georgia, Massachusetts, and New York (use these member names as the names and labels for each).

14. Click the "Save this Dimension" link on the right.

15. Now we're going to create the hierarchy for the organization. We'll need a new member set to create the hierarchy, so click Create Member Set.

16. Name the new member set **Hierarchy**, and click Next.

17. In the next page, select "Create a member set by copying from an existing member set," and select the All Members set in the drop-down field (see Figure 13-15).

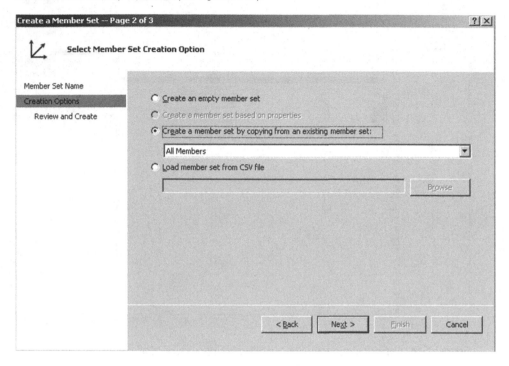

Figure 13-15. *Creating a new member set*

18. Click Next.

19. Click Finish on the final page.

20. You're now in the hierarchy member set; all the members have been copied over, we just need to arrange them.

21. Highlight all the members except for Headquarters, and indent them with the right-facing arrow button (see Figure 13-16).

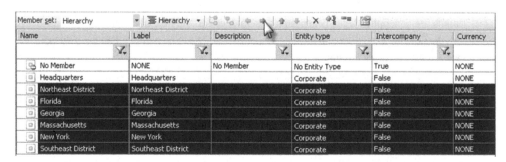

Figure 13-16. *Indenting a selection of members*

22. This indents the members and makes them subordinate to the Headquarters member.

23. Using the up and down arrow buttons, position the members so that Massachusetts and New York are under Northeast District and then indent those two states. Do the same for Florida and Georgia under Southeast District. The results should look like Figure 13-17.

No Member	NONE	No Member	No Entity Type	True	NONE
Headquarters	Headquarters		Corporate	False	NONE
Northeast District	Northeast District		Corporate	False	NONE
Massachusetts	Massachusetts		Corporate	False	NONE
New York	New York		Corporate	False	NONE
Southeast District	Southeast District		Corporate	False	NONE
Florida	Florida		Corporate	False	NONE
Georgia	Georgia		Corporate	False	NONE

Figure 13-17. *The corporate hierarchy*

24. Click "Save this dimension" on the right; then click "Check in" to commit your changes and release the dimension.

25. Now, let's add a dimension for the billing codes of our consultants; click "Create a dimension" on the right.

26. Name the dimension **Billing Codes**, and click the Next button.

27. On the Dimension Structure page, select "Create new dimension structure," and click Next.

28. On the Member Set page, leave the default "Define members later" option selected, and click Next.

29. Click Finish.

30. Click "Create a Member Property" to open the Member Property dialog (see Figure 13-18).

Figure 13-18. *Creating a new member property*

31. Name the property **Hourly Rate**, set the Data type to Money, and click OK.

32. Now add members to the member set, set the hourly rate for each member, and create a hierarchical member set that matches the one shown in Figure 13-19.

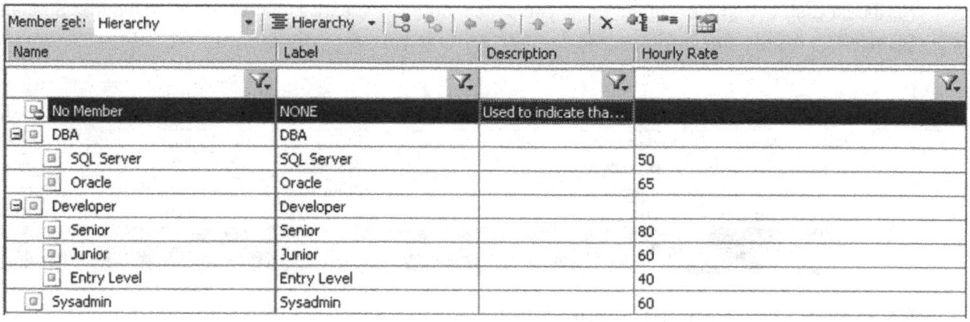

Member set: Hierarchy		Hierarchy								
Name		Label		Description		Hourly Rate				
	▾		▾		▾					▾
No Member		NONE		Used to indicate tha...						
DBA		DBA								
SQL Server		SQL Server				50				
Oracle		Oracle				65				
Developer		Developer								
Senior		Senior				80				
Junior		Junior				60				
Entry Level		Entry Level				40				
Sysadmin		Sysadmin				60				

Figure 13-19. *The billing codes member set*

33. Save the dimension, and check it in.

34. Click the scenario dimension; create members for No Change, Increase 5%, and Decrease 10%. Save the dimension, and check it in. Now, we're going to create the calendar for the model.

Note You have to create a calendar before the modeler will allow you to create a model.

---

35. Click the "Create the Calendar" link in the Dimension Tasks section on the right side of the Planning Business Modeler to open the Create Application Calendar wizard (see Figure 13-20).

36. Click Next.

37. On the next page, you set the calendar requirements (see Figure 13-21). Leave the defaults, but change the past and future years to two each.

38. Click Next.

39. On the period naming conventions page (see Figure 13-22), accept the default frequencies (Year, Month, and Day are mandatory, and the Quarter option is checked by default). Click the Next button.

40. You can indicate how you would like the calendar periods labeled. For example, I delete the prefix for year; if you're using a fiscal year calendar you may prefer to prefix the year with "FY."

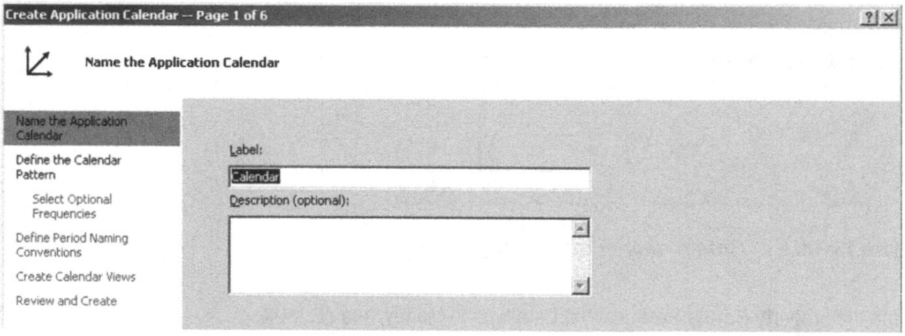

Figure 13-20. *Creating the Application Calendar*

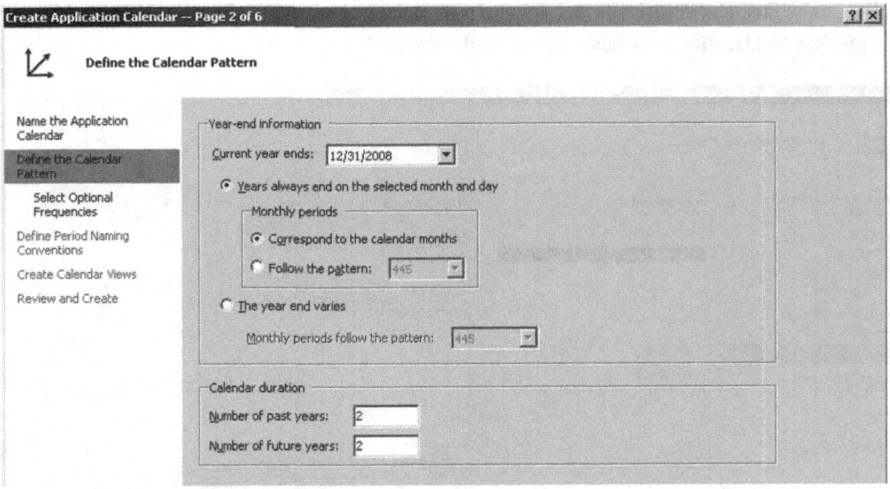

Figure 13-21. *Defining the calendar*

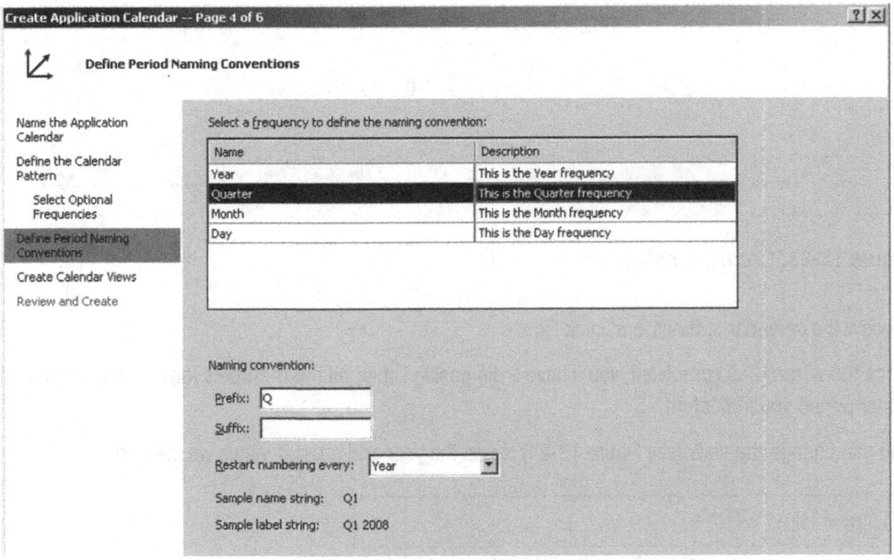

Figure 13-22. *Defining the period marking conventions*

41. Click Next.

42. On the Create Calendar Views page (see Figure 13-23), change the Label to **Quarterly View**, and ensure only the Year and Quarter frequencies are checked. Click Next.

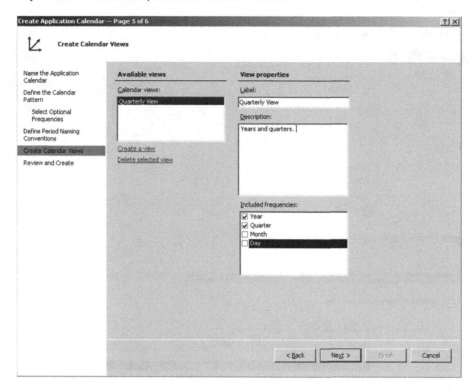

Figure 13-23. *Creating calendar views*

43. Review the calendar settings, and click Finish.

44. Once the wizard has completed, you'll have a dimension listing all the members (one for each day in the calendar period you indicated).

45. You can change the view (see Figure 13-24) to see the year and quarter views we created.

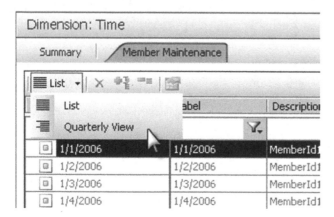

Figure 13-24. *Changing member views*

Adding Users and Roles

46. In the Workspace Browser on the left of the Modeler, click "Security and Roles."

47. From the View drop-down, check each of the views. Note that only Administrative Roles and Users have any members.

48. Select Business Roles Only, and in the Security and Roles Tasks on the right, click "Create a Business Role" (see Figure 13-25).

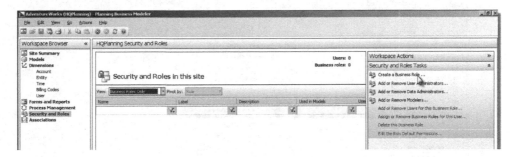

Figure 13-25. *Creating a business role*

49. Name the new role **HQ Financial** in the Create a Role dialog, and the wizard sets the Label field to the same value. Next, move the permissions slider to the bottom to grant read and write permissions (see Figure 13-26).

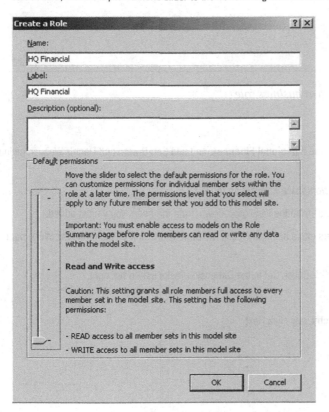

Figure 13-26. *Creating the HQ financial approver role*

50. Click OK.

51. Click the "Add or Remove Users for this Business Role" link on the right of the modeler.

52. Click Bethani Chappell in the Add or Remove Users for HQ Financial dialog, and click the Add Selected button at the top (see Figure 13-27).

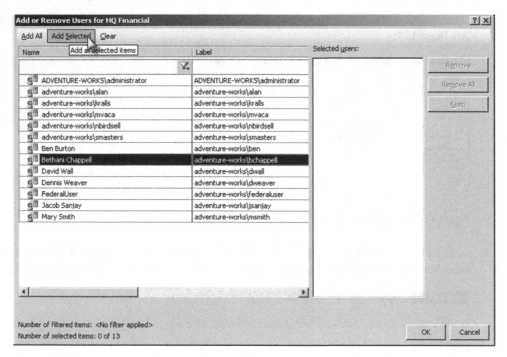

Figure 13-27. *Adding a user to a business role*

53. Click OK.

54. Create another business role, name it **Regional Finances**, and add Ben Burton and Dennis Weaver, giving them read and write access.

55. Click Security and Roles in the Workspace Browser on the left.

56. Select "Business Roles and Users" from the View drop-down. Note the users you've just added.

57. Now, we're going to set the users into a hierarchy. Click the Dimensions link on the left in the Workspace Browser.

58. Click the User dimension, and click Check Out in the Dimension Tasks list on the right.

59. Click Create a Member Set.

60. Name the set **Company Hierarchy**, and click Next.

61. Leave "Create an empty member set" selected. Click Next.

62. Click Finish.

63. Click the Member Sets Maintenance tab.

64. Ensure that Company Hierarchy is selected in the "Member set" field of the Destination Member Set section on the left and that All Members is selected on the right as the "Member set" for the Source Member Set section on the right—you may have to refresh to get them to show up (see Figure 13-28).

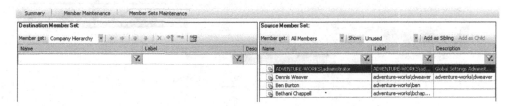

Figure 13-28. *Selecting the members to show*

65. Drag Bethani Chappell from the right pane to the left. Then drag Ben Burton over and drop this user on Bethani Chappell—you'll get a prompt to select "Add as Sibling" or "Add as Child." Select "Add as Child" (see Figure 13-29).

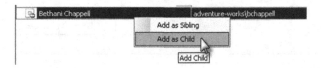

Figure 13-29. *Adding a child member*

66. Drag Dennis Weaver over and add this user as a child to Bethani Chappell as well.

67. Check in the dimension.

Creating the Model

68. In the Workspace Browser, click Models.

69. In the Model Tasks pane on the right side of the Planning Business Modeler, click "Create a Model."

70. In the model wizard, name the model **Personnel Planning**.

71. Click Next.

72. On the next page, leave the defaults selected ("Create a new model"), and select "Generic Model" for the type, and click Next.

73. On the "Define Dimensions and Member Sets" page, select the Entity in the Dimension drop-down and Hierarchy for the "Member set," and click the arrow to add it to the model (see Figure 13-30).

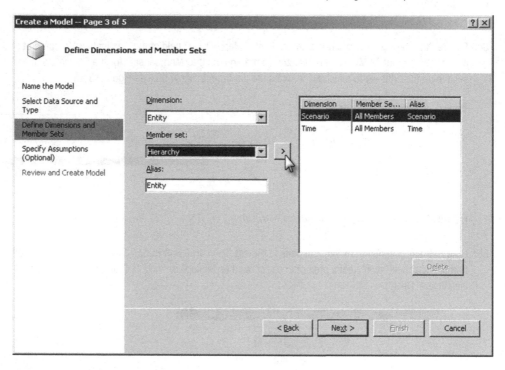

Figure 13-30. *Adding a dimension to the model*

74. Also add the Billing Codes dimension's Hierarchy member set, and change the member set for the Time dimension to "Quarterly view" (see Figure 13-31).

75. Click Next.

76. On the Specify Assumptions page, click Next and then Finish.

77. In the Workspace Actions pane on the right side of the Planning Business Modeler, click "Save this Model."

78. In the Workspace Browser on the left, click Site Summary.

79. In the Workspace Actions pane, click Deploy Model Site.

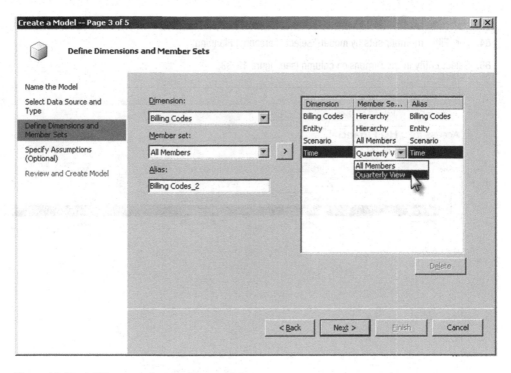

Figure 13-31. *Adding members to the model*

Setting User Security

80. Select "Security and Roles" in the Workspace Browser.

81. Click HQ Financial.

82. Note that the Personnel Planning model is listed, and the access is set to Off—click it, and change it to On (see Figure 13-32).

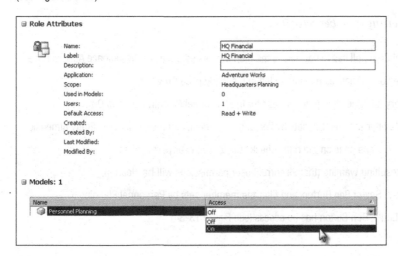

Figure 13-32. *Allowing access to the model for the role*

83. Now click the Role tab.

84. For "Filter member sets by model," select "Personnel Planning."

85. Select Entity in the Dimension column (see Figure 13-33).

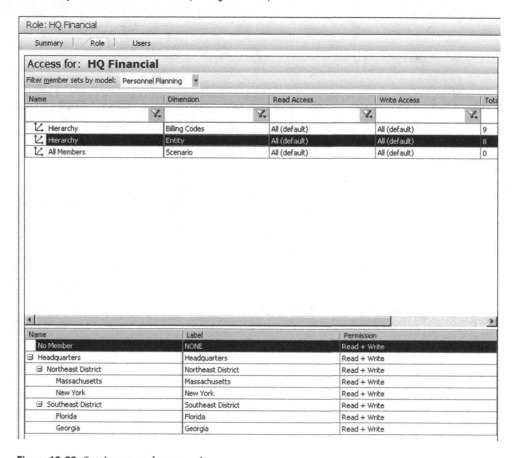

Figure 13-33. *Setting member security*

86. Note that Bethani Chappell has full access to the members listed under the Workspace Actions pane.

87. Now, click the Regional Finances role on the left in the Workspace Browser.

88. Click the Summary tab, and change the access for the Personnel Planning cube to On.

89. Click the Role tab, filter the member sets by Personnel Planning, and then select the Entity dimension.

90. In the Workspace Actions pane on the right, check "Customize user permissions."

91. Click Yes to the resulting warning (that all current user permissions will be cleared).

92. Click the Users tab. Select Ben Burton, and filter the member sets by Personnel Planning.

93. Note that under Entity, Ben Burton has no access (see Figure 13-34).

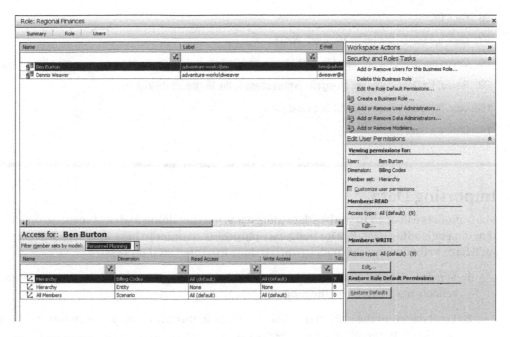

Figure 13-34. *Viewing permissions on member sets*

94. Click the Edit button under Members: READ in the Edit User Permissions pane on the right.

95. Select all four states, giving Ben Burton read access to the full dimension (see Figure 13-35).

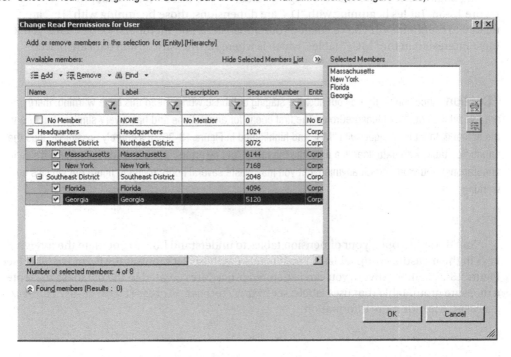

Figure 13-35. *Selecting the read permissions*

96. Click OK.

97. Click the Edit button under Members: WRITE.

98. Check the boxes for Southeast District, Florida, and Georgia, giving Ben Burton write access to his region.

99. Repeat for Dennis Weaver, giving him write access to the Northeast District.

100. Click Personnel Planning in the left-hand pane.

101. Click the Save icon.

Importing Data

Many models will need to work with existing data (whether doing a what-if scenario on current data or loading past data for budgetary purposes). In order to have that data available, we'll have to load it into the model, which is done in a three-step process:

1. Synchronize the model to the staging database, so the structure of the staging database reflects the structure of the model.

2. Load data into the staging database (you can do this with a database import, bulk load, or using SQL Server Integration Services).

3. Load the data from the staging database into the model.

Once you've synchronized the model to the staging database, you can then open the staging database. If you look at the staging database, you'll see a table structure similar to Figure 13-36. Tables beginning with "D_" are dimensions; those beginning with "H_" are related to hierarchies. If you've created your dimensions and members, to load data, you'll be most interested in the "MG_" tables, which is where the measure group data are placed.

■**Caution** Once you've figured out how the staging database works, heed this huge warning: there are two tables noted as MeasureGroup. The first one is for annotations and has a very similar structure to the actual data table (flagged with "MG" and highlighted in Figure 13-36). It's entirely possible to load the annotation table with data, load the data into the model, get no errors, and see no data (because it's all in annotations). You won't break anything, but you may waste several hours trying to figure out why it's not working.

You'll want to open your dimension tables to understand how to populate the foreign keys in the measure group tables. In our staging database, let's look at the D_Entity table (see Figure 13-37). Alternatively, you can use stored procedures created in the database to create a measure group table that uses labels; see http://technet.microsoft.com/en-us/library/bb660591.aspx for more information.

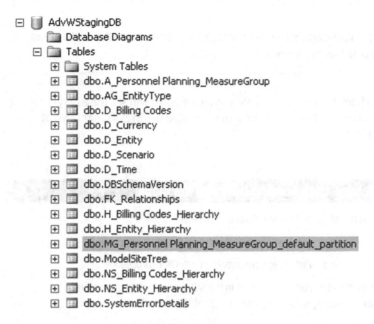

Figure 13-36. *The tables in the staging database*

	MemberId	Label	Description	Name	SequenceNumber	SourceMemberID	CurrencyMemb...	EntityTypeMem...
▶	-1	NONE	No Member	No Member	0	NULL	-1	4
	5001	Headquarters	NULL	Headquarters	1024	NULL	-1	1
	5002	Southeast District	NULL	Southeast District	2048	NULL	-1	1
	5003	Northeast District	NULL	Northeast District	3072	NULL	-1	1
	5004	Florida	NULL	Florida	4096	NULL	-1	1
	5005	Georgia	NULL	Georgia	5120	NULL	-1	1
	5006	Massachusetts	NULL	Massachusetts	6144	NULL	-1	1
	5007	New York	NULL	New York	7168	NULL	-1	1
*	NULL	NULL	NULL	NULL	NULL	NULL	NULL	NULL

Figure 13-37. *Contents of the entity dimension table in the staging database*

To populate our fact data, we need to populate the IDs matching our dimensions and the values. There's one more field to worry about while loading the data—the BizSystemFlag field needs to have a value of 200 (indicating insert this row). The possible BizSystemFlag values follow:

0: Take no action (this is the default value).

200: Add this row.

300: Update an existing row with the data in this row.

400: Delete the indicated row.

After you load the data into the model, the BizSystemFlag will be 100, indicating successful import.

Caution Once you have loaded the staging database into the model, don't disturb the existing rows with 100 values; they must be maintained for future loads.

After you load the data back into the model, PerformancePoint will set the BizSystemFlag for every row, indicating success (100) or some form of error, and the BizValidationStatus will be zero for every successful row.

Let's load some data.

Exercise 13-3. Loading Data into the Model

1. Click the Personnel Planning model in the Planning Business Modeler.

2. In the Workspace Actions on the right, click "Synchronize this model to the staging area."

3. You'll be warned that you may lose data when you synchronize. Click OK to proceed.

4. Now open SQL Server Management Studio, and connect to the SQL Server where you created the staging database. Open the staging database (AdvWStagingDB), and look at the tables.

5. Open the Programmability node, and then open Stored Procedures. Right-click the bsp_DI_CreateLabelTableForMeasureGroup procedure, and click Execute.

6. Fill in the parameters for the stored procedure as follows; these are shown in Figure 13-38:

   - @ModelName: **Headquarters Personnel Planning**

   - @MeasureGroupTableName: **MG_Personnel Planning_MeasureGroup_default_partition**

   - @IncludeExistingData: **F**

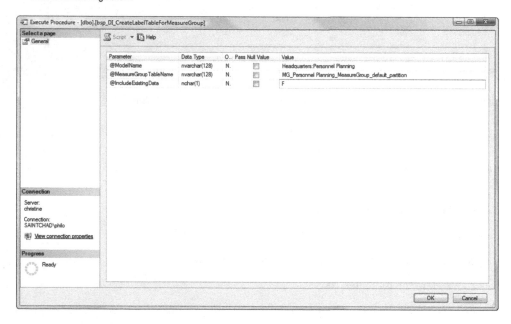

Figure 13-38. *Executing the Create Label stored procedure*

7. This creates the label-based measure group table in the staging database (`MG_Personnel Planning_ MeasureGroup_default_partition_Label`). Right-click this table, and select Open Table; this will open the table and show a single empty row.

8. Copy the cells from the Excel spreadsheet available in the code download from `www.apress.com`, and paste them into the SQL table.

9. Now execute the stored procedure `bsp_DI_ValidateLabelTable` to validate the data. If the stored procedure returns a zero, the data's ready to load. Use the following parameters:

   - @ModelName: **Headquarters Personnel Planning**

   - @MeasureGroupLabelTableName: **MG_Personnel Planning_MeasureGroup_default_partition_label**

   - @AnnotationOnly: **F**

10. Execute the `bsp_DI_ConvertLabelColumnToMemberIDForMeasureGroup` stored procedure to move the data into the MG staging table and convert the dimension labels to IDs. (Indicate "T" for overwrite data, "F" for include validation, and "F" for annotations.)

11. You can open the `MG_Personnel Planning_MeasureGroup_default_partition` table now and see the data and the labels converted to IDs, ready to load.

12. In the modeler, click Models, and select the Personnel Planning model.

13. In the Workspace Actions pane on the right, click "Load this model from staging area."

14. In SQL Server Management Studio, if you refresh the table, you should see that the BizSystemFlag for every row is 100.

15. Now, in the Planning Business Modeler, click the Reprocess Model Data link to rebuild the cube.

16. Finally, select Site Summary in the Workspace Browser, and click Deploy Model Site in the Workspace Actions pane.

17. You can also look at your data by opening BIDS (select Start ➤ All Programs ➤ Microsoft SQL Server 2005 ➤ SQL Server Business Intelligence Development Studio) and selecting File ➤ Open ➤ Analysis Services Database.

18. Select the Planning Server, then the Adventure Works_Headquarters Planning cube.

19. Open the Personnel Planning cube from the Solution Explorer, and open the Browser tab to view the model.

Designing Forms

Once you've created a model and imported the historical data, you'll need to create the forms your users will use to enter data. This is the truly awesome part of PerformancePoint Planning —the forms are Excel spreadsheets. However, instead of filling in spreadsheets and e-mailing them around, Excel is simply the client for the server-side model (cube).

The PerformancePoint Excel add-in (for Excel 2003 or 2007) provides an interface between Excel and the PerformancePoint Planning Server. The interface connects via the Planning Server web services (on port 46787).

Excel forms are useful in PerformancePoint because both the form designer and the form user can take advantage of native Excel features in combination with the data-driven

PerformancePoint planning areas. PerformancePoint Server Excel forms use a data-driven area called a *matrix* to map planning data into a spreadsheet. Those areas are populated with data directly from the model and can write back to the model. Once the matrix is populated, a form designer can add additional Excel-driven content (formulas, charts, graphs, conditional formatting, etc.) outside the matrix areas.

When a user fills in a form in Excel and submits the data, it is written back to the Analysis Services cube behind the scenes, where it can be aggregated, reported on, and shared. Again, this is easiest to understand by doing.

Exercise 13-4. Creating a Data Entry Form in Excel

1. Open Excel (I'll use Excel 2007 for this exercise, but Excel 2003 will work as well).

2. Click the PerformancePoint tab.

3. On the left end of the ribbon, click the Connect button.

4. In the dialog that opens (see Figure 13-39), enter the Planning Server address: `http://[servername]:46787`.

Figure 13-39. *Connecting to the Planning Server*

5. Click OK. This will open the PerformancePoint plug-in (see Figure 13-40).

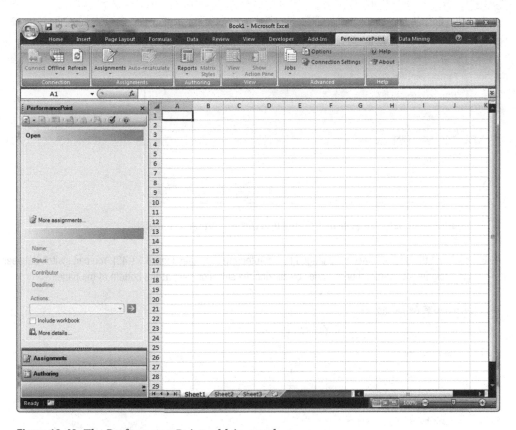

Figure 13-40. *The PerformancePoint add-in panel*

6. In the Authoring group on the ribbon, click the Reports button and then click New (see Figure 13-41).

Figure 13-41. *Creating a new report*

7. In the Choose Application dialog, select the Adventure Works application, and click OK (see Figure 13-42).

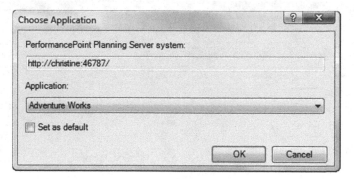

Figure 13-42. *Selecting the application to design a report against*

8. Note that the add-in panel has changed to the Authoring pane (see Figure 13-43). You can switch between the Assignments and Authoring panes by clicking the selection bars at the bottom of the panel.

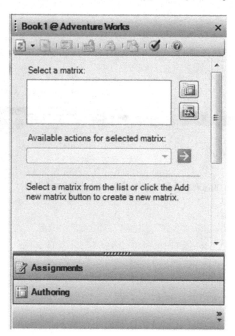

Figure 13-43. *The Authoring pane*

9. Click the "Add new matrix" button (see Figure 13-44) to add a matrix to our spreadsheet.

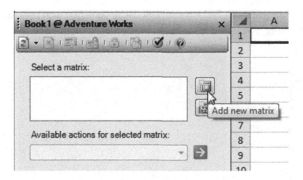

Figure 13-44. *Adding a matrix to the spreadsheet*

10. This will open the New Matrix dialog (see Figure 13-45). Name the matrix **Personnel**, and change the "Start in cell" field to **C4**.

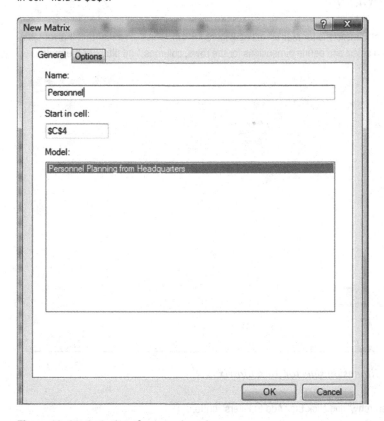

Figure 13-45. *Creating the new matrix*

11. Click the Options tab to look at the options available for data entry members; ensure "Allow data entry" is checked as well as "Merge and center headers."

12. Click OK.

13. Note the matrix has been created and is selected in the PerformancePoint Server pane (you won't see any change in the spreadsheet surface yet). Under "Available actions," select "Select dimensions," and click the arrow (see Figure 13-46).

Figure 13-46. *Matrix actions*

14. This opens the "Select Dimensions for Matrix" dialog (Figure 13-47), which is similar to the pivot table designer in Excel; you select and define dimensions for the rows, columns, and filters of the matrix.

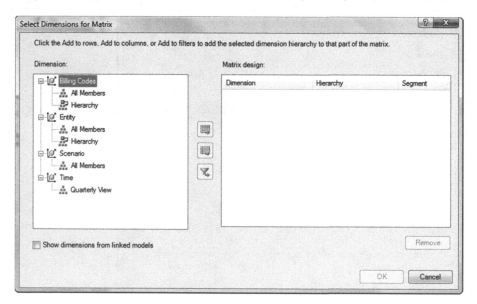

Figure 13-47. *The dimension selector for a matrix*

15. Select "Entity ➤ Hierarchy," and click the "Add to Filters" button.

16. Now select "Billing Codes ➤ Hierarchy," and click the "Add to Rows" button.

17. Select "Scenario ➤ All Members," and click the "Add to Filters" button.

18. Finally, select "Time ➤ Quarterly View," and click the "Add to Columns" button.

19. Your final matrix design should look like Figure 13-48.

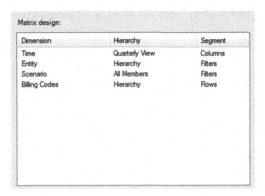

Figure 13-48. *Assigning dimensions to the matrix design*

20. Click OK.

21. The next dialog presents you with the filters and asks you to select default members (see Figure 13-49). For Entity.Hierarchy, select Headquarters, and for Scenario.All Members, select No Change. Click OK.

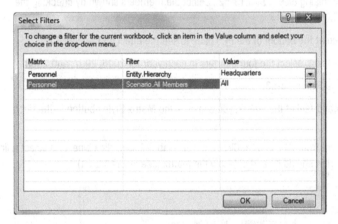

Figure 13-49. *Selecting default filter members*

22. You should have the matrix in your Excel spreadsheet, as shown in Figure 13-50. You may want to resize some columns to see the contents better. Note that the Time and Billing Codes dimensions have defaulted to the All members—let's fix that.

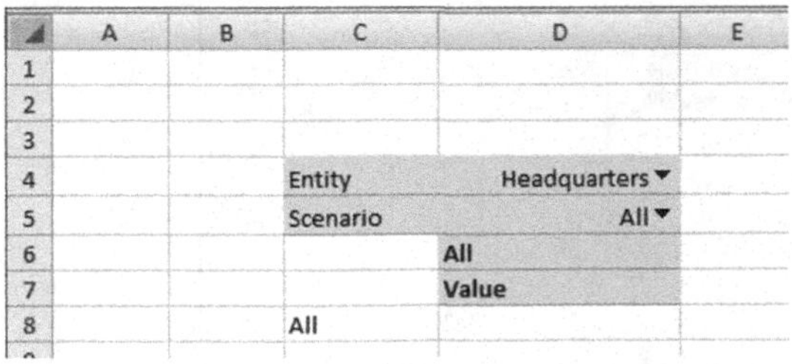

	A	B	C	D	E
1					
2					
3					
4			Entity	Headquarters ▼	
5			Scenario	All ▼	
6				All	
7				Value	
8			All		

Figure 13-50. *The resulting matrix in Excel*

23. In the Rows cell of the PPS pane, click the arrow next to Billing Codes, and select Select Members (see Figure 13-51).

Figure 13-51. *Selecting members for the Billing Codes hierarchy*

24. This opens the Select Members dialog (see Figure 13-52). Select the members shown by checking the boxes next to each. Click the OK button.

25. You can click the Refresh button at the bottom of the PPS pane to see the effect on the matrix.

26. Do the same for the Time dimension; select the four quarters in each year for 2006, 2007, and 2008.

27. Your matrix should now look like Figure 13-53.

28. If you want to change the look and feel of the matrix, you can click the Matrix Styles button in the ribbon and select a different layout style.

29. Finally, click and drag to highlight from C11 to O13. Click the Insert tab in Excel, click Line, and select a line chart. When you select the chart, it should be added below the matrix (see Figure 13-54).

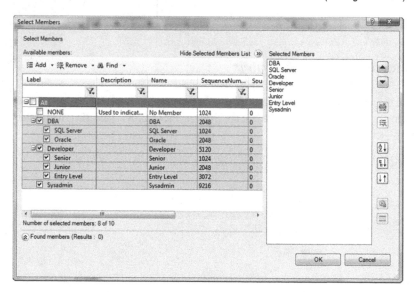

Figure 13-52. *Selecting members for the Billing Codes hierarchy*

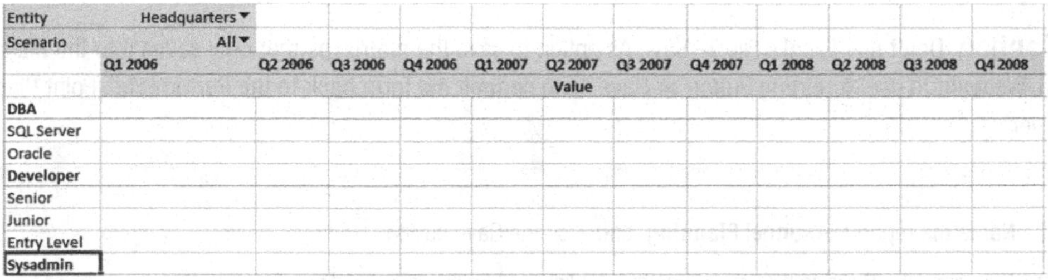

Entity	Headquarters											
Scenario	All											
	Q1 2006	Q2 2006	Q3 2006	Q4 2006	Q1 2007	Q2 2007	Q3 2007	Q4 2007	Q1 2008	Q2 2008	Q3 2008	Q4 2008
	Value											
DBA												
SQL Server												
Oracle												
Developer												
Senior												
Junior												
Entry Level												
Sysadmin												

Figure 13-53. *The matrix after selecting members for rows and columns*

Entity	Headquarters											
	Q1 2006	Q2 2006	Q3 2006	Q4 2006	Q1 2007	Q2 2007	Q3 2007	Q4 2007	Q1 2008	Q2 2008	Q3 2008	Q4 2008
	Value											
DBA	45	46	49	49	47	51	55	57				
SQL Server	21	22	23	23	22	23	23	22				
Oracle	24	24	26	26	25	28	32	35				
Developer	107	108	111	112	113	107	109	107				
Senior	31	30	31	32	31	30	30	30				
Junior	63	62	61	61	61	56	57	55				
Entry Level	13	16	19	19	21	21	22	22				
Sysadmin	29	30	29	28	27	27	25	25				

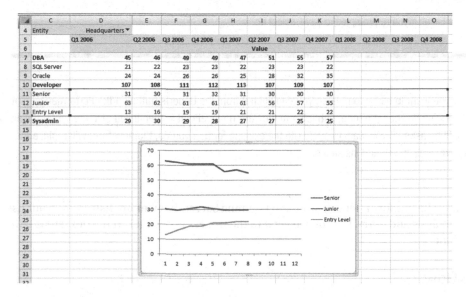

Figure 13-54. *Adding an Excel chart to a form*

30. Now let's save the form; click the Reports button, and select Save As (see Figure 13-55).

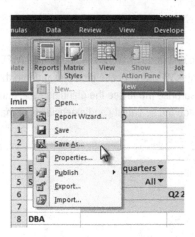

Figure 13-55. *Saving the matrix back to Planning Server*

■**Caution** Don't use Excel's File ➤ Save As option to save the matrix, as that only saves it to the file system. We want to use Reporting Button ➤ Save As to commit the form back to the PerformancePoint Planning Server.

31. Name the report **Personnel Planning**, and click the Save button.

32. Now click the Reports button, and select Publish and As Form Template.

33. Name the report **Personnel Planning**, with the same label. Ensure the Headquarters model site is selected, then click OK.

34. Close Excel; if you're prompted to save, select No.

■**Note** If you want to edit a form later, you can open it from the Reports button in the PerformancePoint tab. Once you've finished the form, publish it to the PerformancePoint server. If you give the report the same name, you'll be asked if you want to overwrite the existing form; if you do, the new form will replace the existing form in all cycles and instances.

Now we have a form (report) stored in Planning Server that we can distribute to our users for data analysis and entry. How do we get it to them? Let's take a look at the next steps—we're almost done!

Workflow

To get our data entry forms out, we need to go back to the Planning Business Modeler and set up a workflow (cycle) for the process we are enabling. For example, this is going to be the personnel planning cycle. Within cycles, we use assignments to notify users of forms they have to review and enter data into.

■**Note** The workflow in PerformancePoint Planning is not based on Windows Workflow Foundation (WF), as PerformancePoint Planning Server (previously BizSharp) predates WF. I don't have direct insight into the planning for the PerformancePoint product line, but it would not surprise me to see the planning cycle and assignment engine replaced with WF in a future version, to leverage the scalability and extensibility of that engine.

Exercise 13-5. Creating a Cycle and Assignment

1. If you don't have it open, open the Planning Business Modeler, and connect to the Planning Server.

2. In the Workspace Browser, click Process Management on the left.

3. In the Workspace Actions pane on the right, click Create a Cycle to open the cycle wizard.

4. Name the cycle **2008 Projections**.

5. Click the [...] button next to Owner. Select Bethani Chappell as the cycle owner, and click the Add Selected button at the top. Click the OK button.

6. Click the Next button on the wizard.

7. On the "Select a Model" page, ensure the Personnel Planning model is selected, and click the Next button.

8. The Data Entry Scope page is where you define what members the users will be entering data for. Click the Edit button next to the Start entry.

9. In the Select Members dialog (see Figure 13-56), select Q1 2008.

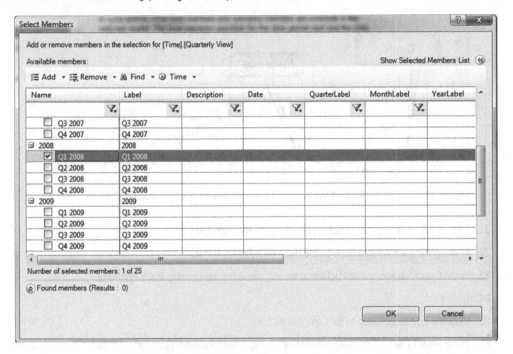

Figure 13-56. *Selecting the starting member*

Note You can set the window to move relative to the current date by clicking the Time button and clicking Add Current Period Reference—this allows you to select a level and offset (for example, "last quarter" or "next year").

---

10. Click OK.

11. Select Q4 2008 for the End member in the same way.

12. Click the Scenario button to open the Select Members dialog for the scenario. Select No Change, and click OK.

13. Click Next on the Define Data-Entry Scope page.

14. The start and end dates for the cycle are the dates during which the assignments will be shown to users—this defaults to starting today and ending in one month. We'll accept the defaults, so click Next.

15. Leave the Notifications check box checked, and click Next.

16. Review the cycle, and click Finish.

17. Click the Save icon.

18. Now that we have a cycle, we need to define individual assignments within the cycle.

19. Click the Refresh button in the toolbar.

20. You should now have a process and cycle, as shown in Figure 13-57.

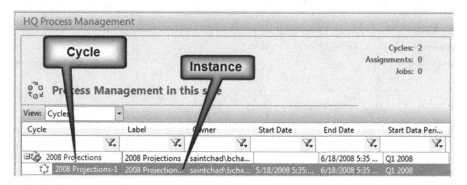

Figure 13-57. *The cycle and instance in the Planning Business Modeler*

21. Click the new instance to select it, and then click the Forms Assignment tab.

22. In the Workspace Actions pane on the right, click Assign Forms.

23. In the Create an Assignment Definition wizard, name the assignment **2008 Planning**.

24. Click Next.

25. Click the Edit button next to the Contributors box.

26. In the Select Contributor dialog (see Figure 13-58), select Regional Finances, and click the Add Selected button.

27. Click OK.

28. Now click the Edit button next to the Forms control.

29. In the Select Forms dialog, you should see the Personnel Planning form we designed earlier; select it and click the right-facing arrow (>) button to move it to selected forms.

30. Click OK.

31. Back in the "Create an Assignment Definition" wizard, click Next.

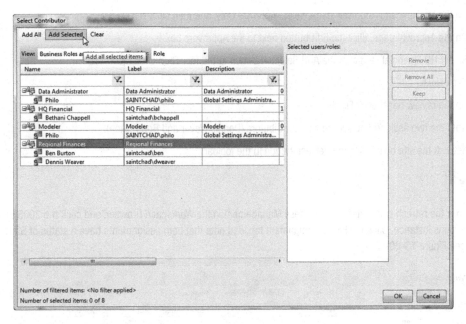

Figure 13-58. *Adding contributors to the instance*

32. The Submission Period page (see Figure 13-59) governs the business rules regarding the instance. Change the Importance to High, and click Next.

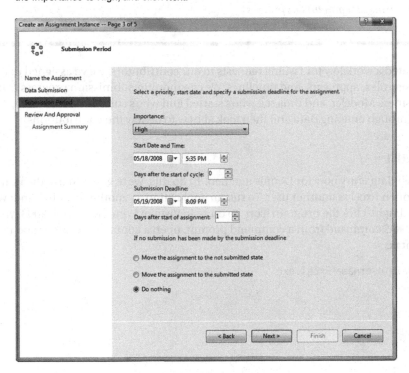

Figure 13-59. *Scheduling the submission period*

33. On the "Review and Approval" page, select Approval Only, and then click Next.

34. On the Approval page, click the Edit button next to the Approvers box.

35. Select HQ Financial, and click the Add Selected button at the top. Then click OK.

36. Click Next.

37. On the review page, click Finish.

38. Note the two assignments for the two contributors (Dennis Waver and Ben Burton).

39. Refresh the site by clicking the Refresh button in the toolbar:

40. After the refresh completes, click Process Management in the Workspace Browser, and click the 2008 Projections instance. Click the Forms Assignment tab, and note that both assignments have a status of Started (see Figure 13-60).

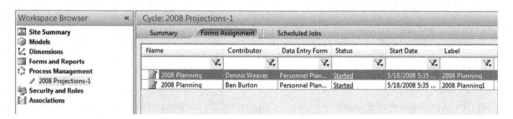

Figure 13-60. *Forms assignments in progress*

So we've created a workflow for issuing requests to our contributors; we've assigned data entry forms to user roles, approvers, and timelines. We can monitor submission progress from the Planning Business Modeler, and thus see who's started and who's submitted their data. Next, we'll walk through entering data and then look at how to review the contributions.

Entering Data

We'll walk through data entry now for Dennis and Ben. To do this, we're going to use the Run As command to open Excel as another user. To run an application as another user in Windows XP, press Shift and right-click the program icon. To do so in Vista or Windows Server 2003, you have to use the RUNAS command from a command prompt; open a command prompt and use the following syntax:

```
RUNAS /user:domain\username Excel.exe
```

Tip For more information on Run As, see http://support.microsoft.com/kb/294676.

Of course, you'll have to either be in the Office directory or have a path mapped to it. Once you run that command, you'll be prompted for the user's password. After you enter it, Excel will open using that user's account.

Note You may have to close all instances of Excel before running the command.

Exercise 13-6. Entering Data into PerformancePoint Server Forms

1. Open Excel as Ben Burton (domain\ben if you followed the earlier user).

2. Click the PerformancePoint tab, and then click Connect to connect to our planning server (http://server:46787).

3. In the PerformancePoint pane, notice the 2008 Planning assignment listed. Click it to open it.

4. When the form opens, you'll see the personnel data and the chart. Notice the entity selector at the top of the spreadsheet is set to Headquarters. Since we're logged in as Ben Burton, we don't have rights to edit at this level.

5. Click the arrow next to Headquarters to open the Select Filters dialog. For Entity.Hierarchy, click the Value column's drop-down arrow, and select Florida (see Figure 13-61).

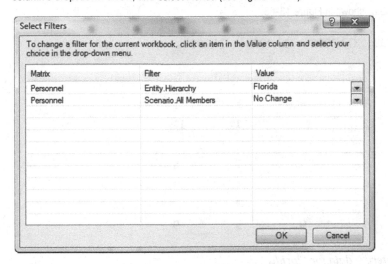

Figure 13-61. *Selecting the entity member filter*

6. When you click OK, the form should recalculate. Since Ben has rights to this region, you'll see yellow high-lighting in the empty cells under 2008 (see Figure 13-62); this is where Ben needs to enter his personnel projections. Note that the Excel chart shows the effects of his projections.

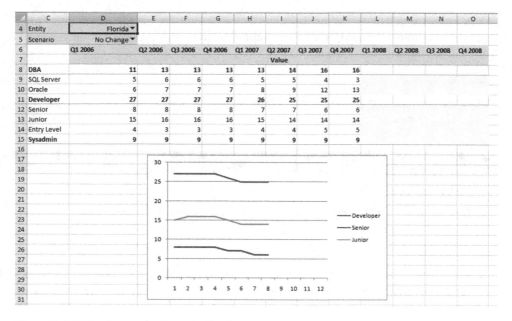

	C	D	E	F	G	H	I	J	K	L	M	N	O
4	Entity	Florida ▼											
5	Scenario	No Change ▼											
6		Q1 2006		Q2 2006	Q3 2006	Q4 2006	Q1 2007	Q2 2007	Q3 2007	Q4 2007	Q1 2008	Q2 2008	Q3 2008	Q4 2008
7								Value						
8	DBA	11		13	13	13	13	14	16	16				
9	SQL Server	5		6	6	6	5	5	4	3				
10	Oracle	6		7	7	7	8	9	12	13				
11	Developer	27		27	27	27	26	25	25	25				
12	Senior	8		8	8	8	7	7	6	6				
13	Junior	15		16	16	16	15	14	14	14				
14	Entry Level	4		3	3	3	4	4	5	5				
15	Sysadmin	9		9	9	9	9	9	9	9				

Figure 13-62. *The data entry form in Excel*

7. Enter data for 2008 as shown in Figure 13-63.

2007	Q1 2008	Q2 2008	Q3 2008	Q4 2008
16				
3	4	4	5	5
13	12	12	11	11
25				
6	6	7	7	8
14	14	14	14	14
5	6	6	7	7
9	9	9	9	9

Figure 13-63. *Entering data for Florida*

8. Once the data is entered, in the PerformancePoint Planning task pane, change Actions to Submit Final, and click the arrow button next to the action.

9. A dialog will open for you to enter comments. Click OK.

10. Click OK on the final action status dialog.

11. Close Excel. Don't save changes.

12. Now open Excel as dweaver using the RUNAS command.

13. Click the PerformancePoint tab, and connect to the Planning Server (http://[server]:46787).

14. Open the 2008 Planning assignment.

15. First of all, notice that for the Headquarters Entity, 2008 now has values (specifically, the values Ben entered).

16. Change the entity to New York. Note that 2008 is now blank, but highlighted yellow for Dennis to enter his data.

17. Enter data for SQL Server, Oracle, Senior, Junior, Entry Level, and Sysadmin for the four quarters in 2008.

18. Submit the form as final.

19. Close Excel, and don't save.

TROUBLESHOOTING PLANNING FORMS

The hardest part of dealing with PerformancePoint Planning Server is getting those cells to turn yellow. As you can see, there is a lot of work up front to get to the point where you are filling in an Excel form. When you open the form and there are no editable cells, it can be a bit annoying.

Here are the main things to look at when troubleshooting writeable regions in a PerformancePoint Planning Server Excel form:

1. Verify the matrix (the cells on the spreadsheet showing the planning cube data) is showing data at leaf level for all dimensions in the measure group. This is a huge gotcha. PerformancePoint Planning Server uses SQL Server Analysis Services's writeback capabilities. One of the caveats of writebacks is that you have to write back to the cell level (this isn't strictly true; PerformancePoint Server can spread data among children of a member, but that's more advanced to set up). For example, in our entity structure, Headquaters and the two regions are not leaf-level members; the states are.

2. Check that the cycle and assignments are configured correctly. Most notably, check the start and end dates of the assignments.

3. Make sure the matrix is using the right model, and that that time dimension of the model covers the assignment dimensions of the matrix and assignment.

4. Check all your user permissions on the members and assignments.

Now that Ben and Dennis have entered their numbers, you should already start to see the benefit of the Planning Server: Ben and Dennis worked in Excel, could set up formulas, play with numbers, create charts, and so on, and when they were ready, they simply submit the numbers, which are applied to the model.

Now let's see what Bethani needs to do to review their submissions.

Exercise 13-7. Reviewing Data

1. Open Excel as bchappell using the RUNAS command.

2. Click the PerformancePoint tab, and connect to the Planning Server (http://[server]:46787).

3. Note that the 2008 Planning link now has an icon indicating there are submissions waiting. Click the link to open the assignment (see Figure 13-64).

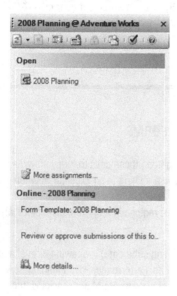

Figure 13-64. *Bethani's task pane in Excel, showing submissions waiting and the review link*

4. We're looking at the Headquarters view; Ben's and Dennis's submissions have been aggregated. Note the "Review or approve submissions of this form" link in the PerformancePoint pane. You can click the "More details" link to see the status of current submissions.

5. Click the "Review or approve submissions of this form" link.

6. The "Review and Approve Assignments" form opens, showing the two submissions from Dennis and Ben (see Figure 13-65).

7. Click Ben Burton's name, and then click the Open icon above the submissions list.

8. This will open Ben's submission for Florida. From here, Bethani can edit the numbers if she needs to and approve or reject the submission.

9. Close whatever copies of Excel you have open, and don't save.

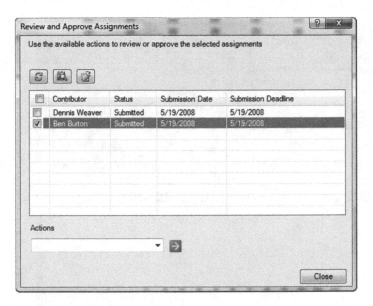

Figure 13-65. *Reviewing submitted forms*

Consider how this would have worked without PerformancePoint Planning: Ben and Dennis each would have drafted two spreadsheets—one for each state. They would've e-mailed them to Bethani, who would have to review them in consideration of each other. She may have edited one and e-mailed it back, then waited for the return, and compared them again. Now multiply that by fifty states.

Hopefully, you can see how Planning Server can greatly simplify consolidation of any form of Excel-type submission, including review and approval, and make the ability to compare and contrast submissions against each other far less painful than the e-mail and copy/paste methodology.

Now what if Bethani wants to prevent submissions where there are more new hires than existing personnel? Or maybe no more than a 10 percent increase in personnel in any one quarter. PerformancePoint Planning Server can enforce business rules as well.

Business Rules

Business rules help model designers add business structure to their data, and they are associated with a specific model (see Figure 13-66).

A number of rules are defined out of the box and presented as templates for you to use when you create a new rule. Some examples of rules are moving averages, net present value, variance between scenarios, year-to-date calculation, and so on. Figure 13-67 shows a new business rule created in the Definition Rule Set based on the variance to the prior year rule template.

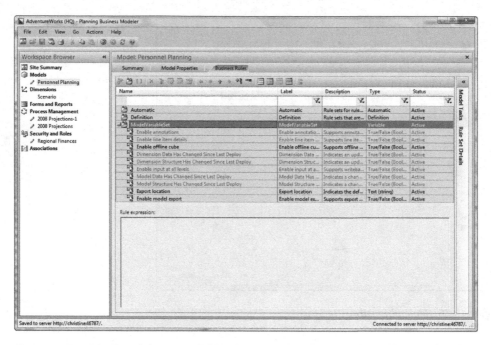

Figure 13-66. *Business rules in the Planning Business Modeler*

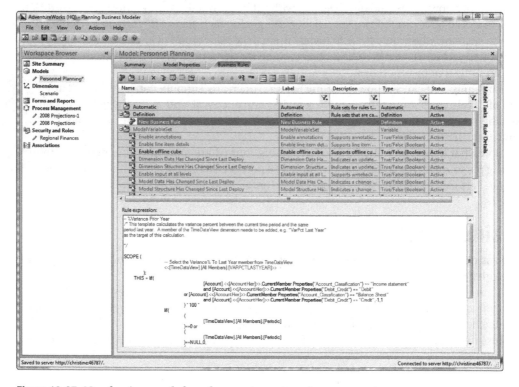

Figure 13-67. *New business rule based on variance to prior year*

Business rules can be designed to do various things, including the following:

- Calculating values that become part of the model

- Calculating standard formulae

- Exporting data to a different PerformancePoint Planning Server application

- Managing the properties of the model

- Distributing values across one or more members or dimensions

Business rules are written in PerformancePoint Expression Language (PEL). MSDN has robust documentation regarding the design and implementation of business rules starting at http://msdn.microsoft.com/en-us/library/bb795339.aspx (alternatively, navigate to msdn.microsoft.com, select the Office Developer Center and then PerformancePoint, and start browsing).

Conclusion

This chapter provided a very high-level view of PerformancePoint Planning. Hopefully, it was enough to pique your interest and help you find your way around well enough to at least know what questions to ask.

We have one last stop on our BI tour. A necessary capability in any financial suite is the ability for financial planners to create their own financial reports—this is where the PerformancePoint Server Management Reporter comes in. We'll take a brief look at it, and then our work is finished!

■■■

CHAPTER 14

Management Reporter

In February 2008, Microsoft added Management Reporter to the PerformancePoint suite. The goal of Management Reporter is to provide a way for financial experts to design their own financial reports in an enterprise business intelligence arena.

Management Reporter was brought over from the FRx product in the Dynamics suite (www.microsoft.com/frx). FRx is a financial analysis and reporting package—the analysis package is very similar to PerformancePoint Planning, so the reporting package fits well on financial cubes created in PerformancePoint. One key thing to remember is that Management Reporter works with cubes as a data source—either FRx or PerformancePoint cubes will work. To report on financial data from other systems, you first need to model it in PerformancePoint and load the data into the cube before you can start designing Management Reporter reports.

Creating Management Reports

At first glance, Management Reporter looks pretty intimidating (Figure 14-1). However, the best approach to working with Management Reporter is to use the wizard. With the wizard, the design of the report is very straightforward, and the interface can be used for tweaking the report once it is nearly complete.

Figure 14-2 shows typical output from Management Reporter. By walking through a simple wizard, you can create a detailed, complex financial report in a few minutes. The report is completely editable and configurable.

The wizard (Figure 14-3) is pretty straightforward once you've walked through it. A number of standard financial templates are available to work from, as well as scenarios for the financial reports. Management Reporter can read data from either PerformancePoint financial models or Financial Data Mart (FDM)–formatted SQL Server databases. FDM is the data repository format used by Microsoft Dynamics NAV (www.microsoft.com/dynamics/nav/).

Once you've selected a report template, Management Reporter gives you a list of accounts drawn from the model or FDM database you chose as your entity (Figure 14-4). You can add accounts to any section to build up your report. This gives you the flexibility to design reports reflecting cash flows as you need them (for one department inventory it may be an expense, while for another it may be revenue or assets).

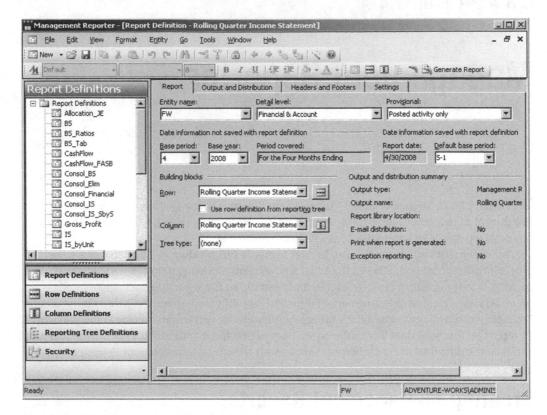

Figure 14-1. *The Management Reporter interface*

FW
Income Statement - Rolling Quarter
Rolling Quarter Income Statement
For the Quarter Ended 4/30/2008

	Current Month			YTD
February	March	April		
			Sales	
556,250	499,234	1,167,656	Sales	2,770,198
739	761	784	Sales - Intercompany	3,000
(32,554)	(33,893)	(34,235)	Sales Discounts	(132,567)
(5,101)	(10,169)	(10,272)	Sales Returns	(35,109)
519,334	*455,932*	*1,123,932*	*Total Sales*	*2,605,523*
			Cost of Revenue	
318,268	814,066	822,289	COGS	2,266,345
318,268	*814,066*	*822,289*	*Total Cost of Revenue*	*2,266,345*
201,066	*(358,134)*	*301,643*	*Gross Margin*	*339,177*
			Operating Expenses	
			Employee-Related Expenses	
89,199	92,644	92,314	Salary Expense	361,826
30,375	31,283	31,599	Officers Comp	123,332
119,574	*123,927*	*123,913*	*Total Employee-Related Expenses*	*485,157*

Figure 14-2. *A management report produced by Management Reporter*

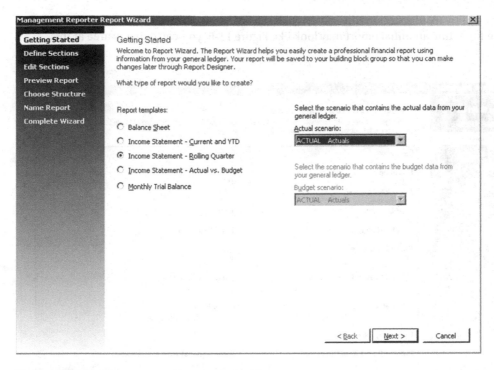

Figure 14-3. *The Management Reporter wizard*

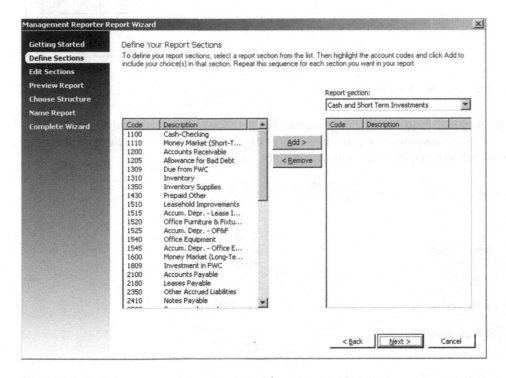

Figure 14-4. *Defining a management report with accounts*

The ability to edit sections directly enables users to ensure the report reflects what they're looking for. While an initial report may look like Figure 14-5, you can edit any area at this point.

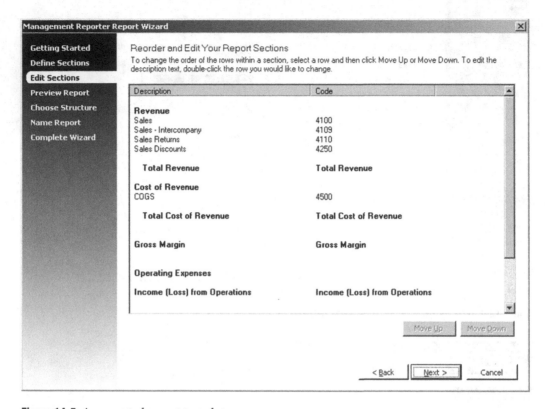

Figure 14-5. *A generated report template*

For example, if you simply change the heading Revenue to Sales, as shown in Figure 14-6, that change also cascades down automatically, as shown in Figure 14-7. You can also use the Move Up and Move Down buttons to rearrange the rows if you like.

Description	Code
Sales	
Sales	4100
Sales - Intercompany	4109
Sales Returns	4110
Sales Discounts	4250
Total Revenue	**Total Reveι**
Cost of Revenue	
COGS	4500

Figure 14-6. *Editing the report template*

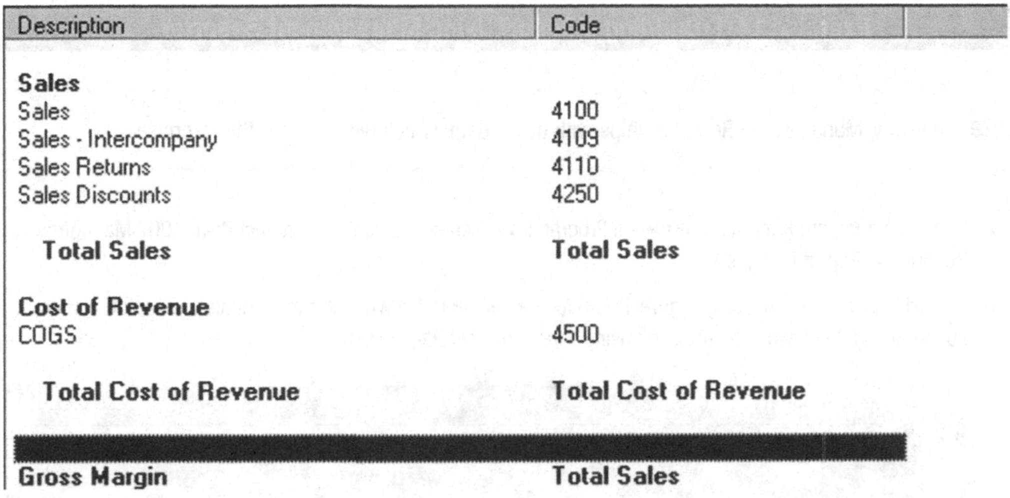

Description	Code	
Sales		
Sales	4100	
Sales - Intercompany	4109	
Sales Returns	4110	
Sales Discounts	4250	
Total Sales	**Total Sales**	
Cost of Revenue		
COGS	4500	
Total Cost of Revenue	**Total Cost of Revenue**	
Gross Margin	**Total Sales**	

Figure 14-7. *Changes propogate as appropriate.*

Once you've finished the report wizard, you can continue to tweak the report in the editor (Figure 14-8). In addition, you can change fonts, sizes, alignments, and formatting, and create formulas for calculated members.

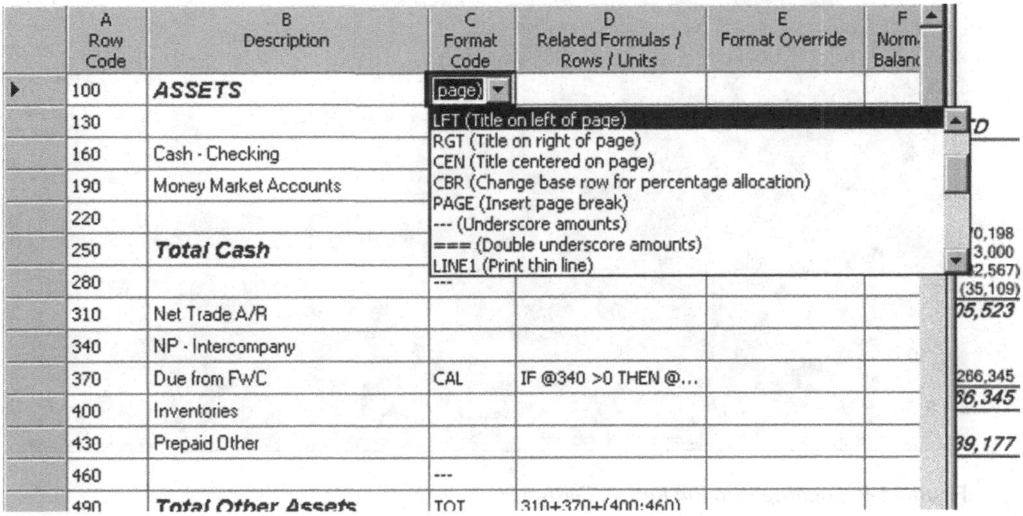

A Row Code	B Description	C Format Code	D Related Formulas / Rows / Units	E Format Override	F Norm Balan
100	*ASSETS*	page) ▼			
130		LFT (Title on left of page)			D
160	Cash - Checking	RGT (Title on right of page)			
190	Money Market Accounts	CEN (Title centered on page)			
220		CBR (Change base row for percentage allocation)			
250	*Total Cash*	PAGE (Insert page break)			0,198
280		--- (Underscore amounts)			3,000
		=== (Double underscore amounts)			2,567)
		LINE1 (Print thin line)			(35,109)
310	Net Trade A/R				5,523
340	NP - Intercompany				
370	Due from FWC	CAL	IF @340 >0 THEN @...		266,345
400	Inventories				6,345
430	Prepaid Other				9,177
460		---			
490	*Total Other Assets*	TOT	310+370+(400:460)		

Figure 14-8. *Editing the report*

The reports in Management Reporter are defined via row definitions, column definitions, and overall report definitions. In addition, there are *reporting trees*, which are hierarchical representations of the organization, so each level displays the appropriate reporting data.

Exercise 14-1. Building a Report Using Management Reporter

Note Currently, Management Reporter ships with demo data, which we'll use for this exercise.

1. Open Management Reporter (Start ➤ All Programs ➤ Microsoft Office PerformancePoint 2007 Management Reporter ➤ Report Designer).

2. This will open the login dialog (Figure 14-9). You can either log in with user credentials or check the check box for using Windows authentication using your current credentials.

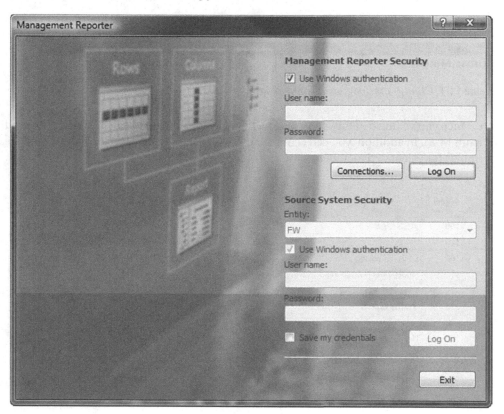

Figure 14-9. *Logging into the Report Designer*

Note The Connections button is where you select which management reporting server you connect to. To connect to a different database, you will have to log out and log in again.

3. Click the Log On button. Once logged on, the Source System Security section in the lower half of the dialog will be enabled. Select FW for the entity and click the lower Log On button.

4. You'll see the Welcome to Management Reporter dialog (Figure 14-10)—click Launch Report Wizard.

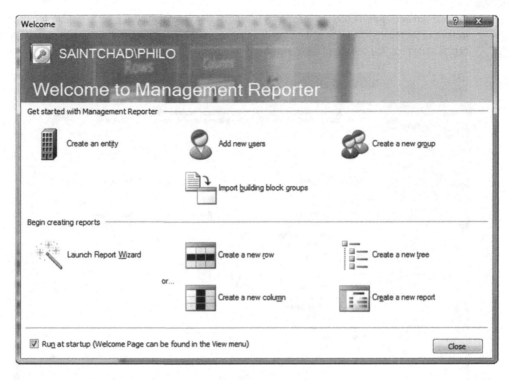

Figure 14-10. *Welcome to Management Reporter dialog*

5. The first page of the wizard (Figure 14-11) provides a few standard financial report templates. The "Actual scenario" drop-down takes scenarios from the data, as does the "Budget scenario" drop-down (currently disabled). Select Income Statement – Rolling Quarter, and click the Next button.

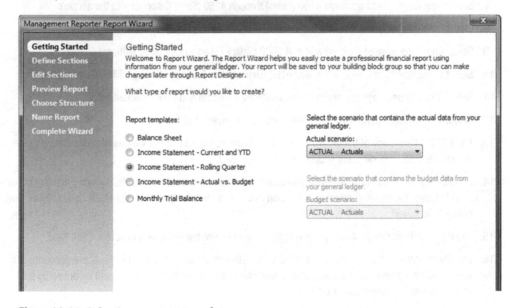

Figure 14-11. *Selecting a report template*

6. The next screen (Figure 14-12) provides a way to indicate which accounts you want to include in various sections of the report. If you look at the drop-down in the upper right, you'll see the standard sections of an income statement. You can select each section and then add the accounts to it.

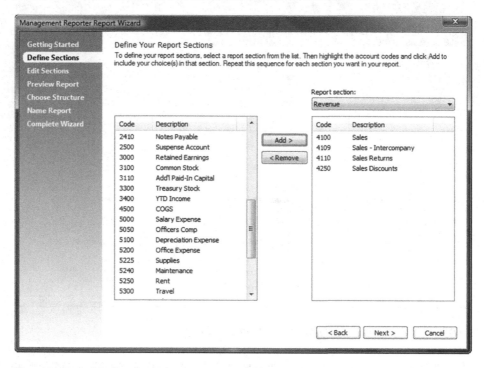

Figure 14-12. *Adding accounts to report sections*

7. Select Revenue and add accounts 4100 (Sales) through 4250 (Sales Discounts) to the section.

8. Change the drop-down, select Cost of Revenue, and add 4500 (COGS).

9. Select Employee Related Expense and add 5000 (Salary Expense) and 5050 (Officers Comp).

10. Select Other Operating Expense and add 5100 (Depreciation Expense) through 5350 (Advertising).

11. Select Other Income Expense and add 5650 (Interest Expense) and 7000 (Interest Income).

12. Select Income Tax Expense and add 5500 (Income Tax Expense). Click Next.

13. The Edit Sections page of the wizard (Figure 14-13) allows you to edit the various sections before the report is generated. You can click any section of text to change it.

14. Double-click the heading for Revenue and change it to Sales—note that the Total Revenue headers change to Total Sales. You can also select sections and move them up and down with the Move Up and Move Down buttons. Click Next.

15. The Preview Report page shows you a rough preview of what the report will look like. Click Next.

16. The Choose Structure page allows you to select whether to create one report for the entire accounts structure, or whether to create multiple reports based on the structure (the breakdown will be driven by the account structure). See Figure 14-14.

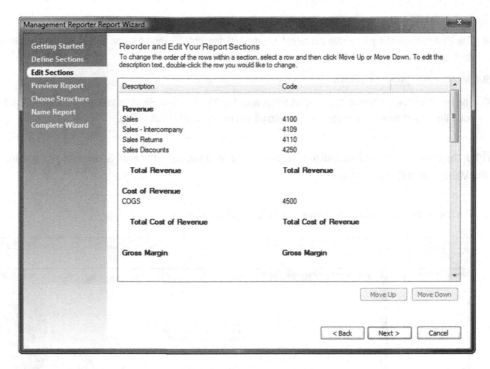

Figure 14-13. *Editing sections of the report*

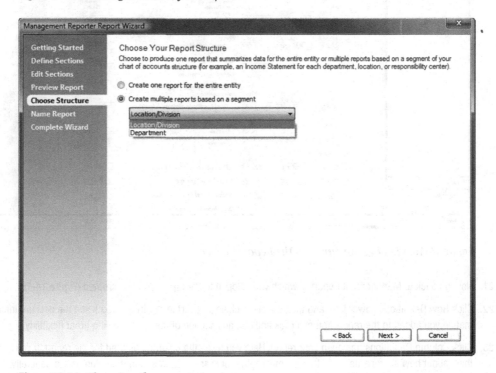

Figure 14-14. *Choosing the report structure*

17. Select "Create one report for the entire entity" and click Next.

18. The final page allows you to give the report a name and description—add a name and description and leave the rest of the options. Click Next.

19. On the review page, click Finish.

20. The report will be generated in the report editor, and then Management Reporter will generate the report and open the Report Viewer. Click the Log On button if you get the credentials dialog.

Tip If the viewer opens and immediately crashes, make sure you have the Print Spooler service running on the Management Reporter server.

The Report Viewer will open showing your report, as in Figure 14-15.

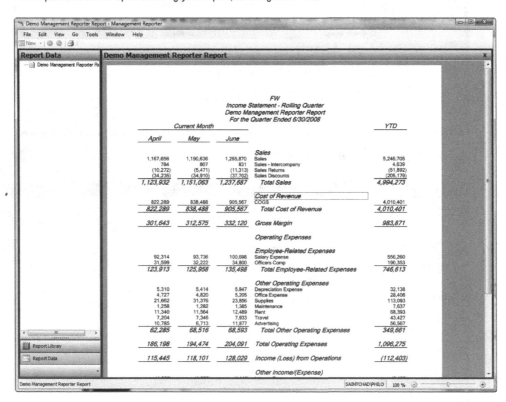

Figure 14-15. *Viewing the report in the Report Viewer*

21. Now go back to Management Reporter, which will be open to the report you just created (Figure 14-16).

22. Click Row Definitions (lower left), and then double-click your report in the tree—you'll see the account information you added to the report. You can click and edit any section of the report, giving great flexibility.

23. Click Column Definitions and open your report. Here you'll see the columns defined for the report. If you think about how scorecards work, this is similar—the rows are accounts, and the columns are generally time periods, but they could be business units, geographic locations, or any other dimension.

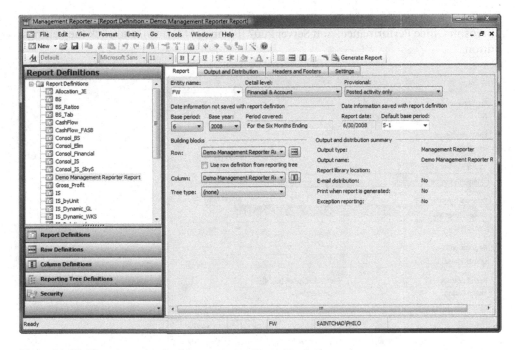

Figure 14-16. *The report in the Management Reporter designer*

24. Close the viewer and designer when you're finished.

Connecting to PerformancePoint Server

You can also connect Management Reporter to PerformancePoint Planning Server models. Once you're logged in, you'll want to create a new entity (Entity menu ➤ Entities—see Figure 14-17).

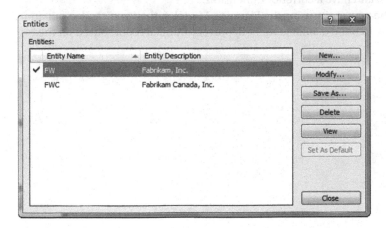

Figure 14-17. *Creating a new entity for a PerformancePoint model*

Once you've opened the New Entity dialog (Figure 14-18), change "Source system" to Microsoft Office PerformancePoint Server 2007 (Financial Models), and click the Settings button.

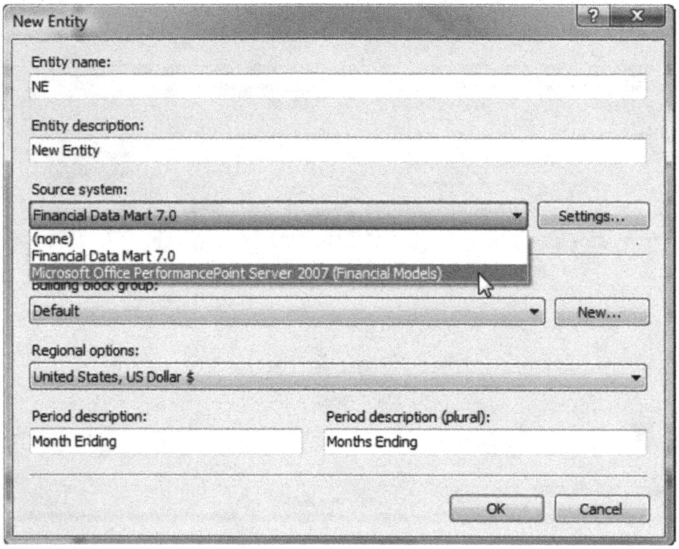

Figure 14-18. *Selecting the source system*

This will open a wizard to connect to a PerformancePoint model. First, you'll need the server address (Figure 14-19). This will be the URL format and port (`http://server:46787/` using the default port). Then click the Connect button and select an application and model site.

The model you use must be a financial model. If you look at the Create a Model dialog from PerformancePoint Business Planning Modeler (see Chapter 13), you can see the types of models available (Figure 14-20). The model we designed in Chapter 13 was a generic model, so we can't use that here. A financial model must be of the financial model type, have a calendar that uses years and months, and have a currency dimension.

Once you've created the new entity using the Planning Modeler, then you can log out and log back in to use that entity to build a Management Reporter financial report based on the data in the model.

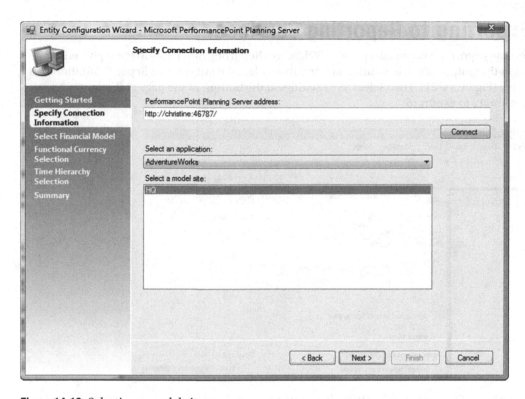

Figure 14-19. *Selecting a model site*

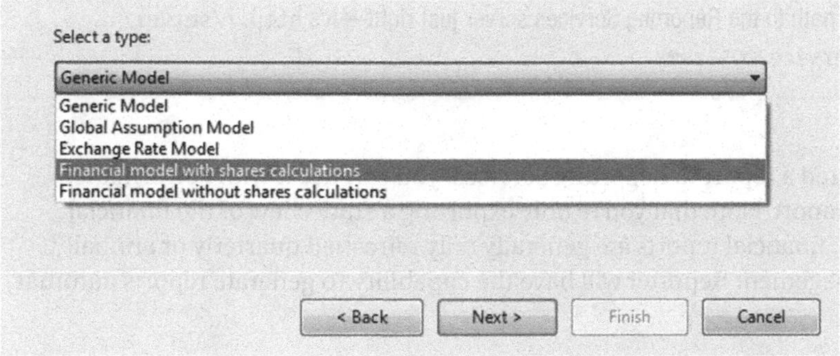

Figure 14-20. *PerformancePoint Business Planning Modeler showing financial model options*

Exporting to Reporting Services

You can export the financial reports to SQL Server Reporting Services—in the report editor, select the Output and Distribution tab, and then select the output type Report Definition Language (Figure 14-21). Then select SSRS Settings at the bottom of the page and set up the server and library to export to.

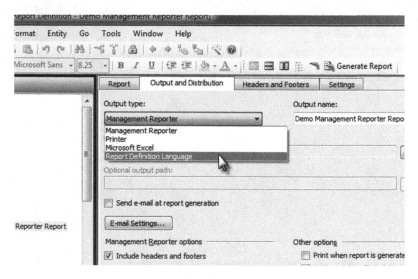

Figure 14-21. *Output to Report Definition Language*

Tip You have to get the path to the Reporting Services server just right—it's `http://server/reportserver/reportservice2005.asmx`.

Once you've exported a report to Reporting Services, you can use it with Performance-Point dashboards as a report. Note that you're only exporting a static view of the financial data. For the most part, financial reports are generally only refreshed quarterly or annually. Future versions of Management Reporter will have the capability to generate reports automatically on a schedule.

Conclusion

This chapter has been very short and sweet—just a basic attempt to familiarize you with what Management Reporter offers. It's part of PerformancePoint, so if it meets your needs, you should take advantage of it.

Index

▮Special Characters

$ format button, 292
+ (expansion symbol), 121
" " (double quotes), 307
' ' (single quotes), 307

▮Numerics

0 BizSystemFlag value, 397
200 BizSystemFlag value, 397
300 BizSystemFlag value, 397
400 BizSystemFlag value, 397

▮A

Access database file (ODBC), 303–307
Accessories category, 334
ActiveX Script task, 71
ad option, 351
Add Current Period Reference option, 409
Add or Remove Programs window, 63
Add or Remove Users for HQ Financial
        dialog, 390
Additional Actions options, 341
administration console, 375
advanced analysis tools
    creating, 236–243
    decomposition trees, 27, 218–219, 236–243
    performance maps, 27, 222
    perspective views, 220–221
Advanced Settings link, 372
AdventureWorks application, 168, 379, 402
Aggregate data flow transformation, 73
aggregating information, 83, 87
Aggregation property, 309
alignment, 8
Analysis Services. *See* SQL Server Analysis
        Services (SSAS)
analytic charts, 222, 334, 345–348
Analytic Grid wizard, 342
analytic grids, 338–344
Analytics Server. *See* ProClarity Analytics
        Server
Analytics Server Administrators Guide, 350
Analytics Server button, 228
Analyze Key Influencers tool, 181
Analyze tab, 181
Application Pool Identity page, 267
Application role, 380
Applications tab, 377

architecture
    Analytics Server, 225–227
    Integration Services, 62–63
    Planning Server, 371
    Service Broker, 45
Assemblies folder, 95
Association Rules engine, 172
attributes, 175
auditing data manipulation, 51
Auditing setting, 380
Authentication extensions function, 134
Authoring pane, 402

▮B

banding
    by normalized value, 286–288
    by numeric value, 288
    by stated score, 289
Batch query processing, 44
.bbk files, 234
Best Practices Analyzer, 49
best practices, XML, 47
BI. *See* Business Intelligence
BIDS (Business Intelligence Development
        Studio), 40–42, 64–66
Billing Codes dimension, 405
Biz# BPM engine, 15, 17, 29
BizSystemFlag field, 397
BizValidationStatus field, 398
blank indicators, 279
Blank Scorecard option, 295
BLOBs, 51
bookkeeping errors, 371
BPM (business process management)
        planning engine, 17
briefing books, 223, 234–236
Browse button, 350
BSM (Business Scorecard Manager), 15, 17,
        189
bsp_DI_ConvertLabelColumnToMemberIDF
        orMeasureGroup procedure, 399
bsp_DI_CreateLabelTableForMeasureGroup
        procedure, 398
bsp_DI_ValidateLabelTable stored
        procedure, 399
BSW files, 271
BSWX files, 271–280
budgets, 369–370
Build menu, 120

business charts, 214–218
Business Intelligence (BI)
    data marts, 11–13
    data silos, 10
    defined, 1
    KPIs, 5–8
    scorecards versus dashboards, 2–4
    strategy maps, 9–10
Business Intelligence Development Studio
    (BIDS), 40–42, 64–66
Business Intelligence Projects option, 94
business process management (BPM)
    planning engine, 17
Business Roles Only option, 389
Business Scorecard Manager (BSM), 15, 17,
    189

■ C

CALCULATE command, 122
calculated measures, 122
Calculation column, 283–284
Calculations tab, 122
calendars, 386–388
CALs (client access licenses), 36
Cell connector, 363
centered indicators, 279
ChartFX software, 161
charts
    analytic, 222, 334, 345–348
    business, 214–218
    Reporting Services, 160–163
Check Out link, 382
Choose Application dialog, 402
Choose the Deployment Location page, 142
Clean Data tool, 183
client access licenses (CALs), 36
clustering, 82, 175
Column Name property, 309
Column Type property, 309
Column Unique Name property, 309
Common Criteria Certification, 45
Compact Edition, SQL Server, 35
Company Hierarchy option, 391
Compare Data command, 273
Conditional Split data flow transformation,
    73
Configuration Manager, 132–134, 264
Configuration Options drop-down, 350
Configure Data Viewer dialog, 69
Configure Error Output button, 78
connected systems, 44
connecting
    Dashboard Designer to monitoring
        servers, 274–275
    Management Reporter to
        PerformancePoint Server, 431–432
Connection link, 376

Connection Manager pane, 76, 97
Connection Properties dialog, 150, 193
connection strings, 60, 81
consolidating budgets, 369–370
containers, 70–71
contextual amplifying information, 30. *See
    also* charts; reports
Control Flow canvas, 67, 70
Copy Shortcut option, 354
Create a Model dialog, 432
Create a Role dialog, 389
Create an Assignment Definition wizard, 410
Create Application Calendar wizard, 386
Create Calendar Views page, 388
Cube wizard, 102
cubes
    building, 91–93
    creating, 114–121
    data source view, 99–102
    data sources, 96–98
    dimensions, 104–114
    overview, 84–88
    projects, 94–95
Cubes folder, 95
custom components, 77
Custom Connection Managers component,
    77
Custom Data Flow component, 77
custom data flow transformations, 77
Custom ForEach Enumerators component,
    77
Custom Log Providers component, 77
Custom Properties section, 277
custom tasks, 77–78
Custom Tasks component, 77

■ D

D_Entity table, 396
Dashboard Designer. *See* PerformancePoint
    Dashboard Designer
Dashboard editor, 333–336
Dashboard Page Template dialog, 356
Dashboard Viewer, 262
dashboards
    defined, 381
    filters, 358–362
    linking items, 362–363
    overview, 207–210, 356–358
    publishing, 363–366
    versus scorecards, 2–4
Data Administrator role, 376
data collection among disparate systems, 44
data connection libraries (DCLs), 190
Data Conversion data flow transformation,
    73
data entry, 412–417
Data Entry Scope page, 409

Data Flow canvas, 74–75, 77–78
Data Flow components
    destinations, 74
    sources, 72–73
    transformations, 73–74
Data Flow Path Editor, 69
Data Flow tasks, 67, 71
Data Flow toolbox, 74
data flow transformations, 73–74, 77
Data Grid display, 222
data manipulation, 59
data marts, 11–13
data mining
    algorithms, 20, 168–176
    defined, 14
    Excel add-ins, 180–185
    implementation of, 166–168
    improvements, 49–50
    in Integration Services, 178–180
    Mining Accuracy Charts tab, 178
    Mining Model Prediction tab, 178
    overview, 165–166
    publishing to Reporting Services, 186
Data Mining Extensions (DMX), 39, 185
Data Mining Model Training destination, 74,
    178
Data Mining Query task, 71, 178
Data Mining tab, 181, 183
Data Mining Transform task, 178
Data processing extensions function, 134
data regions, tablix, 138
data silos, 10
Data Source View Wizard page, 100
data source views, 99–102
Data Source Views folder, 94, 99
Data Source wizard, 96, 98
data sources
    creating, 96–98
    defined, 276
    Integration Services, 59–60
    ODBC, 303–304
    Report Designer, 130
Data Sources link, 379
Data Sources setting, 381
Data Transformation Services (DTS), 53,
    60–61
Data Viewers option, 69
Database Mail (SQL Mail), 45
database mirroring, 37
Database page, 264
Database Setup pane, 133
database snapshots, 47–48
DataReader data source, 72
Date Template option, 109
DCLs (data connection libraries), 190
dd option, 351
DDL triggers feature, 45

debugging, 60
decision nodes, 176
decision trees, 168–172
decomposition trees, 27, 218–219, 236–243
DefaultAppPool option, 372
Definition Rule Set, 417
Delivery extensions function, 134
Dense_Rank( ) function, 44
Deploy Model Site option, 392, 399
deployment, 60
Design Script button, 76
Design the Matrix page, 152
designing forms, 399–408
Destination component, 74
Destination Member Set section, 391
destinations, data flow, 74
Detail Fields Here area, 120
Details pane, 278, 308
Detect Categories tool, 181
Developer Center, SQL Server, 47
Developer Edition, SQL Server, 38
Dewdney, A.K., 176
Dimension column, 309
Dimension Structure page, 385
dimension tables, 90
Dimension Tasks list, 390
Dimension wizard, 104, 106, 116
Dimensional Data Source Mapping dialog,
    313
dimensions
    hierarchies, 113–114
    overview, 89–90, 104–108
    time, 108–112
Dimensions folder, 95, 109
Dimensions link, 390
Display Condition connector, 363
DMX (Data Mining Extensions), 39, 185
double quotes (" "), 307
drill-down hierarchy, 153
drill-through data, 340
Drop Column Fields Here area, 121
Drop Row Fields Here area, 121
Drop Totals area, 120
dt option, 350
DTS (Data Transformation Services), 53,
    60–61
DTS Package Migration wizard, 61
Dundas Reports software, 161

■ E

EDI (electronic data interchange), 66
Edit Banding Settings dialog, 285
"Edit data in Excel" dialog, 310
Edit tab, 273, 345, 349
Edit User Permissions pane, 395
Editor tab, 276–277, 310
electronic data interchange (EDI), 66

embedded connection managers, 81
Enable native SQL/MDX rules box, 378
encryption, 51
Enforced password policy feature, 45
Enterprise Edition, SQL Server, 37
Enterprise Manager, 38
Entity link, 382
error reports, 78, 265
ETL (extract-transform-load), 14, 18, 52, 53
Event and Trace Logs setting, 380
Excel 2007
    add-ins, 180–185, 371, 399–400
    BI in, 191–197
    forms, 415
    scorecards, 255, 295, 315–321
    spreadsheets, 307–314
Excel data source, 72
Excel Services
    configuring, 200–203
    overview, 24–25, 197
    providing functions via code, 199
    publishing, 197–198, 203–205
    reports, 348–349
    running spreadsheets on server, 199
    scorecards, 295
Execute Package task, 71
Execute Process task, 71
Execute SQL task, 72
expansion symbol (+), 121
Explore Data tool, 183
exporting reports to Reporting Services, 434
Express Edition, SQL Server, 35–36
extensibility, 60, 134–136
extensions, 134–135
extract-transform-load (ETL), 14, 18, 52, 53

F
Fact column, 309
facts, 89–90
failover clustering, 47
false positives, 166
Fast Track to MDX, 122
FDM (Financial Data Mart) format, 421
File System task, 71
filestream storage, 51
Fill From Example tool, 182
Filter box, 210
Filter option, 341
filter templates, 361
filters, 358–362
Filters tab, 359
Financial Data Mart (FDM) format, 421
Fixed Values option, 295
Flat file data source, 59, 73
flows, 67–70
Fluent user interface, 272–273, 302
focus, 8

For loop container, 70
Foreach loop container, 70
Forecast tool, 182
Format Numbers dialog, 282
Format Report options, 341
Format section, 345
Forms Assignment tab, 410, 412
FRx financial analysis and reporting package,
    421
fs option, 350
Fuzzy Grouping task, 179
Fuzzy Lookup data flow transformation, 73
Fuzzy Lookup task, 179

G
gauge-style scorecards, 258
geography datatype, 51
Geography view, 116
geometry datatype, 51
Get External Data section, 192
Global Administrator role, 376
Graham, Paul, 174
Granular permission control feature, 45
graphs, 160–163

H
Hierarchies and Levels pane, 114
hierarchies, dimension, 113–114
high availability, 47–48
Home tab, 272
HQPlanning model, 379
ht option, 351
HTTP endpoints, 45

I
i property, 309
Ignore column, 309
IIS 6 management compatibility role service,
    372
Image wizard, 156
importing data, PerformancePoint Server,
    396–399
indicators, 276, 278–281
Initialization pane, 133
Input Columns pane, 74
Inputs and Outputs pane, 76
Installation Options page, 264
installing
    Integration Services, 63
    PerformancePoint, 262–269, 371–374
    ProClarity Analytics Server, 246–254
Integration Services. *See* SQL Server
    Integration Services
isActivated property, 378

K

Kaplan, Robert, 3, 8, 259
Kerberos, 98, 226
Key column, 309
key performance indicators (KPIs)
    actual values, 281–284
    Analysis Services, 122
    defined, 276
    hooking to data
        Excel 2007 scorecards, 315–321
        Excel 2007 spreadsheets, 307–314
        ODBC, 303–307
        overview, 303
    law of unintended consequences, 7–8
    overview, 5–6, 281
    targets, 284–294
Key Performance Indicators: Developing,
        Implementing, and Using Winning
        KPIs, 6
KPI lists, 25, 206
KPI Row connector, 363
KPIs. *See* key performance indicators

L

leaf-level member, 88
Least privilege support feature, 46
linking dashboard items, 362–363
Lookup data flow transformation, 73
looping, 60

M

M&A (monitoring and analytics) module,
        29–30
Maintenance Plan tasks, 72
Management Reporter
    connecting to PerformancePoint Server,
        431–432
    creating reports, 421–431
    exporting to Reporting Services, 434
    overview, 421
Management Studio, 35, 38–39, 80, 398
MAP (monitor, analyze, plan) cycle, 29
Mark Differences command, 273
master time dimension, 309
matrices, defined, 400
matrix reports, 137
Matrix Styles button, 406
MDX (Multidimensional Expressions), 39, 88,
        122, 321
MDX Query filter, 361
MDX Tuple formula box, 314
Member Column connector, 363
Member Maintenance tab, 383
Member Property dialog, 385
Member Row connector, 363
Member Selection filter, 361

Member Set page, 385
Merge data flow transformation, 73
MERGE statement, 51
MG_Personnel
        Planning_MeasureGroup_default_
        partition table, 399
Microsoft Business Intelligence platform,
        13–17. *See also* Business Intelligence;
        Microsoft Office SharePoint Server;
        PerformancePoint Server 2007; SQL
        Server 2005
Microsoft Data Engine (MSDE), 35
Microsoft Office 2007, 14, 190
Microsoft Office SharePoint Server (MOSS).
        See also Excel Services
    document library, 24, 377
    integration, 22, 133, 147, 163, 353
    KPI lists, 25–26
    overview, 206–210
    ProClarity Analytics Server and, 244
    Report Manager, 130
Microsoft scorecards, 295
Microsoft Visio, 136, 259, 336
Microsoft Windows 2008, 372–374
Mining Accuracy Charts tab, 178
Mining Model Prediction tab, 178
Mining Model Viewer tab, 178
Mining Structures folder, 95
mirror servers, 47
mirroring, 47
Miscellaneous folder, 95
mission statement, 8
Model role, 380
model sites
    creating, 377–378
    editing, 378–381
Model Sites tab, 378
Modeler role, 376
modeling and planning module, 31
models
    adding users and roles, 389–391
    creating, 391–392
    overview, 381–388
    setting user security, 393–396
monitor, analyze, plan (MAP) cycle, 29
monitoring and analytics (M&A) module,
        29–30
Monitoring Central web site, 270
Monitoring Server, 262, 274–275
MOSS. *See* Excel Services; Microsoft Office
        SharePoint Server
MSDE (Microsoft Data Engine), 35
Multicast data flow transformation, 73
Multidimensional Expressions (MDX), 39, 88,
        122, 321
multidimensional reports, 147–159
multiple targets, 284

N

naive Bayes algorithms, 172–174
Named Sets filter, 361
neural networks algorithms, 176
New Data Source option, 96
"New data source" radio button, 138
New Dimension, 104
New Entity dialog, 432
New Filter button, 360
New Matrix dialog, 403
No Member default member, 383
"No value" option, 283
nodes, 176
Norton, David, 3, 8, 259
Notifications check box, 410

O

Object Explorer Connect button, 80
objectives, 2
ODBC (Access database file), 303–307
ODBC data source editor, 304
Off by default feature, 46
Office 2007, 14, 190
Office button, 274
Office directory, 413
Office Web Components (OWC), 206, 349
OLAP. *See* online analytical processing
OLEDB data source, 73
OLEDB parameterized command interface, 44
online analytical processing (OLAP)
  actions, 341
  cubes, 11, 225
  data, 18, 338
  scorecards, 327–330
  views, 99
online index operations, 47
Open Items command, 273
optimization, 80
Options dialog, 274
Output and Distribution tab, 434
output matrices, 176–177
OWC (Office Web Components), 206, 349

P

Package Design tab, 68
packages, 58
palettes, 113
parallelization, 79, 82
Parmenter, David, 6
Partition Processing destination, 74
PAS. *See* ProClarity Analytics Server
/pas directory, 350
PBM (Planning Business Modeler), 371, 374, 381–382, 391, 399, 408–409

PEL (PerformancePoint Expression Language), 419
Percentage Sampling data flow transformation, 73
Performance Dashboards, 4
performance maps, 27, 222, 236–243
PerformancePoint
  add-in for Excel, 371, 399–400
  installing, 262–269
  scorecards
    indicators, 278–281
    KPIs, 281–294
    overview, 255–259, 278
    types of, 294–301
  strategy maps, 259
PerformancePoint Dashboard Designer
  connecting to monitoring server, 274–275
  Dashboard editor, 333–336
  dashboards, 356–363
  Details pane, 278
  Editor tab, 276–277
  Fluent user interface, 272–273
  overview, 262, 271
  Properties tab, 276–277
  publishing work, 280
  reports
    analytic charts, 345–348
    analytic grids, 338–344
    Excel Services, 348–349
    overview, 336–338
    PivotChart, 349
    PivotTable, 349
    ProClarity Analytics report viewer, 350–352
    Spreadsheet, 349
    SQL Server, 352–356
  running, 269–271
  saving work, 280
  servers versus workspaces, 272
  Workspace Browser, 275–276
PerformancePoint Dashboard Viewer, 262
PerformancePoint Expression Language (PEL), 419
PerformancePoint Monitoring Server, 262, 274–275
PerformancePoint Planning Server
  architecture, 371
  business rules, 417–419
  designing forms, 399–408
  entering data, 412–417
  importing data, 396–399
  installation, 371–374
  model sites, 377–381
  models, 381–396

overview, 367, 375–376
reasons for, 368–369
scenarios, 369–371
workflow, 408–412
PerformancePoint Planning task pane, 414
PerformancePoint Server 2007. *See also*
    ProClarity Analytics server
    Biz# BPM engine, 15, 17, 29
    Business Scorecard Manager, 15, 17, 189
    connecting Management Reporter to,
        431–432
    overview, 28–31
PerformancePoint Server pane, 404
PerformancePoint tab, 400, 408, 413, 416
Permissions section, 277
Personnel Planning model, 393, 394,
    398–399, 409
perspective view, 220–221, 236–243
perspectives, 2, 123
pipelines, 79
pivot charts, 86
Pivot command, 341
Pivot data flow transformation, 73
PIVOT statement, 44, 93
pivot tables, 148
PivotChart reports, 349
PivotTable reports, 349
PK_Date field, 112
Planning Business Modeler (PBM), 371, 374,
    381–382, 391, 399, 408–409
Planning Process Service setting, 380
Planning Server. *See* PerformancePoint
    Planning Server
Planning Server Configuration Manager
    wizard, 374
Preview button, 273
principal servers, 47
Print Spooler service, 430
Pro SQL Server 2005 High Availability, 47
Pro SQL Server 2005 Service Broker, 44
Process Cube dialog, 120
Process Management option, 409
ProClarity 6.3, 26–28
ProClarity Analytics report viewer, 350–352
ProClarity Analytics Server (PAS)
    advanced analysis tools, 218–222, 236–243
    architecture, 225–227
    business charts, 214–218
    installing, 246–254
    overview, 211–213
    publishing briefing books, 234–236
    SharePoint and, 244
    Web Professional interface, 224–225,
        228–234
    Web Standard interface, 222–224

ProClarity SharePoint viewer web part, 244
Profiler, 42
program flow components
    containers, 70–71
    tasks, 71–72
Programmability node, 398
Properties button, 273
Properties dialog, 144
Properties page, 358
Properties tab, 276–277, 349
Property Type Selector, 291
Publish All icon, 273, 280
publishing
    briefing books, 234–236
    dashboards, 363–366
    to Excel Services, 203–205
    to Reporting Services, 186
    spreadsheets via Web, 197–198

Q
Query Analyzer, 38
Query Builder, 140, 150
query notifications, 45
Query tab, 340

R
Rank( ) function, 44
Raw file data source, 73
RDL (Report Definition Language), 136, 434
reconciling ledgers, 371
Refresh command, 273
Region attribute, 114
Regional Finances role, 394
Regular dimension type, 106
Rendering extensions function, 134
Report Builder, 127, 131
Report Center site template, 22
Report Definition Language (RDL), 136, 434
Report Designer, 127, 130–131
Report Library list type, 206
Report Manager, 129–130
Report Manager Virtual Directory pane, 132
report models, 131
Report Parameters section, 353
Report processing extensions functions, 134
Report Processor, 129
Report Server, 128–129, 352
Report Server Virtual Directory pane, 132
Report Type selector, 341, 345
report URLs, 136
Reporting Services. *See* SQL Server Reporting
    Services (SSRS)
Reporting Services Configuration Manager,
    132–134, 264
Reporting setting, 381
reporting trees, 425

reports
    analytic charts, 345–348
    analytic grids, 338–344
    charts, 160–163
    creating with Management Reporter, 421–431
    defined, 276
    error, 78, 265
    Excel Services, 348–349
    exporting to Reporting Services, 434
    graphs, 160–163
    matrix, 137
    multidimensional, 147–159
    overview, 136, 336–338
    PivotChart, 349
    PivotTable, 349
    ProClarity Analytics report viewer, 350–352
    Spreadsheet, 349
    SQL Server, 48, 352–356
    subreports, 154, 159
    table, 137
    tablix concept, 138–147
Reports button, 408
Reprocess Model Data link, 399
Reverse button, 102
Review Options page, 269
ribbon user interface, 272–273, 302
Role tab, 394
Roles folder, 95
RuleSetsOrRules table, 378
Run button, 141
RUNAS command, 412, 415–416

■S

Sarle, Warren S., 176
scalability, 79–80
Scheduling and Delivery Processor, 129
schemas, XML, 46
Scorecard editor, 296
scorecards. *See also* key performance indicators
    Analysis Services, 321–330
    versus dashboards, 2–4
    defined, 276
    Excel 2007, 255, 295, 315–321
    Excel Services, 295
    indicators, 278–281
    online analytical processing, 327–330
    overview, 30, 255–259
    Reporting Services, 332
    types of, 294–301
Script component, 74, 76
Script data flow transformation, 74
Script pane, 76
Script task, 72
Script Transformation Editor, 74

scripting tasks, 74–76
security, 45–46
Security and Roles Tasks section, 389
Select a Data Source dialog, 100, 306, 312
Select a Data Source Template dialog, 304
"Select a dimension" section, 314
Select a KPI Source page, 327
Select an Indicator Template dialog, 279
Select Build Method page, 104, 109, 115
Select Filters dialog, 413
Select Forms dialog, 410
Select Items tab, 229
Select KPIs to Import page, 318
Select Members dialog, 326, 406, 409
Select the Data Source page, 138
Selected Tables/Views list, 380
Select...Where query, 361
Semantic Model Definition Language (SMDL), 136
Send Mail task, 71
sequence clustering algorithms, 175
Sequence container, 71
Server Options dialog, 275
server reports, 48, 352–356
Server Status pane, 132
Server tab, 275
Service Broker, 44–45
Service Pack 2 (SP2), 48–50
Session Settings, 380
Set Application Pool Defaults option, 372
"Set scoring pattern and Indicator" button, 285–289
SharePoint List option, 295
SharePoint Server. *See* Microsoft Office SharePoint Server
SharePoint Site button, 273
Show Information option, 341
Show Tables/Views button, 379
silos, data, 10
single quotes (' '), 307
slicers, 228
SMART mnemonic, 5
SMDL (Semantic Model Definition Language), 136
snapshot view spreadsheets, 25
snowflake schemas, 90
SOAP-compliant web services, 45
Sort option, 341
"Source data" option, 284
SP2 (Service Pack 2), 48–50
spatial datatype, 51
Specify Assumptions page, 392
Spreadsheet reports, 349
spreadsheets, 197–199
SQL Mail (Database Mail), 45
SQL Native Client, 97
SQL Server 2005

editions of, 33–38
Excel add-ins, 180–185
high availability, 47–48
overview, 17, 33
programmability, 43–45
security, 45–46
Service Pack 2, 48–50
tools, 38–43
XML, 46–47
SQL Server 2008, 51
SQL Server Analysis Services (SSAS)
    BIDS and, 91
    calculated measures, 122
    cubes
        building, 91–93
        creating, 114–121
        data source view, 99–102
        data sources, 96–98
        dimensions, 104, 114
        overview, 84–88
        projects, 94–95
    dimensions, 89–90
    facts, 89–90
    KPIs, 122, 206
    multidimensional expressions, 122
    OLAP scorecards, 327–330
    overview, 14, 18–20, 83, 321–326
    perspectives, 123
    star versus snowflake schemas, 90
SQL Server destination, 74
SQL Server Developer Center, 47
SQL Server Enterprise Manager, 38
SQL Server Integration Services (SSIS)
    architecture, 62–63
    BIDS, 64–66
    custom tasks, 77–78
    Data Flow components, 72–74
    data mining in, 178–180
    data sources, 59–60
    DTS, 60–61
    editions of, 59
    error reporting, 78
    flows, 67–70
    installing, 63
    overview, 14, 18, 53–58
    packages, 80–81
    program flow components, 70–72
    scalability, 79–80
    scripting tasks, 74–76
SQL Server Management Studio, 35, 38–39,
    80, 398
SQL Server Profiler, 42
SQL Server Query Analyzer, 38
SQL Server Reporting Services (SSRS)
    Configuration Manager, 132–134, 264
    exporting reports to, 434
    extensibility, 134–136

overview, 14, 125–128
publishing to, 186
Report Builder, 127, 131
Report Designer, 130–131
Report Manager, 129–130
Report Server, 128–129, 352
reports
    charts, 160–163
    graphs, 160–163
    matrix, 137
    multidimensional, 147–159
    overview, 136, 352–356
    table, 137
    tablix concept, 138–147
SharePoint integration, 163
SQL Server 2005, 21–22
SQL Server Service Broker, 44–45
SQL Tabular option, 295
SSAS. *See* SQL Server Analysis Services
SSIS. *See* SQL Server Integration Services
SSRS. *See* SQL Server Reporting Services
st option, 350
staging databases, 99, 396
Standard Edition, SQL Server, 36–37
standard indicators, 279
standard scorecards, 295
star schemas, 90
stored procedures, 44, 396, 398
strategy maps, 8–10, 259
Submission Period page, 411
subreports, 154, 159
Summary tab, 394
"Synchronize this model to the staging area"
    option, 398
SynchronousInputID setting, 76

■T

table analysis, 181–182
table layout frame, 144
table reports, 137
Table Tools tabs, 181
tablix concept, 130, 138–147
tabular scorecards, 295–301, 315
Tabular Values filter, 361
Target Settings dialog, 301
targets
    calculations, 289–294
    overview, 284
    scoring patterns and indicators, 285–289
tasks, 71–72
tb option, 350
TDE (transparent database encryption), 51
Thresholds editing area, 285
ti option, 350
Time button, 409
time dimension, 108–112
Time Dimension column, 309, 405

time intelligence feature, 309
Time Intelligence filter, 361
Time Intelligence Post Formula filter, 362
time series algorithms, 176
toolbox, Report Designer, 130–131
TOP statement, 44
transaction logs, 371
transactional data, 99, 147
Transfer tasks, 72
Transformation component, 74
transformations, data flow, 73–74
transparent database encryption (TDE), 51
trend arrows, 321
Trustworthy Computing initiative, 45
Try.Catch syntax, 44
tuples, 324

U

UDM (Universal Data Model) concept, 99
Union All data flow transformation, 74
Universal Data Model (UDM) concept, 99
UNPIVOT statement, 44
Update button, 273
URL-based commands, 135–136
"Use calculated values of actual and target to
        compute score" check box, 289
Use Windows Authentication check box, 97
User Administrator role, 376
User Administrator Role link, 378
Users console, 376

V

Validation page, 268
values, 88
vh option, 350
View tab, 311, 349
virtual cubes, 123
Visio, 136, 259, 336
Visual Studio, 40, 64, 84
Visual Studio for Applications (VSA), 76

W

Web Parts page, 268
Web Professional interface, ProClarity, 211,
        224–225, 228–234

Web Service Identity pane, 133
Web Service task, 71
web services, 45, 135
Web Services Description Language (WSDL)
        file, 71
Web Standard interface, ProClarity, 211,
        222–224
weighted averaging, 300
weighting nodes, 176
WF (Windows Workflow Foundation), 408
what-if scenarios, 370–371
WHEN MATCHED phrase, 51
WHEN NOT MATCHED phrase, 51
Whitehorn, Mark, 122
Windows 2008, 372–374
Windows on Windows (WOW), 36
Windows service, 128–129
Windows Service Identity pane, 132
Windows Workflow Foundation (WF), 408
wizard, 421
workflow, 408–412
Workflow Foundation (WF), 408
Workflow setting, 380
Workgroup Edition, SQL Server, 36
Workspace Actions pane, 392, 394, 398, 399
Workspace Browser, 275–276, 382, 389–391
WOW (Windows on Windows), 36
writeback capabilities, 415
WSDL (Web Services Description Language)
        file, 71

X

XML, 46–47
XML datatypes, 46
XML file data source, 73
XML for Analysis (XML/A) queries, 39
XML task, 71
XML/A (XML for Analysis) queries, 39
XQuery, 46–47

Z

Zone Settings option, 358